Investing in Life

STUDIES IN EARLY AMERICAN ECONOMY AND SOCIETY
FROM THE LIBRARY COMPANY OF PHILADELPHIA
Cathy Matson, Series Editor

Investing in Life

Insurance in Antebellum America

SHARON ANN MURPHY

The Johns Hopkins University Press

Baltimore

Johns Hopkins Paperback edition, 2013
2 4 6 8 9 7 5 3 1

The Johns Hopkins University Press
2715 North Charles Street
Baltimore, Maryland 21218-4363
www.press.jhu.edu

The Library of Congress has cataloged the hardcover edition of this book as follows:

Murphy, Sharon Ann, 1974–
Investing in life : insurance in antebellum America / Sharon Ann Murphy.
p. cm. — (Studies in early American economy and society)
Includes bibliographical references and index.
ISBN-13: 978-0-8018-9624-8 (hbk. : alk. paper)
ISBN-10: 0-8018-9624-X (hbk. : alk. paper)
1. Life insurance—United States—History—19th century.   2. Insurance
companies—United States—History—19th century.   3. United States—Economic
conditions—To 1865.   I. Title.
HG8951.M87 2010
368.3200973'09034—dc22   2009043629

A catalog record for this book is available from the British Library.

ISBN-13: 978-1-4214-1194-1
ISBN-10: 1-4214-1194-6

Special discounts are available for bulk purchases of this book. For more information,
please contact Special Sales at 410-516-6936 or specialsales@press.jhu.edu.

The Johns Hopkins University Press uses environmentally friendly book materials,
including recycled text paper that is composed of at least 30 percent
post-consumer waste, whenever possible.

In memory of Mildred Bradley Murphy, one of "the girls" at Metropolitan Life Insurance Company in the 1930s. Her boundless love and indomitable spirit always inspired me.
April 30, 1914–April 24, 2006

CONTENTS

Studies in Early American Economy and Society, a collaborative effort between the Johns Hopkins University Press and the Library Company of Philadelphia's Program in Early American Economy and Society (PEAES), promotes discussions and gatherings of scholars who wish to advance our understanding of the early American economy under the umbrella of numerous disciplines, methodologies, and subjects. In this latest title in the PEAES monograph series, Sharon Ann Murphy traces the development of life insurance in the early republic, both as a new idea regarding the protection of families in the face of calamitous events and as a new kind of business that invested company funds and made judgments about which survivors would be paid and how much they would receive.

Investing in Life traces how early Americans moved beyond earlier mutual aid and benevolent societies, as well as private charities, in their search for better ways to protect families made vulnerable by a dizzying array of social changes. In a nation undergoing deep transformations of households, workplaces, entrepreneurial sites, and cultural arenas, life insurance was touted as a valuable safety net for the emergent middle class. Murphy's meticulous research in company records, advertising literature, and the popular culture reveals that the business of insurance had many layers worthy of our attention. One of these layers involves the savvy entrepreneurs who believed incorporated life insurance would attract myriad small investments from concerned families, which would in turn create available capital for the incorporators to loan to their own businesses. In another layer of Murphy's study, we see how the new insurance company directors developed a discourse about investing in the limits of human life in order to protect loved ones who survived, a discourse that required Americans to contemplate making ethical choices about protecting their families by embracing an untested capitalist enterprise. In yet another layer of Murphy's analysis, readers discover how insurance agents and marketers entered private lives to determine who was eligible to buy policies—the assessments of a person's physical health, examinations of both bank accounts and bodies, and judgments about a potential policyholder's temperance and longevity.

Murphy's study takes a long view of life insurance across most of the nineteenth century, through the challenges of economic depressions, state government interference with insurance company objectives, and a degree of initial public hostility to these novel enterprises. Her careful reconstruction of levels of investment in the major insurance companies demonstrates the tremendous growth of policy sales and Americans' eventual eagerness to secure the peace of mind and guarantee of a payout, should an insured loved one die. At first organized as stock corporations, the transition to mutual insurance companies—in which individual policyholders, not corporation stockholders held the capital—further deepened middle-class commitment to this new business culture. And a deep intellectual change, argues Murphy, was occurring alongside the insurance business's explosive growth in the early republic: insurers carefully crafted and marketed the image of protection for widows and orphans that would come from paying insurance premiums that guaranteed the death of the insured would not become an unbearable burden for survivors. Large numbers of Americans eventually blended the most personal and familial of tragedies with an ethic making matters of life and death the affairs of stockholders, company directors, and state legislators. Indirectly, insuring lives also facilitated the pooling and diffusion of capital into the economy.

If insuring lives caught on slowly in the early republic, the sales of new policies exploded in the post–Civil War decade. Life insurance was evolving by midcentury from an untested means of mitigating the risks of living in the modern world to a perceived middle-class necessity. Yet in a climate of greater corporate competition, new companies became vulnerable to fraud, bankruptcies, and insufficient numbers of new policyholders to survive very long. Murphy's fast-paced narrative and arresting vignettes bring the early republic rise and postbellum catastrophic collapse of life insurance into fascinating relief.

Cathy Matson
Professor of History, University of Delaware
Director, Program in Early American Economy and Society

This project would not have been possible without the financial support of numerous groups including the Library Company of Philadelphia, the Economic History Association, the Harvard Business School, the State Farm Companies Foundation, the University of Illinois Foundation, the University of Virginia Graduate School of Arts and Sciences, and the University of Virginia Office of Research and Public Service. Additionally, the entire Eckert family provided food, shelter, and companionship for a large portion of my research. Through chemotherapy, life-threatening illnesses, and adoption, they always found space for me.

The librarians at several archives were especially helpful to my research. In particular Laura Linard and her staff at the Historical Collections of Baker Library at Harvard Business School, and Elisabeth Proffen and her staff at the H. Furlong Baldwin Library of the Maryland Historical Society, and John Van Horne, Jim Green, and their staff at the Library Company were extremely informative and accommodating.

Throughout this process, my advisor Mark Thomas has provided immeasurable guidance, encouragement, and support both for this project and my graduate experience as a whole. As a lowly undergraduate in his course on American economic history, I first came to his office to discuss the possibility of pursuing graduate work in the field. Neither of us could have anticipated then the long journey on which we were embarking together. I am proud to have been his first Ph.D. student.

Many people read and generously commented on this project. In particular John James, Charles McCurdy, and Peter Onuf all participated in my dissertation defense, furnishing fruitful insights on the entire project. As I began transforming the dissertation into a book, Edward Balleisen's perceptive comments on the structure and argument were invaluable. Additionally, Cathy Matson, Richard John, Gavin Wright, Joe Miller, Robin Einhorn, Cindy Aron, John Larson, Christopher Clark, Leonard Sadosky, Johann Neem, Susanna Lee, Dayo Mitchell, Walter Friedman,

Roderick McDonald, Michelle Craig McDonald, Sean Adams, Dan Wadhwani, Stephen Mihm, Jane Kamensky, Aaron Wunsch, and Melissa Thomasson, as well as the members of the Early American Seminar at the University of Virginia, the McNeil Center for Early American Studies Seminar at the University of Pennsylvania, the Insurance and Society Study Group, the University of Maryland Early American History Seminar, and the Economic History Workshop at Wake Forest University all provided input on selected chapters.

In earlier form, chapter 2 was published in the Spring 2008 issue of the *Business History Review,* and chapter 7 in the Winter 2005 issue of the *Journal of the Early Republic.* The feedback from the anonymous readers for these articles was extremely helpful in refining my prose and argument. Selections from chapter 5 appeared as " 'Doomed . . . to eat the bread of dependency'? Insuring the Middle Class against Hard Times," in the April 2010 issue of *Common-place: The Interactive Journal of Early American Life.*

Special thanks to Bob Katz-Rühl, Maíre Murphy, Johann Neem, Leonard Sadosky, Genevieve Blair, Mary Jo Burke, Jill Johnson, Mariana Martinez, Kathleen Olowin, Wendy Sprigle, and my great colleagues at Providence College. Without their constant friendship, encouragement, and moral support I would never have been able to finish this marathon.

I don't think either my family or my in-laws ever truly understood why a (supposedly) well-educated woman would spend so many years of her life researching life insurance (of all things!) in pursuit of a degree that provides horrible job prospects and even worse pay. But while they often thought I was crazy, they never ceased to be proud of me, and I am thankful for that.

While my husband, Kenny, didn't type a word of the dissertation, darned few socks, and did even less laundry, his love and support (along with countless homemade pizzas, onion tarts, and on-the-fly tech support) has been indispensable to me. He endured long talks about life insurance, even longer research trips, piles of photocopies strewn throughout the house, and my unusual work habits and hours—all with limitless patience and a ready supply of smiles, hugs, and red wine. And whenever I thought of quitting, he promptly sat me back down in front of my laptop and lovingly ordered me to finish. He even assumed the duties of a single parent to our little ray of sunshine so that I could make my final revisions.

Finally, I must thank Amalia Rose for allowing her first year of life to be consumed by this book; she spent many hours sleeping in my arms, soothed by the gentle pitter-patter of mommy typing one-handedly on the keyboard. Looking at her, I developed a much deeper understanding for the emotional pull of life insurance marketing.

Investing in Life

New Risks in a Changing World

A policy of Life Assurance is the cheapest and safest mode of making certain provision for one's family. It is time our people understood and practiced more generally Life Assurance. Many a widow and orphan have great reason to be thankful that the advantage of Life Assurance was understood and embraced by the husband and father. A large amount has been paid . . . to widows and orphans when it formed almost their only recourse.

> —*Benjamin Franklin, writing from London, 1769*

Among the various modes of alleviating the misfortunes and calamities of life, which have been adopted by the inhabitants of Europe, none has more deservedly engaged the attention of the enlightened and benevolent, than the establishment of institutions for insurances on lives and granting annuities . . . The want of a company in the United States . . . has been long experienced, and it is therefore with no small degree of satisfaction, that the existence of such an institution is now announced.

> —*Pennsylvania Company for Insurances on*
> *Lives and Granting Annuities, 1814 brochure*

In December of 1809, a group of prominent businessmen gathered at the Merchants' Coffee House in Philadelphia and decided to create the first for-profit life insurance company in America.[1] When the Pennsylvania Company for Insurances on Lives and Granting Annuities finally received a charter more than two years later, its incorporation marked the birth of an industry that by the postbellum era would become ubiquitous—a quiet pillar of support against the hazards of modern life for families across the entire income spectrum and particularly for those within the emerging middle class. But in 1812, the future success of the life insurance industry was not a foregone conclusion. Despite the positive assertions made by Pennsylvania Company executives in their advertising brochure of 1814, life insurance was neither popular among Europeans nor in high demand among Americans. The few Americans familiar with the idea of insuring a person's life often associated it with gambling, murder, or fraud because of the sensational accounts of such crimes in Europe. The life insurance industry thus faced an uphill battle both to legitimize itself to the American public and to discover—or even create—a demand for its product.

As the leading center of finance and shipping in the new republic, turn-of-the-century Philadelphia was, not surprisingly, the insurance capital of the nation, housing numerous fire and marine insurance entities. While the charters of many of these underwriters permitted them to insure lives as well, they were largely uninterested in entering this sideline and thus rarely sold life policies.[2] Philadelphia was also home to two not-for-profit life insurance companies: the Corporation for Relief of Poor and Distressed Widows and Children of Presbyterian Ministers (established in 1759) and the Corporation for the Relief of the Widows and Children of Clergymen of the Protestant Episcopal Church (established in 1769). These hybrid institutions furnished partially subsidized life policies for the ministers of their denominations, but similar protection was not offered to the public at large.[3] Finally, the city's assortment of fraternal societies often provided burial coverage for their members, but this did little to relieve the ongoing economic stress of the surviving families.[4] The only recourse for the few Philadelphians seeking life insurance was to turn to a British insurer such as Pelican Life of London, which opened offices in major American cities beginning in 1806.[5]

Given this environment, Pennsylvania Company incorporators viewed life insurance as a potentially lucrative business opportunity despite the substantial marketing hurdles. They anticipated "a reasonable prospect of profit" because of the dramatic alterations in "the circumstances of our citizens."[6] The United States had entered a period of extensive industrialization and urbanization, which was fracturing communal relationships and familiar havens in times of need, as well as laying the groundwork for the development of a middle class. Early American women and children had been intimately involved in the successful operation of farms, artisans' shops, and stores. But as men now ventured out into salaried employments, women's domestic duties became increasingly divorced from the breadwinning activities of the family.[7] Rapid urbanization was simultaneously removing the foundations for mutual cooperation and obligation by breaking down social ties. As one historian has remarked, "Once residents of the larger American cities left the small worlds of their neighborhoods, they plunged into a 'world of strangers'—a sea of people, few of whom even residents of long standing could identify."[8] Life insurance would serve as a countervailing force against these dramatic societal changes over the next half century. By quietly pervading the entire fabric of American middle-class life, this new industry would provide a crucial layer of support and stability to a nation in flux, enabling—and even facilitating—the transition from a rural, agriculturally based society to an urban, industrialized one.

With "at present no competition in this particular branch of business," early life insurance entrepreneurs anticipated being able to capitalize financially by offering a novel, for-profit solution to this developing hole in the social safety net.[9] As savvy, successful businessmen, they were always seeking new means of raising capital for investment in their other business endeavors. If they could pool some of the discretionary income of the growing middle class, they could then lend those funds out to their own projects.[10]

As the first mover in the industry, Pennsylvania Company's initial focus had to be educational: "to disseminate throughout the Union . . . some explanation of the objects and views of this institution, in order that a portion of our fellow citizens . . . may have some knowledge of their beneficial effects."[11] Needing to inform the public of its product and convince them of its indispensability for urban families, Pennsylvania Company began by explaining, in the simplest of terms, that "*An Insurance on a Life,* is a contract whereby a premium of a certain per-centage is paid, conditioned that, should the person named die before a specified time, his heirs or representatives should receive the amount of the principal for which the premium was paid."[12] Policyholders could choose to insure for any length of time, including the whole term of life, with the premium "bear[ing] the proper proportion of risk" dependent "upon the age, state of health, profession and residence of the person insured."[13] Reassured that these premiums were based on "a long and studied attention to the bills of mortality in England,"[14] readers were encouraged to consider all of "those accidents and misfortunes to which human nature is so generally exposed" that might render their dependents "reduced to want" and to contemplate how their loved ones would be "rescued from poverty" as a result of a life insurance policy.[15]

As interested as the firm's incorporators were in establishing a profitable business, they were also genuinely concerned with addressing the plight of the widowed and the orphaned in this growing "world of strangers." Around the same time that Pennsylvania Company was initiating operations, the wives and daughters of these insurance entrepreneurs were themselves addressing the same problem through the Orphan Society of Philadelphia. Both institutions claimed as their purpose the protection of the weakest members of society: the latter by providing charitable relief for the helpless victims of an untimely death, and the former by preventing the need for that relief in the first place. Eleven of the twelve directors of Pennsylvania Company (in 1814) as well as the company actuary were married to women who subscribed to the Orphan Society in 1815, and the treasurer of the Orphan Society, Mrs. Mary Yorke, was married to Pennsylvania Company president Samuel Yorke. This intimate connection between the philanthropic and capitalistic responses to the financial consequences of death was likewise present in 1816, when President Yorke and six other company directors made substantial contributions to the erection of an orphan asylum.[16]

Following the lead of Pennsylvania Company, members of New England's wealthiest commercial families—a group historians now commonly refer to as the Boston Associates—organized Massachusetts Hospital Life Insurance Company in 1818 for the specific purpose of raising funds for Massachusetts General Hospital, one of the Associates' pet philanthropic projects. Like their Philadelphia compatriots, the Associates viewed the incorporation of a life insurance company as a means of creating a socially conscious yet profitable enterprise. Therefore, while one-third of the insurer's profits were dedicated to Massachusetts General, a substantial portion of the residual funds were invested in the business endeavors of the Associates.[17]

These firms had barely begun promoting their new product when the Panic of 1819 and ensuing severe depression hit the nation. Banks were largely blamed for the speculative frenzy that led to the panic, but there was a general backlash against corporations of all kinds. Thus it was remarkable that Pennsylvania Company continued in business during the 1820s and that Massachusetts Hospital Life opened its doors at all, selling its first policies in 1823. By 1825 (with fewer than one hundred policies in existence), life insurance was still a virtually unknown product in the United States.

Between 1812 and 1830, seven other American companies were chartered with life underwriting privileges. Of these, two closed their doors within a handful of years, and three others sold few policies, if any. The remaining four firms—Pennsylvania Company (1812–72), Massachusetts Hospital Life (1818–67), New York Life Insurance and Trust Company (1830–65), and Baltimore Life Insurance Company (1830–67)—became the pioneers in establishing this novel industry (see appendix, table A.1). As the country emerged from depression, the sales efforts of these early companies began to bear fruit. Between 1825 and 1840, the amount of life insurance in force (the total death benefit payable on all existing policies) increased at a consistent real rate of 25% per annum (see figure), growing from about $168,000 (in 1860 dollars) in 1825 to $4.5 million by 1840. Mirroring the replacement of Philadelphia with New York as the financial capital of the nation, New York Life and Trust would likewise come to

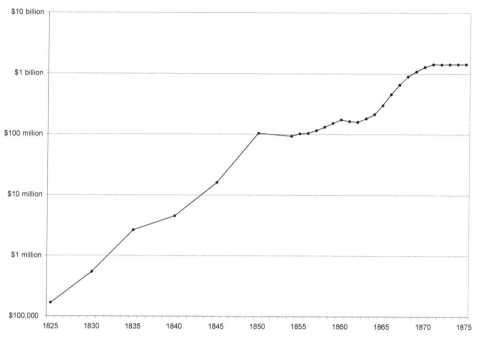

Life Insurance in Force, 1825–75 (log trend). *Historical Statistics of the United States, Colonial Times to 1970* (Washington, DC: Government Printing Office, 1975), 1057. All amounts in 1860 dollars, adjusted according to the consumer price index in Paul A. David and Peter Solar, "A Bicentenary Contribution to the History of the Cost of Living in America," *Research in Economic History* 2 (1977): 16.

dominate the life insurance field during the 1830s, accounting for more than half of all policy sales by 1840.

The express purpose of forming an insurance company was to mitigate risk by spreading it across a large number of people. Yet two main issues plagued the industry during the early years. It had to contend with limited knowledge regarding mortality in the United States (the actual risks they were attempting to underwrite), and it needed to increase sales in order to ensure that mortality risks were adequately spread across the population. New York Life and Trust outperformed its competitors by aggressively addressing both of these issues. During the 1830s and 1840s, company president William Bard was a pioneer in creating more accurate mortality tables and in discerning the proper rate structure for protecting the fiscal soundness of the company while still attracting new business. Cooperation with other life insurance firms as well as with state and federal governments was a key part of these efforts.

Life insurers had always attempted to differentiate themselves from other corporations by stressing their role as the protector of widows and orphans. Thus a third issue facing companies in this period was how to guarantee that these main beneficiaries were not denied their claims. The majority of women were prevented by law or custom from taking out policies on the lives of their husbands, while a policy that a husband took out on himself was considered part of his estate and thus could be claimed by creditors upon his death. This problem particularly came to light during the depression following the Panic of 1837. Paralleling the debates over bankruptcy legislation of the period, various companies (again led by New York Life and Trust) successfully lobbied their state legislatures for laws allowing wives to take out policies on the lives of their husbands that would be exempt from attachment by creditors. Partially as a result of these widow's laws, from 1840 to 1845 insurance in force more than tripled to $16 million.

An important development of the 1840s was the emergence of mutual life insurance companies, whose annual profits were redistributed to the policyholders rather than to stockholders. Although mutual insurance was not a new concept (Society for Equitable Assurances of London had been operating under the mutual plan since its establishment in 1762, and fire and marine companies were commonly organized as mutuals in locations where capital was scarce), the first American mutual life companies were not established until the late 1830s and failed to make significant inroads into the industry until the 1840s. The main impetus for this shift to the mutual model was the Panic of 1837 and the resulting financial crisis, which combined to dampen the enthusiasm of investors for expensive projects ranging from canals and railroads to banks and insurance companies. Between 1838 and 1846, only one new life insurance company was able to raise the capital essential for organization on a stock basis.[18] Mutuals, however, required little initial capital, relying instead on the premium payments from high-volume sales to pay any death claims.[19] By the end of the decade, at least seventeen new life insurance companies would begin operation under the mutual plan.

The few historians who have examined the life insurance industry depict this antebellum growth in very uncomplicated terms. In his book *Marketing Life Insurance: Its History in America*, J. Owen Stalson refers to the sale of mutual policies as the "revolution of 1843" and credits aggressive marketing campaigns by mutual companies during the 1840s with establishing the industry. In *Morals and Markets: The Development of Life Insurance in the United States*, Viviana A. Rotman Zelizer primarily credits changes in religious sermons that first condemned and then promoted the institution with the "unexplained" growth of the 1840s. Both authors start with the basic assumption that the industry was failing prior to the early 1840s and succeeding thereafter.[20] This rather simplistic approach completely ignores the dynamism of the pre-1843 industry, apparent in both the statistical and anecdotal evidence. Indeed, as the figure above demonstrates, the amount of life insurance in force increased steadily during the second quarter of the nineteenth century, with no monumental shift at any point in the 1840s.

The focus on 1843 is mainly due to the fact that mutual companies replaced stock companies as the dominant firms in the industry by the late 1840s. The oldest companies surviving into the twentieth century dated from this period, and (as is often the case) the winners write the history. The focus on 1843 can largely be blamed on the corporate histories of these mutual companies, which almost universally ignore or significantly downplay the role of early stock companies in favor of their own pioneering efforts. While mutual companies clearly built their businesses on the foundation laid by Pennsylvania Company, Massachusetts Hospital Life, New York Life and Trust, and others, they were able to replace these first movers by capturing the optimism of the new middle class. Whereas stock companies focused on the fears of middle-class existence (in particular the ease with which families could become impoverished with the death of the main breadwinner), mutuals were able not only to target these same fears but to cultivate middle-class hopes for the future by marketing life insurance as an investment.

Zelizer's argument that life insurance sales were slowed by religious concerns that it undermined trust in God likewise does not coincide with the historical record. Not only do the roots of the American industry extend back to societies for the protection of the families of ministers, but the sale of insurance to men of the cloth remained high throughout the 1830s and 1840s. Indeed, the area of New York State most touched by the religious revivals of the Second Great Awakening (known as the burned-over district) was the main geographic location of New York Life and Trust sales outside of New York City. Although some sects certainly may have preached against life insurance (just as they preached against the evils of the market as a whole), Zelizer's generalization across denominations does not hold up against actual policy sales. A multidenominational sampling of early nineteenth-century sermons, magazines, and newspapers likewise provides no evidence in support of this thesis.

The alleged triumph of mutual companies after 1843 is further undermined by the growth rate of life insurance subsequent to their emergence as the dominant players in the industry. Sales of life insurance remained stagnant for most of the 1850s. The urban South was the only area to experience a higher than average expansion of sales during this decade, with Baltimore Life making the fateful decision to specialize in underwriting slaves. By the eve of the Civil War, life insurance coverage of urban slaves in the Upper South was approximately equivalent to that of urban white males in the Northeast, although policies on white southerners were far less common.

One factor contributing to the slowdown in policy sales was increased state regulation of insurance corporations during the late 1840s and 1850s. Desiring to protect both their individual citizens from potential fraud or mismanagement and their corporate citizens from the competition of out-of-state firms, states enacted a vast array of taxation laws, deposit requirements, and investment restrictions as well as retaliatory legislation against the acts of other states. Not only did these complicated, constricting, and often contradictory laws depress the sales of the industry during this period, but they pushed company executives to become more involved in the legal process. As lobbying efforts on the state level failed, by the 1860s the industry was actively soliciting relief from the federal government by challenging the constitutionality of state laws in court and by seeking the creation of a national bureau of insurance.

The major boom period in life insurance sales occurred during and after the Civil War. Although the industry had no experience with mortality during war—particularly a war on American soil—and most policies contained clauses that forbade military service, almost all companies agreed to underwrite war risks for a substantial premium surcharge. The goodwill and publicity engendered with the payment of each death claim associated with the conflict, combined with a generally heightened awareness of mortality, greatly increased interest in life insurance. Whereas only 43 companies existed on the eve of the war, the newfound popularity of life insurance resulted in the establishment of 107 new companies between 1865 and 1870.[21] Sales of policies surged from $160 million in 1862 to $1.3 billion by 1870 (in 1860 dollars), a growth rate of about 30% per annum.[22]

But with this increasing popularity also came heightened competition. In direct contrast to the early movers in the industry, new firms of the 1860s were much less likely to engage in cooperative efforts to promote the safety and longevity of the industry as a whole. Rather, they tended to relax the stringent rate structure, selection criteria, and policy restrictions established by antebellum firms. In so doing, these newcomers opened themselves up to increased instances of insurance fraud and risked bankruptcy if the rapid life insurance sales of the immediate postbellum era slackened. When that downturn did begin around 1870, the industry suffered a catastrophic collapse, which marked the end of the first major era in the history of life insurance. The industry would successfully reinvent itself during the Gilded Age by focusing on industrial policies for the working classes, international sales, and more innovative (and risky) investment policies for the middle class. Life insurance of the late nineteenth century was therefore sufficiently distinct from its pre-1870 antecedents to fall outside of the purview of this book.

The American life insurance industry was developed with the goal of protecting widows and orphans from the risks of modern life. Antebellum life insurance promoters achieved success by importing a business model from Great Britain, creating a market for life insurance where none had previously existed and constantly innovating their product to attract an ever-broadening share of the American populace to the industry. In the process, they were forced to combat moral hazards such as gambling policies, murder, suicide, and insurance fraud; to confront legal barriers to the industry's growth; to expand their limited actuarial knowledge; to respond to external shocks such as economic recessions, the Civil War, and emancipation; and to meet the challenges of competition both from within the industry and from other industries such as savings banks. Their success in each of these endeavors depended on the creation and maintenance of a carefully crafted public image and reputation, close cooperation and coordination within the industry as well as between the industry and the public sector, and the insight of entrepreneurs who recognized that the growing class of middle-income families faced unique risks and needs that only life insurance could answer.

PART I

THE CREATION OF AN INDUSTRY

LIFE INSURANCE

In a storm, one night,
When all was fright
'Mongst the passengers and crew;
An Irish clown
Like a block sate down,
And seem'd as senseless too.
Conduct like this
Was much amiss,
And not to be endur'd;
But when ask'd why,
He made reply—
"Good folks, my life's insur'd."

Atheneum, 1823

CHAPTER I

Understanding Mortality in Antebellum America

The Search for a Stable Business Model

In the late 1820s, William Bard of Hyde Park, New York, decided to move his wife and eight surviving children to New York City.[1] A graduate of Columbia College and a lawyer by training, the 50-year-old Bard had spent the majority of his adult life living comfortably on his family's estate in the Hudson River valley as a country gentleman and man of letters. He was a descendant of prominent French Huguenots who had migrated to North America in the early eighteenth century to escape religious persecution. He was also, more immediately, the scion of two of New York City's most respected medical doctors; his father and grandfather had even been called on personally to care for President George Washington when he required treatment for a potentially fatal skin infection in 1789.

Bard fully expected that the family wealth, combined with the substantial fortune brought to the marriage by his wife, Catharine Cruger, would enable him to live out his days in his beloved Hyde Park. Unfortunately, by the first decades of the nineteenth century, a bitter and expensive lawsuit was raging between the Cruger siblings and their stepmother over the dispersal of their late father's estate. As this lawsuit dragged on, Catharine's inheritance was sharply reduced and the Bards were forced to reconsider their considerable living expenses. The Bard children encouraged their father to sell Hyde Park and return to New York City, where they could enjoy the many diversions and amenities of city life. William Bard reluctantly complied.

Whether because of financial necessity or mere boredom, Bard arrived in the city seeking employment. Having no interest in practicing law, he appears to have considered pursuing the recently vacated post of president of Columbia College. But his attention was quickly diverted by a proposal to establish a life insurance company in New York City. Prominent businessman Nathaniel Prime, the father of Bard's new son-in-law, informed him of this venture and encouraged him to become involved. And while the extant record provides little indication of why he found this particular avenue so appealing, Bard immediately devoted his full energy to the creation and success of the proposed New York Life Insurance and Trust Company (NYL&T), serving as the first president from its incorporation in 1830 through 1843 and as actuary from 1830 until just before his death in the early 1850s. Later in life, Bard would accurately remark: "While I presided over it, it rose to be a great and important company . . . I first suggested the plan of the institution. I had been almost exclusively the creator of its business in life insurance."[2] With Bard at the helm, NYL&T would revolutionize the way life insurance companies operated in the United States, creating—virtually from scratch—the statistical basis for the long-term safety of the industry.

Before the incorporation of NYL&T, Pennsylvania Company for Insurances on Lives and Granting Annuities and Massachusetts Hospital Life Insurance Company held monopolies on the sale of life insurance in their respective regions. Each company pursued this new business enterprise very conservatively in order to ensure its long-term safety and viability. Since knowledge of American mortality rates was close to nonexistent, they each based their premium charges on established British tables, adding a substantial surcharge in case the American experience was less favorable. They were also extremely vigilant in selecting risks, requiring that all applicants make a personal visit to the home office and that policyholders be people known and respected by the company directors. But despite the novelty of the new product and the companies' cautious approach to sales, life insurance grew steadily with each passing year as urban businessmen and their families became more familiar with the concept. By the end of the 1820s, both companies were regarded as sound, stable financial institutions within their local regions.

As the true first movers with established track records in the life insurance industry, Pennsylvania Company and Massachusetts Hospital Life should have had a distinct advantage over new entrants to the field. Yet by the end of the 1830s, Baltimore Life Insurance Company (chartered 1830) and Girard Life Insurance, Annuity, and Trust Company of Philadelphia (1836) would quietly surpass them in sales. But all four of these firms would be dwarfed by the rapid growth and success of NYL&T (1830), which by 1840 would account for more than half of all policy sales in the country; Bard could confidently (if somewhat prematurely) declare the following year that it would "have the monopoly for a long time."[3] NYL&T's success was the direct result of the business model pursued by Bard. Instead of passively accepting the conservative methods of the earlier companies and merely applying them to a new location, NYL&T completely reinvented how life insurance was sold in America, establishing the model followed by all subsequent nineteenth-century competitors.

Led by Bard, NYL&T subjected the methods employed by Pennsylvania Company and Massachusetts Hospital Life to a complete reappraisal. Rather than ensuring the stability of the industry, Bard determined that their approach in fact exposed the industry to greater risk of failure. By severely limiting the number of policyholders through high prices and strict selection criteria, they also limited their ability to spread mortality risks across a wide segment of the population; the laws of probability, upon which all insurance is based, are most accurate when applied to large groups of people.[4] But even more disturbing to Bard was their complete lack of knowledge about the American mortality experience in general and their blind faith in the British tables. Although the high premium rates *might* be required to safely underwrite American risks—and might even underestimate the true death rate—they might just as easily be unnecessarily high, pricing out a large number of potential policyholders. The critical foundation of the industry was built on mere guesswork and was thus little better than playing the lottery or engaging in financial speculation.

Although his efforts to understand the mortality experience of Americans would not come to full fruition until decades after his own death, during the 1830s and 1840s Bard was a pioneer in compiling and promoting the compilation of data on mortality by age, occupation, geographic region, gender, and even marital status. Simultaneously, Bard sought to extend life sales to as wide a population base as possible—while still maintaining vigilant oversight over the quality of the policyholders. This second objective was intimately linked to his mortality project. Understanding which factors tended to increase or decrease life expectancy better equipped NYL&T to judge individual applications. Bard ultimately hoped to use these data to discern the optimum rate structure for protecting the fiscal soundness of the company while keeping prices low enough to attract a maximum number of potential applicants.

Bard's vision and leadership were essential for the success and dominance of NYL&T, yet Bard was by no means merely a profit-maximizing capitalist. He was a family man who truly believed in the benefits of life insurance and worked first and foremost for the success of the industry as a whole. He would recruit rival insurance entrepreneurs, prominent citizens from around the country, and state and federal governments in his quest to create the safest, most scientifically accurate basis for the sale of life insurance. Perhaps this obsession was due to paternal concern for his own fourteen children, six of whom died in infancy and four as young adults. Or perhaps it was the experience of raising five grandchildren who were orphaned—all under the age of nine—when their own parents died within a year of each other. Or perhaps it was the example of his mother and wife, both of whom devoted considerable time, energy, and money to helping the less fortunate. Whatever his motivation, most of Bard's efforts benefited—and were intended to benefit—the industry as a whole.

The Price-Setting Quandary

More than any other component, what differentiated life insurance from fire and marine insurance was the certainty of the risk it underwrote; death was inevitable, and the main question facing people was not *if* but *when* the loss would occur. Therefore, the core requirement for the success of any life insurance company was accurate evaluation and management of its mortality risks. The fiscal soundness of the industry was predicated upon setting premium rates at a level high enough to cover the risk of insuring as well as overhead costs and to provide an adequate return to stockholders. The greatest proportion of an insurance company's costs was death claims on its policies—a cost that it could only estimate with accurate mortality tables. While individuals could not estimate the time of their demise with any degree of accuracy, European mathematicians as early as the seventeenth century understood that, with the proper data, the average life expectancy for a given age group could be predicted quite precisely. To maximize predictability, minimize costs, and maintain public confidence, companies had to compute accurate mortality tables to assess the average risk incurred for insuring different age groups.

The development of accurate mortality tables was a problem that plagued the American industry for the majority of the nineteenth century, since the information necessary to compute such tables was difficult to obtain. Ideally, a mortality table would be constructed from a continuous registry of births and deaths combined with periodic census enumerations to account for migration. Less precise tables could be calculated from vital statistics alone, particularly in the case of relatively stationary populations, or from data provided by two or more censuses if the time between enumerations was not too great.[5] Unfortunately, few American towns attempted to track birth or death records during the first half of the nineteenth century, there was no established church to record baptisms and burials for the population as a whole, and the large number of immigrants and internal migrants made the construction of an American life table an especially daunting task. Early American life insurance companies thus were forced to turn to the tables used in England, although they initially had little means of assessing the applicability of these tables to the mortality rates of the United States.

The two most important early mortality tables for the history of American life insurance were the Northampton Table, based on the registries of christenings and deaths from 1735 to 1780 for the parish of All Saints in Northampton, England,[6] and the Carlisle Table, based on observations of births and deaths collected by Dr. John Heysham for the parishes of St. Mary and St. Cuthbert in Carlisle, England, from 1779 to 1787.[7] Although some contemporary observers were highly skeptical of the accuracy of these tables in predicting mortality of the general population,[8] several major British life insurers employed them with great success well into the mid-nineteenth century.[9]

The relationship of these tables to mortality rates in the United States, however, was unexplored. The best analysis in America prior to 1850 was attempted by Dr. Edward Wigglesworth on the mortality experience of sixty-two towns in New Hampshire and Massachusetts from 1789.[10] His table suffered from two crucial defects, however. First, he examined mortality in only one year although mortality rates can fluctuate widely from year to year. Second, he constructed his table based on a stable population model and then overcorrected for the fact that births greatly outpaced deaths, while ignoring the effect of migration.[11] Early life insurance companies recognized the limitations of the Wigglesworth Table, and none ever adopted it for their premium calculations. In his 1853 chapter on mortality tables, American life insurance historian Moses Knapp commented that the Wigglesworth Table was "imperfect" and contained "fallacies"; Knapp did not mention the table again and quickly turned to an extended discussion of the applicability of the various British tables for the American life insurance industry.[12]

Despite these drawbacks, for the first decades of the American life insurance industry the Wigglesworth Table was the main point of comparison between the American and British mortality experiences. The only other American tables (for which I have found evidence) were two tables on life expectancy in Philadelphia constructed by Pennsylvania Company in 1814 based on records from the Episcopal Church and the Philadelphia Board of Health—although Pennsylvania Company would never adopt either of these tables.[13] Given the limited statistics on American mortality available at that time, the Northampton Table most closely emulated American life expectancy. Compared with the Wigglesworth Table, the Northampton appeared to underestimate the American experience over the entire adult age range, while the Carlisle Table greatly overestimated it until the age of 50. But both of Pennsylvania Company's tables demonstrated life expectancies even lower than that predicted by the Northampton Table (see appendix, table A.2).

Notwithstanding these misgivings about the Northampton and Carlisle tables, the American industry quickly adopted them as the industry standards for determining rates; they had no other options. Following the lead of the Society for Equitable Assurances on Lives and Survivorships of London (established 1762), both Pennsylvania Company and Massachusetts Hospital Life[14] began business using the more conservative Northampton Table, adding 10% for loading (expenses, profits, and contingencies).[15] However, as this conservative approach translated into high premium rates, both companies encountered difficulty through the 1820s acquiring a number of policyholders adequate to render any table safe.

Following the lead of their American predecessors, both NYL&T and Baltimore Life began business in 1830 employing the same rate structure. Yet NYL&T had been in business less than a year when President Bard began reexamining the underwriting practices of these companies and questioning the use of this table. Writing to Pennsylvania Company in January 1831, Bard expressed his concern that the premiums charged under the Northampton Table were too high and his hope that the more extensive experience of Pennsylvania Company in the life insurance field could shed some light on the true rate of American mortality. "To an Office it is a disadvantage to have the rates higher than a just estimate of human life makes prudent," he wrote, "in as much as high rates prevent Insurance & the safety of the Office depends more on the numbers insured, than on extravagant profits."[16]

Bard was especially concerned that NYL&T—and by extension Pennsylvania Company and Massachusetts Hospital Life—had not written sufficient numbers of policies for *any* mortality table to be accurate, yet he was averse to making a haphazard change in rates without sound statistical backing for his decision: "I have myself been inclined to the opinion that our rates were too high, but have been unwilling even to propose an alteration with the little experience we have here on the subject." Having been informed that Pennsylvania Company was in the process of reexamining its rate structure, Bard hoped that the more-established company would share its knowledge and conclusions.[17]

By 1832, Bard was becoming increasingly frustrated as sales of life policies remained slower than he thought prudent—and as Pennsylvania Company refused to respond to his repeated inquiries. The only means of ensuring that the firm's costs in death claims did not exceed its revenue in premium payments was to increase the number of policyholders, yet he believed that this actuarial ignorance was severely curtailing policy sales and thus undermining the safety of the entire industry: "It was thought we discovered in the high rates of their premiums a sufficient cause for the trifling amount of their business . . . It is plain, that the business of a Company is likely to be extended in proportion to the cheapness with which the inhabitants of the Country can obtain the benefit of the comfortable & safe practice of Insurance."[18] According to one London actuary with whom he consulted, the company would need at least 300 to 500 active policies to operate safely, but as of May 1833 NYL&T still had less than 250. Bard noted: "If a large number can be secured it is a safe and profitable buisiness [*sic*] but numbers are requisit [*sic*]."[19] As he investigated the matter further, Bard learned that "the scientific Gentlemen of England" believed that the Northampton Table overestimated mortality—providing some credence for his criticism of the rate structure.[20]

Despite being well versed and up to date on the question of British mortality tables,[21] Bard had no way of knowing how well any of these tables applied to the American experience. At one point, he wrote to Pennsylvania Company that "unless it can be shown that the Climate of America is more unfavourable to life than that of England, [the tables] are more favourable to the Office than modern experience proves necessary."[22] However, this was more conjecture than a statement of fact. In reality, Bard had no way of knowing how the American mortality experience compared with that of the British. He had hoped that Pennsylvania Company "would have taken the lead in lowering the rates" based on its more extensive experience, and on several occasions he requested that friends in Philadelphia inquire as to the status of these alleged new tables.[23] He even wrote directly to Joseph Roberts Jr., actuary of Pennsylvania Company, to ascertain whether the tables had yet been prepared and when they would be published.[24]

But Pennsylvania Company seemed uninterested in collaborating with the newest entrant into the life insurance field. Although the company was willing to discuss premium rates with Massachusetts Hospital Life,[25] the New England firm posed little threat to Pennsylvania Company's mid-Atlantic monopoly, never having infringed upon its local market. Almost 80% of Massachusetts Hospital Life's sales through 1831 were in the state of Massachusetts, 93% were in New England, and only one policy was ever sold in Philadelphia. As late as 1841, the secretary of Massachusetts Hospital Life stated that the object of the company was "to insure on the lives of persons remaining in and about New England."[26] In contrast, NYL&T demonstrated no signs of limiting its business operations to the immediate New York City area, stating unequivocally in 1833 that "the great increase of our population promises to us success and situated as we are we shall by and by command a share of buisiness [sic] from other States."[27] But even if NYL&T had intended to confine itself to the immediate vicinity of New York City, its relative proximity to Philadelphia alone would have made it a threat.

Just as Bard had surmised, during the 1820s Pennsylvania Company had found that its premium charges were "quite favorable to the Company,"[28] and it had indeed begun reevaluating these rates in an attempt to attract more business and undercut the emerging competition from New York. By the end of 1831 the company decided to lower its rates by approximately 9% (still employing the Northampton Table, but now with only 1% for loading).[29] Pennsylvania Company wrote to inform Massachusetts Hospital Life of this decision during the winter of 1831–32 but deliberately continued to ignore NYL&T.[30]

Unaware of the rate cut by Pennsylvania Company, the frustrated Bard and his NYL&T directors decided in January 1832 that this youngest of the American life insurance companies would make the bold move to unilaterally lower rates. As Bard explained to one board member, "the reduction must be eventually to the advantage of the Co[mpany], by increasing its business & adding to its security; for it should be remembered that a Co[mpany] doing business on just principles, is insecure only while the members is small, & that every additional ins[urance] adds to its security."[31] NYL&T concluded that by expanding sales, the use of a more liberal table such as the Carlisle would actually increase the safety of the institution by spreading the mortality risk over a larger base. Bard wrote to President Nathaniel Bowditch of Massachusetts Hospital Life and President Thomas Astley of Pennsylvania Company to inform them of NYL&T's decision to switch to the Carlisle Table, with 35% added for loading.[32] This was a significant rate cut for the company, particularly for customers under the age of 50. The Carlisle rates undercut the new premiums of Pennsylvania Company by as much as 20% for the youngest insurers; only those over the age of 50 benefited more from the new Pennsylvania Company table (see appendix, table A.3).

The following year, both Massachusetts Hospital Life and Baltimore Life (the only other major competitors in the field) likewise lowered their rates, but they chose to follow the lead of Pennsylvania Company (still the preeminent American life insurer) by remaining on the Northampton Table with 1% loading.[33] A third minor competitor, United States Insurance Company of Maryland, continued at the original rates, using the Northampton Table with 10% loading. Writing in 1833, the Washington, DC, agent of United States Insurance (who was then in the process of switching his agency to Baltimore Life) expressed his disgust upon learning that United States Insurance was charging higher rates than the rest of the industry: "Such was bad policy in the Company, as it defeated the very object of the agency, by reducing the number of applicants, who would of course apply elsewhere."[34] By June of that year, United States Insurance had ceased writing life insurance and its twenty-eight existing policies had been reinsured with Baltimore Life.[35]

Remaining on the Northampton Table in any manner proved disastrous for both Pennsylvania Company and Massachusetts Hospital Life, with NYL&T benefiting. By 1835, only five years after its incorporation, NYL&T's life insurance in force approached $2 million. This accounted for more than half the amount insured by the industry as a whole, and it was three times greater than the industry total had been in 1830. The growth of other companies was much more moderate during those same five years; insurance in Pennsylvania Company grew from $302,000 to $482,000 and in Massachusetts Hospital Life from $185,000 to $319,000.[36]

Although Baltimore Life continued to use the Northampton Table as well, the company was able to move into second place in the industry as early as 1833 by marketing its product to segments of the population underserved by its competitors—including government bureaucrats, military personnel, southerners, and slaveholders; by 1835 it was responsible for 24% of the life insurance in force—and yet it still underwrote less than half the amount of NYL&T. In 1835 Baltimore Life reconsidered its rates, especially as it attempted to expand into the northeastern market. In correspondence with a potential new agent in Hartford, Connecticut, by the name of Thomas Perkins—who simultaneously served as the Hartford agent for NYL&T and Massachusetts Hospital Life[37]—the president of Baltimore Life admitted that "our rates are somewhat higher in the younger ages than the New York Co."[38] Only two months later, in June 1835, the company decided to make its rates conform to those of the now dominant firm in the industry, NYL&T.[39] Pennsylvania Company likewise finally adopted the Carlisle Table for its premium rates in March 1837.[40]

Girard Life of Philadelphia began business in 1836 using the Northampton Table (following the lead of its main local competition), but in May 1837, President B. W. Richards of Girard Life wrote to President John J. Donaldson of Baltimore Life—with whom Girard Life had a standing agreement to reinsure large risks—to inform him that Girard Life was also switching to the Carlisle Table.[41] During the remainder of the antebellum period, most new companies likewise employed the Carlisle Table as the basis for their operations, including New England Mutual Life (1835), Mutual Life Insurance Company of New York (1842), Nautilus Insurance Company (1841, later renamed New York Life), Mutual Benefit of New Jersey (1845), North Carolina Mutual Life (1849), Mutual Life Insurance Company of Baltimore (1849), Manhattan Life Insurance Company (1850), and American Life and Trust of Philadelphia (1850).[42] These companies underwrote more than half the life insurance in force in 1850. Massachusetts Hospital Life was the last major company to switch to the Carlisle, clinging to the Northampton Table until 1845 or 1846.[43]

Pennsylvania Company made two decisions during the early 1830s that critically damaged its ability to compete in the life insurance industry. First, it chose to ignore a new competitor rather than asserting its position as the dominant company in a highly concentrated industry. If Pennsylvania Company had informed NYL&T of its decision to lower rates in 1831, the correspondence of NYL&T gives every indication that it would have followed Pennsylvania Company's lead rather than making its own unilateral—and more drastic—cuts (although it is impossible to say for sure that NYL&T would not have adopted the Carlisle Table regardless). Second, Pennsylvania Company (as well as Massachusetts Hospital Life) failed to meet the price cuts of NYL&T, effectively relinquishing to the new company leadership in the industry. Unlike Baltimore Life, neither company attempted to increase demand through marketing campaigns or to justify its higher prices through product differentiation. As Massachusetts Hospital Life's corporate biographer states, the company was "nonaggressive in spirit,"[44] and a similar comment could be made about Pennsylvania Company.

In 1836, Pennsylvania Company gained a charter extension allowing it to enter the trust business for the first time;[45] Massachusetts Hospital Life was already in the trust business, and by the late 1830s both companies were concentrating their operations in that sector. Although Massachusetts Hospital Life and Pennsylvania Company continued to write new life policies until 1867 and 1872, respectively, their share of the industry dropped precipitously. Pennsylvania Company's market share was reduced from about 50% in 1830 to 13% in 1835 to just 2.5% by 1845, while Massachusetts Hospital Life's share went from 31% in 1830 to 9% in 1835 to 1.5% in 1845.

In Search of an American Mortality Table

Throughout the antebellum period, insurance executives publicly touted the Carlisle Table as "represent[ing] the average laws of mortality in England with very considerable accuracy, and . . . approximat[ing] that of the northern United States."[46] An 1845 *Treatise on Life Insurance* extended its applicability, stating: "It may be relied upon in all calculations wherein the tenure of life is concerned, throughout the Middle and Eastern States, also the Western, and a portion of the Southern."[47] One insurance promoter even declared that "it is the result of long experience and minute observations on life insurance establishments, and may be relied on for general accuracy. The exceptions to its assumptions are found to be so trivial as to supersede the exercise of much consideration as to calculations."[48] North Carolina Mutual's 1849 brochure assured potential clients that "its calculations are found to apply with exceeding minuteness to the present experience of Insurance Companies in the middle States of our Union, and all that have adopted it, seem to be doing a safe and profitable business."[49]

Notwithstanding these assertions, "seem to be doing" was the proper phrasing, since firms still had little knowledge of the applicability of the Carlisle Table to the American mortality experience. Current profitability was an extremely inaccurate indicator of the safety of employing this table for two crucial reasons. First, the pool of policyholders was subject to a selection advantage; since applicants had to pass a medical exam and answer a series of questions about their own and their family's health history, policyholders were likely to be healthier than the aggregate population. But as companies strived to expand their business in the face of increasingly stiff competition, they would find it more and more difficult to limit themselves to those perceived as the best risks and would have to start insuring those they considered merely better than average risks or, eventually, just average risks.

Second, companies operated under a level premium system, whereby annual premium payments remained constant for the life of the policy. In the case of a one-year term policy, the premium reflected the risk of insuring a person of that age for one year. For example, the cost of a one-year term policy for a 20-year-old under the Carlisle Table would be $9.10 per $1,000 of insurance, while the same policy would cost a 55-year-old $23.20. But for a whole life policy, members paid more than the rate dictated by their age for the early years of the policy but less than their risk would indicate during the later years. A $1,000 whole life policy taken out at the age of 20 would cost $17.70 per year for the life of the policy, or $8.60 more than required by the initial risk ($17.70 minus $9.10). But by the age of 55 the person so insured would still be paying $17.70 per year, $5.50 *less* than his risk level would have required for a term policy.

This level premium system worked to the advantage of both companies and policyholders. Owners of term policies often were required to repay their application fee (usually $1.00) and to retake their medical exam with each new application, thus racking up fees and increasing the risk of rejection. Additionally, term premiums increased with age—gradually at first for those in their twenties and thirties but rapidly in middle age. By the age of 60, a term policyholder would owe $43.50 per $1,000 of insurance, compared with the $23.20 charged just five years earlier. For their part, companies received premiums sooner and could invest them for a longer term, increasing profits and potentially lowering the cost to policyholders (if the companies chose to charge lower rates reflecting this increased investment income). Lapsed whole life policies also left the company with more money to invest and apply to profit or the payment of other claims. Thus the level premium system inflated corporate profits as long as the majority of policyholders were new and in their overpayment years (when the proportionate difference between term and whole life prices was to the largest benefit of the company). For young companies, it was still unclear whether those premium rates would be sufficient once policyholders aged and policies began to mature.

Despite their public pronouncements of confidence, early life insurance executives were well aware of their ignorance in these matters, privately questioning both the long-term effect of medical selection and the overall safety of the tables. John J. Donaldson, president of Baltimore Life, expressed his doubts regarding the new rates in a letter to his Richmond agent in 1837 (just two years after switching from the Northampton to the Carlisle Table): "The regular rates of the New York & Balto Offices are low, *perhaps too low*" (emphasis added).[50] Similarly, in a long 1832 letter to NYL&T board of directors member Thomas Ludlow, President Bard revealed his continued misgivings about the Carlisle Table, which the company had just adopted. British actuaries considered the table "to be more correct & probably as correct as any [in] existence." Yet the question still remained whether this "moderate size town, & a very healthy one" really reflected the mortality experience of the United States. "The enquiry has given great trouble," Bard wrote, "nor have we been able to come to a decision on any very accurate or determinate basis. We have no accurate tables for showing the waste of human life in this Country, & the materials for forming an opinion of its comparative health; nor have scientific men nor medical men entered into the examination in any way to give decided information." Bard was thus forced to rely on anecdotal evidence and a "general opinion" that "the Climate of the U[nited] States north of Virginia is as favourable to human life as the Climate of Europe & of the State of N[ew] York as that of England."[51] For a man determined to place the life insurance industry on a solid, statistically sound footing for the long term, such guesswork was unacceptable.

By June 1832—less than six months after switching to the Carlisle Table—Bard began to act on his dissatisfaction with the existing mortality tables. For the next decade, he engaged in an effort to procure the data necessary to construct an accurate picture of mortality for the United States as a whole, as well as for specific American cities and occupation groups. First, he solicited the advice of Charles Babbage and John Finlaison,[52] two preeminent British actuaries, regarding the type of information necessary for the construction of such tables.[53] The initial focus of his attention was on the data provided in the United States and New York State censuses: "It will answer my hopes, if [Mr. Finlaison] will examine the census of the U[nited] States (1800, 1820, 1830) and [New York] State (1825, 1835), and say whether any and what columns of enquiries can be added, which would enable a skilfull [*sic*] actuary at some future period to draw accurate information, and form tables of Life for this Country, which may be depended on."[54] On several occasions, both Bard and members of NYL&T's board of directors expressed their intention to lobby the United States Congress and the New York legislature to add any suggested columns to their respective censuses, but these lobbying efforts were delayed by Finlaison's slow response.[55] In March 1839, after several years of corresponding with the British actuary (and in the context of "the President [of the United States] calling upon Congress to provide for the taking of the next census"), NYL&T entreated its investment house in London to find out from Finlaison "if in this matter anything further is desirable than what is contained in the census of 1830 which he now has, for if so we would exert ourselves to obtain it through the persons who will be appointed to take the census for 1840."[56]

When Bard finally received Finlaison's advice in September 1839, he promptly forwarded it to Secretary of State John Forsyth—whose office was in charge of conducting the federal census at that time—requesting that he consider adding several additional columns of information to the 1840 census.[57] Although this lobbying effort came too late to effect a mortality schedule for the 1840 United States census, the mortality schedule that was added in 1850 provided extensive detail on all deaths occurring during the twelve months prior to June 1850, including age, sex, nativity, color, marital status, cause of death, occupation, length of illness, and month of death. The superintendent of the 1850 census estimated that at least one-quarter of all deaths still went unrecorded, but the schedule was an important step toward collecting accurate mortality statistics; the information gained could still be compared with the data on the living population to create a preliminary mortality table for various demographic groups within the United States.[58]

Alterations to the census would provide the life insurance industry with accurate mortality information in the future, but Bard attempted to collect data for more immediate use, particularly regarding specific states and cities where life insurance was growing in popularity. As he wrote to his agent in Baltimore, "I am doing what I can to form a correct opinion of the value of Life in the different States of the Union." He continued to consult with Finlaison, who had requested information on "the annual deaths in our Chief City's [*sic*] and any other documents relating to their health and Climate. That I may do so I have written a circular to the Mayors of our chief Cities which I hope may elicit some information."[59] Bard also homed in on the various parts of New York State where the majority of applicants to NYL&T resided; during the late 1830s Bard sent out five thousand letters to "Clergy, Physicians, men of science, mechanics and farmers" throughout New York to gather more accurate birth and death information.[60] Copies of the nineteen hundred responses he received were sent to Finlaison in February 1840 to help him "form a correct estimate of the value of life in this state."[61] Bard was thus attempting to gather information on numerous levels and from a wide variety of sources. While each of these snapshot methods had potential flaws, the information provided could be overlaid and compared until a more accurate picture of American mortality began to emerge.

Other individuals not directly related to the life insurance industry also attempted to compile mortality data on various American cities at this time, though not nearly on the scale of Bard's efforts. With the stated goal of "establish[ing] a basis for premiums on life insurance," Philadelphia physician James Mease argued in 1841 that the existing bills of mortality greatly inflated the urban death rate over that of the English countryside. In order to accurately compare the healthiness between locales, he proposed that these bills should be adjusted to exclude deaths not directly related to "salubrity," including those caused by accidents, alcohol abuse, syphilis, murder, suicide, epidemic diseases, smallpox, and unknown causes. While he justified these omissions on the grounds that their effect "would operate equally in one place as in another," by so greatly understating the true mortality of a region his resulting tables would be of little use for life insurers.[62] In contrast, University of Georgia mathematics professor Charles F. McCay combined data on interments for Baltimore from 1826 to 1848 with the census returns from 1830 and 1840 to create a mortality table based on a stable population. However, the insurance industry dismissed this table because it included slaves and free blacks and was thus not restricted to the segment of the population in whom the industry was most interested.[63]

Several states passed legislation during the 1840s and 1850s requiring the registration of all deaths with a central state authority. Massachusetts passed the first such law in 1842, followed by New York in 1847, New Jersey and Connecticut in 1848, New Hampshire in 1849, Pennsylvania in 1851, and Kentucky and South Carolina in 1852.[64] By the early 1850s, the actuary of Mutual Life Insurance Company of New York had convinced New York's secretary of state to include mortality questions on its 1855 state census forms.[65] Although there is no clear evidence that Bard or any other life insurance promoter exercised direct influence on the changes to the 1850 federal census or the state death registration laws, the coincidence of this public interest in mortality statistics with the lobbying efforts of the industry—as well as the rapid increase in importance of life insurance and new insurance company incorporations during the 1840s and 1850s—suggests that the life insurance industry may have been a driving force behind the collection of these data.

Several things are striking about Bard's actuarial crusade. First, the creation of accurate tables was *not* an attempt to undermine the business of competing life companies. By lobbying for changes to the federal and state censuses rather than compiling the data independently, he was attempting to create a public record that would be to the long-term advantage of the entire industry. Of course, by 1840 NYL&T underwrote more than half of all life insurance in force; facing no strong competition, the firm was operating from a position of strength, and Bard had every reason to believe that his company would be the chief beneficiary of this information. Yet Bard's main goal was accurate statistical information that would place the entire industry on a solid financial footing. Companies could compete in areas such as service and marketing, but it was not safe to compete on price.

Second, Bard believed that the collection of such data was in the public's interest. Not only could state and federal governments gather such information in a more efficient manner than could any one individual or company (or so the industry initially thought), but that information could shed light on areas where the government could be better serving the public. For example, the superintendent of the census believed that from the compilation of mortality statistics in 1850 "a mass of information must have resulted relating to the sanitary condition of the country, attained as yet in no other part of the world."[66] Third, the compilation of data for mortality tables was of necessity a long-term project that would result in few short-term gains to the life insurance industry. Statistics would have to be collected and analyzed over several years, or several censuses, before sufficient data would be available to formulate mortality tables. Thus, Bard and NYL&T were laying the groundwork for the future success of the still immature industry.

But by the early 1840s, Bard's ultimate purpose also had shifted. In 1831—when the company was first trying to break into an oligopolistic industry with a relatively small overall market—his foremost concern was with safely lowering prices in order to increase demand for insurance. A decade later, when NYL&T had become the dominant firm in a thriving industry, he was more interested in providing NYL&T stockholders with an ample dividend. Bard wrote in 1841 to George Atkinson, a London actuary, that NYL&T need not reduce rates until "rivals" began offering lower rates: "This is not likely to be the case for many years. The Citizens of this abused Country are less likely now [in the aftermath of the Panic of 1837 and the ensuing depression] to trust new Offices or new experiments than they have been and I believe we have the monopoly for a long time." Thus, while he still desired Finlaison's expert opinion "as to the lowest rates to which they may go and yet be safe, which may be of future service," Bard also requested that the actuary estimate conservatively, taking "all drawback and unfavorable circumstances into consideration, and mak[ing] the most ample allowance for all."[67] The major interest of NYL&T in discerning American mortality accurately had thus become estimating future costs in order to safely distribute profits to the shareholders, not necessarily to lower costs to the public.

Understanding Other Factors Affecting Mortality

While age was the main characteristic considered in most mortality tables, life insurance executives understood that many other factors could bear on a policyholder's mortality. Particular parts of the country were believed to be more susceptible to disease; travel on newer conveyances such as steamboats and railroads as well as long-distance voyages by land or sea placed an individual at higher risk of injury; and certain occupations exposed their practitioners to greater hazards than the average person. Even gender or marital status could influence one's chances of death at any given age. While life insurers initially denied coverage to people living or traveling outside of the Northeast or working in hazardous occupations, companies were soon forced to reconsider these regulations as the travel requests of policyholders increased, as companies began targeting a more middle-class clientele, and as geographical competition within the industry induced firms to seek policyholders outside their local region. To tap into this wider applicant pool, companies cautiously began to place a surcharge on premium rates for policyholders in imperfect environmental situations.

Initially, these surcharges were mere guesswork. As applications arrived from people residing outside of the northeastern urban centers or engaged in employments of uncertain safety, companies such as NYL&T would quickly attempt to gather both anecdotal and statistical information regarding the mortality rate of the climate or occupation in question. As the industry matured, life insurers would also try to compile more accurate statistics based on their own underwriting experiences for a given region or occupation. For example, in advertising literature from both 1847 and 1857, New England Mutual remarked that it was "especially difficult to estimate the extraordinary risks from climate, hazardous employment, and any extraordinary circumstances, on account of the want of sufficient and accurate statistics of such risks, which can be derived only from long experience." But to address this problem, the company proudly assured the public, "Our company has, from its commencing business, taken care to preserve the statistics of such risks, in a form to be conveniently used in determining a just rate of additional premium, so soon as a sufficient number of cases shall have been recorded."[68] Unfortunately, the necessity of "a sufficient number of cases" meant that for the present, companies still had to rely on educated guesses in their decision making.

Occupation

While the majority of early policyholders were merchants, lawyers, or other professionals employed in nonhazardous pursuits, applicants for insurance were engaged in a wide range of occupations even during the earliest years of the industry. They included farmers, laborers, blacksmiths, carpenters, supercargoes, shipmasters, tallow chandlers, mechanics, mariners, brickmakers, distillers, and military personnel. Life insurance executives were wary of underwriting people employed in occupations that might expose them to greater health risks or physical danger than faced by the average policyholder. President Bard advised his Paterson, New Jersey, medical examiner in 1831 that applicants "must not be engaged in any unhealthy manufacture, of this latter point we shall depend on your judgment very much." He was particularly concerned that "a pursuit which shortens life by too much confinement or by the poisonous substances employed by the insured or by any other circumstances would make it unsafe to insure the party so employed at least at the usual rate of insurance."[69] In a statement typifying the attitude of the industry as a whole, National Life Insurance Company of Vermont specified in its 1856 rules and regulations that "premiums will be increased from the rates of the Tables, if the applicant is in the Navy, Army, or is a manager of, or connected with the business of Steam Engine, or Railroad Locomotive, or Steamboat, or in the manufacture of Gun Powder, or any business or occupation particularly hazardous to life." Even existing policyholders could not switch into these professions without "obtaining the consent of the Company and paying the increased premiums."[70]

Bard approached the acquisition of mortality statistics for different professions almost as tenaciously as he sought to create a life expectancy table for the United States, asserting in 1835 that "before we could make any offer for the Insurance of a particular class we should have some means of judging whether the lives of that class are better or worse than the average of lives on which our present rates are formed."[71] As applications came in from people engaged in potentially unhealthy or dangerous occupations, Bard compiled information to determine the safety of insuring them. Even if this knowledge only pertained to one individual applicant, Bard believed that it would contribute to the long-term understanding of mortality by occupation. For example, in 1833 he consulted several doctors regarding the hazards of house painting for one applicant from Paterson, New Jersey: "Dr. Thackrax agrees with Dr. Marsh that house painting is not a healthy employment. Such cases will require double caution." However, Bard also weighed the above-average risk of this particular occupation against the below-average risk of the individual applicant: "As Mr. Whitly is but 31, is healthy now and is attentive to his person and only wishes a 7 years insurance, I think he may be taken. I therefore send you a Policy."[72] While some professions placed their practitioners in imminent danger of death, the exposure to hazardous fumes associated with house painting created a long-term rather than a potentially impending risk. With a relatively young and healthy applicant, Bard was willing to underwrite this risk for a limited period of time, but not for the whole term of life.

That same summer, Bard researched the various dangers of working with brass for another applicant, Darius Cole from Rochester, New York, and noted that "the author on whom I depend says Brass founders are short lived. Turners Fellers and dressers of Brass are not short lived. The former suffer from the inhalation of the volatilised metal. Copper Smiths he adds are considerably affected by the fine scales which rise from imperfectly volatilised metal and by the fumes of the Spitter or solder of Brass. The men are generally unhealthy suffering like the Brass founders." On his application form, Cole listed his occupation as associated with the manufacture of brass, but he did not specify the exact nature of his involvement with the industry—a crucial detail for Bard: "Now if Mr. Coles occupation is such as to expose him to the inhalation of the volatilised metal, we would not insure him: if he is a burner, feller, and dresser of Brass only we would unless his constitution is manifestly feeble. Will you ascertain how this is and let me know."[73] Whereas Pennsylvania Company or Massachusetts Hospital Life would probably have rejected this applicant based purely on his occupation, Bard sought to increase the business of NYL&T by underwriting all applicants with potential life spans that had a high probability of conforming to the mortality tables. By consulting the most current experts in the field, Bard was able to differentiate between an average risk and a potentially unsafe applicant. Darius Cole received a $2,000 policy for the term of seven years, which he would renew for another seven years in 1840.[74]

But Bard did not limit his inquiries to blue-collar professions. In 1834, as applications from clergymen began arriving at the head office, Bard decided that it would be beneficial to research their mortality rates as well. While the general opinion was that "Clergymen are as good lives as the average at least," Bard was concerned that "in looking round I see but few old Clergymen this is however but a poor way of judging." Repeating his oft-stated refrain that "tables can alone give the truth," Bard sought to uncover any useful data that existed for the formation of such tables. He asked G. W. Clinton, "Could you ascertain from the Revd Mr Wilber Hoag [of Canandaigua, New York] whether there could be obtained from an examination of the records of one or more conferences a table of the Clergymen of those conferences for the last thirty or forty years, their ages when they entered on their duties as Clergymen, their present ages if alive or if dead their ages at the time they died."[75] This information would become increasingly important to NYL&T, as approximately 12% of all its policies were underwritten on the lives of clergymen during the 1830s.[76]

Physicians also fell within Bard's purview. In 1836, two doctors involved with quarantining immigrants coming into Quebec applied for insurance with the company.[77] President Bard returned the policies to his local agent, William D. Dupont, with a request for him to "inform me if any peculiar mortality has existed among that class of Gentlemen at Quebec." Once again, Bard faced the problem of analyzing the life expectancy of a small subset of the population. The little information he had indicated that "a large proportion of the Quarantine Physicians at N.Y. died 20 years since," yet he had "not understood that this had been the case of latter years." Reluctant to reject underwriting potentially good lives, Bard instead preferred to limit the policy amount to no more than $5,000 and to adjust the premium rates "depend[ing] on the information I receive from you."[78]

The occupations of greatest concern for life insurance companies were military positions. A standard condition inserted into policies for insurance stated that "insurances will be made on the lives of military and naval officers, off or on duty, in time of peace; the premium in every instance will be determined according to the more or less hazardous nature of the risk to be taken"[79] and that policies would be rendered void if the insured "enter[ed] into any military or naval service whatsoever, the militia not in actual service excepted."[80] In its initial prospectus of 1830, NYL&T stated that military risks would be taken "at an increased rate of premium, and by special agreement."[81] This additional premium ranged from $10 to $70 per $1,000 of insurance—a considerable increase over the standard premiums.[82] However, Bard was still wary of underwriting these risks. In 1832 he informed one applicant that the company would only "insure Naval or Military men not exposed to those peculiar risks. We will issue policies . . . not to be good against the Company during War or Civil Commotion by which the party is bro[ugh]t into active Service."[83] During the 1840s the company still did "not insure any person under any circumstances against the chances of battle, even upon the payment of an additional premium."[84] The contingencies of war were of particular concern, since the likelihood of mortality was nearly impossible to quantify.

Even during peaceful times, military men were potentially exposed to greater rates of mortality than civilians. Thus, as with all other risks, President Bard endeavored to learn the true rate of mortality among this population. He was particularly concerned with members of the navy, who spent long periods of time confined to ships at sea. In 1835, his agent in Washington, DC, suggested charging only a small additional premium upon naval risks in hopes of attracting more applications from this population. Bard was reluctant to go along with this proposal, since "no Office that I know of ventures to insure Naval Officers over the World at one rate nor at any thing like the small increase you suggest."[85] In a follow-up letter to the agent, he added: "If we adopt your proposal it would probably add to our business, but if we make a mistake in the rate at which we insure it would do us great injury if not ruin us."[86]

But Bard did not merely decline his agent's suggestion; instead, he took the opportunity to add to the company's knowledge of naval mortality. First, he sought all available data on the topic: "I am endeavoring to procure a statement of the deaths as they have taken place in the Naval Service," he wrote to the agent. "I am inclined to think they have been much more rapid than among the same number permanently on land." Second, rather than the small, flat surcharge proposed by the agent, Bard preferred to vary the charge depending on the particular situation of the applicant: "If the party insured is ordered abroad, the increase will depend on the position to which he is ordered and whether he has been acclimated or not. The increase will vary from ½ to 6 per cent" ($5 to $60 per $1,000 of insurance). However, he left open the possibility of adjusting the policy as more data became available: "Should the Gentleman I have employed be able to furnish me the proposed table the whole subject will be reconsidered."[87] In the end, Bard's hunch that military lives were a bad risk proved correct, as his investigation would eventually reveal unfavorable mortality among this population. By the 1850s, NYL&T had made the decision to deny policies to all military personnel, stating in 1850 that it did "not insure persons in the Navy at any rate of premium"[88] and in 1852 that it did "not insure the lives of Officers in the Army."[89]

However, a small number of companies were willing to take on war risks during the antebellum period—particularly those operating in the Baltimore and Washington, DC, area where there were high concentrations of military men. For example, Mutual Life Insurance Company of Baltimore actively advertised: "Parties belonging to the army and navy, insured with war and sea risks, on liberal terms."[90] In addition to the standard stories employed by virtually all companies in the promotional literature of the 1840s and 1850s, Mutual of Baltimore added that during the 1846 war with Mexico, "many officers and soldiers in the army and navy were insured with this company, with war and sea risks." In particular, its advertising highlighted the experience of one "gallant and distinguished officer, himself a member of this company." The officer informed the company "that as he saw his men falling on every side during a *sortie* from the walls, by the Mexicans, the thought occurred that some of the widows would be presenting policies at our counter for payment."[91] Thus like NYL&T's Washington, DC, agent, Mutual of Baltimore viewed military men as a target population for sales—people who faced mortality on a regular basis and therefore more readily appreciated the protection offered by a life insurance policy.

Although not as liberal in its terms as Mutual of Baltimore, Baltimore Life also advertised that "Officers of the Army and Navy by an insurance of their lives can make provision for their families,"[92] although these applicants would be required to pay a higher premium. Baltimore Life routinely placed an endorsement on every military policy indicating whether death in battle was covered by the company. During the summer of 1836, captains Erasmus D. Bullock and Benjamin L. Beall of the Second U.S. Dragoons (an army regiment stationed in Jefferson Barracks, Missouri, in preparation for the Second Seminole War in Florida) applied for and received policies with Baltimore Life. Captain Bullock's $500 policy was endorsed: "This Policy is made with privilege to assured to continue in the service of the United States wherever called, provided if he be killed in Battle the Policy is void."[93] Captain Beall's $1,000 policy additionally covered him in case of death during battle: "This Policy is made with permission for assured to remain in the Military Service of the United States, and to cover any risk of Battle."[94] However, Captain Beall paid a considerable surcharge to obtain this superior protection.

These Baltimore-based companies were the exceptions in an industry that generally opted—like NYL&T—to avoid underwriting military lives. In an 1837 article from the *Army and Navy Chronicle,* the author strongly encouraged military men to purchase policies: "Exposed as they are to more than ordinary perils and hardships, no class of citizens should be more prompt to secure to their families a competency, in the event of their being cut off." However, the writer warned that some companies would not underwrite military lives, citing the example of an applicant to Massachusetts Hospital Life who was "refused in rather an ungracious manner, on the ground that the Company declined insuring upon the lives of those who belong to the profession of arms." Readers were instead encouraged to apply with more local offices, "which will not hesitate to insure the lives of the defenders of their country."[95] Not until the Civil War would most other companies be forced to reconsider their rules regarding war risks.

Climate and Travel

The early life insurance industry was dominated by companies headquartered in the Northeast that were wary of the allegedly higher rates of mortality in the southern and western states. Executives were also concerned that the risks posed by traveling on certain modes of transportation would increase mortality rates. With the frontier being pushed farther and farther west and the population becoming increasingly mobile, insurance companies found it all the more difficult to deny coverage based on climate or to forbid policyholders to travel; thus obtaining accurate information on the true risk of these factors became particularly important.

As NYL&T attempted to expand its sales outside of New York City, the firm immediately had to face the question of how life expectancies were different in these new regions. For example, while Bard believed the climate of Halifax, Nova Scotia, to be "as favorable to life as that of any other state" and consequently appointed an agent there in 1833,[96] he was much more cautious about risks in western New York or the midwestern states. That same year, Bard requested more information on the climate of Syracuse, New York, before he would appoint an agent there; he asked B. Davis Noxen, who eventually became the local agent, "whether Syracuse is a healthy place or whether its neighborhood to the salt works and a marshy County does not make it liable to intermittents and fevers."[97] By the end of the year, Bard was satisfied with the safety of the city; he appointed agents not only for Syracuse but for cities throughout the interior of New York—many of which were along the course of the recently completed Erie Canal, including Albany, Auburn, Bath, Binghamton, Buffalo, Claverack, Cooperstown, Elmira, Genesee, Geneva, Ithaca, LeRoy, Lockport, Mayville, Oneida, Rochester, Salem, Saratoga, Troy, Utica, and Watertown.[98] As Bard affirmed in 1833, "Life Insurance is extending rapidly and is a safe business if conducted prudently."[99]

NYL&T was less confident about the safety of insuring residents of the Midwest. It placed a $5,000 limit on policies in the region and charged an "additional from 1 to 2 per cent [$10 to $20 per $1,000] on insurances in some parts of Ohio, Kentucky, Indiana, Illinois, Missouri, below the South line of Virginia to the 31st degree of North latitude."[100] Bard settled on this policy "after inquiry as to the health of Michigan, Indiana, Illinois, or the new Western States."[101] Because of the necessity of charging these higher rates, and perhaps also because of the more rural nature of this region, Bard did not expect life insurance to be popular in these areas. In 1833, his cousin Nathaniel Greene Pendleton of Cincinnati wrote NYL&T requesting advice regarding the establishment of a life company in Ohio. While Bard said he was happy to "send you all the documents in this Office, and will give you every information from time to time which you require," he was extremely pessimistic as to the prospects of such a company: "I should however I confess scarcely think Cincinnatti [sic] a situation in which Life Insurance could be made profitable or even a safe buisiness [sic] . . . in this large and buisy [sic] place we shall after a few years find enough to do, but in Cincinnatti I should doubt your success." Bard continued with a statement that could be construed as either supportive or condescending: "When you have made the trial if you relinquish the buisiness let me know & we will appoint you, or some one you will reccomend [sic] as our Agent for Life Insurance in Cincinnatti tho alone it may not aford [sic] a business for a Company, it may afford assistance worth having to the Office here."[102] Although there is no indication that Pendleton pursued the establishment of a life firm, another company—Ohio Life and Trust, formed in 1834—did indeed find it difficult to support a life business in Ohio. In 1837, it reinsured all its life risks with NYL&T, just as Bard had predicted.[103]

Throughout the antebellum period, northern life companies refused to extend their normal rates to applicants wishing to travel or reside beyond the southern border of Virginia and Kentucky (approximately 36.5° north latitude). South of this line, unacclimated policyholders were permitted to live or travel between the first of November[104] and the first of June—upon requesting permission from the company and paying an extra premium. A company would perhaps allow acclimated persons to live in the South year-round with an additional climate premium.[105] Initially, NYL&T added a ½% to 1% ($5 to $10 per $1,000) surcharge for an acclimated person, while the charge for unacclimated policyholders wishing to reside south of Virginia was at least an additional 5% ($50 per $1,000).[106] A policyholder in New Orleans who wished permission to travel throughout the South in any season was assessed a 10% ($100 per $1,000) supplement.[107] But by 1834, Bard decided that even these premiums were too liberal, increasing the surcharge to 2% ($20) for acclimated persons, 2% to 6% ($20 to $60) for unacclimated persons, and "declining altogether Insurances for the whole year in New Orleans or in other Southern or particularly unhealthy places."[108]

At first, additional premium rates were based mainly on anecdotal evidence regarding the disease environment in the South. In 1835, President Bard complained: "We have very few insured to go to the South during the summer months, yet of the 5 losses we have met with two of them were South and South West, and we were very near losing another last summer."[109] Companies were particularly concerned with "remitting and bilious fevers" (most likely referring to typhoid and yellow fever) during the summer months, although they admitted that consumption (tuberculosis) appeared to be much more prevalent in the North than the South.[110] Bard was absolutely positive of the necessity of southern surcharges, explaining to William Atkinson of the British House of Commons, "There can be no doubt that Life is not so good in the Southern States as it is in those North of Virginia . . . Life is not quite as good to South as to the North."[111]

However, by the 1840s and 1850s, more precise comparisons of mortality rates between states were being undertaken—largely as a result of additional questions that had been added to the federal census. In 1846, *Hunt's Merchants' Magazine* published life expectancy tables divided by both state and age cohort, which were based on the population schedules of the 1840 census. To the industry's surprise, these tables concluded that life expectancy was as good (if not better) in North and South Carolina, Maryland, and Virginia, as in most of the states of the Northeast. Interestingly, the Deep South states of Georgia, Alabama, and Mississippi demonstrated greater longevity than northern cities such as New York and Boston (where the greatest number of policyholders was concentrated).[112] In the winter of 1855–56, the *United States Insurance Gazette and Magazine of Useful Knowledge* published a similar analysis of mortality rates based on the 1850 census returns but refused to acknowledge that the results for the South were accurate, declaring that "the real mortality is obviously much larger."[113]

Because of the skepticism regarding tables drawn from the census returns, some life companies attempted to justify their surcharges by presenting their own data. Mutual Life of New York, for example, compiled a table of risks by nativity based on its experience in New Orleans through 1857. A discussion of the table stated: "The risks of life are nearly double in some latitudes what they are in others . . . Compared with New York or Baltimore, the risk of life in New Orleans is more than 2 for 1 . . . Taking well-known facts into view, our Life Insurance Companies will feel bound, in duty to their own customers, to enhance their rates on lives South of Richmond, Virginia."[114] In 1859, New York Life likewise reported that the mortality rate among its southern policyholders was much higher. Death claims from southern policyholders consumed more than half of total premium payments, although they represented only one-quarter of the policies.[115] Of course, the experience of Mutual of New York and New York Life in the South did not represent a random sample of that region's population. Given the relatively small number of those insured, interest in life insurance among southerners may have been confined to a riskier segment of the populace, while life insurance had become more generally accepted in the North.

While northeastern firms remained wary of underwriting southern lives without an additional premium charge, there were also eighteen southern life companies operating during the antebellum period. Two-thirds of these endeavors were short lived, but several did a significant amount of business, including Baltimore Life (1830–67); Mutual Life Insurance Company of Baltimore (1845–57); North Carolina Mutual Life Insurance Company (1849–62), Kentucky Mutual Life of Covington, Kentucky (1850–67); Greensboro Mutual Life of North Carolina (1853–65); and Southern Mutual Life of South Carolina (1854–68).

The southern life insurance companies tended to be more lenient with regard to travel and residency restrictions, although they still adhered to the same belief that the South was generally less healthy than the North, particularly for unacclimated persons in the summer months. Mutual of Baltimore forbade policyholders from going south of 34° north latitude (Columbia, South Carolina) and required "those residing in the States of North Carolina, Tennessee, South Carolina, Mississippi and Arkansas . . . to keep 50 miles distant from the Mississippi river, and from the Atlantic Ocean."[116] Similarly, North Carolina Mutual Life set the southern boundary of South Carolina and Tennessee and the eastern shore of the Mississippi River as the limits for its policyholders between June 15 and October 15.[117] Although Baltimore Life most resembled its northeastern counterparts on paper—forbidding policyholders from venturing below the southern border of Virginia or Kentucky—in practice it was more flexible regarding these risks. In a letter to its Richmond agent regarding a policyholder's request to travel to Texas, President John J. Donaldson was confident that Baltimore Life's terms were the most reasonable, since "the Philadelphia & New York offices . . . have a greater dread of the Southern risks than we."[118]

Baltimore Life did a thriving business in Virginia, with a few active offices in Kentucky as well. As a consequence, its policyholders were more likely than those of more northern companies to request permission to travel beyond the stated limits. For example, one potential policyholder from Kentucky objected to the boundary limits because he lived only forty miles from the border. The company permitted him to travel within fifty or one hundred miles of his residence, "not to exceed two days at a time."[119] William F. Davis, a businessman in Petersburg, Virginia, gained permission to travel to North Carolina year round with only a small extra premium. The company initially insisted on the standard ½% ($5 per $1,000) charge, stating, "We are sorry that the Limitation of Travel in Policy shou'd be an obstacle to the adoption of Insurance with you. We cou'd not well repeal it. It is the case in every other Office North of the Potomac."[120] However, after additional negotiations in which Davis presented his policy with American Life and Trust Company of Maryland as evidence of the leniency of other companies, Baltimore Life agreed to waive the extra charge between November 1 and June 1, requiring only ¼% ($2.50) if Davis desired a year-long privilege. Company president Donaldson noted, "This we suspect gives more than any other office in the United States does. No office that we know gives the privilege at all seasons without some additional prem. and if they charge, it certainly is more than our charge ¼ pC."[121] Precautions regarding travel to or residence in the South were thus subject to a great deal of interpretation and negotiation by the companies.

California Risks

One of the biggest antebellum challenges to the industry occurred as a result of the California gold rush. Beginning in late 1848, requests for insurance from people seeking their fortunes on the Pacific Coast poured into the life offices. The industry cautiously embraced these risks as an expansion of its business, but the practice was soon abandoned as the claims far surpassed the premiums paid on these policies. By the mid-1850s, the only companies willing to underwrite these risks were small institutions attempting to capture a greater market share.

Although William Bard had stepped down as president of NYL&T, he continued to serve as the company actuary and was thus intimately involved in the firm's decisions regarding California applicants. As with each other class of mortality risks, Bard carefully gathered all available data on this population and constantly reevaluated the firm's rates as new information emerged. In January 1849, NYL&T president David Thompson informed his Washington agent of the company's initial decision to underwrite these applicants with specific travel restrictions and at an extremely steep surcharge: "We shall not insure parties going by Panama, but only those going round the Cape. We take no risk over $1000. The charge is double that shown by the tables at each age and ½ percent [$5 per $1,000] for going and ½ percent for returning."[122] But less than two weeks later, NYL&T had already concluded that these policies were too risky, as the company's Baltimore agent was informed that "the Company have discontinued insuring persons going to California"[123]—a decision that remained in effect throughout most of 1849.[124] This appears to have been a judgment reached in conjunction with several other "Northern Offices," including Connecticut Mutual and Mutual Benefit of New Jersey, which simultaneously decided to "refus[e] all California risks."[125]

In response to rapidly changing travel, work, and living conditions in California, NYL&T would reverse this decision several more times over the course of the next two years. Beginning in the fall of 1849, the company again underwrote California lives with substantial premium and travel surcharges.[126] However, the experience of NYL&T with California risks remained unsatisfactory. By mid-1851, Bard was informing agents of another alteration to the official policy: "After our experience [with] California risks the Board have determined to accept them only in very special cases, and in no case to do so unless the applicant himself applies at the Office, where the circumstances of his constitution, habits and future employment may be ascertained by personal examination of the Officers of the Company. We shall in future decline applications made through our Agents unless it may be some extraordinary case."[127]

The experience of Baltimore Life with California risks proved similar to that of NYL&T. In December 1848, Baltimore Life secretary R. B. Dorsey informed its Fredericksburg, Virginia, agent that California risks would be taken with a 2% ($20 per $1,000) surcharge on the amount insured,[128] but by February 1849 it had raised this to 3% [$30], which gave "the party the option of going by any route he please by sea or land & of residing in California."[129] The company also limited the policies to $2,500, although this limit was lowered the following month to $1,500, raised back to $2,500 by November, and again lowered to $1,000 in March 1850.[130] Between December 1848 and May 1850, California policies accounted for 43% of non-slave policies written by Baltimore Life. Yet by May 1850, the company had officially decided to cease writing policies for California risks,[131] although it did continue to accept a limited number of applicants on a case-by-case basis. While data on Baltimore Life's experience with these risks do not exist, it is unlikely that the company would have abandoned such a large portion of its business if it had not proven unprofitable or overly risky.

Although older companies like NYL&T and Baltimore Life approached these risks with extreme caution, newer companies were more willing to underwrite Californians—with a much more moderate premium surcharge—as a means of expanding their policyholder base. New York Life (originally chartered in 1841 as Nautilus Insurance Company) was disposed to accept policies on people going to California, although it initially only permitted policyholders to travel by sea.[132] In its 1851 brochure, the company reported several examples of policyholders dying en route to or while in California, including a man who drowned in the San Francisco harbor, another who died from cholera aboard a steamship on the Rio Grande, and a third who died from "coast fever" in Panama.[133] During the mid-1850s, Albion of London advertised "California risks taken at a moderate extra premium";[134] British Commercial Life of London informed interested policyholders of "California, Australia, and special risks taken";[135] State Mutual Life Insurance Company of Worcester, Massachusetts (1844), accepted "good lives for California . . . at reduced rates of premium";[136] and the newly formed Howard Life (1852–56) and Knickerbocker Life (1853) of New York both announced "California, Australia, and other Foreign risks taken at a reduced extra premium."[137]

By the end of the 1850s, the rapid population growth and improvements in living conditions on the West Coast had induced even some of the older companies to reconsider accepting California applicants. Connecticut Mutual, which previously had declined underwriting these risks, declared in its 1859 annual report, "Risks in all the various forms of Life Insurance, and for residence in Australia, California, and the gold regions of Kansas, as well as in foreign countries, taken by this Company at the usual *mutual* rates."[138] A decade later, the *Insurance Monitor* would observe, "Life insurance companies have regarded California as a placer, and nearly every company is represented there. The State is literally overrun with life insurance, and the business largely overdone . . . a much larger proportion of the men are insured than in other parts of the country."[139]

Marital Status and Gender

Although most efforts to understand mortality focused on age, occupation, and geographic factors, some life insurance executives believed that factors such as marital status and gender could also affect life expectancy in the long term. Although no statistics exist regarding whether people were declined insurance based on their marital status, the anecdotal evidence suggests that marriage was considered an attribute in the applicant's favor in the overall evaluation of the application package. Gender was initially not a factor regularly considered by insurance companies, but by the middle of the nineteenth century many companies began charging females an additional percentage on their premium rates (when they insured them at all). The question of whether females were riskier lives to insure than males was a regular topic of debate in insurance circles throughout the second half of the century.

Along with age, occupation, and health history, the earliest application form of NYL&T asked potential policyholders their marital status[140] because "a married person has a better chance of life than an unmarried one."[141] In 1835, the NYL&T agent from Somerville, New Jersey, wrote to inquire whether the marriage of an existing policyholder would nullify his policy contract, as he had declared himself to be single in his initial application. In reply, President Bard expressed his opinions on the positive benefits of marriage: "I wish all our insured unmarried men would marry immediately. Marriage is a security to the virtue and, of course, to the health of the Individual and I consider Mr Von Vighten a better life by 5 or 10 years since he was wise enough to marry. His having done so makes no alteration in the State of his Policy."[142]

Persons desiring insurance with Baltimore Life regularly included marriage among their low-risk characteristics when writing to the company. For example, a clerk of the House of Representatives declared in 1837: "I was 36 years of age in August last, seldom troubled with indisposition of any kind. Am a married man."[143] Walter Smith wrote the company in 1841: "I am a Surgeon in the U.S. Navy in the fortieth year of my age, of sound constitution and in good health: am a married man."[144] In contrast, there were no cases of unmarried inquirers including their single status among positive attributes.

The only extant nineteenth-century statistics of the relationship between marital status and mortality of men were compiled in the 1860s by the Register General of births, deaths, and marriages in Scotland. The report, issued in 1867 and published in an American insurance journal, concluded that the life expectancy advantage of married over single men was startling, with young bachelors dying at twice the rate of young married men. Although this extreme advantage decreased with age, "it decreased slowly and regularly, showing the difference in favor of the married men at every period of life." The article thus asserted "that bachelorhood is more destructive to life than the most unwholesome trades, or than residence in an unhealthy house or district, where there has never been the most distant attempt at sanitary improvements of any kind."[145] Not only did marriage apparently extend the life of the husband ("The married man is, in general, not only more healthy, vigorous, and free from disease than the unmarried, but he is also more regular in his habits, is better housed, better fed, and better attended to"), but bachelorhood could serve as an indicator of ill health or the undesirable habits life insurance companies sought to avoid. The Scottish report thus concluded: "Indeed, the married men may, in one sense, be accounted as selected lives; for the weak, the delicate, those suffering from disease of any kind, the dissipated, the licentious, do not marry."[146] However, since the percentage of unmarried men in the population was relatively small—particularly among the age group most likely to seek insurance—this factor was unlikely to have a dramatic effect on life insurance selection.[147]

The relationship between gender and mortality was of much greater potential importance. The Equitable Society of London initially levied premium surcharges on women under the age of 50.[148] Yet considering the scrupulousness of American companies with regard to other characteristics and their adherence to the policies endorsed by their English predecessors, it is somewhat surprising that early American firms do not appear to have considered gender as a factor potentially affecting mortality. In an interview given to Massachusetts Hospital Life in the mid-1820s, Pennsylvania Company stated that it did not differentiate in its rates between risks on males and females.[149] And from their initial incorporation through the closure of their life insurance divisions in the 1860s, Massachusetts Hospital Life, Baltimore Life, and NYL&T all charged identical rates to males and females of the same age.[150]

In all the correspondence of these three institutions, the issue of gender was only mentioned on a handful of occasions. Delineating the policies of NYL&T to a new agent in 1833, President Bard stated, "The prem[iu]m is the same for a man and a woman."[151] The only distinction among these early companies was in regard to the application of a pregnant woman for insurance with Baltimore Life. Writing to his agent in Leesburg, Virginia, President Donaldson explained: "In the present situation of Mrs. Carter, the Board considers the risk as increas'd by her Pregnancy. Of course a higher rate will be ask'd. We ask 3 PrCent [$30 per $1,000] for the first Year and Two prCent [$20] for the remainder."[152] Both the tone of the letter and the rates charged on the lives of other women indicate that this was an exception to the general practice of the company of not differentiating between the sexes. The policy applications of these early stock companies similarly adopted a gender-neutral tone.

The first application forms of New England Mutual employed masculine pronouns; for example it inquired about the applicant's "age at his next birthday,"[153] but by the early 1850s, the company had simplified its questions to reflect the possibility of female applicants: "Age at next birthday."[154] The language of many company brochures and prospectuses (both stock and mutual) was completely gender-neutral, always referring to "the assured," "the insured," "the person," or "the party," unless they were giving specific examples of people who benefited or would benefit from insurance. One rare exception was a section from the 1837 Girard Life brochure, which advertised: "Females will be waited on by the physician of the office at their own houses, when requested."[155] But for the remainder of this brochure, potential policyholders were not discriminated by gender.

The extant evidence regarding gender during the first half of the nineteenth century indicates that females had a longer life expectancy than males. The British government's tables, compiled in 1829 by the national actuary John Finlaison, "establishe[d] the fact of the *longer duration of female life*" for all cohorts above the age of 10.[156] In 1843, the Register General of Britain released a report comparing the mortality rates by gender of people throughout England that reaffirmed these findings. The study concluded that even women of childbearing age had a greater life expectancy than men because young men were exposed to other hazards. As the nineteenth-century observer Moses L. Knapp noted, "The violent deaths of men, in rivers and the sea coasts, in mines, in the streets, in traveling, in their dangerous occupations, the mental agitations and anxieties, terminating, unhappily, sometimes in suicide, the accumulation of workmen in ill-ventilated shops, or the service in unhealthy climates, counterbalances the dangers and sorrows of child-bearing."[157] As a result of this discrepancy in life expectancy, during the 1850s one British company operating in the United States (Eagle of London) even tried to capture the market in female lives by offering "distinct and reduced rates of premium for the assurance of female life,"[158] while National Life Insurance Company of Vermont began to advertise that it insured females at the same rates as males.[159]

Even though the data seemed to indicate higher life expectancies for women across all age groups, most American companies remained cautious. At some point during the mid-nineteenth century, the attitude of insurance companies toward underwriting women changed dramatically from indifference to extreme caution. For example, on the same redesigned application form (from the early 1850s) in which New England Mutual questions became gender-neutral, the company also added eight questions specifically for female applicants:

> If the proposed life is a female, the applicant, or some physician or friend, will answer the following additional questions, viz.:—Is she single or married? . . . Or engaged, and, if engaged, how soon expected to be married? . . . If married, how long since? . . . Number of children she has borne, if any? . . . Date of the birth of her last child? . . . How long ago her last pregnancy? . . . Is she now pregnant, and

if so, how soon expecting to be delivered? . . . Is there any reason to apprehend unusual difficulty of labor?[160]

By 1861, it would add a ninth question, "If any former labor, was the last one difficult? If so, from what cause?"[161] As these questions indicate, New England Mutual was primarily concerned with the potential hazards of childbirth.

By the end of the 1860s, few companies were willing to insure females at any rate of premium. An 1869 article in the *Insurance Monitor* summarized companies' attitudes toward such policies: "Female risks are not sought by any of the life companies. Some of them decline to write on female lives *in toto*. Others take them under certain restrictions, as on joint policies for a widowed mother having children dependent upon her; but none of the companies [seek?] female risks, while all are eager for males." The article went on to explain that this position was "simply the result of unfavorable experiences[;] . . . at regular rates the results have been found adverse, and consequently the risks are not sought, as a general thing."[162] Thus, while the life expectancy of females in the general population was favorable, the actual experience of the companies with the much smaller group of women who sought insurance proved otherwise. A study of the entire mortality experience of twenty English life companies published in 1869 found that the death rate of women *with insurance* far exceeded that of men until the age of 45.[163]

Life insurance observers offered several theories as to the reason for this discrepancy between the mortality rates of women in the general population of England and that of insured women in the United States and England. Most assumed that the higher than expected mortality reflected adverse selection against the industry rather than real differences in female mortality between the two countries. An 1869 *New York Times* editorial concluded: "If all women would insure, that is as generally as men do, the risks on them would pay." However, the number of insurance policies on women was extremely few: "But it is a fact that, as a rule, healthy women don't apply for policies. It is when a woman feels a premonition of some disorder, or has some trouble that may or may not be apparent to the examiner, that she applies, and, the companies say, that in such cases neither she nor her husband are apt to disclose the real state of the case."[164] An additional factor was the dilemma of conducting a thorough health evaluation on female applicants. In 1865, the assistant secretary of Manhattan Life informed Massachusetts insurance commissioner Elizur Wright: "We have recently concluded that it is inexpedient to insure the lives of women. The difficulty of obtaining an adequate personal examination from the delicacy necessary in such cases, the superior ability of husbands to judge of peculiar hazard affecting the longevity of wives, and the general fact that pecuniary loss is rarely sustained in such cases are some of the objections."[165] Thus the small numbers of women seeking insurance, combined with the difficulty of adequately discerning the actual risk associated with their lives, made the industry wary of underwriting females.

Based on the results of the 1870 federal census, Director Alexander Delmar of the United States census office criticized the industry's policies on insuring females, noting that "insurance companies are incorrect in assuming that women, during their child-bearing period, are subject to greater risk of death than men during the parallel period of life. Such an opinion is not founded on facts."[166] But the industry was quick to refute this conclusion, admitting "that women were longer-lived than men, but that the particular class of women who resort to insurance on their lives are not so. This has been proved beyond any question whatever, which is the cause of charging that class one-half of one percent. [$5 per $1,000] more than the rate for men of the same age."[167]

Whether because women sought insurance less frequently or were more likely to be declined by the companies, policies on females formed only a small fraction of all policies both in America and in England.[168] Over the course of their existence, the percentage of policies on women was 4% for NYL&T, Massachusetts Hospital Life, and New England Mutual (through 1853 only) and 6.5% for Baltimore Life; only 11% of the policies used to create the 1869 British Experience Table were on females. Furthermore, the expectations of antebellum companies became self-fulfilling. Their marketing specifically targeted men, and they made no effort to expand their policy sales to women. By charging females a higher rate (usually $5 per $1,000 of insurance),[169] companies actively discouraged healthier women from insuring.

As one observer correctly pointed out:

> The laws of trade obtain here as well as elsewhere. The dearer you make an insurance, and the more you discriminate against any particular description of lives, the greater will be the inducements forced upon the healthier and more robust to insure themselves, and the greater the liability,—if conscious weakness forces itself upon a party to so great an extent as to compel him to resort to insurance,— that you will have a delicate and short-lived assurant; and the higher you make the rate, the further will this process of winnowing be carried.[170]

Just as William Bard understood earlier in the century, price *did* matter in the sale of life insurance. If companies wanted to ensure that the mortality tables were accurate by expanding policy sales across a substantial subset of the population, they could not overcharge applicants. Of course, it is also possible that demand for life insurance among women would have remained low regardless of the price of insurance, in which case the companies were wise not to expose themselves to unnecessary risks.

The Allure of Statistics

For William Bard of NYL&T, the compilation of accurate data on mortality was the key component in establishing a fiscally stable life insurance industry. In pursuing this objective, Bard was participating in a much larger social phenomenon. As historians such as Theodore M. Porter and Patricia Cline Cohen have documented, the early decades of the nineteenth century witnessed a rapid increase in the use and acceptance of statistics in daily life. On both sides of the Atlantic, people began subjecting to quantification not just economic questions but civic, social, and moral issues as well. The burgeoning reform movements turned to statistics to buttress their calls for temperance pledges or for funds to combat pauperism, while community boosters compiled data on the population, climate, and economy of their areas to promote business development and attract migrants. Americans were becoming more numerically literate, and they increasingly associated data with objective truths.[171] Thus for Bard a statistical understanding of the factors contributing to mortality would not only ensure the long-term viability of the industry but would create confidence among the general public that life insurance premiums were based on scientifically sound principles and were not merely a matter of chance.

Although both Pennsylvania Company and Massachusetts Hospital Life enjoyed an advantage as first movers in the emerging life insurance industry, their lack of statistical curiosity largely hampered their ability to capitalize on that position. Profiting from virtual monopolies in their local markets, these early firms were able to adopt rate tables that comfortably covered their risks and returned a profit even with only rudimentary knowledge of American mortality. NYL&T rejected this business model and sought instead to rapidly expand sales by charging premiums that more accurately represented the risks underwritten. And by appealing to a more extensive group of potential customers through lower prices—and thus spreading its risks over a greater client pool—the firm seemed to benefit from a more stable financial basis. For the second movers in the industry such as NYL&T, knowledge of average mortality was crucial to walking the fine line between fiscal soundness and bankruptcy. Yet despite the best efforts of Bard and his actuarial descendants in the industry, this statistical knowledge was never complete. While publicly touting the scientific rigor supposedly underlying the permanence and financial stability of life institutions, throughout the nineteenth century the American life insurance industry privately struggled to understand what the average rate of mortality for Americans really was; a newfound respect for statistics did not alter the inherent difficulty in obtaining such information. But even though this lack of knowledge about mortality could have delayed the development of a viable life insurance industry, the pressing need for a means of mitigating the risks of untimely death in a burgeoning urban environment far outweighed the risks to policyholders and insurers.

CHAPTER 2

Selecting Risks in an Anonymous World
The Development of the Agency System

In the summer of 1832, Levi A. Ward Jr. of Rochester, New York, wrote to President William Bard of New York Life Insurance and Trust Company in New York City requesting an appointment as local agent for the company.[1] The firm's two older rivals—Pennsylvania Company and Massachusetts Hospital Life Insurance Company—rarely sold policies outside their respective home bases of Philadelphia and Boston. Each instead preferred to restrict its sales to individuals whose application responses could be verified by people known and respected by the company's board of directors and who could be visually examined (in person) by the company's officers. Furthermore, a company strategy of minimizing risks through strict selection would theoretically help to compensate for the absence of accurate mortality tables by driving the rate of mortality among policyholders well below that of the population as a whole. Since New York was the largest city in the nation, with a population more than 2.5 times that of Philadelphia or Boston by 1830, NYL&T could have pursued a similarly risk-adverse business strategy. Instead, President Bard recognized that "the safety of the Office depends more on the numbers insured"—that *prudently* spreading the company's risks across greater numbers of policyholders would actually place the firm in a more secure financial position.[2] Thus Ward's request to expand the geographic reach of the company into this rapidly expanding city in western New York caught Bard's attention.

While NYL&T already had several representatives spread throughout the state—including in Monroe County, where Rochester was located—these agents were mainly charged with assessing the property of rural landowners requesting mortgage loans from the company. Loan agents occasionally forwarded to the head office requests for life insurance, but rural farmers were not the primary target of policy sales. Rather, the company anticipated that middle-income urban professionals (small merchants, lawyers, clerks, store proprietors, teachers, doctors, and clergymen) would be most interested in its product. This emerging middle class consisted of people with little real estate or investment income whose family livelihood depended instead on the earnings of a single breadwinner and whose economic security thus would be completely erased with the untimely death of that breadwinner. However, the more disconnected a company was from these applicants, the harder it would be for the firm to obtain the information essential for accurately evaluating the risk of insuring them. As Bard well knew, without a careful selection of lives, even the most accurate mortality table would be rendered useless, since the greatest demand for insurance most likely came from those facing the highest risk of death.

When Ward's letter arrived, the board of directors of NYL&T had just recently "proposed that the Agents of the Company for life insurance should be distinct from the Agents for making loans," in order to ensure that the agent was in regular contact with the target clientele and that he possessed the necessary capacity for judging applicants.[3] Levi Ward would be one of the first people considered for such a position, but the mere desire to represent the company as agent was hardly an adequate qualification. Bard had in mind very particular characteristics for the men who would make up this new agency system, characteristics that would limit the company's exposure to instances of adverse selection and moral hazard. He sought to appoint highly respected men with extensive connections within their communities, whom the company could trust to make honest and informed evaluations of applicants.

Local agents would be obliged to act as the home office's eyes and ears on the ground; they initially would be charged with weeding out poor risks rather than soliciting new customers. As Bard instructed Ward in response to his initial inquiry: "The Agent has not much to do that is troublesome. He is to *see* the party applying for insurance & *judge* from his appearance of his health . . . The point of most importance indeed only importance is his health at the moment of insurance" (emphasis added). In addition to this visual evaluation, directors also expected the agents to possess broad knowledge of the applicants themselves, in order to assess more accurately their health history and habits: "He must not be of a family liable to consumption or other hereditary disease, must be perfectly sober & of sound constitution & regular habits[;] such individuals we insure without hesitation." Finally, to build a more accurate risk profile of each applicant, these agents would need to verify their own conclusions by tapping into the knowledge base of the wider community, "address[ing] the letter enclosed to the parties [*sic*] friend whom *he must know* to be a respectable individual & also the letter to his family or a reputable physician"[4] (emphasis added). By providing an informed (if subjective) mortality risk profile on his family, friends, neighbors, and colleagues, the agent would be serving as a proxy for the type of oversight of applicants exercised by the board of directors at the home office.

In considering Ward for this essential yet sensitive position, Bard first sought the opinion of Frederick Whittlesey. Whittlesey was a lawyer from one of the wealthiest families in Rochester, who was then representing the twenty-seventh district of New York (Rochester's district) in the United States Congress as part of the Anti-Masonic Party.[5] "I am told [Ward] is a very respectable man," Bard began. "Will you say to me whether you think his appointment will be a proper one." By "proper" Bard did not mean an able salesman or an active solicitor of policies.[6] As he explained to Whittlesey, "Good sense, prudence & integrity are necessary in the agent for life insurance."[7]

The few historians who have examined the life insurance industry depict its early agency system in very critical terms. For example, J. Owen Stalson disparages the agency system as a "passive mode of marketing" that "was almost completely lacking in initiative, [and] was low in selling intensity." In assuming that early company agents should have been (or were intended to be) active salesmen, these historians fail to understand the original purpose of agencies. Employing soliciting agents could have created a principal-agent problem for the company, as the interests of the agents in acquiring large numbers of applicants (to increase their own bottom line) might have outpaced the ability of executives to consider the entailed risks adequately. Active sales agents would have overwhelmed an industry that was still trying to flesh out the general guidelines for risk.

While a basic understanding of mortality rates by age for the American population was critically important for the industry, applicants were a self-selecting group that did not necessarily represent the whole accurately. Firms particularly feared adverse selection, whereby the people most likely to seek out an insurance policy were those with reason to suspect a below-average life expectancy; reasons for adverse selection could range from a feeling of general unease that induced the person to apply for insurance to outright fraud. Company actuaries made predictions based on the aggregate population, and executives knew all too well that poorly selected risks might mean bankruptcy, while careful selection meant greater profits for their stockholders or higher dividends for mutual policyholders. Companies certainly sought to expand their client base, but they needed to do so conservatively—within the confines of the extant knowledge of mortality.

In Levi A. Ward Jr., scion of one of Rochester's leading families, NYL&T found its ideal agent. One local historian refers to the senior Ward as "a village father," a doctor who was instrumental in founding the town's first library in 1822, its first bank in 1824 (serving as the second president), and the Rochester Athenaeum in 1829 (serving as its first secretary), in addition to occupying one of the front pews at the First Presbyterian Church.[8] At the age of 31, the younger Ward was himself an esteemed member of Rochester society with commercial and social aspirations independent of his father. During the 1830s and 1840s, he would likewise rise to a position of prominence in the Presbyterian Church, as well as being appointed director of two local banks and the gaslight company, serving as president of the first school board in town, and then representing the Whig Party as supervisor, alderman, and finally as mayor in 1849.[9]

Writing to NYL&T in 1832, the already well-connected Ward was in a good position to judge the respectability and veracity of both insurance applicants and the physicians and friends testifying on their behalf. He additionally had a reputation to protect and cultivate, which company directors believed would prevent him from abusing his position as an agent either for monetary gain or to enhance his personal and professional relationships with the applicants. One of the first representatives chosen to form NYL&T's new agency system, Ward would remain the company's agent through the 1860s, and Rochester would produce more policyholders for the company than any other location outside New York City and Brooklyn. By early 1833, Ward would be joined by agents carefully appointed in twenty-one other cities throughout New York State, as well as in ten out-of-state cities in the Northeast and eastern Canada, creating the industry's first widespread system of agents. By the mid-1840s, NYL&T was a presence in most major cities of the Midwest and Upper South and had agents as far south as Macon, Georgia, and Puerto Rico.[10]

Beginning in 1833, the Baltimore Life Insurance Company (also chartered in 1830) began creating its own agency system in the cities of the Mid-Atlantic and Upper South, employing criteria similar to those of NYL&T; all newly chartered companies in the 1830s and 1840s would follow this model as well. For example, upon commencing business in 1844 New England Mutual Life Insurance Company immediately appointed fifteen agents throughout the country and continued to expand this system rapidly in the ensuing years.[11] Each of these agency systems was initially developed not as a sales force but as a means of *re*personalizing the connection between corporate headquarters and the individual applicant—in effect creating a subjective mortality risk report for each individual who applied for a policy. The system would allow companies to navigate successfully between the worlds of personal relationships and anonymity during the antebellum period.

Avoiding Adverse Selection

Throughout the first half of the nineteenth century, life insurance executives believed that the fiscal soundness and long-term profitability of their firms depended upon the careful selection of lives to underwrite; thus the risk of mortality for every individual applicant needed to be thoroughly assessed. In addition to age, occupation, and geographic location, actuaries also considered more distinctive characteristics such as health, family history, and personal habits as they formed an educated opinion about the chances of life for each potential policyholder. The goal of all insurance companies was to restrict their sales to people "of sound health, and of sober habits, without hereditary disease, and not belonging to families remarked for short lives."[12] These individual traits were the most relevant details for ascertaining specific risk levels, but they were also the most prone to problems of asymmetric information, since their accuracy relied primarily on the word of the applicants.

The process of selecting lives with better than average prospects for longevity began with the health questions on the application. Early insurance companies all asked nearly identical questions of applicants:

> Is he now in good health, and does he usually enjoy good health, or how otherwise? . . . Has he at any time been afflicted with gout, asthma, consumption, scrofula, convulsions, palsy, or any other disease likely to impair his constitution? . . . Has he been vaccinated, or had the small pox? . . . Is he of a sedentary turn, or accustomed to much exercise? . . . Do you know of any circumstance which renders an insurance on his life more than usually hazardous?[13]

In addition to questions such as these—all asked by Pennsylvania Company, Massachusetts Hospital Life, and Baltimore Life—NYL&T was also concerned about "dropsy [edema], . . . or spitting of blood," the latter being a common symptom of tuberculosis.[14] Although these questions were written in the third person, candidates would personally fill in the answers, forcing life firms to rely on the applicant to provide honest, precise, and complete responses.

The two diseases of most concern to life insurance companies were smallpox and tuberculosis (consumption). Smallpox was highly contagious and resulted in a significant number of deaths during the eighteenth and nineteenth centuries; medical historians estimate that at least 80% of the population would contract the disease at some point in their lives and that between one in ten and one in seven cases would end in death.[15] In response to this threat, NYL&T initially stated that it would charge an extra premium in cases where the applicant had never been afflicted with or vaccinated for smallpox (following the example of more mature British companies, such as Equitable Life Assurance Society of London).[16] But all American companies, including NYL&T, eventually developed a much stricter policy with regard to the disease, declining to insure in all cases where the applicant had not yet been exposed to the virus.[17]

Unlike many other diseases, smallpox was a binary condition. Once a person had suffered from either smallpox or the related but weaker cowpox virus, or had been vaccinated with the cowpox or kinepox virus, he or she was believed to be immune to further outbreaks (although as early as 1846, applicants to New England Mutual commonly replied to the question, "Has he been vaccinated, or had the small pox?" with "Has been twice vaccinated").[18] Thus the application form itself provided ample protection for life firms against the risk posed by smallpox. Anyone with prior exposure to the virus knew and would readily disclose that fact. If, on the other hand, an applicant lied about his or her exposure and later contracted the disease, the company would have ample grounds (based solely on the inaccurate application response) for canceling coverage or denying the payment of a death claim. While companies usually "declined insuring" when an applicant had no prior exposure to the disease, in a few cases firms issued a policy with the caveat "in case he should die by the small pox, the Company not to be held responsible."[19]

While smallpox could be avoided by only insuring those protected against the disease, consumption was the greatest fear of the industry. Anyone could potentially be stricken (young adults appeared to be particularly susceptible), the early symptoms were easy to hide (or misinterpret), and prior exposure most likely raised rather than lowered the probability of future infection.[20] At midcentury, tuberculosis was the leading cause of death in the United States, accounting for between 15% and 25% of all fatalities.[21] In 1834 President Bard estimated that between 0.3% and 0.5% of the population of New York City died of the disease each year (approximately 725 to 1,200 people), leading him to comment: "Consumption is the disease which in our office we have most to dread. From it are our greatest dangers. It is the disease of the Country."[22] One history of Mutual Benefit Life estimates that almost 20% of claims between 1845 and 1857 were for deaths from consumption,[23] while the medical examiner for United States Life reported that consumption was the cause of more than one-quarter of all death claims made to the company between 1850 and 1873.[24]

During the first half of the nineteenth century, most people believed consumption to be primarily a hereditary disease that mainly struck underweight individuals.[25] Companies thus attempted to minimize their consumption risk by declining insurance to people falling into one of three groups: those showing any symptoms of the disease, including anyone who had "had continued coughs or is liable to colds" or who had "ever spit blood or had pains in his chest"; applicants with a family who had "been liable to the disease" or whose "parents or relations died of it"; and those presumed to be more susceptible to the disease because of their frail body structure, particularly applicants with "a delicate complexion, of a thin make, with a narrow chest, and high shoulders."[26] Firms believed that while application questions could serve as a first defense, these questions were woefully inadequate for discerning who might be at a higher than average risk for developing consumption (or a wide variety of other maladies that could potentially shorten life).

To reduce their exposure to this disease, early companies relied on a visual inspection of all potential policyholders in the main office and on their personal knowledge of the candidates or letters of reference to verify the applicants' overall health and the truthfulness of their responses. Massachusetts Hospital Life in particular stressed throughout the 1830s and early 1840s that applicants had to make a "personal appearance" or "personal application" at the office in Boston, a rule that it "deviated from only in cases where the sum insured is small and the person well known to us here."[27] Pennsylvania Company, Massachusetts Hospital Life, and Baltimore Life all required that "the family physician, or other respectable physician, or, in case neither can be had . . . any known respectable persons in the neighborhood" also sign the application form, stipulating to the veracity of the statements.[28] Similarly, applications for insurance with NYL&T had to be accompanied by letters from both a doctor and a "respectable friend" regarding the health of the applicant.[29]

In all cases, it was imperative that both the physician and the family friend confirming the responses be persons known and respected by the company's officers. If not, some third party had to verify their respectability. For example, Charles Little of Washington, DC, an applicant to Baltimore Life in 1832, advised the company: "For the character of Thomas Sim my family Physician I beg leave to refer you to Doctor N Potter of Baltimore."[30] Little was confident that Dr. Potter would be sufficiently known and respected by the officers of the company and that he would vouch for the ability and integrity of his own local physician.

Acquiring information from a variety of sources was crucial to the firms, since none of these safeguards alone was foolproof. In many cases, a person was declined merely for appearing to be weak or frail with no actual signs of disease or other risk factors. Bard responded to one applicant, for example: "I know that sometimes a delicate constitution makes old bones & I sincerely hope it may be so in your case. Yours is a delicate Constitution . . . I am therefore obliged to decline the assurance you proposed of your Life at this Office."[31] Other seemingly healthy candidates were refused because of their family history. "A Gentleman has this morning applied for an insurance healthy in appearance," Bard reported, yet "the Physician says he has had nine brothers & sisters who have all died of the Consumption."[32] Application questions, visual inspection by and the inside information of company officers, and third-party knowledge and corroboration all combined to protect companies from problems of adverse selection.

During the 1840s, newly chartered mutual companies would quickly replace the older stock companies in leadership and innovation within the life insurance industry; however, despite the assertions of historian J. Owen Stalson to the contrary, the mutuals persisted in emphasizing the importance of personal knowledge of applicants.[33] On all application forms, starting with its initial policies in 1844 and continuing throughout the 1850s and 1860s, New England Mutual inquired if the applicant was "acquainted with any person whom he understands to be a member of the Company?"—a member being anyone holding a policy with the company— and "If so he will please to name one or two most likely to be known to the officers of the Company."[34] Even as the mutual companies sought to capitalize on the differences in business form between themselves and their stock competitors, they recognized the value of attaining third-party information about all applicants. New England Mutual wanted to ensure that it could verify the soundness of the responses on the application form through its personal contacts—even if that verification involved several degrees of separation between the company officers and the applicant.

Insurance companies believed that this type of outside knowledge regarding applicants was vital to forming an accurate assessment of the potential risk. During the 1840s, the directors of New England Mutual regularly discussed the health and habits of individual applicants, often noting their impressions and opinions on the back of the application form itself. In 1847, director Charles P. Curtis questioned the wisdom of underwriting Rufus Choate of Boston based on his own personal knowledge of the applicant. Although Choate made no mention of experiencing headaches in his application form, Curtis thought it prudent for the company to solicit the advice of a respected doctor, since, he pointed out, "It is known to the Bar, that Mr Choate is frequently confined to his room, & his bed, with sick head ache, or something else. Postponements of business in Court often take place in consequence of Mr Choate's illness." Although Curtis was not himself a doctor, he conjectured that "this seems to indicate something wrong in stomach or brain. I have no doubt he over works himself, a species of intemperance as false as any." Director Theophilus Parsons agreed, stating, "I know nothing whatever against Mr Choate's fair chance of life, except that he seems to be working himself to death. It has appeared to me, and I have sometimes intimated to him, that he was throwing his life away by the intensity of his mental labour." The issue was then presented to Dr. C. G. Putnam for his professional evaluation; after examining Choate, the respected doctor assured the directors that these headaches, "though productive of discomfort, [do] not tend to shorten life." Yet although New England Mutual ultimately agreed to underwrite Choate, its continued misgivings based on the personal observations of these two directors led the company to proceed cautiously, charging him a higher premium than his age would require.[35]

The association of Choate's tough work schedule with intemperance was no accident, since the one *habit* upon which antebellum companies focused their attention was alcohol consumption. Historians estimate that the average American adult was consuming approximately four gallons of alcohol per year by 1830, and many contemporaries believed that drunkenness accounted for numerous social ills.[36] In Dr. Benjamin Rush's well-known words from 1784, "We see poverty and misery, crimes and infamy, diseases and death, are all the natural and usual consequences of the intemperate use of ardent spirits."[37] Life underwriters were profoundly influenced by the arguments of the temperance movement—one of the largest reform efforts of the second quarter of the nineteenth century—believing that alcohol consumption not only directly reduced life expectancy through disease or accident but was also an indicator of a person's generally unhealthy lifestyle. Alcohol consumption thus served as a proxy for numerous other habits that might contribute to premature death; on the other hand, people who did not imbibe alcohol were perceived as likely to be more cautious on all health-related fronts.

All early companies stressed the importance of temperance in those wishing to insure, yet firms initially did not even bother to inquire with the applicant himself regarding the temperate nature of his habits (perhaps assuming that he or she would not be honest). Instead, this was one of the most emphasized pieces of information sought from outsiders. On the application forms of Pennsylvania Company, Massachusetts Hospital Life, and Baltimore Life, there were only five questions asked of the family physician or "respectable person." The first three—"Do you know the person mentioned in the above application, and how long have you known him?" and "When did you see him last?"—established the relationship of the reference to the applicant. A fourth question attested to the truth of the statements regarding health history given by the applicant. In the final question, the reference was asked, "Is he sober and temperate, or are his habits such as usually tend to shorten life?"[38] This was the only issue initially raised about the person independent of the applicant's own answers. Later companies, such as New England Mutual, would also ask the applicants themselves if they were "of temperate habits," and eventually would inquire if they had "always been so," but the only means of testing the veracity of these statements was the observation of others.[39]

After tuberculosis, overindulgence in alcohol was probably the characteristic most feared by life insurers. President Bard repeatedly stated that applicants had to be "perfectly sober" in order to be accepted as a risk.[40] Bard immediately declined one applicant because of his sporadic lapses of judgment: "One of the answers in the case of Eugene Decaix is 'that he is Generally temperate but occasionally drinks too freely' this forbids his insurance at this Office, perfect and absolute sobriety being a requisite never dispensed with."[41] Baltimore Life was likewise vigilant in its underwriting of only sober risks, as exemplified by President Donaldson's declaring in the case of one particular applicant: "We cannot insure any <u>intemperate</u> man. No calculation can be made of the risk. We therefore decline the application of Mr. Barton."[42]

The insuring public likewise believed that a temperate lifestyle positively affected longevity. Along with other characteristics believed to lower mortality, inquirers to Baltimore Life often stressed their sobriety in their correspondence with the company. One clerk from the War Department in 1832 described his status as "health good, free from hereditary or other disease, of correct and regular habits, from all and every kinds of drink, fermented or distilled, I observe total abstinence."[43] Ten years later, a naval lieutenant informed the company, "I am a member of a total abstinence society, not because it was necessary for me to join on account of my habits (which have always been temperate) but in hopes that my example might have a favorable effect on my younger brother officers."[44] In view of the fact that liquor was part of the daily food ration for both the navy and army, military men felt particularly compelled to vouch for their own self-control.[45]

With the stress placed on sobriety by antebellum life insurance companies, the industry welcomed the growing strength of the temperance movement in the decades prior to the Civil War. One temperance reformer, Edward Cornelius Delavan, was one of the incorporators of NYL&T in 1830. Just two years earlier, Delavan had joined with the Presbyterian minister Eliphalet Nott to create the New York State Temperance Society, based in Albany.[46] In Rochester, New York, activists in the temperance movement regularly applied for life insurance with NYL&T. In 1830, for example, attorney Hestor L. Stevens was elected secretary of the Monroe County Temperance Society; in 1840 he began paying premiums on a $1,500 policy on his life.[47] Agent Levi Ward was himself selected in 1828 by the First Presbyterian Church as one of its representatives to the Rochester Society for the Promotion of Temperance.[48] And as the Baltimore Life agency of Robertson & Branda in Norfolk, Virginia, wrote optimistically in 1842: "It is to be hoped the great increase of the Temperance cause will induce many to apply to the Insurance of their Lives, part of what they formerly appropriated to the Insurance of their deaths."[49]

One company even attempted to benefit directly from the popularity of this reform movement. In 1851, American Temperance Life Insurance Company was established in Hartford, Connecticut, with the express purpose of only insuring people who absolutely abstained from alcohol. The main inducements to insure with American Temperance were its lower rates—reflecting the lower risk of under-writing teetotalers—as well as greater potential dividends, since temperance was assumed to be associated with greater longevity. However, its actual policy toward drinkers remained in line with that of the remainder of the industry. While its name served as a marketing ploy to appeal to a specific segment of the population, the company miscalculated the popularity of the reform movement.[50] American Temperance was never able to gain more than a 2% market share, even at its antebellum height in the mid-1850s. Only one other antebellum company appears to have attempted to attract customers by charging reduced rates for nondrinkers. In 1852, Eagle Life and Health Insurance Company of New Jersey (chartered 1847) advertised: "Teetotalers Insured at Five per Cent. less than the regular rates."[51] But the company never made significant headway in the industry and by 1853 had closed its doors.

The Need for an Agency System

For applicants living in major metropolitan areas—especially before the surge in urban growth beginning in the 1830s—it was relatively easy to supply supporting evidence of their health and habits by appearing in person for examination and establishing a chain of references from themselves back to one of the company's officers. But for applicants from smaller towns or rural areas, it was much more difficult to find local references that were known and respected in the cities. For example, in 1828 Nathaniel Bowditch, president of Massachusetts Hospital Life, wrote to a gentleman in Osborn, New York, requesting his input on the health and appearance of a potential policyholder: "I wish to know whether you are acquainted with Mr. Chs. De. Forest of New York, who has written to us to make insurance on his life . . . as we were not acquainted with his physician, Dr. Gibb Smith, & could not find any one *here* who did know him" (emphasis added).[52] Without adequate verification of Dr. Smith's credentials, his statement on behalf of the applicant was meaningless to the company; Massachusetts Hospital Life had no way of confidently assessing the possible risk attached to underwriting De Forest. The further removed applicants were from the inquisitive eyes of company directors, the more easily they could adversely select against the company by unintentionally omitting details relevant to their potential longevity, by deliberately lying on their applications, or by committing more serious crimes to swindle the company.

Establishing a direct chain of references was the main means by which early life companies attempted to reduce this risk of adverse selection. In response to Samuel Mather's 1846 application to Massachusetts Hospital Life, actuary Francis Cabot

Lowell informed the Cleveland resident: "We shall require in addition to the above [application] some evidence that the Physician is really a Physician in good standing in Cleveland. This you might obtain from some magistrate or from some resident of Cleveland *known in Boston*" (emphasis added).[53] In assessing the risk of underwriting applicants like De Forest and Mather, each firm initially insisted that the chain of references ultimately had to lead back to the company's home office: someone known and respected in Boston (or New York, Philadelphia, or Baltimore, depending on the company) had to be able to vouch for the applicant or the people writing on his or her behalf. But as urban populations surged and interest in life insurance spread beyond the professional classes of the major port cities, establishing an acceptable chain of references became increasingly difficult for the average applicant; companies would either have to decline a growing number of applicants for lack of adequate third-party information or find an alternative means of monitoring their risks.

Massachusetts Hospital Life alone selected the former option, choosing to limit its policy sales to applicants who lived in the immediate vicinity of Boston or had adequate ties within the city. As late as 1850, company executives still required almost all applicants to appear personally at its offices in Boston. When Samuel Mather of Cleveland wrote the company in 1846, he proposed "to insure my own life with you & perhaps apply for the agency of your Co. at this place."[54] While Massachusetts Hospital Life willingly forwarded an application form, Lowell added that the company had no interest in opening agencies: "We have no agency & of course can not avail of your good offices."[55] Even in the case of renewals, Massachusetts Hospital Life executives would rather send applicants to competitors than risk underwriting unverifiable applications. When George Rivers of Providence, Rhode Island, attempted to obtain a renewal of his existing policy with the company, the secretary responded: "As we have no agent in Providence to whom we can refer, it would probably be your easiest way to effect the insurance with the N. E. Mutual Co of this City, through their agent in Providence."[56] With this strict policy, however, Massachusetts Hospital Life was the lone holdout in the industry, which greatly inhibited its ability to grow and compete with other companies as interest in life insurance expanded.

The remainder of the industry—led by NYL&T and Baltimore Life—began to appoint agents who would serve as the personal contact between the applicant and the company. In many cases, the same respectable citizens the companies initially relied on to vouch for the identity of local residents would later be recruited as agents for the companies in their hometowns. But it was just as often the case that prominent community members (such as Levi Ward) would write directly to company executives, suggesting the establishment of an agency in their location. With the creation of this extended agency system, the point of reference for respected friends and physicians was no longer the big city but the local community, which now had local agents in place to attest to the respectability of applicants and their references.

Like Levi Ward, the men appointed to this agency system overwhelmingly were leading citizens of their communities, often serving as local mayors, postmasters, justices of the peace, or prominent businessmen. During the 1830s and 1840s, more than 80% of NYL&T agents operating within the state were lawyers; of these, more than one-third eventually served as county, New York Supreme Court, or federal circuit court justices. Lawyers were especially attractive candidates for this position because of their unique function within the community. When soliciting candidates for one new agency, NYL&T wrote to the treasurer of the local savings bank, specifically asking him to "recommend . . . some judicious upright Gentleman not under 30 who would answer to our purpose and be willing to accept the appointment, to some young lawyer perhaps it would be acceptable."[57] On one hand, a lawyer's practice would bring him into frequent contact with the citizens of his local community, particularly with the businessmen, professionals, and the salaried middle class who formed the target clientele of the industry. On the other, life insurance firms hoped that by hiring young lawyers with a reputation to build and uphold, they could avoid a potential principal-agent conflict—the problem, for example, of an agent being more interested in earning policy commissions than in providing honest, accurate assessments of the risk posed by applicants.

For a small-town lawyer, a strong relationship with a major big-city company like NYL&T added to his local and regional reputation and represented potential future business with the expanding company. But more important, particularly for local lawyers with political aspirations, the relationship signified contacts with the business and political elites of the state who comprised the board of directors and stockholders of the company, as well as with his peers throughout the state who occupied similar positions as agents within the company. This desire to create and maintain reputation collateral for long-term political and economic advancement—rather than a more basic need for immediate monetary gain—made lawyers and other leading citizens of local communities the ideal prototype of the insurance agent.

Almost all of these agency men were politically active. More than half of NYL&T's in-state agents were elected members of the New York state legislature or the United States Congress; many served these terms concurrently with their service to the firm. A similar percentage of out-of-state agents were elected to local, state, or federal offices, functioning as mayors, town managers, state legislators, or United States congressmen. Running as Crawford Republicans, Jacksonian Democrats,

Anti-Jacksonians, Anti-Masons, and Whigs, these agents represented the full spectrum of American politics at the time.[58]

These political connections were exemplified by the NYL&T agency in Buffalo, New York. In 1840, company executives approached Millard Fillmore—then a United States congressman—regarding the establishment of an agency in his hometown. Fillmore was acting informally as an agent at the time, forwarding policy applications to the company and collecting the normal commission.[59] Although Fillmore declined to assume that role formally, in all likelihood it was he who recommended his former classmate Nathan Kelsey Hall for the position. Hall would represent the company in Buffalo throughout the 1840s while also serving as an Erie County judge (1841–45), a New York state assemblyman (1846), and a United States congressman (1847–49). He only left the employment of NYL&T to assume his duties as the United States postmaster general during the Fillmore administration (1850–52).[60]

Political connections also directly benefited the company, as the presence of directors, stockholders, and agents in the New York legislature would ensure that the company's interests were represented in Albany. In discussing new agency appointments with Erastus Corning, a prominent member of the board of directors from Albany (as well as a future mayor of Albany, New York, state senator, and United States congressman),[61] President Bard remarked that one potential agent "would be of service to us as he was a member of the legislature," although Bard was quick to add: "not that he would be appointed with that view." Although Bard recognized the benefits of political connections, he also realized that "character and judgement" were more important traits than mere connections. For example, elsewhere in the letter he acknowledged that whereas "Mr. R" had been helpful to the company as a member of the legislature in the year it received its charter, NYL&T soon discovered that he was "not a suitable" agent and had "done very little" in that role.[62] The firm ultimately sought out agents whom they could trust to serve the interests of the company within their local communities; while additional attributes (such as service in the state legislature) were certainly desirable, firms could not replace the more indispensable characteristics related to one-on-one contact with the applicants. As President Bard cautioned when seeking a recommendation for a Montreal agent, "He should be a gentleman not only of integrity but of prudence and judgment."[63]

The Agency System in Practice

The creation of these agencies was not initially intended as a method of increasing insurance sales through personal sales efforts, as some historians of life insurance contend, but was rather meant to protect the company from high-risk applicants who resided far from the home office: "Very much of the safety of this Company in this branch of its buisiness [*sic*] depends on the prudence and caution of the agent."[64] Although agents were encouraged to "recommend" life insurance "in conversation and letter on all suitable occasions," and to "take pains to extend the Business by explaining its objects," the duty most stressed by company executives throughout their correspondence with agents was that of personally evaluating the health of the applicant when they delivered the final policy.[65] As President Bard stated to Levi Ward, "The point of most importance indeed only importance is his health at the moment of insurance."[66] Executives advised their agents to make sure that "when you deliver the policy you will see the party is in the same state as the date of the declaration" and "if there should be any change you will not deliver the policy."[67] The companies were concerned both that they might have made a mistake in their initial assessment and that the applicant could have experienced some significant change in his or her state of health; no company wanted to be bound to a long-term contract with a questionable risk.

Agents were expected to possess intimate knowledge of, and have significant connections with, the people in their community, and they were to use that knowledge to form an opinion about potential risks to aid the main office in making decisions. James H. Causten, a Washington, DC, agent for Baltimore Life, often commented on applicants who appeared to be particularly good risks. In 1833, he contended that William P. Zantzinger "is in good health now and is usually so having an excellent constitution, and free from gout and other complaints that impair the constitution . . . I am acquainted with the Gentleman. He is intelligent, prudent, and respectable, of good habits and of close calculation in all his movements. I consider the risk (as to the person) one of the very best."[68] Although an agent's estimations were not always as detailed and personal as this, companies took an agent's input seriously, particularly once he had developed a reputation with the firm's officers as an observant and reliable judge.

Perhaps even more important than their ability to verify information and to vouch in favor of applicants was the degree to which agents employed their local knowledge to caution against certain risks or to recommend the discontinuance of existing policies. On one occasion, Causten became aware of the drinking habits of a Baltimore Life policyholder named Thomas Randolph. Randolph was a couple of days late in the payment of his annual premium, and Causten believed that it would be beneficial for the company to seize the opportunity and cancel the policy due to "Randolph's habits of intemperance."[69] President Donaldson readily accepted the verdict of the agent: "Our practice is that if annual premium be not paid at that day, not to receive it, if any change has occurred in the health or habits of the assured. In the case of Randolph, it would be advisable not to receive the premium if tendered now, and to let the policy expire."[70] Causten's prudence in staying aware of the habits and reputation of local policyholders was invaluable to the company.

A similar situation occurred in 1851 when Levi Ward expressed his concerns that a new policyholder of NYL&T and his "respectable" friend had both lied about the drinking habits of the applicant. William Bard directed Ward to "ascertain . . . the truth of the facts, whether Burnett had been intemperate and at what period, and how long before the date of his policy he was considered among his acquaintances an intemperate man."[71] Since both Bard and Ward believed that Burnett's statements on the application "show[ed] fraudulent intention," Ward was instructed to cancel the policy: "When the premium is tendered you will decline it, saying the Office had desired you to do so, on the ground of misrepresentation in the declaration, and in the friends certificate as to the Sobriety Health of Mr. Burnett."[72] Lacking these personal connections, company executives in New York City would have been severely handicapped in accurately evaluating both the potential risks of underwriting applicants and the ongoing risks associated with existing policyholders.

Even if the agent had no personal knowledge of the candidate himself, he could still judge the reputation and respectability of the people vouching for the applicant. Thomas Gold, New England Mutual's agent in western Massachusetts, warned the board of directors in 1846 that he did "not have as much confidence in Dr. Mason . . . as in . . . Many physicians," explaining that "his mode of practice is peculiar." Yet even if Dr. Mason's ability as a physician was in doubt, his honesty was not in question: "I am . . . told that he would not make a certificate other than he believes true & correct." Gold was likewise able to vouch for the integrity of the other people submitting letters on behalf of the applicant: Mr. Sayles was "a respectable lawyer," while Henry C. Plunkett, "a large Manufacturer & Merchant, is a sensible man & highly respectable." The latter gentleman could attest that "he never knew or heard of any constitutional difficulty, any pulmonary affection & would say that full confidence could be put in [the applicant's] representation."[73] Without Gold's intimate knowledge of and connections with the people in Berkshire County, New England Mutual would have had to make decisions blindly, assuming that all applicants, physicians, and references were of equal honesty, integrity, respectability, and judgment.

No longer able to inspect each individual applicant themselves, companies were often forced to rely upon the final assessments of their agents. In 1833, Bard entrusted the NYL&T agent in Halifax, Nova Scotia, with the decision of whether to insure a woman of questionable health: "With regard to Mrs Mary Ann Harvie the physicians certificate states at the time she has a cold and that she is a lady of delicate constitution. At this distance the propriety of giving her a Policy for seven Years must be left to your Judgment."[74] Similarly, when an applicant in Hartford, Connecticut, reported that he had only experienced "spitting of blood once in his life" and did not believe it to be related to consumption, Bard advised the local agent to "exercise your judgment," instructing him to evaluate the applicant visually for signs of consumption and then to advise the company on how to proceed.[75] Once a life firm committed to expanding beyond its home base, it necessarily forfeited some degree of control over decisions regarding applicants. Company executives placed their faith in the careful process of initially selecting agents. They also continued to remind agents of the hazards of poor selection and in particular of the symptoms of consumption.

Agents knew they possessed the confidence of the home office, but they also worried that if they recommended what turned out to be poor risks, it could undermine this trust. In 1847, A. C. Robbins of Brunswick, Maine, placed his reputation as a New England Mutual agent on the line to vouch for the prudence of underwriting George Dunning. Dunning came from a large family, two members of which had died of consumption. Robbins asserted that the Dunning family was not "one of those where consumption has its origin in any hereditary Difficulty." He then continued: "I consider George (the Insured) no more likely to Die of Consumption than myself, and I should think his chance for Long life as good as my own . . . that is my opinion of Mr. Dunning & he is a person whom I see Daily & have associated much with for some years past." Yet Robbins, a relatively new agent, was also concerned that this assessment (if incorrect) would hurt his standing with the company: "I know not how far you hold me accountable for an opinion upon a risk and I should not like to be blamed if any of the risks I have certified for, terminate as bad ones."[76] Of course, if Robbins displayed a pattern of recommending bad risks, he would probably be relieved of his duties as agent. But a company would be unlikely to blame the agent for individual cases unless it suspected that the agent had acted irresponsibly or in an intentionally misleading fashion. Thus it was ultimately the company that would have to bear the cost if an agent's decision about a particular individual turned out to be wrong. Insurance executives really had no choice in the matter; without a more objective means of assessing risk, firms were forced to rely on the subjective opinions of local agents.

While agents did not want to be held responsible for making poor decisions, they did take credit when their instincts turned out to be correct. Dr. Beverly Wellford of Fredericksburg, Virginia, wrote the Baltimore Life president regarding one such "narrow escape" in 1835 in which his intuition saved the company: "[Fackett] is since dead. I congratulate myself and the Co. that I did not induce him to take [the policy] which could have been readily done. But I did not like the risque although there was no apparent reason to anticipate his death for a much longer period than that at which it occurred."[77] Although life insurance companies frequently advertised that the business was conducted on a scientific basis—and had no relation to the unpopular lottery or other forms of gambling—in reality, decisions on questionable applicants often came down to personal testimonies, anecdotes, intuition, and gut instincts.

Most agents treated their role as the linchpin in a company's chain of references very seriously, taking the initiative in examining each individual case that applied through their agencies and being especially vigilant with regard to consumption. Yet on many occasions, the available evidence regarding the risk of underwriting a specific applicant was mixed. Although none of the responses on Thomas Coggeshall's 1846 application to New England Mutual would have given company executives cause to question his fitness for life insurance, agent William Taylor of New Bedford, Massachusetts, took a more cautious approach, considering both his personal knowledge of Coggeshall and the applicant's visual appearance. His conflicting observations and confused conclusions indicate the difficulty of rendering judgments on such a complicated disease:

> Mr Coggeshall is a slight built man . . . This fact, and my knowledge of his having been unwell several times within a few years, induced me to address Doct Bartlett. [Mr. Coggeshall] is a man who habitually takes good care of his health, and on this account I would prefer writing on him, rather than on some persons of more robust appearance. Doct. E. W. Greene the Postmaster, under whom Mr. Coggeshall is employed, is of opinion that he is free from disease now, but thinks his form, size &c indicate a liability to disease of the lungs, but he also considers the great age attained by his parents &c. as entitled to some weight in estimating the probability of an attack of pulmonary disease. Instances are rather rare where the offspring of long lived parents become the victims of consumption.[78]

The thoroughness of Taylor's efforts (including consulting two different doctors familiar with the applicant) demonstrates the active role taken by agents to discern the potential risk to their companies of underwriting specific individuals. Taylor understood that he and his fellow agents functioned as a company's eyes and ears in the community, revealing information that the impersonal application might hide.

Similarly, Newton Fitch of Amherst, Massachusetts, commented that he had known applicant Zebina Eastman ten years earlier, when he was "a young man of good habits and tolerable good constitution, always rather poor in flesh, and somewhat round shouldered." Although both of Eastman's parents as well as three of his five siblings had died of consumption, it was unclear whether or not Zebina was similarly prone. "I know Mr. Eastmans brothers, men between 40 & 50, strong healthy men I should think, but they also are round shouldered and have that appearance peculiar to those inclined to consumption complaints." In the end, Fitch abdicated his role as adviser to New England Mutual, concluding that the company itself would be able to "judge better in this matter."[79]

These two episodes expose the complexity of the subjective system of evaluating risks. How should the company have gone about assessing the actual risk of accepting Coggeshall's or Eastman's application? Both possessed (what were believed to have been) consumption-prone builds, and Coggeshall had been ill on several occasions; these were factors likely to lead to an outright rejection of their applications. While Coggeshall's heredity indicated longevity, Eastman's family had been riddled with tuberculosis in the past, although his surviving family now seemed to be robust. On the other hand, both men had the visual appearance of health (despite their skeletal makeup) and took good care of themselves. Which factors were more important in determining potential mortality? Were the directors in the main office—looking at two-dimensional applications and letters—really better equipped to judge these risks than the agents themselves, who could consider the flesh-and-blood reality of the applicants? Even as the agency system helped life insurers to repersonalize the relationship between the company and the applicant, the industry recognized the limitations of this system and desired the development of more precision (beyond mere anecdotal experience) in considering similar applicants; this would force companies to move toward both obtaining better information on questionnaires and ascertaining the actual, precise risk associated with various attributes.

Firms did begin to quantify risks when they solicited expert medical opinion. As early as the 1830s, companies started hiring doctors to examine each applicant and certify the statements made by the applicant's personal physician. Although the nineteenth century witnessed the emergence of more systematized training for doctors in the United States, there was still no central oversight of the profession either on the state or federal level. As one historian of the profession writes, colleges with rigorous academic standards competed with institutions that "were blatantly commercial in conception and execution, inadequately staffed but offering degrees at cut-rate investment of time and money."[80] Thus life insurers worried that even "respectable" local doctors might not have adequate training and experience to assess the life expectancy of individual applicants. By hiring medical examiners to oversee the statements submitted by local physicians, companies added an extra layer of oversight to the process. And while applicants to New England Mutual had always been asked for the names of any physicians they had consulted in the previous five years, by 1847 they were also requested to indicate if any such physician was "not a regular physician," and, if not, "what class is he?"[81] In this way, the company might better assess the doctor's training and experience in deciding how much weight to put in their judgments.

One of the first medical examiners for the industry was Dr. E. J. Marsh, appointed by NYL&T in 1831 to scrutinize individuals making application in their Paterson, New Jersey, office.[82] By the 1840s, NYL&T expected all agents to "select a physician of experience, and one in whose character entire confidence can be placed. His opinion will be taken in every case."[83] In some instances, a doctor was selected to fill both roles. For example, from 1833 to 1854 Dr. Beverly Wellford served as both the agent and the medical examiner for the Baltimore Life office in Fredericksburg, Virginia. In this way, he could directly apply his expertise when evaluating the applicants who presented themselves in his office.

Whether the doctor was the personal physician of the applicant or a hired medical examiner for the company, he was expected not only to comment on the applicant's specific health condition but to provide some quantifiable opinion as to his potential life span. New England Mutual regularly sent a form letter to local doctors asking whether a given applicant was "as good a life for insurance as the average of persons of his age, of good constitution, in good health? or better, or not so good, and in what degree?" Many of the responding doctors focused on the ambiguous term "average," commenting that an applicant's "chances for life are equal to those of the most healthy individuals of the same age, in this locality," "better . . . than the average of persons," or "as good as the average of men."[84]

But a few doctors took seriously New England Mutual's request that they determine to "what degree" the applicant deviated from the average, anticipating later attempts by the industry to quantify the specific risk attached to each individual applicant. Dr. A. A. Hobert of Somerville, Massachusetts, declared that he thought Edmund C. Flagg to be "5 per cent. at least better than the average," while Dr. Daniel Collins believed that the scrofula suffered by Ellsworth H. Hyde of Williamsburg, Massachusetts, "diminishes the chance of his living to old age about twenty five per Cent, compared with persons in good health of the same age."[85] Even Francis C. Lowell, a prominent member of New England Mutual's board of directors (as well as the actuary of Massachusetts Hospital Life), was not immune to having his health history closely examined and quantified; his personal physician opined that his health and family history "might perhaps justify an addition of ten per cent to the premium on the best risks."[86] However, these early attempts at quantification remained merely a mirage. Doctors were still basing both their qualitative and quantitative judgments on personal experience and anecdotal evidence. Both inadequate knowledge of the causes of specific diseases and the lack of statistical data on the effect of particular conditions or habits on an individual's mortality prevented a true quantification of risk. It would not be until the postbellum era that life insurance companies would be able to develop more sophisticated and objective means of assessing mortality.

Abuses of the Agency System

In developing a system that depended so heavily on the knowledge and observations of the local agents, life insurance companies necessarily opened the doors to potential principal-agent problems. Could the companies really trust agents to be truthful when expressing opinions regarding their friends, neighbors, and colleagues? Would agents place the best interests of the company ahead of their own financial, political, or social aspirations? The companies attempted to mitigate some of these concerns through their selection of agents with a reputation for honesty and integrity to uphold and who might desire to leverage positive relations with the company for future political or commercial aspirations. Despite these cautions, abuses still emerged. While extant company records do not reveal the reasons most agents left (or were relieved of) their positions, letters to and from company agents disclose some of the major points of contention. The main concerns expressed by company executives had to do with late submission of premium payments, unproductive agencies, and agents working for multiple companies. But there were also a few accusations that agents were blatantly misusing the power and trust of the company.

The majority of complaints against agents by company executives related to delays in forwarding premium payments to the head office. On repeated occasions, the company had to remind agents that "the nature & success of our Life Insurance business depends upon the punctual payment of premiums."[87] In most cases the agents were merely delinquent in making their returns, eventually forwarding the money to the head office. But in a small number of instances, the company was forced to replace negligent agents, particularly in the most productive markets.

Peter Lythoff was one of the first agents for NYL&T and served conscientiously as its Newark, New Jersey, agent from 1831 to 1846. Yet by 1846, a number of "infirmities" and "troubles" caused him to neglect his duties. Although the company "felt a great regret that [his] latter years have been filled with sorrow," Lythoff's personal problems were "to this Company unimportant." His "former and present neglect in remitting Insurance premiums" forced the company to "withdraw [his] Agency." Yet, giving "every consideration for [his] long and honourable life," the company did offer "to do this, with as little pain to [him] as possible," offering to accept his resignation if tendered within the week.[88] The same year, NYL&T similarly accused the firm of Hale and Welbasky, which had been in charge of its Boston agency since 1842, of "some irregularity . . . in making monthly returns"; with much less sympathy for this agent, the company summarily revoked its agency.[89]

By the mid-1850s, Baltimore Life's most lucrative agency was in Richmond, Virginia, where John Darracott had expanded the business from 1853 to 1855 through his advocacy of slave insurance. Yet while Darracott was highly innovative, he was also fiscally irresponsible. Baltimore Life wrote him repeatedly, complaining that his records were in a "state of confusion" and "his manner of conducting business . . . very loose and unsatisfactory."[90] Despite the company's reluctance to "withdraw the agency" of such a successful representative, it could not overlook the fact that "his conduct has been so very strange and so directly in violation of all rules of business men that we are compelled to it. Our letters are never answered, and but seldom acknowledged, while his accounts are always sent in such a confused manner that they are of no use to us."[91] Despite the firm's best efforts to convince the agent to reform his ways, after fifteen months of continued problems the company finally forced Darracott to resign.[92] The financial liquidity of the company was dependent upon the regular payment of premiums, and the failure of agents to forward these funds—whether because of fraud, incompetence, or incapacity—could quickly turn trusted and lucrative agencies into liabilities.

Company executives also frequently complained when their agents were unproductive: firms depended on steady growth in policy sales to ensure their stability. Although agents received payment on a commission basis, the head office had to pay for incidental expenses associated with local advertising and was responsible for local taxes on the agencies of out-of-state companies. For these reasons, NYL&T either replaced its agent or closed the agency altogether in Cincinnati, Ohio; Burlington, Vermont; Halifax, Nova Scotia; Macon, Georgia; and Petersburg, Virginia; Baltimore Life similarly closed agencies in Annapolis, Maryland, and Richmond, Virginia.[93]

The extant records provide only one instance of a flagrant abuse of power by an agent. In late 1838 and early 1839, Baltimore Life exchanged a series of letters with its agent James H. Causten of Washington, DC, on the subject of policies issued on the lives of debtors. Causten was not only the company's agent at the time (representing the firm in that crucial market from 1833 to 1846) but was also one of Baltimore Life's biggest customers. Between 1831 and 1847, he held thirty-one policies on the lives of nineteen different people (including himself) worth a total of over $45,000. Company president John J. Donaldson first wrote Causten in November

1838 to express his concern that the agent was taking out so many policies for his own benefit: "You know it is the rule of all Life Insurance made on the Life of another, that there is an interest in the Life to the amt insur'd."[94] Although the company stopped short of making an outright accusation, it in effect implied that Causten was taking out policies on people for whom he did not possess the insurable interest required by all American companies, meaning a continuing interest in the life of the party insured as opposed to a gambling interest in his or her death.

Rather than defending his interest in the lives underwritten, Causten instead attacked the company rules themselves, which he viewed as "untenable," asserting: "As you insure the Life and not the Debt of the assured, I do not see how the amount or validity of the debt can be drawn in question; or, if it be the thing actually covered by the policy, then, you would of course be responsible for the whole debt, even though it exceed the amount insured."[95] Despite Causten's protest, Baltimore Life refused to budge on the topic of insurable interest: "The principle to which you object, is that which governs every Life Insurance in the World . . . I consider this as the definitive action of the Board."[96] Although Causten reluctantly accepted this decision and appears to have exercised his power more responsibly during the 1840s, he would eventually resign in 1846 over another disputed policy claim he held against the company.[97]

Overall, despite these complaints expressed by company executives, the benefits of the agency system far outweighed the negative experiences of the companies. While many abuses may have gone unnoticed (or unrecorded) by company executives—for example, if agents gave special consideration to family and friends when making their recommendations—it is interesting to note that firms never accused agents of intentionally or unintentionally making poor recommendations or providing bad advice. Even as they sought more objective means of evaluating applicants, firms seemed to do so more out of a desire for better precision than from the perception of a widespread principal-agent problem within the system.

Replacing Subjective Agents with Objective Profiling

The companies clearly believed that careful monitoring of the health and family history of their applicants gave them a selection advantage over the average mortality rates predicted by the tables, thus lowering their risk level, reducing their overall costs, and increasing their profits. Yet even as they were developing this elaborate agency system to help them in their selection process, insurance entrepreneurs realized that more in-depth knowledge about mortality was necessary in order to better understand the precise risks. Just as Bard had sought to quantify the risks associated with age, gender, occupation, and geography, life insurers of the 1840s and 1850s wanted to replace the subjective assessments of their agents with more precise, objective analyses of the health and family history of applicants. By embedding their growing knowledge of mortality risks within the policy application itself, companies could more accurately quantify the risk of death of each individual—choosing to reject the applicant, accept him or her at the published rates by age, or accept him or her at an additional rate of premium.

Throughout the antebellum period, life insurance applications became increasingly detailed and, in the opinion of some observers, intrusive. The original application form of the Baltimore Life asked a mere seven general questions, which were then supplemented by the knowledge and observations of the respected friend, family physician, and local company agent who would provide empirical opinions regarding the prudence of underwriting the applicant. This firsthand knowledge of the applicant far surpassed in importance the black-and-white answers on the application form.

Over the course of the next thirty years, these application queries would become increasingly detailed, as companies attempted to statistically quantify the risks attached to each individual applicant. The original New England Mutual application from 1844 was similar to those of earlier companies, with only a few differences. First, it inquired directly of the applicant regarding the temperance of their habits, rather than relying solely on the opinion of the references. Second, the company broke down the question regarding health conditions into eight distinct queries, thus forcing the applicant to consider separately each disease, symptom, or family of diseases. Lastly, New England Mutual added two questions regarding family history, asking the "Age of his parents, if living, or at what age, and of what disease, both or either died, as nearly as can be recollected," with a similar question regarding elder siblings.

Responding to the Temperance Question

While applicants had little difficulty answering most of these new questions, the temperance query created a great deal of confusion, since many people were unsure exactly what constituted temperate habits. This confusion mirrored a central problem with the temperance movement itself: it was not always clear what the movement was against. First, the word *temperance* implies moderation, yet temperance reformers often equated it with total abstinence.[98] Second, temperance as an idea is not exclusively about alcohol but can be applied to any number of activities. Thus while active members of temperance societies would assume that the question "Is he of temperate habits?" on a life insurance form really meant "Does he *totally abstain from alcohol?*" the responses given by applicants to New England Mutual indicate that the average person was not necessarily aware of or in agreement with this emerging definition. In theory, this question only required a yes or no answer, yet in practice many applicants felt it necessary to qualify their answers, and it is these qualifications that reveal the confusion of Americans regarding the meaning of *temperance,* even two decades after the establishment of the American Temperance Society in 1826.

First, did temperance imply total abstinence from alcohol or merely moderation in its consumption? While several applicants[99] specifically stated that they were "total abstinence" men, "teetotalers," or "cold water" men, others responded according to the more traditional definition of moderation. Benjamin King of Boston did not deny taking an occasional drink, but asserted that he was "Never *addicted* to the use of intoxicating Spirits" (emphasis added), while W. H. Mackintosh of West Newton, Massachusetts, stated that he was temperate "but not strictly a tea totaller."[100] Similarly, Joseph Dylan of Cincinnati, Ohio, was "temperate tho not strictly abstemious," while Ellsworth Hyde of Williamsburg, Massachusetts, said he was "moderately" temperate "but not strictly." But lest this latter response be misunderstood, the local agent qualified Hyde's response for the home office: "He is, I suppose what may be termed a strictly temperance man, he may once in a great while drink spirituous liquors, but not habitually, by any means, he made this answer so that he might err on the safe side."[101] For these respondents, alcohol was only a problem if it became addicting. Thus many applicants to New England Mutual viewed temperance as a form of moderation, with total abstinence or teetotalism entailing a more extreme form of that moderation.

In his tongue-in-cheek response to the same question, Charles Sedgwick (youngest scion of the famous Sedgwick family and a future agent for the company) stated, "I say emphatically & unequivocally yea, a Tetotaller wd. probably say no."[102] Yet while Sedgwick intended to mock the question, John Mead of Newton, Massachusetts, was perfectly serious when he responded that Edward Ryan (born in Ireland) "Is as temperate as the average of his countrymen. Not noted for intemperance. Have not known him to be so intoxicated that he could not walk. Have known him to drink too much only on public days."[103] Obviously, New England Mutual agreed that this was acceptable, since each of these men received a policy with the company.

But even more than the question of moderation versus total abstinence, the question "Is he of temperate habits?" gave no actual indication that the company was referring exclusively to alcohol, or even that it meant to include all types of alcoholic beverages. Many respondents assumed that the question was limited to "intoxicating" or "ardent spirits" but that it did not refer to less intoxicating beverages such as beer, wine, or cider.[104] John S. Tyler of Boston attested to "a natural antipathy to alchoholic [*sic*] liquor, but like[d] a glass of wine occasionally."[105] Likewise, Augustine Haines of Portland, Maine, declared himself to be temperate, although he admitted to using "wine, & distilled liquor, when I please";[106] based on his answer, it is unclear whether Haines believed any beverage to be problematic.

But even more applicants broadened rather than restricted the meaning of the question, going well beyond temperance merely with regard to alcoholic drinks. Some respondents indicated in their answers an adherence to the health system of Sylvester Graham, referring to caffeinated beverages, tobacco, medicine, work and sleep habits, diet, exercise, and bathing as reflecting on a person's "temperance," in addition to their comments on alcohol.[107] Pliny Jewell of Winchester, New Hampshire, said that he "drinks teas and coffee but no intoxicating liquors; uses no tobacco in any shape."[108] William Fisher of Lacon, Illinois, also "occasionally" drank "coffee & Tea," but "never any *other* stimulant" (emphasis added).[109] In contrast, Amos Townsend Jr., of New Haven was a "tetotaler as to all intoxicating drinks & to tea & coffee."[110] For these men, all alcohol unquestionably fell within the temperance rubric, while only milder drinks like tea and coffee were subject to interpretation.

For several other applicants, whether to include smoking was the controversial element. While these men were nondrinkers, they qualified their responses by indicating that they smoked or used tobacco. Francis George Shaw of Roxbury, Massachusetts, declared himself to be a "Washingtonian but smokes," while John H. Norris of Newport, Maine, said he "uses tobacco however."[111] Even Francis Cabot Lowell, one of the company's directors, was unsure how to accurately answer the question, declaring himself to be temperate "unless in Smoking which some people might not consider temperate."[112]

In a number of instances, diet was included in the understanding of the term. Augustus C. Robbins of Brunswick, Maine, stated: "I am temperate in my habits. In the words of Young Beecher, 'No bone, muscle or fibre in me ever felt the power of Alcohol.' I never used tobacco in any form or shape. I am abstemious in my diet, living almost entirely upon vegetable food, & seldom eating meat, & never with my food or at any time Drinking anything except cold water."[113] Edmund R. Peaslee, MD, of Hanover, New Hampshire, likewise included food in his definition of temperance, saying he "intend[ed] to <u>eat</u> to <u>live</u>, & not <u>live</u> to <u>eat</u>," while H. Seymour of Deerfield, Massachusetts, was temperate "in eating and drinking."[114]

But quite a few people interpreted temperance to mean more than what (or how much) one ate, drank, or smoked. Benjamin H. Barnes of Chelsea, Massachusetts, was "accustomed to daily bathing," while Samuel Osgood of Providence, Rhode Island, was "Studiously regular in all habits of diet, sleep, study, exercise & bathing."[115] And when company director Charles Curtis brought Rufus Choate's headaches to the attention of the other directors, he determined that this was due to his "over work[ing] himself, a species of <u>intemperance</u> as false as any."[116] Perhaps Jonathan Pratt Robinson of Roxbury, Massachusetts, was the most perceptive when he honestly responded: "Hardly know how to answer this question as there are so many different opinions as to what constitutes temperance nowadays; but would respectfully refer to Peter Wainwright Esq, one of your Directors."[117] Despite this ongoing confusion, New England Mutual never rephrased this question on later application forms.

Expanding the Application Form

New England Mutual would further refine its policy application over the next two decades. In 1847 it added several more health questions, queried whether the applicant "had always been" temperate and whether the applicant's attending physician was "a regular physician, or what class is he," and asked for the details of applications for policies with other companies. By the early 1850s, the company was additionally concerned about any injuries the applicant had suffered and whether he had ever traveled outside of the United States or south of 30° latitude, and it asked specific questions of female applicants regarding their marital status and reproductive history.

These changes often reflected the evolving scientific knowledge about the nature of disease and mortality or the industry's efforts to understand the statistical implications of various risks. For example, several companies, including Mutual Benefit Life of New Jersey and United States Life of New York, conducted inquiries into the relationship between consumption and weight, the latter concluding by 1873 that there was "a tendency to leanness, especially noticeable among the tall individuals" who had died from consumption.[118] As a result of earlier studies like this one, in 1858 Mutual Benefit began asking applicants to list their weight along with their health history, thus providing one objective measurement to consider along with the personal observation of an applicant's physical constitution.[119]

New England Mutual's 1861 application most thoroughly reflected the industry's movement toward complete discovery of risk factors. For the first time, the company asked the marital status of all applicants (no longer limiting this question to females) as well as their height—for further evaluation of their consumption risk. In addition to alcohol, the firm was now also concerned about the use of opium as a stimulant. The form listed thirty-nine conditions and asked applicants to indicate "Whether now, or heretofore, and when, and how long, or how frequently, and to what degree, subject to, or at all affected, or suspected to be so, by any of the following diseases and infirmities." Every known disease or symptom of disease that the company suspected might affect mortality was included on this list. And finally, the application widened its inquiry into the health history of the applicant's family, asking, "Has either of the parents, or have any of the paternal or maternal grandparents of the proposed Life, or any of their descendants, so far as known, had consumption, or asthma, or been affected with insanity, or mental derangement, and if the latter, please to state the cause, kind, degree, duration, and other circumstances?"[120]

While it was still possible for the applicant to provide fraudulent answers to these questions, the company believed that such a detailed form enabled accurate assessment of the mortality risk associated with each applicant, based on carefully compiled mortality statistics as well as the most current scientific knowledge regarding disease. The agency system had allowed companies to navigate successfully between the worlds of personal connections and anonymity from the 1830s through the 1850s, but profiling risks through detailed application forms began to supplant this function.

Whereas companies believed these detailed questions to be necessary, applicants were finding them increasingly intrusive. By the mid-1850s, articles mocking life insurance applications began to appear in the press. One writer for *Harper's New Monthly Magazine,* noting the "number, variety, and troublesomeness of the questions," suggested several additions to the insurance application, including "Are you a polite man, who does not mind running out of a hot opera-house to get up a carriage on a wet night?" and "Was any member of your family ever swallowed up by an earthquake?"[121] In 1866, humorist Josh Billings (born Henry Wheeler Shaw) published a short story entitled "Josh Billings Insures His Life." In it, the title character is asked a series of ridiculous questions by the insurance agent, ranging from his gender (and how long he has been that gender) to his precise number of ancestors and his legal opinion on the constitutionality of the Ten Commandments.[122] Similarly, an 1867 journal printed what was purported to be the application form of a new life insurer:

> Great advances have recently been made in the medical examination of candidates for the benefits of Life Insurance . . . What he does on rising and retiring is . . . regarded as essential to be known, and still more so whether he takes his tea and coffee weak or strong, with sugar or without. What does he wear next to his skin? is another of these vital questions. Does he always wear a shirt, or go with-

out on washing days? . . . Has, the would-be insured ever bathed? if he has, when will he do it again. What is his exact height and weight, fighting and otherwise. Are his nasal passages large and free? or, in other words, is he like Lord Dundreary "a difficult sneezer," or, like David Crockett, a "regular snorter?" How is he "complected?" and, above all, what is the color of his eyes? for how can his destiny be foretold without this indispensable clue? Upon the color of his hair a still greater emphasis is laid, because, we suppose, if it be so red as to drive him to desperation, he may be induced to fly in the face of his Maker by dying. But to resume this medical catechism:—Is the applicant married or single? if single, has he proposed? if he had, has he been accepted or rejected? if accepted, when is the wedding to come off and what will be the sex of the first pledge of affection? Is the applicant's moral character unexceptionable? Did he ever murder his grand-mother? if not, what is her present age, the "size of her bones," and the number of the spectacles she wears. What is the name and what the length of the neck of the candidate's great grand aunt on the mother's side? Are the applicant's features large or small? Is his nose rubicund, Roman, Grecian, or pug? Is his beard light or heavy? Is his mouth capacious? Is his an open countenance? Is his hair of the same color as his sister's? Does he resemble his father or his mother? if neither, why not?[123]

This spoof would have resonated with mid-nineteenth-century Americans because, in spite of the ridiculous nature of the questions, it came awfully close to mimicking the reality of applying for insurance by the 1860s.

Conquering Anonymity

Like life insurers, most other businessmen during the early decades of the nineteenth century also had to rely on direct knowledge of a person's reputation and past experiences in making sound commercial judgments. Eastern businessmen routinely rooted their decisions of creditworthiness on knowledge obtained "through a network of kin, friends, business acquaintances, and longtime customers." When such direct connections were unavailable, creditors often put their faith in "letters from local attorneys, merchants, and clergy attesting to the good character and sound business habits of the applicant."[124] Establishing a direct chain of references was the main means by which all early businessmen attempted to reduce the risk of adverse selection. For insurance applicants, the necessity of proving their identity and trustworthiness through personal references fell well within the accepted custom of providing letters of introduction for new arrivals to a location or references for credit seekers.

As cities rapidly expanded and market connections spread beyond the local sphere, both creditors and insurers had to find new ways of protecting themselves from unsafe, speculative, and fraudulent risks. Credit-reporting services met the needs of many businessmen in the 1830s and 1840s. In acting as a creditor's eyes and ears on the ground, reporting agencies created a proxy for personal knowledge and relationships. In her fine study of the antebellum credit-reporting industry, historian Rowena Olegario reveals that during the 1840s Lewis Tappan's Mercantile Agency would rely on leading citizens of local communities to supply relevant information for its credit reports on individuals and businesses. The majority of these correspondents were attorneys, who occupied a "central position in the commercial life of towns and localities" and who "functioned as a nexus between outsiders and locals."[125] The same traits that made lawyers attractive as agents for life insurance companies also made them desirable as correspondents for the Mercantile Agency. Tappan himself pointed out that these lawyers had reputations to uphold and were motivated as well by a desire to form business contacts outside their local communities, making it particularly likely that they could be trusted to act "honestly and competently" for the company.[126]

Paralleling the emergence of these credit-reporting services were changes in the selection process for life insurance. The same breakdown of communal ties that was driving the demand for life insurance also rendered a careful selection of lives to be insured more difficult: the more disconnected a company was from applicants, the harder it became for the firm to obtain the information necessary to accurately judge the risk. Life insurers thus developed the agency system to *re*personalize the relationship between their boards of directors and the individual applicants, minimizing the problem of asymmetric information. Companies selected highly respected local citizens who were expected to serve as their eyes and ears in the community, evaluating the appearance of applicants, unearthing evidence of unhealthy family histories or questionable habits, and attesting to the respectability of the people writing testimonial letters on the applicant's behalf. In short, like credit-reporting agencies, the initial purpose of the life insurance agency system was to recreate the glass-bowl mentality associated with small towns or city neighborhoods. It would not be until the postbellum period—when companies would finally be able to begin breaking down mortality into its component factors—that insurers would develop a more objective profile of the ideal policyholder. In many ways, such an objective profile would eliminate the need for agents' subjective evaluation. Then, rather than judging risks, agents could concentrate their energy on actively soliciting new applicants.

CHAPTER 3

Lying, Cheating, and Stealing versus The Court of Public Opinion

Preventing Moral Hazard and Insurance Fraud

In the summer of 1836, New York Life and Trust received a letter from Gardner Lawrence, one of its new agents in Syracuse, New York, regarding the death of Nathaniel Knowles. Knowles had applied for a life insurance policy with the company earlier that summer before allegedly committing suicide, and Lawrence sought the company's advice about how to handle the case. President Bard was initially unconcerned. While he believed, based on Lawrence's account, that "there can be no doubt that the unfortunate Knowles put himself to death," the company would not have to prove that Knowles had violated the suicide clause in the contract because no policy had ever been issued. Although Lawrence had forwarded to the home office Knowles's application along with all of the necessary supporting documentation— "the declaration of the party & the letters of a physician & friend"—the company board had not yet accepted the application when the death occurred.[1]

Yet this case would not be closed so easily because, unfortunately for the company, the novice agent had made a serious error. Rather than waiting for the official approval of the board before proceeding, Lawrence had broken company protocol and had accepted the first premium payment from Knowles—thereby implying to the applicant that his policy was already in force. NYL&T sent the premium payment back to Lawrence and reminded him that "no person is authorized by us to insure an individual." And, recognizing the firm's potentially precarious position as a result of this mistake, Bard further chastised the agent: "Why you rec[eive]d the premium before it was determined that the Ins[urance] would be made & before the policy was returned to you, I can not explain."[2] But the damage had already been done. Denying that Knowles had committed suicide—and believing that the policy contract was valid—his beneficiaries chose to fight the company for the proceeds of the policy. Writing through well-respected Syracuse lawyer James R. Lawrence (who was of no known relation to agent Gardner Lawrence), the family demanded immediate payment of the policy.[3]

Although all the facts seemed to support NYL&T, the company needed to weigh carefully how contesting the family's claim would be perceived in the court of public opinion. Even as it took responsibility for agent Lawrence's poor decision and acknowledged the existence of the policy contract—stating that "whether Mr. Lawrence was as prudent as he ought to have been in making the insurance, will not be made a ground of assignment between Mr. Knowl[e]s family and the company"[4]— Bard still believed that the policy was void "on the ground of intentional fraud on the part of Mr. Knowl[e]s."[5] Since Knowles had applied for the policy immediately before committing suicide, NYL&T was sure that Knowles's actions were premeditated. Additionally, the policy contract clearly stated that the company was not liable in instances where the policyholder "die[d] by his own hand."[6] However, the burden was on the company to positively demonstrate that Knowles had committed suicide. If the public believed that NYL&T was dealing unfairly with the family—challenging an honest claim and dragging the grieving family through the time, cost, and emotion of unnecessary litigation—then the company risked damaging its carefully crafted reputation in the community.

On the other hand, the firm would only remain fiscally sound as long as its mortality tables accurately reflected the risks it was underwriting. Companies predicted from the tables that, on average, a given number of people would die each year from a given age group, but *which* individuals would die was a random event over which the companies had no control, and thus they could only avoid losses by selecting good risks when writing policies. Crimes such as murder, suicide, or fraud—when committed for the express purpose of collecting on a life insurance policy—specifically targeted individuals *because* of the money value of their demise, thereby rendering the actuarial tables useless as long-term predictors of risk.[7] Gambling policies, by which the party assuring would benefit from the death of the insured, were merely temptations to negligence and outright murder; whereas gambling was defined as a risk-bearing activity with a positive outcome (for the gambler) resulting from the risk coming to fruition, insurance was distinguished as a risk-avoiding endeavor.[8] Instances of insurance fraud—ranging from lying on applications or violating policy restrictions to faking death—impaired a company's ability to avoid underwriting individuals with questionable health histories or who engaged in risky behaviors. Life insurers thus needed to walk a fine line between gaining a reputation for being overly litigious and undermining their long-term stability by being too lenient in weeding out fraudulent claims.

Bard was well aware that the Knowles case, if handled incorrectly, might either undermine the firm's growing business along the Erie Canal corridor or expose the company to increasing instances of fraud. He thus sought the advice of B. Davis

Noxen—a prominent local lawyer, a known associate of James R. Lawrence, and the company's leading representative in the town since the opening of its first Syracuse agency in 1833.[9] Noxen was instructed to weigh all the evidence regarding Knowles's death and determine whether "there was reason to believe that before a jury, the evidence of suicide would be so clear, that an honest jury would have doubt." Understanding that "the feelings of a jury would be in favour of the family and against the Office," Bard knew that "the evidence must be undoubted to attain a verdict in our favour." Barring such overwhelming evidence of suicide and "under all the circumstances" surrounding the case, the company would consider it "fair to offer a compromise" to the family in order to keep the matter out of court. If Noxen determined that it would be "imprudent to contest the whole claim," Bard hoped he would be able "to negotiate a little for us" with the beneficiaries.[10] If the situation could be kept out of the public sphere, then perhaps the damage could be contained to this one claim.

But the Knowles family refused to go down without a fight. Before Noxen could engage in any negotiations, James Lawrence again wrote to NYL&T, using language that Bard interpreted as "uncivil," "rude," attacking the company's "fairness," and containing "threats which tho[ugh] denied are meant to be understood." Despite Bard's outrage, these tactics appear to have been effective, since the president quickly assured the family's representative that "unless Mr. Noxen thinks there is good and sufficient ground to believe it was a case of suicide, and the insurance made with the intention of defrauding the company, we have no wish to delay payment an hour."[11] With Knowles's beneficiaries indicating that they would rally public opinion to their side, NYL&T was forced to abandon even a compromise settlement.

American life insurance companies of the nineteenth century were faced with a virtually impossible task. Because the industry dealt directly with consumers, maintaining a positive public reputation was crucial. However, this reputation was based on morality—that is, paying all just claims and not promoting questionable practices such as wager policies—as well as on financial soundness; policyholders wanted to be sure that they were paying premiums to a company that would be able to honor their future claims. While fiscal responsibility required companies to strictly enforce policy restrictions and root out all potential cases of gambling, suicide, and fraud, public perception of companies' morality necessitated the prompt and uncontested payment of claims except in cases where an *obvious* fraud had been committed. Throughout the antebellum period, the industry would seek a delicate balance between preserving its actuarial foundations and maintaining a reputation for equity and fairness.

Maintaining Insurable Interest

One of the chief objections to the sale of life insurance in both the United States and continental Europe was its reputation as a gambling contract and its association with crime. During the sixteenth and seventeenth centuries, speculative insurance policies had become increasingly popular throughout Europe. A person could secretly acquire a policy on the life of another person whose payment was contingent on the outcome of almost any event—ranging from loss of virginity, divorce, the birth of a child, or the outcome of a scandal to death from drinking gin, the death of a nobleman or famous statesman, or the number of immigrants to die within a given week. While many of these gambling policies were harmless diversions (for example, during the 1770s Londoners wagered thousands of pounds on the actual sex of a cross-dressing French diplomat named Chevalier D'Éon), these speculative life policies too often resulted in the murder of the insured.[12] Critics thus maintained that life insurance created a moral hazard by either providing a new profit opportunity for criminals or "tempt[ing] good people to do wrong."[13] In response to such crimes, between the sixteenth and eighteenth centuries many governments (including those of Amsterdam, France, Genoa, Germany, the Netherlands, Rotterdam, and Spain) passed laws prohibiting life policies outright.[14] England, on the other hand, attempted to reform the system when it passed a 1774 law (St. 14 Geo. III, c. 48) banning life insurance policies "except in cases where the persons insuring shall have an interest in the life of the persons insured"[15]—that is, an insurable interest.

Early British court rulings initially favored a conservative reading of this law. In the landmark case of *Godsall v. Boldero* (9 East, 72), the courts enforced the idea that a creditor could not collect more on an insurance policy than the amount of debt owed. When British prime minister William Pitt died insolvent in February 1806, Parliament allocated funds to pay all of his debts, including £1,000 owed to his coach makers. The coach makers, who in 1803 had taken out a £500 policy on Pitt's life, sued Pelican Life Insurance Company for payment on the policy (for an additional £500 above the £1,000 paid by Parliament) but were rebuffed by the court: "It was held that this assurance, like every other to which the law gives effect, was a contract of indemnity as distinguished from one by way of wagering or gaming . . . that if the debt, which was the foundation of the indemnity, is paid, it matters not from what source the fund is derived."[16] Several companies stated specifically in their rules that insurable interest must exist at the time of the death of the insured. For example, the conditions of insurance of Scottish Widows' Fund and Life Assurance Society, published in 1814, "provid[ed] . . . that the assignee shall have an interest in the life upon the *termination* of which the benefit arises" (emphasis added).[17] Such strict adherence to the concept of insurable interest served to preserve both the integrity of mortality tables and the reputation of the industry in the public mind.

As life insurance increased in popularity in England and new companies emerged to challenge the British giants, competition drove many companies—particularly those newly entering the market—to relax these rules. By the mid-nineteenth century, insurable interest in England was ascertained only with the initial application for insurance and rarely challenged once a claim was made.[18] At first glance, this development may seem counterintuitive, since the principle of insurable interest was a protection to companies against people criminally driving up mortality rates as well as a protection of the life of the insured. However, a reputation for settling claims swiftly and with few legal challenges attracted business both from those with a gambling or criminal instinct and from legitimate policyholders who feared a prolonged, expensive, unfair court dispute over their claims. And if the companies themselves refused to contest questionable claims, there was little the British courts could do to enforce the spirit of the law.[19]

As a result of this emerging leniency among British companies, gambling policies soon reappeared in England. The most prevalent offense to the idea of insurable interest was the auction of life insurance policies by legitimate policyholders to speculators. To raise money, elderly, sick, and poor policyholders would gather every week at the Royal Exchange in London and auction off their policies. By considering the age and physical condition of the policyholder, bidders would attempt to estimate the number of premiums remaining before the death of the insured to determine the net gain from payment of the policy's face value to the new owner. These auctions were regularly reported in both the English and American press as matter-of-factly as the sale of cattle, grain, or American slaves.[20] Although the bidders held no insurable interest in the life of the insured, these claims were declared legal because, by the mid-nineteenth century, the British law was interpreted as only requiring insurable interest at the time the policy was issued; once issued, policies could continue as legal contracts even after such interest had ceased to exist.

Early American insurance companies were well aware of the association between life insurance, gambling, and crime in Britain and, from the very beginning, sought to prevent the same abuses in the United States. Thus the idea of insurable interest became central to the industry's early development, as it helped to preserve the actuarial foundations of the fledgling industry and to create a reputation for life insurance in the United States that was free from any taint of moral hazard.[21] American companies' rules or conditions of insurance reflected the wording of the 1774 British law: "Every person desirous to make assurance with the Company must sign a declaration, . . . in case such assurance is made upon the life of another person, that the interest which he has in such life is equal to the sum assured" (Pennsylvania Company, 1814);[22] "A person must have an interest in the life he insures, if it be not his own life" (Union Insurance Company and Massachusetts Hospital Life Insurance Company, 1818);[23] " No person can insure the life of another, unless he has an interest in such life" (NYL&T, 1830).[24] But whereas English companies interpreted the law with a strict adherence to its wording, American companies and courts embraced the spirit of the law by rigorously enforcing the idea of insurable interest from the moment a policy was issued through the payment of the final policy claim.

In practice, the most common instances of insurable interest involved debt contracts. A creditor who insured the life of a debtor could only collect payment up to the amount owed at the time of the insured's death (as the 1806 case of *Godsall v. Boldero* had decided), with the remainder of the policy claim being remitted to the estate of the insured. Nathaniel Bowditch, president of Massachusetts Hospital Life, stated as much in 1831 to one potential customer: "The insurance could be made payable to creditor, & if the am[oun]t should exceed his debt, he to pay over the balance to the Ex[ecutor]s or Adm[inistrator]s of the assured."[25] A similar letter from President Bard of NYL&T advised a creditor in 1833, "This Company will insure the Life of your debtor and pay on his death the sum insured . . . You can only insure the amount due by him. On his death reasonable advice will be required of the amount of your Interest."[26] And again in 1834 Bard wrote: "If I understood your question and understood the law, a party insuring the life of another can not recover more than the other owes him at the time of his death, what that is the insuring party will have to show."[27] In each of these cases, the companies determined that their financial soundness as well as their reputation as an industry serving the public good depended on a strict enforcement of the principle of insurable interest.

Although this basic rule was an industrywide standard in the United States, some policyholders (such as James H. Causten, Washington, DC, agent for Baltimore Life) considered it unfair, arguing that policies underwrote "the Life and not the Debt of the assured" and that by paying premiums on that policy, the owner was entitled to the full claim upon the death of the person in question.[28] In court cases throughout the antebellum period, state supreme courts were divided on the subject. At issue was whether the 1774 British statute stating the doctrine of insurable interest was an expression of common law, which would have rendered it applicable in the United States, or a statute addressing a topic not covered or contradicted by common law, which would require the enactment of similar laws in each of the states for it to be relevant.

The Supreme Court of New Jersey in the 1854 case of *Trenton Mutual Life and Fire Insurance Company v. John Johnson* ruled that the demonstration of insurable interest on life policies was unnecessary unless a law was specifically passed to that effect: "Until the legislature shall think proper to interfere, the courts can only adhere to the common law as they find it established."[29] In 1856, the Supreme Court of Massachusetts reached a similar conclusion in the case of *Loomis v. Eagle Life and Health Insurance Company,* stating: "As the English statute in terms has never been in force in this country, the case must be governed by the principles of the common law."[30] But that same year, the Vermont Supreme Court ruled that a creditor "can not retain the surplus" of a life policy above the amount of the debt,[31] and in the 1861 case of *Ruse v. The Mutual Benefit Life Insurance Company* (on appeal from the New York Supreme Court), Judge J. Selden stated, "My conclusion, therefore, is, that the statute of 14 George III, avoiding wager policies upon lives was simply declaratory of the common law, and that all such policies would have been void, independently of that act."[32]

During the 1850s and 1860s most states eventually incorporated the necessity of insurable interest into their insurance laws, but even without these laws—and despite the contradictory state court rulings—the companies themselves consistently required such interest to remain present upon the death of the insured. An 1846 article describing the operation of the American life insurance industry encouraged creditors to insure the lives of their debtors but warned: "It is necessary in this case, however, that the party insuring should have not only a legitimate interest in the person whose life is insured at the time the policy is taken out; but that the interest should continue down to the hour of his death."[33] This would remain the accepted industry practice in America throughout the antebellum period.

Demonstrating a direct *financial* interest in the life (and not the death) of another was virtually the only means of establishing insurable interest in the early years of American life insurance. Instances of creditors insuring the lives of debtors were probably the simplest cases of insurable interest, since pecuniary interest (in the form of a debt contract) would be relatively easy to prove. As an article entitled "Illustrations of Life Insurance" from the October 1846 issue of *Hunt's Merchants' Magazine* declared, there were only two means of obtaining a life insurance policy, the first being to insure one's own life. "The second," the article stated, "is, that all persons having a pecuniary interest in the existence of a life, can secure that interest."[34] Thus a family member (such as a husband or father) who wanted to insure the life of another family member (such as his wife or children) needed to establish the specific monetary benefit to him of their continued existence.

In numerous letters to potential policyholders written during the 1830s, William

Bard stressed this point: "It would be well for you to state your interest in your daughters life independent of that you have as a parent,"[35] he wrote to one, and to another, "According to the laws of this State a husband cannot insure the life of a wife, unless she has a separate Estate in which he has an interest dependent on her life."[36] Bard particularly rejected the idea that a parental or marital bond rendered such policies safe, stating repeatedly that a father or husband "must have some other interest in [the insured's] Life than that of affection."[37] He warned one applicant attempting to insure the life of his daughter: "From your statement to me it appears doubtful whether you have such an interest in her life as can be insured." While the daughter owned stock in her own name, Bard was not convinced that "the income from the Stock is payable to you during her life," which would have given the father "such an interest as can be insured." Rather, it appeared that "the stock & the interest arising from it is absolutely hers & you have no claim till her death," in which case "the contract would not be binding on us."[38] All of the early companies were extremely strict in the application of rules regarding pecuniary interest, repeatedly turning down inquirers with inadequate proof of interest or insuring them for less than they requested.

In theory, a vigilant application of pecuniary interest should have been adequate both to protect the insured from falling victim to crime as a result of the life insurance policy and to preserve the actuarial soundness of the industry. In practice, however, the need to demonstrate a direct monetary interest worked to the disadvantage of those intended as the prime beneficiaries of life insurance: women and children. For a wife to take out a policy on the life of her husband (through the mediation of a trustee), she had to demonstrate that she possessed a specific monetary interest in his continued existence—despite her status as an economic dependent. Although the Massachusetts Supreme Court in the 1815 case of *Lord v. Dall* had ruled that a child could obtain a policy on the life of a parent (or a sister on the life of a brother when he acted *in loco parentis*) without demonstrating a direct monetary interest, life insurance companies did not extend this privilege to wives insuring the lives of husbands. Both companies and the insuring public appear to have remained largely ignorant of the ruling during the first decades of the industry's existence.[39] It would not be until 1840, with the passage of a New York law specifically addressing this issue, that wives would be able to insure the lives of their husbands without providing proof of insurable interest (see chapter 5).

An important corollary to the idea of insurable interest involved the assignment of life insurance policies. A person who took out a policy on his own life could assign that policy to a specific beneficiary—whether it be to a family member, friend, creditor, institution, or even an anonymous stranger. In the early years of American life insurance, such assignments were promoted as one means of evading the rules regarding insurable interest. Nathaniel Bowditch of Massachusetts Hospital Life advised one potential policyholder in 1828: "If the policy sh[oul]d be made in the name of Mr. Ingham & he will assign it to you, it will save you the trouble of proving your interest in case of his death, & in this case you will not be under the necessity of signing the additional declaration stating your interest in his life."[40] While such policies were considered part of the insured's estate and subject to the claims of creditors, in effect the assignment served as an extension of a will by designating the person or persons who were to receive the proceeds of that policy.

This interpretation was repeatedly upheld by the courts. In the 1855 case of *Milton St. John v. The American Mutual Life Insurance Company of New Haven,* the company challenged payment of a claim based on the fact that the assignee had no insurable interest in the life of the insured. The judge, however, disagreed: "It seems to me it cannot be doubted, but that the assured might legally assign the policies to the plaintiff. It has been said, that without the right to assign, insurances on lives lose half their usefulness." In the view of the courts, the only person required to demonstrate interest in the life of the insured was the specific person named as the insurer on the policy: "The whole proof shows that Mr. Noyes effected the insurance upon his own life; it was not done by the plaintiff; he had no agency in procuring the policies to be issued; neither does it appear that the assured was even indebted to the plaintiff at that time."[41] Thus the assignment of a life insurance policy was considered merely a contract between the assignor and the assignee independent of the insurance company and therefore subject to the laws regarding contracts and not life insurance.[42] This was just one of several instances in which antebellum courts attempted to preserve individual property rights while at the same time discouraging threats to the public welfare.[43] Such rulings distinguished between the need to protect innocent lives from being threatened by wager policies and the right of individuals to stipulate the parameters of insurance on their own lives.

Lying on Policy Applications

Because of the strict observance of the principle of insurable interest, documented instances in which a person was murdered to obtain the proceeds of an insurance policy were almost nonexistent in the United States during the antebellum period. But whereas murder to procure a life insurance settlement was clearly illegal, fraud proved to be much more problematic for the industry. There were three different types of insurance fraud: lying on the initial policy application, breaking restrictions once the policy was in force, and faking death. While there were some cases of applicants lying about their insurable interest in the life of another, this type of fraud was rare in the United States, as policyholders were required to produce proof of such interest upon the death of the insured.

The most common type of fraud was lying on declaration statements, particularly about current or past health history or age. Since careful selection of risks was crucial to the success of an insurance institution, even the oldest American companies stipulated "that if the declaration . . . shall be found in any respect untrue, then and in such case, this Policy shall be null and void."[44] Although the burden was on the company to demonstrate that a misstatement on an application constituted a breach of contract, such blanket provisions opened all policyholders to potential challenges to their claims for even the minutest errors in their applications.

Strict enforcement of policy contracts was in the best interest of the policyholders, since it minimized premium costs. But as interested as policyholders were in low costs, they also sought equity and fairness (as they perceived it) from the insurance companies. They feared that any accidental misstatement on an application form or a death without an obvious cause could result in a disputed claim for their beneficiaries. One midcentury critic of life insurance cautioned that for-profit companies sought any excuse for refusing a claim: "Though the corporation may have the husband's money in its coffers, it will not have the 'soul' to relieve [the 'poor widow's'] distress, because all the crooked conditions of the policy have not been lived up to." In particular, this author was concerned that "it often happens that persons die in such ways as to render it difficult and expensive, if not impossible, to furnish proof that they have died at all!" Rather than providing comfort and relief for a "poor widow," the battle over the insurance claim would only increase her pain and suffering.[45]

While it is unclear how often companies contested seemingly valid claims, doing so always excited public clamor. In one article entitled "Heartless Injustice to the Widow and Orphan by a Life Insurance Company," the writer editorialized: "We trust that [the beneficiary] will recover [the amount claimed], and that the [Chicago Life] company will be branded for its attempt to evade, by litigation, the just claim of a poor woman."[46] Acquiring a public reputation as a company likely to contest valid claims was exactly what all institutions sought to avoid. Again, they needed to strike a balance between several competing forces. The need to maintain a strong financial foundation while keeping premium costs low drove companies to contest claims based on any intentional or unintentional falsehood. But in an industry extremely sensitive to changes in public perception, companies had to weigh the actuarial costs of fraud against the negative effect each contested claim had on their reputations.

In 1851, Philadelphia actuary Harvey Tuckett wrote one of the first accounts of the life insurance industry as a whole. While his book largely celebrated the benefits of insuring with a sound, well-respected company, it also critiqued the conduct of several companies. In particular, Tuckett warned, "Of all the evils of Life Insurance most to be dreaded—and to which small Proprietaries are peculiarly prone—is an inclination to LITIGATE." For Tuckett, the most egregious instances of litigation involved cases where the policy was declared void despite the fact that the erroneous or missing information was *"not material* to the cause of death." For example, "a man drowned at sea, having omitted to state that he had had an attack of gout, would void the policy; though the fact of his having had the gout, is not material to his being drowned." The author warned potential policyholders to investigate the company before acquiring a policy to determine the likelihood of its protesting a claim, since "no man desires to leave a lawsuit as an inheritance to his widow and children."[47]

Tuckett cautioned insurance companies not to acquire a reputation for being overly litigious, particularly when "no fraud was intended or reasonably suspected." Although some companies had "succeeded in inducing claimants to forego a part of the whole of their demands, without the office injuring itself by appearing to be of a litigious character" (at least for the moment) and others *"boasted of their power to litigate a claim for three years,"* the author believed the short-term gains from these tactics would eventually lead to long-term damage by undermining the reputation of life insurance in the public's mind.[48] In a few instances, insurers tried to empha-size their rejection of these underhanded tactics; Mutual Benefit Life, for example, asserted in 1850 that it had "never had a lawsuit with any one, and all its affairs are managed in an honorable and business-like manner."[49] However, statements re-garding litigation were relatively rare in antebellum advertisements and only be-came commonplace in the highly competitive postbellum industry.

Tuckett's concerns over unnecessary litigation raised questions of whether a pol-icy could be legally or ethically voided in cases where the misstatements were not intentionally fraudulent or materially related to the cause of death and whether there was (or should be) a statute of limitations with respect to companies finding fault with applications. Most of these debates emanated from particular court cases involving contested claims and were therefore subjected to public scrutiny.

In one such case from 1852, the American Mutual Insurance Company refused to pay a claim when a postmortem on the deceased found a preexisting condition that physicians testified "could not have been known during life." While the com-pany conceded that the deceased had answered all questions on his declaration honestly, it "insisted that because of this latent bodily defect they were not bound by the policy." Not surprisingly, the jury sided with the beneficiaries; they "were out thirteen minutes, just long enough to compute the interest" on the original claim.[50] The public, as represented by the jury, would not tolerate contested claims unless a company could prove beyond a reasonable doubt that the insured acted in an intentionally fraudulent manner.[51] And it was not uncommon for juries to side with a claimant despite evidence of fraud (though such verdicts were usually overturned by a higher court on appeal).[52] Jurors, especially those who owned life insurance policies themselves, could understand how easily some small item of a person's health history or details of the cause of a parent's, grandparent's, or sibling's death could be misstated on an application form.

The industry was well aware of the public relations problem of contesting claims, and by the late 1850s and early 1860s, promoters of life insurance were trying to educate the public about the necessity of some litigation. The editor of the *Insurance Gazette,* in reporting the case of a woman who allowed her policy to lapse and then allegedly misrepresented her health on the new declaration, supported the efforts of the company that disputed her claim: "Knowing, as we do, the dangers to which Life Insurance Companies are so frequently exposed, by the ignorant and designing, we think the offices of the United States Life should be praised rather than blamed for the watchful vigilance they displayed in the present case."[53] Later in the same edition, the editor stated with regard to another company: "And we can say, without fear of contradiction, that there is not a Life Insurance official who is more willing, at all times, to devote his time, trouble, and expense in prosecuting Insurance frauds, and assisting others in bringing criminals to justice, than the respected President of the Union Mutual." In direct contrast to Tuckett's critical view of litigation, this editor explicitly cast the perpetrators of fraud in the role of criminals (rather than merely innocent misstaters) and the president of Union Mutual as the industry's chief defender: "The whole profession is under a deep debt of gratitude to him for his perseverance and disinterested labors in these respects."[54] The *Insurance Monitor* likewise editorialized on the 1869 case of *Monk v. the Union Mutual Life* that "no respectable life office ought to be intimidated or deterred by fear of popular prejudice or clamor, from thoroughly educating the community up to the *judicial fact* that it is no more *safe* than just to attempt to swindle."[55]

The industry attempted to inform the public about the financial risk taken by insurance companies in *not* contesting questionable claims, but many policyholders and potential customers feared that theirs would be the policy claim unfairly treated. Despite their best efforts, most companies found it nearly impossible to strike a reasonable balance between litigation and maintaining the perception of fairness to their policyholders. As one 1863 article accurately portrayed the situation, "A sound company will rather submit to an occasional loss by fraud, than injure its reputation by a lawsuit, where the sympathies of the jury are sure to be on the side of widows and orphans against a wealthy corporation."[56] By the postbellum era, this fear of litigation would open up the entire industry to rampant cases of fraud.

Violating Policy Restrictions

Another common type of fraud occurred when a policyholder violated a restriction written into a policy such as those with respect to travel, health habits, occupation, or manner of death. While companies would contest policies when they had evidence that a policyholder traveled to a forbidden climate or by a banned mode of transportation,[57] cases in which the insured demonstrated a habit of intemperance[58] or engaged in a dangerous occupation without paying an additional premium[59] were rare because evidence was often difficult for the insurance companies to come by unless the insured had actually died in the process of breaking the contract restrictions.

Claims disputed because of broken restrictions commonly involved policyholders' failing to make premium payments on time. Because of the leniency of many debtor-creditor relations of the eighteenth and early nineteenth centuries, some of these delinquent policyholders may not have realized the importance of making prompt payments. Massachusetts Hospital Life faced this problem not only among its insurance customers but also in its extensive mortgage investments. As historian Tamara Plakins Thornton has ably documented, Massachusetts Hospital Life expended significant time and energy attempting to persuade mortgage recipients of the virtues of punctuality.[60] But late premium payments created a much bigger dilemma than late loan payments, opening up the question of precisely when an insurer's liability for a death claim actually terminated.

Among the earliest American companies, it was an accepted practice to reinstate lapsed policies at the original premium rate if customers signed a new declaration stipulating that they remained in good health—as healthy as they had been under the original declaration. For example, Massachusetts Hospital Life stated in its 1835 brochure that "the annual premiums must be paid the day they fall due, otherwise the Policy expires," but it was willing to restore the policy "at any time within fifteen days, the person on whose life the assurance was made being then alive and in good health, by the payment of said premium, together with an additional sum of ten per cent. upon such premium."[61]

Later companies placed greater emphasis on affirming the health of the insured before reinstating a policy. United States Life Insurance Company instructed its agents during the 1850s: "When a premium is past due, and is not paid, the party remains at his own risk until said premium be paid; but when payment is offered, let it be an *invariable* rule not to accept it until satisfactory evidence be given that the party is living, and in his usual good health."[62] This new declaration was open to dispute, and it was not uncommon for companies to contest a claim on the grounds that the person was no longer in the *same* state of health as in the first declaration. If the new declaration was not signed within fifteen to thirty days (depending on the rules of the company), the policy would be considered forfeited. The insured would then be required to reapply completely and, if accepted, pay the higher premium rate associated with his or her more advanced age.[63]

Much more serious disputes arose when policyholders died soon after allowing their policies to lapse; the beneficiaries in these cases often protested the forfeiting of the policy—particularly when the policy had remained in force for several years. The *Christian Advocate and Journal* decried one such instance: "Witness the case of Rev. W. B. Tappan, of Boston, who recently died of the cholera, but who happened to have neglected paying up his annuity for a few days; and thus his family were left destitute of the very money which for years he had flattered himself he was saving and securing for them!"[64] While the conditions of insurance clearly stated that a company was not liable as long as a premium payment remained overdue, claimants argued that they deserved payment of the face value of the policy minus the overdue payment (or some other compromise payment of the policy). This placed the companies in an extremely difficult position; while they were not legally bound to honor such claims, the public was more interested in being treated equitably and fairly (as they viewed it) than in specific policy clauses.

In many ways, this dilemma reflected the conflict between legal and moral debt obligations in the early republic. Legislation such as the bankruptcy acts of 1800 and 1841 legally relieved struggling debtors of their monetary commitments, thus promoting economic recovery and entrepreneurial risk taking, but this did not release them from an unwritten moral responsibility to repay even cancelled debt contracts. While only a rare bankrupt actually honored these obligations (usually only repaying particular creditors with whom they sought to reestablish a commercial relationship), the public generally—and creditors specifically—embraced such repayment as the honorable way to cleanse oneself of the taint of failure.[65] The public took a similarly nuanced view of the life insurance contract. Failure to pay a premium on time might release the company from any legal obligation to continue the contract, but many policyholders interpreted cancellation on such grounds as an opportunistic ploy on the part of a large, profitable corporation to release itself from its underwriting responsibilities (represented by all the previously paid premiums). It was unclear to companies how they could protect themselves from the additional risk of remaining liable for lapsed policies while still acting responsibly in the eyes of the public.

By the end of the 1850s, British companies had adopted a policy of permitting thirty days' grace on premium payments to assuage public opinion. Several of the British companies with branches in the United States also allowed a grace period. As early as 1845 Albion of London accepted payments made within fifteen days on its American policies,[66] and National Loan Fund Life permitted a thirty-day delay in payment "should even the life assured cease to have existed during the said days of grace."[67] North Carolina Mutual was one of the only American institutions to offer leniency in the payment of premiums, allowing forty days for payment as of its 1849 brochure.[68]

The majority of American companies were adamantly against such a policy. When the *Insurance Gazette* surveyed companies' opinions of the new British practice in 1858, all fourteen that responded stated that under no circumstances should companies allow grace periods. Manhattan Life Insurance Company asserted that "the practice of giving grace in the payment of life premiums is a pernicious one, detrimental to the interests of both parties to the contract," while American Mutual Insurance Company declared: "Thousands of dollars are lost to families by the neglect of the father to pay his last premium. There must be a time fixed, when the liability of the Company terminates, for it would never do to have it become a matter of uncertainty."[69] By 1860, however, Girard Life was also allowing fifteen days' grace on its policies.[70] And a decade later, the policy of permitting thirty days' grace—which companies had so steadfastly opposed during the antebellum era— had become the norm, although the insurance press dubbed it "the worst improvement that has been introduced in a long time," as it only encouraged policyholders to be negligent.[71]

The institution of a specified grace period struck a balance between the need for certainty on the part of life insurers and the desire for leniency among policyholders, but it did not address a company's moral responsibility toward longstanding customers who had allowed their policies to lapse. While life firms universally denied any obligation in such cases, several state regulators would see otherwise, with Massachusetts being the first to pass a nonforfeiture law in 1861 (see chapter 9). The Civil War itself would likewise raise questions regarding late payments and the reinstatement of lapsed policies, particularly among southerners insuring with northern firms, forcing the Supreme Court to weigh the responsibilities of the parties to incomplete contracts (see chapter 10).

Suicide

The suicide clause was another common reason for a company to contest a claim. While companies always assumed that a person applying for insurance on his or her own life had a risk-avoiding interest in that life, even the earliest American institutions recognized that this insurable interest would not exist in all cases or might cease to exist over time. Mimicking the language of British policies, the first policy issued by Massachusetts Hospital Life in 1823 stipulated that if the insured "shall die by his own hand, in, or in consequence of a duel, or by the hands of justice, or in the known violation of any law of these States, or of the United States, or of the said Provinces, this Policy shall be void, null, and of no effect."[72] Despite similar clauses in all life insurance policies, preventing suicide claims was not easy.

The first problem encountered was proof; the burden was on the company to demonstrate that a death occurred by suicide. One unusually straightforward case occurred in York, Pennsylvania, in 1851. A man by the name of William Callender, who made his living by capturing fugitive slaves, had obtained a $5,000 policy on his own life on the afternoon of March 26, before dying the same evening. The company was able to demonstrate conclusively that during the morning of the same day (before obtaining the policy) Callender had purchased arsenic, which was found in his stomach during the autopsy. The man had even told several people of his "intention to commit suicide." Given the blatant nature of this case, the court concluded that the policy would be considered void even without the suicide clause, since the man had clearly committed fraud against the company.[73] But the clear-cut nature of the Callender case was exceedingly rare. And since every contested claim was tried in both the court of law and the court of public opinion, in practice companies preferred to settle with the beneficiaries (as in the case of Nathaniel Knowles) unless there could be little doubt as to a conclusion of suicide.

A second problem was interpretation. Even where suicide could be demonstrated adequately, the courts began to rule that suicide was a specific legal term that implied both intent and knowledge of the consequences. In the 1843 case of *Breasted v. The Farmers' Loan & Trust*, the Supreme Court of New York declared that an insane person who committed suicide could not be held liable for his own death and that the insurance company was obligated to pay such claims. The justices concluded that the wording of the policy exclusion only pointed to "a criminal act of self-destruction," similar to the person's dying as a result of a duel "or by his execution as a criminal." While an insane person might take his own life, this action fell outside of the formal definition of suicide: "Suicide involves the deliberate termination of one's existence, while in the possession and enjoyment of his mental faculties. Self-slaughter by an insane man or a lunatic is not an act of suicide within the meaning of the law."[74] The *New York Journal of Medicine* and the *Boston Medical and Surgical Journal* both concurred with this interpretation.[75]

While the burden of proving insanity technically rested with the beneficiaries of the insured, in practice claimants found insanity relatively easy to demonstrate. Verdicts of suicide by insanity were common, with many jurists having a difficult time discerning instances when suicide would *not* be associated with insanity.[76] Companies on both sides of the Atlantic alluded to this problem. One British insurance executive complained: "Suicide has been held to render a policy invalid, but so many questions have been raised in the law courts as to the cause of suicide—as to whether it proceeded from mental derangement or from desire to destroy life—that an infinitude of trouble has been caused to Assurance offices."[77] The American companies likewise asked in frustration: "What is the clause voiding the policy in cases of suicide worth? Is it worth while for our life companies to spend any more money contesting its validity?"[78] The monetary and reputational costs of litigation, along with the low likelihood of success in these cases, only further discouraged companies from disputing suicide claims.

It was not until 1872 in the case of *Mutual Life Insurance Company v. Terry* that the United States Supreme Court would definitively rule that a sane person *could* commit suicide, but this did not prevent juries from accepting insanity pleas in cases involving suicide.[79] The irritation of the industry was evident in an 1872 article in the *Insurance Monitor* entitled "Another Case of Suicide Lost by the Company," which stated that "the *usual* verdict was returned. The judge ruled that the company was liable if the jury found that the deceased killed himself in a fit of insanity, which overpowered his consciousness and reason" (emphasis added).[80]

More than a decade later, the question of insanity with relation to suicide remained in debate. In an 1883 article discussing the case of *The Manhattan Life v. Broughton,* the Supreme Court reaffirmed its 1843 opinion that suicide by insanity did not void a policy but left open the possibility of a sane person committing suicide. The *New York Times* editorialized about the problematic nature of this distinction: "There are eminent men who hold that the act of suicide alone is sufficient proof of insanity, and that no perfectly sane man destroys his own life. If every person who commits suicide is insane, then, under this decision, it is useless to insert in any policy of insurance such a condition." In the author's opinion, "an insurance company will save time and money by promptly settling with an insured sui-cide's heirs" rather than quixotically trying to contest such claims with juries.[81]

Companies experimented with various strategies to address this persistent prob-lem. Several, including Knickerbocker Life and Berkshire County Mutual Life, in-serted clauses voiding the policy in all cases of suicide, "sane or insane."[82] Though the Supreme Court upheld the legality of such a clause in 1876,[83] the public rela-tions problem of challenging claims where the deceased did not intentionally com-mit a fraud (as well as the appearance of punishing innocent widows and orphans for the acts of an insane father) drove many companies to seek alternative solutions.

In response to the image problems caused by contesting claims on the basis of application misstatements and broken policy restrictions (including suicide), sev-eral companies began to liberalize restrictions once the policy had remained in force for a certain amount of time. Antebellum institutions commonly advertised that they were "prompt in the payment of losses,"[84] but later companies began to state that they would not dispute claims after the passage of a certain number of years. For example, National Life Insurance Company stated that "all of our policies are incontestable after five annual payments,"[85] and Great West Mutual Life declared in 1869, "Policies are incontestable after five years duration, except for intentional fraud."[86]

Some companies vowed not to contest claims after the stipulated period had expired even in cases where the insured violated the policy restrictions or lied. North American Life Insurance Company was one such company, advertising in 1864 that "suicide, dueling, or change of residence or occupation, error on preliminary appli-cation regarding family history or condition of the health of the applicant, do not work any forfeiture of the policy after seven years."[87] While such policies did not elimi-nate the challenging of claims before the designated passage of time, they did limit the number of contested claims, thus soothing public opinion. Additionally, actuar-ies concluded that the detrimental effect of misrepresentations—both accidental and intentionally fraudulent—on the accuracy of mortality tables diminished over time and disappeared altogether as soon as five years after the application. But this growing leniency on the part of life insurers would expose them to ever-increasing levels of risk by the postbellum era.

Faking Death

Policyholders who faked their own deaths to collect on a life policy were clearly engaging in a criminal act to swindle insurance companies—even in the eyes of the severest critics of the industry. Faking one's own death was difficult because it required the help of accomplices and the creation of a new identity in a new locale. However, during a time when immigrants and internal migrants alike flocked to the growing cities or set out for the western frontier, the appearance of a stranger in town with no prior connections or local references was common. Before social security numbers, fingerprint databases, and DNA testing, this type of insurance crime had a much higher probability of success.

There were two main ways a policyholder might attempt to fake his own death. The first was to recruit a doctor to sign a death certificate on the insured (in exchange for a cut of the proceeds), stipulating that he had either been present at the death or had examined the body soon afterward. Then a casket would be filled with logs, rocks, and assorted debris to approximate the weight of the insured,[88] or the body of an already dead John Doe would be placed in the coffin. In the second and more elaborate method, the insured would set up his own accidental death in front of witnesses who might either be accomplices or innocent bystanders. Deaths by drowning were most commonly staged, since the body of a drowning victim was often never found, and if a corpse was planted, the distortions to the waterlogged body helped mask the deceased's true identity.[89] Days later, remains might be discovered washed up on shore, which the "widow" or another "grieving" family member would identify as the insured. While in rare cases murder was committed to obtain a corpse, it was much more common to dig up the body of a recently interred person.[90]

For both methods of faking death, a funeral and burial would ensue—often attended by the accomplices as well as innocent acquaintances who truly believed the person to be dead. In cases where the insured was later apprehended, he (the insured in these cases was almost invariably male) often admitted to attending the funeral himself as one of the mourners. While it is impossible to ascertain the frequency of such crimes, extremely few cases of faked deaths were discovered in the antebellum period, and most of these were reported from abroad. But just as the number of documented cases of murder associated with life insurance rose dramatically during the 1860s, so did the reported instances of faked deaths.

We the Jury

Soon after the creation of the Interstate Commerce Committee in 1887, its new chairman remarked that railroads could not get a fair hearing in jury trials because most jurors viewed the industry "as a creature standing apart from human nature, soulless, heartless, grasping, an arrogant representation of monopolizing wealth."[91] Likewise, in reflecting on the process of jury selection in 1933, the famous defense attorney Clarence Darrow averred: "Jurymen seldom convict a person they like, or acquit one that they dislike. The main work of a trial lawyer is to make a jury like his client, or, at least, to feel sympathy for him; facts regarding the crime are relatively unimportant."[92] For the burgeoning corporations of the mid-nineteenth century, both statements were unfortunately true. Whether the case involved the liability of a local government for a defective bridge, an injured railway passenger, or an allegedly fraudulent life insurance claim, juries almost universally sympathized with the individual plaintiff (a person with whom they could likely relate) against the impersonal corporation. Thus unless the evidence was sufficiently solid to warrant the risk, many large entities chose to settle rather than expose themselves to the dual punishment of negative publicity and compensatory damages at the hands of an unfriendly jury.[93]

This inclination to settle placed American life insurance companies of the nineteenth century in a particularly difficult position. Because they dealt directly with consumers, maintaining a positive public reputation was crucial to the success of individual companies as well as of the industry as a whole. However, this reputation was based both on morality (paying all just claims, not promoting questionable practices such as wager policies, and not becoming associated in the public mind with murder) and on financial soundness (policyholders wanted to be sure that they were paying premiums to a company that would be able to honor their future claims). While fiscal responsibility required companies to be strict in enforcing policy restrictions and extremely active in rooting out cases of gambling, suicide, murder, and fraud, public morality necessitated the rapid and uncontested payment of claims except in cases where an *obvious* fraud had been committed.

By the middle of the nineteenth century, the industry had reached a delicate yet still imperfect balance between preserving the actuarial foundations of the business and maintaining a reputation for equity and fairness in their dealings with policyholders. In some ways, the industry thrived *despite* an inability to find that elusive perfect balance. Life insurance companies were able to shake neither an indirect association with criminal acts such as murder (see chapter 8) nor a reputation for being overly litigious nor the general distrust that surrounded all big businesses by the end of the century. And as the industry grew more competitive during the 1860s, the necessity of attracting new business drove many companies to relax their level of vigilance—opening the door for increased instances of moral hazard and insurance fraud (see chapter 11).

CHAPTER 4

The Public Interest in a Private Industry

Life Insurance and the Regulatory-Promotional State

Following the Panic of 1837, the American economy sank into a deep depression that lasted from 1839 to 1843. Yet even as unemployment rose and countless businesses declared bankruptcy, contemporaries believed New York Life Insurance and Trust "to be above the common ills of our condition," with its stock "quite above par, and accounted better than old gold."[1] NYL&T had accumulated substantial profits during the 1830s, and in 1841—even in the depths of the depression—the firm confidently began making plans to declare its first dividend. President Bard conservatively calculated that the company could safely pay stockholders a minimum 14% return on their investments annually for the next five years, spreading the profits out over a series of years so that "the public, who would not consider that we have been ten years working it up, should not be shocked by a very large dividend." This cautious approach would also ensure the continued fiscal soundness of the company and guarantee that dividends would persist unabated into the future. These dividend payments, which were mainly based on profits "understood to be derived from Life Insurance," were slated to begin in early 1843.[2] The ongoing success of the company provided contemporaries with a ray of hope during the otherwise gloomy economic times: "Whatever else might go wrong, it was never doubted that in this powerful institution everything would be right."[3]

Then, in the late fall of 1842, a scandal rocked NYL&T, resulting in "the severest shock to confidence in corporate institutions which has been felt for a long time." Adding to a long list of economic ills—"depreciation in prices, bankruptcy of debtors, mismanagement of agents, blunders, embezzlements, and frauds of every possible device," all of which had "dissipated the surpluses of the rich, and the little savings of the poor"[4]—NYL&T became just one more example of a capitalist system gone awry. The dividend plans of the nation's leading life insurer were quickly suspended as the scandal wiped out the company's cash surplus and undermined its pristine reputation with current and potential policyholders, investors, and—most critically—the State of New York.

In December 1842, President Bard received two anonymous letters informing him that the company secretary, Edward A. Nicoll, had "abstracted" company funds and was "engaged in dealing in lottery tickets."[5] Bard initially expressed his confidence that the company would not be affected by Nicoll's personal transgressions: "We have not however after the most careful examination of Mr. Nicoll, and of such means as are immediately within our reach any reason to believe that Mr. Nicoll has taken any thing from this Co or done more than committed a folly ruinous to his reputation and destructive of his high standing."[6] Unfortunately, this optimism was premature; just two days later Bard was reporting that Nicoll had stolen between $40,000 and $50,000 from the company. As the investigation continued into early January, this amount rose precipitously to $300,000.[7]

Combined with the effects of the ongoing depression, the crime was disastrous for the company: "This loss and the deficiency on some of our securities occasioned by the times, will we fear take our accumulated surplus from all sources, which we have estimated at about $450,000 and not leave much more than our Capital clear." Thus the first casualty of the scandal was necessarily the dividend: "Prudence will probably oblige us to forego our dividend, but I trust that increased economy and double vigilance will soon bring us to a better position before long."[8] The second casualty was President Bard; although no blame had been directly laid at his feet, he was symbolic of the failure of managerial oversight at the company. He tendered his resignation on January 21, 1843 (although he would stay on as company actuary until the early 1850s).[9]

In addition to forgoing its dividend plans, the company was forced to quickly rebuild its capital stock and cash reserve. On January 10, 1843, the finance committee resolved to call in over $100,000 in outstanding loans (ranging in amount from $233.36 to $18,000).[10] New president Stephen Allen then continued the effort to cut costs, writing to the editors of nine newspapers to cancel subscriptions "merely as a matter of retrenchment of expenses,"[11] and advising policyholders attempting to surrender their policies for a cash value that "after the Nicolls [sic] robbery, a resolution was passed, not to buy back policies at present, nor till further ordered."[12] Almost overnight, the firm had been transformed from a successful enterprise flush with cash to a struggling corporation with a major public relations problem.

The scandal quickly became public knowledge. Noting that "no man ever possessed the confidence of his associates more fully than the delinquent Secretary,"[13] the press focused attention on the ease with which Nicoll was able to accomplish his theft. Abstracting from this incident, newspapers such as the *New York Herald* immediately went on the offensive against the institution as a whole, striking at the fiscal responsibility central to the safety of all insurers: "The unbounded and unwarantable confidence reposed in this man [Nicoll] by the directors, in suffering to make way with so large an amount of property, leads to the inference that the same negligence has extended to all the investments."[14] With the scandal threatening to shake the confidence of policyholders and stockholders alike, President Allen wrote numerous letters directly to investors in an effort to calm their fears. One read: "Let me caution you against the reports you see stated in the public papers. There is scarcely one of them, that is true. Our newspapers are with a few exceptions, not to be depended on, and are freely used by the unprincipled to promote their own interests."[15] But while the company could make accusations of biased reporting, the facts to which it was willing to concede were enough to severely damage its reputation as a fiscally sound corporation.

But while the company was certainly apprehensive about its standing with customers and investors, its officers' primary anxiety involved its relationship with the state. As in most early commercial endeavors, the creation, growth, and success of the life insurance industry intimately depended on the sanction and oversight of state governments. Life underwriters embraced state charters as a means of acquiring the rights and privileges of the corporate form. They presented themselves as quasi-public enterprises in order to gain the acceptance of both the government and the citizens to whom they were marketing. Among the many virtues of life insurance appreciated by the state was the protection it offered to widows and children, relieving the community of the obligation to support them in the event of the death of the family breadwinner.[16] Life insurers also promoted the idea that their product mitigated some of society's worst problems by removing the economic rationale underlying many crimes. The product of this for-profit industry provided benefits to the commonweal as a whole.

Early life insurance charters often assigned specific public duties to the firms in exchange for their corporate privileges. As part of NYL&T's 1830 charter, the company was charged with the responsibility of guardianship for the estates of orphan children entrusted to them by the Court of Chancery. The company agreed to guarantee each estate annual interest of at least 4% on the principal and to assume sole risk for the investment of the funds. If the company should ever be dissolved, the claims of these estates would hold preference over all other petitioners.[17]

This guardianship obligation led New York State to assert significant regulatory power over NYL&T. The company was required to submit an annual report of its affairs to the state chancellor, the official from whom they received estates in trust. By the provisions of the charter, the chancellor was empowered to inaugurate, at will, a full investigation into the affairs of the company and "to report his opinion in relation to the ability and integrity with which its affairs are conducted, the prudence and safety of its investments, the security afforded to those by whom its engagements are held, and the advantage derived by the *public* from its operations" (emphasis added), all at the expense of the firm. Based on these findings, the chancellor could recommend any changes in the regulations and by-laws of the company that "he shall deem to be required by the *public good*, and a just regard to the security of the creditors" (emphasis added), and he had the authority to file a report with the state legislature if the company failed to comply with or reply adequately to his recommendations.[18] State governments universally recognized the need to regulate life insurance in the interest of citizens and the state itself—even as the nature of this regulation changed over time. Insurance companies received corporate privileges because their services were believed to benefit the citizens of the state, and they maintained those privileges as long as it was to the continued advantage of the public.

In the aftermath of the Nicoll scandal, the company's reputation with potential policyholders could be rebuilt over time, the cash reserve could be replenished, and dividends could eventually be paid to stockholders; though wounded, the *private* corporation did not necessarily receive a fatal blow. However, the scandal was potentially devastating to the quasi-public entity with obligations to the state. Since the state had the power to substantially alter or even revoke the firm's charter if its operations failed to benefit the citizens of New York, NYL&T knew that the scandal placed its very existence in a perilous position. Controlling damage to its relationship with the state would have to be the company's main priority.

Upon learning of the potential embezzlement, Bard's first action was to quickly inform the state chancellor of the brewing problem. Writing on Christmas Eve, Bard assured Chancellor Reuben Walworth he would receive "daily reports of our proceedings and discoveries, and of course as soon as the facts shall have been ascertained, a complete statement thereof, and of the condition of the Co[mpany] shall be made to you and the public."[19] Bard kept his promise, regularly updating the chancellor as the company uncovered the true extent of the crime. He also stressed the continued soundness of the firm with regard to its obligations to the citizens of the state: "The stock-holders will be the sufferers, but those who confide in us, among whom you are the most important, are perfectly safe."[20] Since the Court of Chancery held the fate of the company in its hands, it was imperative that NYL&T executives show themselves as open, cooperative, and competent in handling the crisis.

The relationship between corporations and the state went well beyond careful oversight and regulation. The state also played a more positive, promotional role in the private success of quasi-public entities like life insurers.[21] The long-term nature of an insurance policy left policyholders vulnerable to both unscrupulous insurers and well-intentioned but fiscally unsound firms. As one editorial warned after a company declared bankruptcy in 1826, "There is something horrible in the very idea of the failure of an *insurance company* . . . But the failure of a *Life Insurance* is perhaps more wicked than any other . . . the only provision secured by its [policy-holders being] a lodging in the alms-house."[22] With potential applicants wary of making a long-term financial commitment to the emerging industry, companies welcomed a certain degree of state oversight as a way to gain the trust and confidence of the public. While not guaranteeing the longevity and profitability of a company, the imprimatur of a state charter reassured investors and potential customers of the basic soundness of the institution.

The court's entrusting sensitive funds with NYL&T buttressed this crucial appearance of stability. Just two years prior to the scandal, a prominent article promoting the benefits of life insurance specifically cited NYL&T's relationship with the state as irrefutable evidence of its soundness: "The vast confidence which the Court of Chancery reposes in its management, by intrusting it with the disposition of those immense sums of money over which this court exercises a control . . . conclusively show[s] with what fidelity every trust reposed in it would be executed, and with how much engagement which it entered into would be performed."[23] This association with the power of the state enabled an untested company in an emerging industry to command a much greater degree of respectability than it could on its own.

Short of instigating formal investigations and making recommendations to the legislature, the chancellor thus had the power to sway opinion of the company merely through his public reaction to the scandal. Therefore, while promising to supply Chancellor Walworth with daily updates, Bard also requested discretion in the matter: "In the meantime as a measure of prudence and precaution, we keep the matter from all unnecessary notoriety, and would respectfully suggest the expediency of such a course for your Government, until our final publication."[24] Bard hoped the company's candor and transparency with the state would encourage the chancellor to refrain—at least in the short term—from exercising his latent influence over the opinions of current and potential policyholders and investors.

By the end of January, NYL&T was finally confident that it had properly addressed its obligations to the state by demonstrating that it had handled the crisis expeditiously and that the funds entrusted to its care had never been in jeopardy. Shifting focus to damage control among customers and investors, President Allen petitioned Chancellor Walworth to use his influence positively in the company's defense: "If the reports of the condition of the company are sufficient to secure confidence on the part of yourself, and those who have monies in your Court, the

Company is safe, beyond the chance of accident, from any further inquiry to its credit . . . I would . . . leave respectfully to ask your aid, and assistance, and your assurance, to the numerous parties that are likely to apply for the removal of the monies from the company of your belief in their entire safety."[25] In receiving state charters, corporations were expected to operate in a manner that would benefit the citizens of the state—even as they sought to earn a profit for their stockholders. The state, in recognizing the beneficial role played by the corporation, had a reciprocal obligation to promote its successful operation. Company executives believed that their prompt, thorough, and honest handling of the scandal had restored NYL&T's position as a corporation acting in the public interest, and it would now behoove the state to aid in the recovery of its reputation with the insuring and investing public.

As the nineteenth century progressed, this regulatory-promotional relationship between the states and corporations would evolve. As life insurers continued to promulgate themselves as socially responsible citizens whose product had positive externalities for the state, the states attached fewer and fewer formal obligations to their charters. Yet the need for regulation never waned. Initially, the primary concern of state regulation was to ensure the long-term stability of life insurance firms so that policyholders could pay their annual premiums with a level of confidence that the company would be fiscally sound when their death claim came due. As the industry matured, state regulation expanded to include consumer protection rules to level the arguably uneven playing field between large corporations and individual policyholders.

At the same time, states began to recognize the citizenship rights of the corporations as well. With the development of the agency system, it became relatively safe and easy to sell life insurance anywhere in the country, creating an intensely competitive environment not experienced by most other antebellum industries. In-state corporations sought to manipulate the apparatus of state regulation to limit competition from new or out-of-state companies. By the middle of the century, there was a growing tension between regulation for the welfare of individual citizens and regulation for the welfare of corporate citizens, resulting in a regulatory environment that often operated to the detriment of one or both types of citizens.

Regulation by Charter

The emergence of an American life insurance industry was intimately linked to the development of the corporate form. In the early nineteenth century, business enterprises increasingly sought the benefits associated with incorporation. First, corporations possessed the capacity to operate "as a single corporate entity irrespective of changes in ownership"[26]—the emerging idea of corporate personhood.[27] In contrast to partnerships, the corporation itself (and not the individual investors) was responsible for buying and selling property and appearing in court. And unlike partnerships, which immediately dissolved if one of the partners died or otherwise chose to leave the firm, the life of the corporation existed independent of the individual owners.

In its 1812 charter, Pennsylvania Company was ordained "a body politic and corporate in fact and in law . . . capable of suing and being sued, pleading and being impleaded, answer[ing] and being answered unto, defending and being defended, in all courts and places whatsoever, in all manners of actions, suits, complaints, matters and causes, whatever."[28] Charters for Massachusetts Hospital Life (1818), Baltimore Life (1830), Ohio Life Insurance and Trust (1834), and North Carolina Mutual Life (1849) all contained similar provisions. For an industry in which customers paid in the present (and then continuously over time) in exchange for a benefit that they would receive at some unknown future time, the continuity and longevity inherent in the corporate form was imperative to success.

The second major advantage of incorporation was that it facilitated the acquisition of capital from investors beyond the initial company executives.[29] The second and third decades of the nineteenth century witnessed the rise of limited liability laws in numerous states, freeing investors from risks beyond their initial investment.[30] Like other major business enterprises of the time (such as transportation companies), life insurers required a large initial investment of capital before they could begin operating. Without limited liability provisions, few people would be willing to assume the risks associated with investing in an untested company (in a newly emerging industry) unless they had direct control over the operations of that firm. Limited liability enabled capital-intensive enterprises such as life insurers to attract large numbers of small to medium investors.

Although a limited liability clause was not included in the Pennsylvania Company charter, such provisions became commonplace later in the decade. Massachusetts Hospital Life's charter of 1818 stated "that in case the amount of the said capital stock actually paid in, shall at any time prove insufficient for the payment of the just debts due from the said Corporation, each original stockholder shall be liable for the debts due by the said Corporation, to an amount not exceeding that part of his original subscription, which shall, at such time, remain due and unpaid."[31] This clause was particularly important for a Massachusetts company, since that state did not universally recognize limited liability as a privilege of corporate stockholders. While most New England and Mid-Atlantic states had adopted limited liability laws by the 1820s, until 1830 the Massachusetts legislature more often assigned *un-limited* liability to corporate stockholders.[32] The inclusion of a limited liability clause in the 1818 Massachusetts Hospital Life charter was a special privilege not extended to most other state corporations at that time.

Baltimore Life's charter of 1830 contained a clause similar to Massachusetts Hospital Life's and further stipulated "that no stockholder shall be liable for any debts, contracts, nor engagements of said corporation, but that the money, property, rights and credits, of the company, shall alone be liable for the same."[33] The rights of corporate personhood and limited liability were granted to all New York companies by state law, as consolidated in the Revised Statutes of 1829 and 1836. These statutes were specifically referred to in the charters of NYL&T (1830) and Mutual Life Insurance Company of New York (1842).[34]

During the early national period, the regulation of business enterprises was generally limited to the terms and conditions of the corporation's state charter. In addition to the basic privileges that rendered the corporate structure so attractive, early companies received charters from their respective states outlining the explicit rights granted to the corporation, the procedures for initially setting up the firm including the precise processes for subscribing shares and electing officers, and the rules regarding the investment of funds. Supreme Court decisions in *Dartmouth College v. Woodward* (1819) and *Providence Bank v. Billings* (1830) guaranteed the sanctity of corporate charters, ruling that legislatures could not alter the provisions of a valid charter granted to either public institutions or private businesses.[35] Yet in the former case, Justice Joseph Story implied that the state could change an existing charter if the legislature had included that right in the original agreement.[36] Thus while the charter formed a type of contract between the state and the corporation, the state was not necessarily signing away its ability to regulate the corporation for the greater benefit of the public welfare.

Even before the decisions in the *Dartmouth College* and *Providence Bank* cases, some state legislatures were careful to protect their right to alter or repeal charters in the future. As early as 1812, the Pennsylvania legislature included a provision permitting repeal of the Pennsylvania Company charter, although the company would be allowed "a reasonable time to bring their accounts to a final settlement and termination."[37] Likewise, the New York legislature declared in the 1830 charter of NYL&T that it would "have the power, at any time hereafter, to repeal, alter, or modify this act, or any of its provisions" and included a similar provision in the 1842 Mutual Life charter.[38]

Other state legislatures guaranteed that the provisions of charters would remain unchanged for a set period of time. The charter of Baltimore Life was guaranteed until 1860, although the State of Maryland retained the right to levy taxes identical to those imposed on other corporations or individuals "by license or otherwise, upon all the property, estate and funds, in which the capital stock of said company shall be invested."[39] The act chartering North Carolina Mutual was to remain intact for fifty years,[40] while the charter of Ohio Life and Trust stated that no legislature would "repeal, amend, or alter this act" until after 1870, although Ohio retained the right to tax the company at rates identical to those levied upon banking institutions within the state.[41]

Only in the Massachusetts Hospital Life charter did a state fail to include some provision for future control over the institution, neither reserving the right to alter or repeal the charter nor legislating a termination date for the act in question—in effect, guaranteeing the corporation's charter in perpetuity—although the charter was successfully amended in 1823 and 1824 with the approval of the company. In 1831, the commonwealth passed a general law to make all future acts of incorporation "which contain no express provision limiting their duration . . . subject to alteration, amendment, or repeal."[42] Although this provision did not explicitly include preexisting corporations, the Massachusetts legislature generally proceeded as if it did.

Beyond the fundamentals of incorporation, charters also defined life insurance companies as institutions cloaked in the public interest. Although they were private companies with obligations to their stockholders, the state legislatures also viewed them as servants of the citizens of the state—making them quasi-public institutions.[43] Thus the state legislature of Pennsylvania reserved the right to revoke the charter of Pennsylvania Company if "at any time it shall appear to the legislature, that the charter privileges hereby granted are injurious to the public welfare."[44] This public aspect was reflected not only in the general language of the charters, but also in the investment restrictions, oversight provisions, and additional obligations imposed on the companies by the state.

Investment requirements for both capital stock and insurance premiums were imposed as a means of ensuring the fiscal soundness of companies for the benefit of policyholders as well as shareholders, although the guidelines were relatively lenient in the early years. The charters of Pennsylvania Company and Massachusetts Hospital Life contained nearly identical clauses to this effect, permitting them to invest "in the funded debt of the United States or of this Commonwealth, or in the stock of the bank of the United States or of any of the banks incorporated within this Commonwealth, or in the purchase of ground rents, or mortgages on real estate." They were allowed to alter their investment portfolio "at their discretion, as the safety or welfare of the said Corporation, as the President and Directors thereof may deem expedient."[45]

By the 1830s, these rules had been relaxed for NYL&T and Ohio Life and Trust, allowing these institutions to invest in the public stocks of any state or city, "or in such real or personal securities as they may deem proper, or loan the same to any county, city, incorporated town, or company," as long as their investment in any one private company did not exceed twenty-five thousand dollars.[46] The Maryland legislature endowed Baltimore Life with complete carte blanche, empowering the president and directors "to provide for the investment of funds of the corporation in such manner as they shall deem most safe and beneficial."[47]

In contrast to the restrictions that would be placed on insurers later in the nineteenth century, few common investment opportunities were forbidden by these clauses. The one prevalent avenue specifically prohibited for both Pennsylvania Company and NYL&T was the issuance of bank notes or the lending of money on interest in a manner similar to a bank loan.[48] Massachusetts Hospital Life and Baltimore Life, however, were both permitted "to make all kinds of contracts in which the casualties of life, and interest of money are involved."[49] Baltimore Life employed this privilege to extend its business by issuing general loans using insurance policies as collateral (see chapter 6). Ohio Life and Trust alone was specifically empowered "to issue bills or notes to an amount not exceeding twice the amount of the funds deposited with said company for a time not less than one year" until the year 1843, effectively making it both an insurance company and banking institution.[50]

Very little information exists regarding the actual investment portfolios of early life insurance companies. The balance sheets of NYL&T indicate that between two-thirds and three-quarters of its assets during the 1830s and early 1840s were held in "bonds and mortgages." Unfortunately, company ledgers provide no further breakdown of this asset category.[51]

Corporations in the Public Interest

In several instances specific public obligations were written directly into the charter agreements. The main reason for the establishment of Massachusetts Hospital Life was to provide funding for Massachusetts General Hospital.[52] To this end, the company was directed annually to pay one-third of its net profits from all life insurance sales to the hospital. All future companies incorporated in Massachusetts with the privilege of selling life insurance would likewise be required to support the hospital, or the obligation of Massachusetts Hospital Life would cease.[53] In 1823—when Massachusetts Hospital Life first began active business—its charter was amended to permit the company to hold money in trust, and the overwhelming success of this arm of the business led the legislature to further amend the charter in 1824; Massachusetts Hospital Life would thereafter be required to pay the hospital one-third of its profits arising from all forms of contracts—not just life insurance. However, when some directors expressed concern that this limitation would suppress the interest of investors, the charter was again amended to stipulate that such profits would be determined *after* all stockholders had been paid "legal interest" (6%) on their paid-in capital.[54]

The clause guaranteeing that all future insurance companies chartered in the commonwealth would similarly hold obligations to Massachusetts General Hospital protected Massachusetts Hospital Life from being placed at a competitive disadvantage. However, the clause did not anticipate the rise of out-of-state competition or mutual insurance companies. In 1835, New England Mutual Life became the first mutual company chartered in the United States, although it would not begin selling policies until 1843. As promised to Massachusetts Hospital Life, the New England Mutual charter contained an identical clause requiring the payment of one-third of all profits to the hospital; similar provisions were also included in the charters of State Mutual Life of Worcester (1844), Equitable Life Assurance Society of Boston (1845), Berkshire County Mutual Life (1851; renamed Berkshire Life Insurance Company of America in 1855), and Massachusetts Mutual Life (1851). However, the president and directors of both New England Mutual and State Mutual believed that this clause was moot, since a mutual company, by definition, never accumulated a profit; dividends paid to policyholders were merely the refund of excess premium payments.[55]

In 1847, the Commonwealth of Massachusetts responded to this discrepancy of opinion by passing "an act in addition to the several acts incorporating mutual life insurance companies," which specifically defined the profits to be partitioned as "the excess of the dividend over six per centum annually, payable by the said companies respectively to the holders of the guaranty capital stock actually paid in."[56] While it appears that most companies chose to comply with the law and pay the stipulated amount to the hospital, at least one—State Mutual—continued to refuse. It considered the 1847 law unconstitutional because it was being applied retroactively to its original 1844 charter.

In 1855, Massachusetts General Hospital went before that commonwealth's supreme court to compel State Mutual to pay the money in question. The ruling of Judge J. Dewey reaffirmed the rights of a state with regard to corporate law by siding with the hospital. He concluded that, in the aftermath of the 1831 law reserving to the commonwealth the right to amend all future acts of incorporation, the charter of State Mutual was "accepted by the corporators subject to the provisions of" that law. Thus the commonwealth was well within its rights when it passed a later law defining profits for mutual insurance companies.[57] In its annual report issued the following year, State Mutual reported paying $2,323.89 in "taxes" to Massachusetts General Hospital, stating that the decision of the court "will be as faithfully observed by the Company as though they found reasons satisfactory therefor."[58] By reserving the right to amend or repeal all acts of incorporation, states could ensure that the rights and privileges granted to these for-profit enterprises were in exchange for duties and obligations that directly benefited the citizens of the state.

Other insurance companies were likewise given obligations within their states. As noted above, NYL&T's 1830 charter required the company to serve as guardian for the estates of orphan children. The State of Ohio conferred a similar obligation on Ohio Life and Trust: "In all cases where any court hath jurisdiction for the appointment of a trustee or guardian of any infant, lunatic, or other person, the annual income of whose estate shall exceed the sum of one hundred dollars, such court shall have power to appoint the said company trustee or guardian of the estate of such infant, lunatic, or person." Like NYL&T, the latter company also had to guarantee the interest and principal of such estates.[59]

A direct result of these public commitments was state oversight of the operations of life insurance companies. While Pennsylvania Company, which was not charged with any specific public responsibilities, fell outside the purview of direct state regulation, the other early life companies were all required to periodically report to the state on their fiscal status. Massachusetts Hospital Life had to make an annual statement of its "real estate, funds and investments," which would be presented to the governor and his council, while the state legislature was granted free access to the company's records. Massachusetts General Hospital trustees were also empowered to inspect and verify the books of Massachusetts Hospital Life to ensure that they were receiving funds in accordance with the charter agreement.[60] Baltimore Life—with no direct public burdens—was required to compile a similar annual report, although this was merely for the benefit of the stockholders; the state did not reserve the right to conduct independent examinations or to verify the contents of the reports.[61]

The guardianship obligations placed on NYL&T and Ohio Life and Trust led their respective states to move beyond mere oversight and assert greater regulatory power over these corporations, resulting in the significant power of the state chancellor over the affairs of NYL&T. Employing the same language regarding the protection of the public good, the charter of Ohio Life and Trust granted to the Supreme Court of Ohio, which disseminated that state's guardianship trusts, almost identical privileges to investigate the company and recommend regulatory changes. Yet unlike the Court of Chancery of New York, which could only file reports and make recommendations to the state legislature, the Supreme Court of Ohio possessed the additional power to disband Ohio Life and Trust outright if it failed to comply with the orders of the court.[62] The rights granted to these private enterprises were contingent on continued fulfillment of their public duties, and failure to do so abrogated those rights.

While life insurers sometimes chafed at the public obligations written into their charters, they understood that state legislatures and individual citizens alike would find for-profit companies more acceptable if their operation resulted in positive benefits for the community as a whole. For example, as an outgrowth of the argument that life insurance protected families from destitution, insurance promoters predicted that the social ills of the nation would be resolved once life insurance pervaded the middle and (eventually) lower classes. In the early advertising literature of NYL&T, President Bard avowed that he was promoting the company's product because he was "persuaded that the general habit of Life Insurance would contribute to the economy, virtue, and happiness of our citizens." Not only was it a for-profit company "affording to the Court of Chancery, and to the widow and orphan, and to the wealthy, a place of safe and convenient deposit for their funds," but it was also a quasi-public entity "promoting the agriculture, the improvement, and the best interests of the state" as well as "supply[ing] the means of rendering the enterprise of its citizens secure, and free from hazard."[63]

As life insurance sales spread during the 1840s and 1850s, insurance brochures claimed an ever-increasing role in "ameliorating the state of society, and elevating its moral character."[64] Referring to life companies as "great public benefits" and "truly benevolent," promotional literature for the industry repeatedly cited not only the potential "great mass of misery [that may] be avoided by the sacrifice of a very small portion of annual income" but also actual instances of "disbursements . . . to families which would have been left in destitute circumstances."[65] But no company waxed more eloquently on the topic than Nautilus Insurance Company in its 1848 brochure:

> Cheered onward as they are, by the confidence and favor of the public, the Officers and Directors, to whom its management is confided, feel that they can render no higher service to the cause of humanity, and to society at large, than by urging all who have the power to do so, to place the helpless members of their families under the protection of this society. Every philanthropist is interested in promoting Life Insurance; inasmuch as destitution and suffering are diminished, wherever its influences extend. In city and country, in every town and village in the land, families are to be found whose circumstances have been straightened and

reduced, by the death of their natural protector. If the kindness of friends and their own exertions, enable the survivors in some of these families to sustain themselves, to educate their children, and to secure for them a respectable position in society, there are many others less fortunate, who sink under the pressure of adversity to a humbler level, where they and their little ones, are surrounded by want and ignorance, and moral degradation. Yet in all these cases, the struggle and the disaster might have been saved them, by a timely resort to Life Insurance.[66]

A decade later, the same company (now renamed New York Life) prophesized: "When [life insurance] should become universal . . . we shall no more hear of destitute widows and orphans being thrown upon the cold charities of this world. Suffering and want, hunger, cold and nakedness, wretchedness, misery, distress of body and mind, and, we might add, crime in some of its most revolting forms . . . will be strangers, where now they stalk abroad, around us, and in our very midst."[67] Life insurance would thus serve not only as the private protector of individual families but as a solution to the most pressing problems of urbanization and industrialization.

Regulating in the Interest of Individual and Corporate Citizens

By midcentury, states began seeking to assert greater control over all businesses operating within their boundaries, regardless of whether they were required to perform specific public duties. Discriminatory legislation was often adopted to give in-state corporations a competitive edge, but these in-state firms were expected to contribute actively to the well-being of the state and its citizens. The case of *Bank of Augusta v. Earle* (1839) represented the beginning of this period, since it gave a state legislature permission to exclude foreign (i.e., out-of-state) corporations from operating within the state.[68] The life insurance industry was not immune to this regulatory activity. Legislation regarding insurance companies addressed two separate issues: the need to provide a protected business environment for in-state corporations and the need to guarantee that these corporations continued to serve the best interests of the public.

Legislators sought to ensure that companies incorporated by the state were not at a competitive disadvantage vis-à-vis larger foreign firms. Many lawmakers believed that the payment of premiums to foreign insurance companies would drain much-needed investment capital out of the state. Legislatures therefore passed a variety of (sometimes competing) regulatory laws in an effort to protect both their individual and corporate citizens. While states in the South and the West often justified these laws by arguing that they were protecting their businesses from the northeastern power structure, New York was the actual leader in the passage of such legislation. The most potent weapons employed were discriminatory taxation, licensing fees, and security deposit requirements—all of which were permitted based on the Supreme Court's decision in *Earle*. By making it expensive for foreign companies to do business within their jurisdiction, states attempted to create more favorable environments for domestic firms.

Discriminatory Taxation and Licensing Fees

During the 1830s and early 1840s, state laws in Massachusetts and Pennsylvania regarding the sale of life insurance were designed to protect the market of Massachusetts Hospital Life and Pennsylvania Company (and later, other companies in those states) from their chief rival, New York Life and Trust, which had rapidly expanded throughout the Northeast and had come to dominate the industry. In 1840, with agencies already active throughout New York and New Jersey, as well as in Providence, Rhode Island; Hartford, Connecticut; Baltimore, Maryland; Washington, DC; Montreal and Halifax, Canada; and as far west as Detroit, Michigan, NYL&T proposed opening its first Massachusetts office: "The applications to this Office for Life insurance from Boston and its neighborhood have become so frequent, that we are desirous of establishing an Agency there." However, President Bard was concerned "that the Laws of Massachusetts might so far interfere, as to impose a tax on the amount insured, which would be a fatal objection, unless the insured paid the tax, which would lessen the business."[69] He was referring to the provision in Massachusetts Hospital Life's charter obligating all future life insurance companies to contribute one-third of their profits to Massachusetts General Hospital. But while this law clearly pertained to all life insurance companies chartered in the state of Massachusetts, NYL&T executives did not believe it applied to companies based outside of the state. As Bard stated: "I should think the [Boston] Agency would not come within the Law, as the insurance would be completed, and the contract entered into here [in New York]."[70] Feeling confident in its ability to evade this tax, NYL&T opened its first office in Boston in 1840, establishing a second in western Massachusetts (Pittsfield) in 1842 and a third in north-central Massachusetts (Greenfield) in 1844.[71] Apparently, the Commonwealth of Massachusetts initially chose not to challenge these agencies, allowing NYL&T a significant competitive advantage.

The situation in Pennsylvania was much less tractable, since the wording of its statutes specifically targeted out-of-state insurers. At first, Pennsylvania banned all insurance by foreign companies, yet by 1829 it permitted out-of-state competition on the condition that these firms pay a hefty 20% tax on insurance premiums and have a minimum $200,000 capital stock.[72] Regarding Baltimore Life's establishment of a life agency in Pennsylvania, John J. Myers—a property insurance salesman based in Carlisle, Pennsylvania, for North American Insurance Company of Philadelphia—wrote the company in 1840: "I believe quite a large business could be done. I know several gentlemen that would at once avail themselves of an opportunity."[73] Yet while Baltimore Life was certainly interested in expanding into Pennsylvania, President Donaldson was concerned about the state's law regarding agencies of foreign life companies, responding to Myers: "We have no agencies in Pensylvania [sic] as we understood the Laws forbid them except on terms too onerous. Whether the Law cou'd be maintained or not, is a question."[74]

Four years later, Baltimore Life, still with no agency in Pennsylvania, was approached by the Pittsburgh partnership of Blakely & Mitchel. President Donaldson advised the firm to investigate the law regulating foreign agencies, so that the company would "be better able to judge of the propriety of establishing an agency."[75] The Pittsburgh firm quickly realized that the provisions of the law were too burdensome for any out-of-state company to accept, and it tried in vain to effect a revision of the law. It quickly learned that the discriminatory legislation had the support of politicians in "Philadelphia City & County & all the influence which they could bring into the field."[76] As a result of this law, neither Baltimore Life nor NYL&T ever established agencies in Pennsylvania, leaving control of that market to an increasing number of in-state companies. The 20% premium tax was finally repealed in 1849, being replaced with a licensing fee for all agents of foreign companies.[77]

In the aftermath of the *Earle* decision, other states began passing legislation to tax the agencies of out-of-state companies, although none was quite as onerous as the Pennsylvania law. For example, in 1842 the Virginia legislature enacted a law—targeted at foreign property insurance companies but encompassing the insurance industry as a whole—that required all foreign agencies to pay an annual licensing fee of $100.[78] Unwilling to pay this tax, Baltimore Life immediately discontinued its agencies in Petersburg and Richmond and declined the establishment of a new one in Winchester.[79] But the company did not leave the state altogether; its two larger agencies in Fredericksburg and Lynchburg continued in operation with some minor modifications. In the aftermath of the new legislation, Dr. Beverly Wellford of Fredericksburg informed the company that he would "now act rather as the Agent of the insured than of the Co[mpany]." By this he meant that he would accept premiums on behalf of the policyholders and forward them to the home office, rather than accepting the premiums on behalf of the company[80]—a trivial distinction, but one Dr. Wellford hoped would enable him to maintain his agency without paying the tax. The Fredericksburg agency successfully operated under this scheme until 1853, when the state "threatened prosecution against [Wellford] for action as [Baltimore Life's] Agent."[81] Dr. Wellford gave up his agency and moved to Richmond in 1854, but not before being subject to "annoyance & expence [*sic*] . . . in consequence of our state tax on insurance companies."[82]

While this arrangement permitted the Fredericksburg agency to remain in service, it would not allow Baltimore Life to actively promote its business in Virginia. As it informed its Petersburg agent upon revoking his agency, "We are much oblig'd to you for your interest for our Co[mpany] and hope the Legislature will see the propriety of making an exception of Life Insurance Companys, and that we may be enabled again to command your Services."[83] To that end, the firm solicited its Lynchburg agent, attorney Charles L. Mosby, to plead its case with the Virginia legislature: "Your Legislature being now in Session, would it not be as well to call the attention of some influential member to the Law respecting Agencies of Insurance Companies. I presume upon a proper representation, the Legislature wou'd make an exception of the Life Insurance Agencies."[84] Since Virginia had no in-state life companies, Baltimore Life believed that the inclusion of life insurance in a law targeted to protect in-state property insurance firms was a clear oversight.

Out-of-state life companies were caught in an awkward position in Virginia. E. H. Williamson of Petersburg advised President Donaldson that a repeal of the law was unlikely as long as the demand for life insurance was low: "Such an attempt would be useless until the benefits resulting from Life Insurance became generally known, which would doubtless turn man to remove the prejudice which now exists against foreign insurance of all kinds." But the reluctance of Baltimore Life to pay the tax without an assurance of success—and the absence of any life insurers native to Virginia—prevented the advertisement and spread of life insurance in that state. Williamson nonetheless encouraged Baltimore Life to take the risk (paying the tax while simultaneously lobbying for its repeal) before the aggressive NYL&T moved into the market:

> I have had interviews recently with very many on the subject, all of whom think favorably of it, & I heard the assertion that were an agency now <u>Legally</u> established here for any life insurance office, there would be issued in less than 18 months 500 policies varying from 3 to 10,000$ . . . should you be the first one [to pay the tax], I have no doubt that the N. York office [NYL&T] would be dissuaded from it . . . There are very many persons who are now waiting the establishment of an agency here to effect an insurance on their lives.[85]

By the spring of 1845—with Baltimore Life still showing no signs of reopening a Petersburg agency—Williamson again wrote the company president, encouraging him at least to make arrangements to bypass the law even while refusing to pay the tax: "If not an agent, advertise in some one of our Papers here giving information & referring our Community here to some one through whom applications can be forwarded." Williamson remained confident that Virginians were on the cusp of embracing the growing industry and that the first company to take advantage of this new market would reap great profits: "Our people are now waking up on the subject of life insurance & I am now of the opinion that within the next two years it will be as common here for a man to have his life insured as it is now for a person to have his house insured." He likewise assured company executives that a revision of the law was in the works: "I do not doubt but that in twelve months the present onerous & unjust tax on Foreign Insurance offices will be taken off." In the meantime, Williamson encouraged the firm to "advertis[e] in our papers here at a cost probably of some 15 or 20$ per annum" and to engage "some person here through where applications may be forwarded to you in Baltimore."[86]

Baltimore Life finally relented. In an arrangement similar to the one maintained by Dr. Wellford of Fredericksburg, the company appointed W. E. Hinton, the agent for Merchant's Fire Company of Baltimore, as its Petersburg representative. Hinton was less sanguine than Williamson regarding the potential for life insurance, but he agreed to the terms offered by the company: "I will accept of your offer, though I fear but little can be done in life Insurance in this place, and there is a tax of $100 on each office, but if all signatures are made by you I think the Law will not exact a tax."[87] In the meantime, just as Williamson had warned, NYL&T made the decision to pay the tax and maintain its Petersburg agency—first established in 1839.[88] Not until 1851 would NYL&T decide to discontinue the agency "owing to the tax imposed by your Legislature."[89]

Despite the lobbying efforts of Mosby (who would himself be elected to the Virginia legislature in 1847)[90] and the establishment of forwarding agencies for Baltimore Life in Fredericksburg and Petersburg, the tax remained in force—being raised twice during the next decade to $250 and then to $300.[91] Some cities also imposed their own licensing fees above and beyond that of the state. Richmond, for example, charged another $50 plus 0.75% on premiums received.[92]

These fees greatly restricted the willingness of Baltimore Life to actively promote its business in Virginia. As one potential agent noted in 1854, "I am convinced that we can build up a good business here if we take out a license, and advertise . . . Without advertising we can not get Insurance on the lives of white persons. By doing so we should hope to do quite a good business in this way."[93] Without the ability to advertise and educate the public about their product, life insurers would be unsuccessful in attracting policyholders in the southern market, and their forwarding agents were wary of being prosecuted under the law if their tax evasion tactics became public (as happened to Dr. Wellford in 1853). As the Richmond medical examiner wrote to Donaldson in 1854, "What insurances we have effected [have] been entirely among our acquaintances, and we have been afraid to attempt much for fear of legal prosecution for acting without license."[94]

It would not be until 1856, through the initiative of a new generation of agents specializing in policies on the lives of slaves, that the Virginia legislature would finally replace the flat licensing fee with a graduated tax of 0.5% on premium payments.[95] While this tax still placed foreign life insurers at a competitive disadvantage, the cost of operating in Virginia was now directly linked to the agency's level of success—to the potential benefit of both the state and the foreign company. Life insurers would be more willing to establish agencies and promote insurance when faced with lower up-front costs. At the same time, with the successful spread of life insurance across the state, a premium tax would bring in more revenue than a flat licensing fee in the long term.

Baltimore Life was not the only company to employ unofficial agents, and tax evasion was a problem faced by several states. Both the 1852 Vermont statute and the 1858 Maryland statute went to great lengths in defining agents liable under the law in order to close any interpretive loopholes.[96] For example, the 1846 insurance law for Maryland required agents of foreign companies to pay a $100 annual licensing fee, but by 1858 the state had amended this law to specifically define what types of activities fell under the purview of an "agent." The new law required a state agency license for anyone authorized "to receive or transmit offers for insurances to their principals, or to receive or deliver policies of insurance, or any instruments in the nature or to the effect of policies of insurance, or to advertise or offer to make such insurances, or to receive and transmit such offers, or to receive or deliver such policies, by publication in any paper, or by any card or circular, or to open any office for the transaction of such business."[97] Additionally, an agency applicant would now have to "make affidavit that he is not indebted to the State of Maryland for the annual license fee . . . and that the company for which he makes application, as agent, is not so indebted." Anyone in violation of the 1846 licensing requirement would have to pay the past-due taxes before being able to obtain a license under the new act.[98]

Pennsylvania attempted to remedy tax evasion by passing "An Act for the Better Securing to the Commonwealth the Payment of Taxes Due by Incorporated Companies" in 1858.[99] The problem of foreign companies ignoring Pennsylvania tax laws was apparently ongoing; wrote one incensed editorialist: "On what principle, *Foreign Insurance* Companies and other *Foreign* Agencies, who come here to transact business and ask to compete with our home companies doing a similar business, claim to be exempted from taxation, we cannot imagine." The author observed that discriminatory legislation against foreign companies was common in most states, and he defended such measures taken by legislatures who "wish to protect our citizens."[100] While minimum capital requirements helped to ensure the stability of foreign insurers for the benefit of in-state policyholders, licensing fees and premium taxes benefited corporate citizens by placing out-of-state companies at a competitive disadvantage. As this author correctly asserted, taxes on foreign insurance corporations were widespread throughout the nation, and they only continued to multiply as the century progressed (see appendix, table A.4).

In fighting these discriminatory laws, some companies returned to the argument that they were quasi-public entities whose businesses operated to the general benefit of all citizens.[101] The 1856 annual report of Union Mutual Life of Maine emphasized the central duty of life insurers "to protect the widow and orphan." To help the company effectively fulfill this role, Union Mutual encouraged its policyholders (as well as the policyholders of its competitors) to "exert their influence in endeavoring to repeal all such laws as tax funds set apart for the 'sole use and benefit' of the widow and orphan."[102] Since life insurance reduced the public burden by providing for widows and orphans who might otherwise require public relief from the state, Union Mutual argued that fees and taxes restricting life insurance sales ultimately taxed these most vulnerable members of society.

Similar arguments emerged when Congress proposed a federal tax on insurance to help raise funds during the Civil War. Meeting as the American Life Underwriters' Convention in 1862 to object to this proposal, industry leaders pledged their "willing[ness] to bear their full and just share . . . of the burdens occasioned by the present war." However, they protested that "taxing the funds of a life company to any extent is tantamount to laying a tax on good intentions and forethought" by "diminish[ing] the amounts to be received by the widow and orphan," and that such a tax would "impair" the "security, stability, and permanence of these institutions."[103] While they stopped short of declaring how they *would* contribute to the war effort, these insurers were attempting to demonstrate that the ultimate purpose of the life insurance contract made them unique among for-profit firms.

Deposit Requirements and Retaliatory Legislation

Along with protecting in-state corporations, states also wanted to ensure the safety of the life insurance business conducted within their state—which sometimes had the added benefit of further discouraging foreign competition. The very nature of the insurance contract generated the need to guarantee the long-term or perpetual existence of companies, particularly in the area of life insurance. Therefore, the states felt compelled to ensure that these companies were fiscally sound and operating to the full benefit of their citizens—and not merely lining the pockets of company officers and shareholders. As one editorial in the *Cincinnati Price Current* of 1851 declared:

> The majority of persons who insure, do so for life, and the public should, therefore, have some assurance of the *permanent* safety of all Life Insurance Companies . . . what would be thought of a Legislature that would now charter banks, without doing anything to protect the public against fraud, or secure note-holders against loss, in the event of a failure. We cannot, in this respect, see any great difference between a bank and a Life Insurance Company . . . and we do not see any more reason to doubt that frauds *will* be practiced by one, than that they have been practiced by the other. In the case of Life Insurance Companies, the gates are wide open, and the road perfectly free to corruption.[104]

As more and more mutual life insurers sought charters during the mid-1840s, some states (likely prodded by the stock companies directly competing with this new corporate form) adopted legislation to ensure such companies would remain fiscally sound. For example, on April 10, 1849, the New York state legislature passed a law requiring all new insurance companies either incorporating or planning to do business in New York to possess $100,000 of capital stock—regardless of their corporate structure.[105] Two years later, the legislature passed a more stringent law obligating all life insurance companies (including those chartered prior to the passage of the law) to deposit with the comptroller of New York $100,000 "in public stock of the United States, or of this State, or stocks, or bonds of either of the incorporated cities of this State; . . . or in bonds and mortgage on unincumbered improved real estate situate within this State." The comptroller would hold this capital as security for the in-state policyholders of the company. The law also authorized the comptroller to conduct or to have conducted periodic examinations of the affairs of any life insurer within the state.[106]

While this capital requirement was readily met by in-state stock companies (whose charters already mandated that they possess at least this amount) as well as the established New York–based mutual companies, it made it extremely difficult for new mutual companies to form and thus effectively dampened the movement toward mutualization in the state until the 1890s. But beyond the minimum capital stipulation, the deposit requirement gave a competitive edge to in-state companies. The rationale for this mandate was that the state would maintain sufficient funds to compensate their insured citizens in the event a company went bankrupt. But as these funds were deposited with New York, they were no longer available for claims in other states, thus requiring a $100,000 deposit *in addition to* the minimum capital stipulated by the companies' own state charters. Upon passage of the New York law, twelve out-of-state companies ceased doing business in the state altogether, leaving only New England Mutual and Mutual Benefit of New Jersey to compete with the New York companies in one of the largest markets in the nation.[107]

Finally, this law placed greater restrictions on the types of investments permitted. Whereas the 1830 charter of NYL&T had allowed funds to be invested in the stock of the federal government or any state or incorporated city,[108] Mutual Life of New York's charter of 1842 stipulated that the company invest at least half of its premiums "in the bonds and mortgages on unincumbered real estate within the State of New York."[109] Coming on the heels of the speculative land frenzy of the 1830s and in the midst of the ensuing depression, this New York law was specifically a protective measure to ensure that capital did not leave the state. By 1851, New York mandated that the required $100,000 deposit had to be made in federal stocks, securities of the state or municipalities of New York, or in-state mortgages.

Although mutual and foreign companies were the main targets of the 1851 New York legislation, NYL&T particularly took exception to this law. In a long letter to the state comptroller, President Bard delineated the board's reasons for choosing to ignore the law. Citing the clause in NYL&T's charter permitting future amendment of the act, Bard argued that a general act with regard to insurance companies could not pertain to the "special act of Incorporation" for NYL&T unless that latter act was specifically mentioned.[110] Bard then went on to list all the elements of the original charter that served to satisfy the intentions of the new law. For example, the operation of NYL&T was overseen by the Court of Equity "for the purpose of providing that security to the public for the providing which the law of the 8th was passed." He objected to the fact that NYL&T would be subject to examinations by the state comptroller, in addition to the chancellor, which would "put the Company in the points of labour and Expense in a much worse situation than any other Life Insurance Company in the State[.] We should my Dear Sir as willingly be under your control as under the control of the Court of equity, but I think you will see there are very serious and important objections to being under the control of both."[111] Despite this plea, the state comptroller remained firm in his opinion that the new law applied to all insurance companies, and by the summer of 1851 NYL&T was forced to comply.[112]

Several foreign companies attempted to combat this law by organizing and lobbying the New York state legislature. In January 1852, Baltimore Life received a confidential letter from an insurance executive in Boston soliciting a donation of between $100 and $500 in support of this effort: "I am authorised to correspond with the Life Insurance Cos. in the U.S. relative to contributions to a movement for the repeal or modification of the present objectionable NY Life Insurance Law." In addition to losing out on the lucrative New York market—"New York City being the London of America (to whose greatness all the states have & are contributing) it is desireable [*sic*] that Life offices in the U.S. have the right to establish Branches in her precincts upon equitable principles"—this committee was likewise concerned about "evidences of a determination by several Legislatures passing Laws of retaliation this season: the effects of which must be disastrous, the great safety of Life Offices consisting [in] the dissemination of their risks over an extended territory." The writer claimed that the protest effort was "guided by a man of consummate ability who has held one of the highest positions in the N.Y. legislature & who has now the confidence of all" and that most of the northeastern life companies had already agreed to participate in the campaign.[113]

While this movement failed to achieve a repeal of the New York deposit law (and may even have been a hoax designed to extort money from the insurance companies), the writer was correct in his fear that states would pass retaliatory legislation as their only means of fighting back. As table A.4 suggests, deposit laws passed during the antebellum years in other states including New Jersey, Iowa, and Wisconsin only further multiplied the burden of the 1851 New York law. And as in New York, often accompanying these deposit laws were new requirements that a portion of premiums and capital be invested in the state as a means of preventing the outflow of capital from their borders; New Jersey, California, Illinois, Iowa, Kansas, Kentucky, Ohio, and Wisconsin all passed such laws during the 1850s and 1860s.[114] The Ohio state legislature contemplated deposit laws so onerous that the insurance press could only conclude that they were "intended, and would have the effect to drive out all outside Companies, and make a close corporation of those Companies now incorporated."[115]

Interestingly, several southern states and insurance companies began to take a regional rather than strictly state-centered view of investing. For example, the 1849 brochure of North Carolina Mutual Life queried: "Why should the citizens of the Southern States leave *home* to seek insurance elsewhere? . . . It is estimated that more than $100,000 are annually sent from this State to be invested in life Policies; and the same amount, or more perhaps, from South Carolina, Georgia, Tennessee and Virginia. Surely these investments have not been made abroad from preference."[116] The 1860 charter of the Virginia Life Insurance Company stipulated that half of the assets of that company "shall be invested in the stocks of the State of

Virginia, or any other slaveholding State, or of any incorporated city in the said States, or in bonds guaranteed by any such State or city, or in bills receivable, satisfactorily secured by personal or collateral security."[117]

But while some states retaliated with deposit requirements or investment restrictions, others merely reflected back on out-of-state companies the same discriminatory laws in force in those companies' home states. Although Massachusetts had passed such a reciprocity law as early as 1844, other states began adopting this tactic in the wake of the New York law. For example, Connecticut in 1852 stipulated: "Insurance Companies of other States, doing business in this State, to be subject to the same liabilities as Insurance Companies of this State, doing business in such other States."[118] This sort of legislation could be devastating for companies. For instance, in 1899 Wisconsin collected $8.52 in taxes from two small Illinois companies. But because of Illinois' reciprocity law, Northwestern Mutual of Wisconsin was required to pay Illinois $17,694.63 in return. Although many companies (including Northwestern Mutual) lobbied their own state legislatures to reduce discriminatory taxation of foreign companies in order to relieve them of this retaliatory burden, many states chose to ignore their complaints. In an address to the Wisconsin Assembly in 1905, Governor Robert M. LaFollette declared: "The legislature of this state should not be moved to the rejection of a just law when proposed, by the consideration that an unjust law might be enacted in some other state in retaliation."[119] Legislatures of the mid-nineteenth century agreed with this contention.

Although some of this legislation (particularly deposit requirements and some investment rules) served to protect policyholders from undercapitalized, fraudulent, or otherwise fiscally unsound companies, much of it (including discriminatory taxation, some investment rules, and retaliatory legislation) mainly served as protection for in-state firms—and may in fact have reduced the overall stability of the industry. For many small companies, out-of-state policy sales were a primary means of increasing their customer base and spreading their risks, but as a result of these laws only the largest companies could afford to operate outside their home states. As State Mutual of Worcester, Massachusetts, commented in its annual report for 1856: "The legislation of most of the other States of the Union upon the subject of Life Insurance, has become so stringent that the Company is almost necessarily confined in its operations to the Commonwealth of Massachusetts."[120] And as a result of such barriers, citizens of states with a less developed insurance industry were forced to purchase policies from newer companies without proven track records. By forcing citizens to choose in-state companies, some legislatures actually exposed the insuring public to greater risks of company default—thus not necessarily acting in the best interests of their constituents.

The Regulatory Quandary

As historian William J. Novak observes: "The early nineteenth-century American business corporation was understood as a special creation of public power subject to special regulation and control by the state that created it. Even after the opinion of John Marshall in the Dartmouth College Case and the increasing use made of general incorporation laws, states never relinquished their general police powers to regulate business corporations for the public safety, morals, health, and welfare."[121] The regulatory history of the life insurance industry exemplifies many of the main trends in nineteenth-century regulation. By continuously promoting themselves as corporations in the public interest, life insurers gladly assumed public duties in exchange for the rights and privileges attendant to a corporate charter. Their quasi-public status as protectors of the most vulnerable members of society helped them earn a level of respect among the public and legislators that a purely for-profit company could not expect.

However, if the purpose of regulation was "to further the welfare of the whole people and community,"[122] states soon encountered the problem of determining *whose* welfare took precedence when the needs of diverse groups of citizens clashed. Whereas early insurance regulation was primarily concerned with ensuring the long-term safety of the industry for the benefit of policyholders, by midcentury the states began taking on much more complex regulatory roles—desiring both to protect individual citizens from potential abuses of corporate power and to protect corporate citizens from the rigors of out-of-state competition. This bifurcation of purposes in regulating the industry often resulted in contradictory legislation, leaving corporate as well as individual citizens exposed to greater risk.

PART II

REACHING OUT TO
THE MIDDLE CLASS

This illustration, which accompanied an 1845 article on the necessity of life insurance for a newly married man, depicts the sorrow of a widow with her two young children upon the death of their husband and father. While little can be done to mend their broken hearts, the Greek goddess of abundance watches over them as the proceeds of their loved one's life insurance policy pours forth from her cornucopia, relieving the family's economic needs. *New England Family Magazine,* December 1, 1845: 239. Photo courtesy of The Newberry Library, Chicago (A5.4105).

CHAPTER 5

Protecting Women and Children "in the hour of their distress"
Targeting the Fears of an Emerging Middle Class

Go with us among the poor of our large towns and cities—yes, go with us among the poor in our very midst. Behold the widows and orphans suffering for the want of the most common necessaries of life, made so from a neglect to effect an insurance upon their only property, their only resources, now entirely and forever cut off, viz: the life of a husband and father. Behold the misery, the want, the suffering, the cold and cheerless prospects, the excessive toil, the deficiency of food, clothing, and comforts of life. Hark! hear those dear ones, who once had a fond father to caress them, now crying for bread. Witness the pang that shoots through that anxious and careworn mother's breast, as she raises her eyes to heaven, and with a broken heart and suppliant tone pleads for her innocent offspring. She murmurs not; but she feels that her burthen is more than she can bear. Witness all the horrors of poverty attendant upon a neglected widow, whose greatest exertions are remunerated only with a miserable pittance, surrounded, as she may be, with her helpless children—suffering for the necessaries of life; and then but for a moment reflect that our own families, our own wives, and dear ones, are daily exposed to the same sad fate, so long as we live without providing a certainty against their future want. This is not an overdrawn picture. In the capacity of a physician for the last fourteen years, we have witnessed numerous instances of families reduced to penury and want by the death of a husband and father, whose former circumstances were in every respect as good as many of ours; and far better than some who imagine themselves rich in this world's goods.[1]

This quintessential piece of advertising copy from the 1858 brochure of New York Life Insurance Company (established 1841 as Nautilus Insurance)[2] exemplifies the principal marketing technique of all antebellum life insurers: targeting the fears of an emerging urban middle class. The setting is any of the many ballooning "large towns and cities" of the mid-nineteenth century, and the central figure in the ad is a "neglected widow" and "careworn mother" who in vain tries to procure "the most common necessaries of life" for herself and her "innocent offspring." While this Dickensian picture closely resembles the numerous calls for donations by charitable institutions such as widows' and orphans' societies,[3] the writer is careful to reveal the woman's genteel roots; if not for the death of her husband, this poor widow's station in life would have remained no different than that of the (presumably middle-class) reader's own wife. The whole purpose of the ad was to drive home viscerally the idea that the average middle-income family was a mere heartbeat away from being reduced to the "horrors of poverty."

Although the woman "raises her eyes to heaven" and "pleads" for help, neither a wrathful God, nor a personal moral failing, nor the unpredictable caprices of fate are blamed for her tragic reversal of fortune. Even the machinations of the market system itself, which might arguably have been accountable for the vast inequalities of wealth in the urban centers and the widow's inability to receive more than a "miserable pittance" in exchange for her "greatest exertions," emerge uncritiqued in this scenario. Indeed, the *sole* responsibility for the fate of this family lay with the failure of the father to fulfill his duties as breadwinner from beyond the grave. A paternal presence overshadows the ad like the ghost of what should have been—the "fond father" who should be "caress[ing]" his children by providing them with "food, clothing, and comforts of life." Thus even in death, the husband's obligation to "provid[e] a certainty against their future want" did not cease. This was the intended message for the reader—who was assumed to be himself a middle-class husband and father.

Life insurance companies employed ads such as this one to market protection of a lifestyle to the emerging middle class—people who had economic and social aspirations but were dependent on a regular income and generally eschewed risk for fear of failure. In the words of one early life insurance ad, "It is only natural, that those, who by their virtues and industry *have* acquired a competence, should be *anxious* to preserve their children from *actual* suffering."[4] As Americans moved from agricultural regions into the burgeoning anonymous cities, as families became dependent on the income of the head of household rather than a more holistic family economy, and as businessmen became aware that their economic fortunes were as much dependent on the booms and busts of the business cycle as on their own abilities, the fate of families after a breadwinner's death became increasingly uncertain and fraught with anxiety, particularly since he was a middle-class family's "only property, their only resource."

The industry understood that this growing segment of the population faced opportunities and anxieties that made them unique among Americans. Life insurance thus appealed not to their status consciousness—as people "who imagine themselves rich in this world's goods"—but to their recognition of the fragility of that status. By providing not just "a certainty against future want" but also the "comforts of life" for families, life insurance offered a hedge against the economic vicissitudes of middle-class life. It freed middle-class breadwinners to take more risks during their lifetimes by protecting their wives and children from the ultimate risk of death.

In recent years, a number of works have greatly enhanced our understanding of both risk and failure in nineteenth-century America, as well as of the emergence of the middle class. Edward Balleisen, for example, analyzes commercial failure and the evolution of bankruptcy laws to encourage entrepreneurship during the ante-bellum period, while Naomi Lamoreaux's work on banking demonstrates the importance of kinship networks for spreading investment risks. Mary Ryan and Stuart Blumin take a different approach and create portraits of middle-class America focusing on the *mentalité* of this group and how its members differed (or believed they differed) from those above and below them. The latter historians uncover a group of people who are largely concerned with their own status. Although Balleisen briefly analyzes the intersection between risk and class in arguing that the experience of bankruptcy drove many from the middle class to seek the "stability" of salaried employment, these two schools of historiography rarely engage each other. Yet it is only at the point where middle-class hopes and fears meet the realities of a modern economy that a fuller picture of this class can emerge.

As numerous historians have pointed out, the middle class cannot be defined solely as an income level: one must also consider its conduct—its movement into salaried, nonmanual occupations; its embrace of reform movements; its assertion of control over family size; its segregation of public and private sectors of the home; its consumption patterns, etc. Modern American life insurance was embraced by the same people who constituted this inchoate class. As one 1837 article asserted, "Public attention has, of late years, been drawn to the great advantages which life insurance holds out to persons in *middling circumstances* as an easy means of providing for those who may survive them" (emphasis added).[5] Its growth over the course of the nineteenth century paralleled the development of a middle-class *mentalité* by providing a new safety net to protect middle-class widows and orphans from the risks of modern life and by facilitating the aspirations and lifestyle they sought.

In particular, the shifting role of women in urban middle-class families not only made them especially vulnerable in the case of their husband's untimely death but gave them greater decision-making power with regard to the needs of the household. Among the many industries that viewed women as an important market segment was life insurance. Firms increasingly recognized that, as the moral guardians of the family, middle-class women were not just passive victims. As they increasingly asserted control over all aspects of household consumption and governance, whether to purchase a life insurance policy on the main breadwinner often fell under their purview. However, women faced two basic problems: their inability to contract for insurance on their spouses (because of the legal bar on signing contracts in the coverture system and the industry's strict rules regarding insurable interest) and the legal status of a policy as part of the deceased's estate. During the late 1830s and early 1840s, life insurance companies spearheaded lobbying efforts to pass legislation removing each of these barriers in order to attract the attention of the female head of household. Being thus empowered to take control of her own economic future, the potential "neglected widow" might be more likely than her husband to seek the protection of an insurance policy.

Casting a Wide Net around the Amorphous Middle Class

The first life companies operating in America saw homing in on potential applicants and convincing them that they needed this new and untested product as the key to success. Some early life insurance promoters focused on the most dangerous occupations, presenting their product as perfect protection for the families of "husbands and fathers, who in the pursuit of their living are obliged to expose themselves to the perils of the ocean"[6] or for men who "are drawn in the pursuits of business, into every part of the world, exposed to all the hazards and vicissitudes of the land and the sea, the changes of climate, and the contagion of disease."[7] Of course, high-risk occupations were exactly what the incipient industry needed to avoid, since their mortality knowledge was not yet sophisticated enough to accurately predict the level of risk involved.

As urban salaried and professional employments would not expose the companies to unpredictable rates of mortality, life insurers turned their attention toward the emerging middle class, and insurance advertisements stressed how dependence on the income of a lone breadwinner placed families in a particularly precarious economic position. Thus Pennsylvania Company's 1814 brochure recommended insurance for any man "who maintains his family by the annual or daily produce of his industry" or "who receives a salary sufficient for his support, but has no resources or expectation for his family after his death." As the brochure went on to explain, "His expenses are numerous, and he is not able, with all his endeavours, to provide the means for the *comfortable subsistence* of his family in case of his early death" (emphasis added).[8] The short-lived Union Insurance Company similarly advertised in 1818 that a policy would benefit men "possessed of fixed incomes, which will terminate with their own lives."[9] These companies were attempting to point out the higher consequences of death associated with certain urban occupations. While a solvent businessman could rest assured that his firm would provide for his family after his demise (either through continuance by another family member or profitable liquidation), the salaried man could take no such consolation, since his money-earning potential died with him.

These early companies also recognized that urbanization was removing the economic and social safety nets present (at least in theory) in rural societies. In the countryside, several options were available for widowed and orphaned families. Under the common law of dower, widows received a fixed share of the real property owned by their husbands; under the law of most states they received lifetime use of one-third of the husband's landed property. Thus fatherless households could continue running the family business in his absence—particularly when older sons were available to help on the farm or continue his trade. The assistance of family and neighbors was vital to this transition, while children and paid farmhands provided long-term stability. Even families lacking the economic, emotional, or human capital necessary to continue without a husband and father were not left out in the cold. Neighbors and relatives readily incorporated victims of loss into their own household economies.[10] As historian Jack Larkin has pointed out, "The chances for early death made for many widows and widowers who frequently found places in the households of their children or of their married brothers and sisters. Kinfolk came into their relatives' families as paid or unpaid domestic help, apprentices and employees, and even paying lodgers."[11] Thus the very nature of the household economy in rural America helped to shield families from sudden economic dislocations when the family head died.

Urban families dependent on the wages of the father, however, could not easily replace his labors themselves. As Shawn Johansen's history of middle-class fatherhood emphasizes, the transition of the home from a place of production (with responsibilities shared by all family members) to exclusively one of consumption put considerably more pressure on the role of the primary male breadwinner, who now "keenly felt the responsibility to provide[;] . . . without [his income] the family economy collapsed." Families who lost their fathers and husbands faced a dismal fate because "the few jobs available to women paid such low wages that widowhood usually meant a decline in class status."[12] A similar pattern emerges from Mary Ryan's study of midcentury Oneida County, New York. Respectable paid employment for women was largely confined to taking in sewing and laundry, teaching school, or running a boarding house (assuming she had the means to afford such an enterprise). For many, remarriage—and a return to the dependent confines of the private sphere—was the only means of maintaining their middle-class status.[13]

Nineteenth-century fathers similarly experienced growing expectations about establishing the middle-class foundations of their children. Whereas rural offspring were likely to follow directly in the footsteps of their parents, the urban father now needed to ensure adequate education and training, as well as possibly capital investments, for his son's future career. His daughter, as well, needed the appropriate literary and musical skills to be considered marriageable within middle-class society. In his history of fatherhood, Stephen M. Frank concludes: "By the 1830s, if not earlier, providing children with the means to an education was, in the minds of many urban middle-class men, among their most important functions as fathers. Indeed, the desire and ability to keep children in school quickly became a sign of middle-class respectability and a marker of class boundaries."[14] A father's untimely demise thus might force his children to enter the workforce prematurely, sacrificing the education that was becoming increasingly necessary as the basis for a middle-class lifestyle.

Direct support from family or neighbors was much more limited in the cities as well. Urban residents were not heartless, but connections were more fluid in this highly mobile environment. Whereas taking in the needy in rural communities added productive units to the household (at least partially compensating for their additional consumption), in urban areas they would essentially become extra mouths to feed—placing undue strain on household budgets. Thus in the mushrooming towns and cities of antebellum America, the plight of the widowed and the orphaned emerged as a new concern, particularly as the removal of work from the home decreased their opportunities for independent survival.[15]

To fill this void, several charitable organizations such as the Society for the Relief of Poor Widows with Small Children, the New York Female Guardian Society, and the Association for the Relief of Respectable or Aged Females, emerged during the early nineteenth century to provide aid for the "deserving" poor—among whom were included "females once in *comfortable circumstances* who have been reduced to poverty by the death or misfortune of their husbands and relatives" (emphasis added).[16] Yet while these charitable organizations certainly performed a crucial function for nineteenth-century Americans in need, no moderate-income father wanted his family to become "dependent upon the cold charities of the world" after his demise.[17] Rather, he found it "indispensably necessary . . . that some sure and unfailing provision should be made to those who are dear to him, a sufficient competency to place them beyond a miserable dependence upon public charity after his death."[18] Indeed, even though most charities targeted those considered most deserving, the idea of receiving charity remained stigmatized, and many poor widows refused such handouts.[19]

Life insurance companies tried to capitalize on this shifting economic situation of urban families, emphasizing the real fears of middle-income households and the potential solution offered by their product. As Nautilus Company proclaimed in its 1848 brochure, "The man who has the power, but neglects the opportunity of providing in this way for the comfort and independence of his family, in the day when the hand that labored, and the head that thought for them, and the heart that loved them, are cold in death, fails in the duty which he owes to them and to himself."[20] A life insurance policy was the investment of funds by a father during his lifetime to provide for the needs of his family upon his death. It was neither the social obligation of rural society nor the pity of urban charities but a market solution for a market dislocation.

Building on the marketing foundation of the earliest life firms, one of the most important pieces of life insurance advertising literature was created in 1832 by President William Bard of New York Life and Trust Company. It was an essay written in the form of a letter to David E. Evans of Batavia, New York, who had remarked that life insurance would not meet with much success in New York State. The board of NYL&T decided that Evans's pessimism provided the company with an opportunity to address the critics of life insurance as well as educate the public about the numerous people in many situations who would benefit from a life insurance policy. Although several of his arguments had been made at various times by earlier companies, Bard brought them all together in the most comprehensive and persuasive fashion.

With Evans's permission, the company published its response to him in various New York newspapers and had ten thousand copies printed in the form of a seventeen-page pamphlet that it distributed to the company's agents and potential customers.[21] For the next several years, this letter would continue to be reproduced in its entirety in newspapers across the country.[22] By employing the genre of educational pamphlet literature in an epistolary form, a medium similar to that used by the numerous reform movements of the 1820s and 1830s, Bard aligned his crusade to protect widows and orphans alongside those calling for religious revival, temperance, and education reform. Life insurance was more than just a profitable new commodity for sale in the marketplace; it was a movement that promised to bring about the betterment of society as a whole. This one letter would form the model of life insurance advertising literature for the entire antebellum period.

While the first three pages of the letter were educational—detailing for the reader how a life insurance contract worked—the main portion of the message (about five pages) was devoted to examples of the types of people who would benefit from a policy, including "gentlemen in the army, the navy, the church, the law, or in office, medical, and other professional men, annuitants, tenants for life, tradesmen, *and all other persons, whose income depends upon their lives*" (emphasis added). Bard was trying to cast a wide net to reach as many middle- and upper-income Americans as possible. Even during the very first years of NYL&T, he envisioned a broad customer base for life insurance: "It concerns the rich, the mechanic, the farmer, the man living on income, or the land-holder, the professional man, or the merchant— in short, all classes of men whatever."[23]

But despite this vision of a world where life insurance was ubiquitous, Bard and other early American promoters always returned to that core group for whom they believed life insurance would have the greatest appeal: "The most general use made of a Life Insurance, is, by persons living on income; to secure a family, by its means, a *comfortable support* after the death of its head or parent" (emphasis added).[24] In short, they believed that the emerging middle class had the most to gain from their product. Not only were its members dependent on the income of a lone breadwinner, but their aspirations for their families went beyond the provision of bare necessities. The middle-class father sought a "comfortable subsistence" for his family so that his wife need never work and his children would benefit from a solid education and the prospects of their own proper middle-class careers.

Throughout the remainder of the antebellum period, the hypothetical conditions outlined in *A Letter to David E. Evans* were reiterated in the advertising literature of all companies. For example, Baltimore Life (1830) and Ohio Life Insurance and Trust (1834) both aimed their initial sales brochures at "the salaried officer, men in public offices, the clergy, clerks, and every other person whose family is dependent on his personal services for support." Through the payment of only a small premium, this type of man could "make a *comfortable provision* for his family at his death and save his wife and children from pecuniary distress" (emphasis added), all in an effort to guarantee "independence to families."[25] Drawing directly on the fear of failure that plagued middle-income fathers, the 1837 brochure of Girard Life Insurance Company asked: "What greater obligation can exist for a husband or parent than to make provision for the *comfortable support* of a wife or children who are dependent upon his earnings for subsistence?" (emphasis added).[26]

By the 1840s these hypothetical predicaments were given increased potency as companies began to provide specific (real or composite) examples of people who insured in each category, including their age, occupation, date and amount of insurance, and whether they died prematurely. Over the years, these examples became standardized across company brochures. There was the "highly respectable and wealthy merchant" who had the misfortune of going bankrupt and then dying within two years of taking out his insurance policy, the widow in Indiana who "was so forcibly impressed with the advantages of life insurance" after the death of her husband that she took out a policy on herself, a bookkeeper who died within ten days of contracting scarlet fever, and the farmer in Dutchess County, New York, who "died very suddenly, from an attack of apoplexy."[27] By presenting such a wide array of people and situations, all of which ended with a premature death and the prompt payment of the insurance claim, companies hoped that at least one example would resonate with the reader and prompt him or her to consider the prudence of taking out a life insurance policy.

While each of these companies clearly sought to insure people of all economic backgrounds, they focused the majority of their effort on people of moderate means who they felt would benefit most from the protection of life insurance—and who thus made up the core of their potential market. Both Bard's *A Letter to David E. Evans* and Pennsylvania Company's 1837 brochure described as their sole specific example a 30-year-old married man with an annual income of $1,000, while Girard Life's 1837 pamphlet spoke of a man "whose income enables him to support his family *in comfort,* but is so limited as not to allow him to save more than $23.60 a year" (emphasis added)—the annual premium necessary for a 30-year-old man to obtain a $1,000 policy.[28] (As Walt Whitman wrote in 1858, "The most valuable class in any community is the middle class, the men of moderate means, living at the rate of a thousand dollars a year or thereabouts.")[29]

A middle-income man could just as easily scrape together this moderate amount for insurance as he could fritter it away on "an unnecessary journey, an idle amusement, a few wasted days in each year." More pointedly, the "tobacco chewer," could give up "his two cents a day," and the "tippler" who "drinks one shilling a day" should be ashamed of his "indulgence [in] that most filthy of all habits" when the expense forces him to "sacrifice . . . the education and clothing, and food, of objects the nearest and dearest to us all."[30] As Connecticut Mutual asserted in 1851, "No man is too poor to insure his life."[31] All antebellum companies thus believed that their most lucrative business would come from middle-income fathers, whose death would leave their families in "pecuniary distress,"[32] "in want,"[33] in a state of "poverty, in the hour of their distress,"[34] suffering "sacrifice and loss,"[35] or exposing them "to insult and poverty" or "the horrors of destitution, of want, and of misery."[36]

In reflecting the most basic anxieties of middle-income Americans, these bleak descriptions resonated throughout urban society. Incoming letters from potential policyholders to Baltimore Life have survived, providing a rare (albeit brief) glimpse at people's motives for insuring. A lawyer from Sanford, Virginia, desired a $3,000 policy "to insure a living to my wife,"[37] while another Virginian, in anticipation of making a marriage proposal, wanted "to secure to a <u>Lady</u> if she shall survive me, $10,000, if not then to my children."[38] John O. Lay, who would later become Baltimore Life's local agent in Richmond, Virginia, wrote in 1833: "It has since occurred to me that having a Family of young Children dependent in a great measure on my exertions it would be a matter of prudence to effect a Life Ins[uranc]e. Say to the am[oun]t of $3000 for their benefit."[39] Merchants and small proprietors, in particular, were well aware of the high rate of failure among American businesses and thus sought insurance to protect their families against the risks of their livelihood.[40] "I have been raised to the mercantile business, and think I have the capacity and opportunity to employ capital advantageously," explained John P. Trezevant of Memphis, Tennessee, in 1845. "And in obtaining it," he continued, "would be very glad to avail myself at the same time of the protection afforded by such an Institution as yours, against the vicissitudes of trade, and the sufferings to a young and helpless family which might result from my death in a state of poverty."[41] Middle-class inquirers to Baltimore Life sought life insurance to secure the economic future of their families, thus freeing them to pursue their professional aspirations with less fear of the consequences of failure.

Because of its location near the nation's capital, Baltimore Life targeted sales among Washington's growing military and bureaucratic workforce. In April 1831, Michael Nourse, a colonel in the United States Army and the first registrar of the treasury, wrote to George Carr Grundy, secretary of Baltimore Life, expressing his interest in becoming an agent of the company in Washington. Nourse proposed that the company solicit insurance from the rapidly increasing number of salaried federal employees: "At present, with few [ex]cepting, they expend all their income as received. Upon the plan of insurance they would . . . be laying up something for the support of a family when they should be called away; for the want of which, some are now aproximating [*sic*] to pauperism."[42] Although Nourse was not hired by the company, his suggestion to target the growing white-collar workforce—many of whom were probably young clerks with higher professional aspirations—piqued the firm's interest.

When Baltimore Life did officially open a Washington agency in March 1833, its new agent's main objective was to sell insurance policies to government clerks. In his acceptance letter, agent James H. Causten declared that he was "located in the midst of the public offices, & have an intimate acquaintance with nearly all the officers of the Departments, a class of persons of all others the best suited to the object of your Company," because of their status as middle-income salaried professionals.[43] He felt that these federal employees, like emerging pockets of white-collar workers all along the eastern seaboard, were a prime target for the life insurance industry. In an 1839 letter to the company president, Causten stressed that "many of the clerks are notoriously improvident, most of them receive inadequate Salaries; and very many leave their families at their death in a most deplorable State of destitution."[44] These clerks lived on the cusp of middle-class existence. While their white-collar employment and their long-term aspirations placed them firmly within the middle-class *mentalité,* their modest incomes left them particularly vulnerable to losing that precarious social status.

Indeed, Causten was interested in providing life insurance to as many of these salaried clerks as possible. Having spoken to several officers in various departments regarding their insecure financial situation, he believed that the diverse federal departments should jointly petition Congress to provide that "an annual additional Salary of 100$ be allowed to each officer, for the purpose of securing a life policy of Insurance for the benefit of his wife and children." In this plan, the money would be paid by the paymaster directly to Baltimore Life for the purchase of said policies. Causten argued: "It is supposed that such a measure would be highly acceptable to the American people, and would afford a most salutary stimulant to the drudging clerk while living, and a happy relief to his surviving family, who are usually subjected to great distress from poverty, and his children thrown upon the world uneducated and helpless."[45] As the underwriting agent, Causten would clearly be a prime beneficiary if such legislation were passed. Though potentially self-serving, however, his line of reasoning was pulled directly from the arguments of the company brochures themselves. Life insurance would protect middle-class families from a loss of class status, allow them to continue educating their children for advancement up the socioeconomic ladder, and alleviate the burdens of local municipalities to provide for destitute widows and orphans.

Causten was several decades ahead of his time in suggesting the underwriting of a group of employees by their employer, and President Donaldson of Baltimore Life was particularly wary of the risks inherent in such a novel undertaking: "If the risks were good, it wou'd be greatly to our advantage. But there might be some in office whose health was imperfect these necessaryly [*sic*] wou'd be excluded." In an industry still struggling to fully comprehend the American experience with mortality, the idea of underwriting a group of people without the benefit of an application and selection process seemed particularly risky. And as turnover inevitably occurred within the bureaucracy, Donaldson wanted to know "what then becomes of the Insurance?" in the event of an insured worker leaving his position. Despite these misgivings, Donaldson expressed his willingness to consider "some plan . . . to obviate these objections" (although I have found no evidence to indicate that this request was ever presented to the Congress).[46] This early attempt at group insurance—which would have amounted to a $4,000 policy for a 30-year-old clerk—exemplifies the optimism of life insurance promoters about the long-term success of their industry, as well as their belief in the protection life insurance could provide to middle-income Americans.

By midcentury, insurance advertisements increasingly went beyond mere mentions of poverty or sacrifice to embrace fully the emotional turmoil that was becoming a central part of middle-class life. A blatant example of this type of psychological marketing tactic came from the 1848 brochure of the New York branch of Eagle Life Insurance Company of London. In it the firm painted a picture of one thousand young healthy males who dreamed of marrying and passing on their middle-class status as "successful independent operatives" to their offspring. During their lifetimes, these men would easily be able to support their families in a middle-class existence, yet Eagle Life estimated that half would die an early death: "The children of five hundred are doomed in some way, to eat the bread of dependency. There is no effort of ordinary economy which can save them from such a contingency," which would leave them "a hunger-driven herd of shiftless individuals."[47]

The closing paragraph of this description brought home to the reader the nightmare scenario dreaded by every middle-class father—that his children would fall out of the middle class and have to repeat their father's and grandfather's struggle up the ladder. Upon his premature death "his heirs and representatives must instantly descend many grades in the scale of comfort, if not of respectability; to feed on husks and breathe in corners, and find in scattered places, and among varied chances a vague hope of attaining in after years a snug hearthstone like their father's."[48] Thus these advertisements created a classic metaphor whereby the sin of the father (in failing to protect his family adequately through life insurance) became a yoke born by his children.

Another article from 1863 even more explicitly detailed the fate of middle-class families "who have been delicately nurtured, unaccustomed to labor, and inexperienced in privation" upon the death of their main breadwinner: "The widow must take boarders; the daughters must seek employment as teachers; the sons must beg for subordinate positions in stores or workshops, or emigrate to the Far West." Despite their best efforts to maintain their middle-class status, they would inevitably fail: "Self-respect is seldom preserved; the destitute must solicit aid from friends, and this is but a euphemism for beggary." While the author callously declared that "poverty is not so great a hardship to those who have always been poor," the middle-class family was less adequately equipped to survive the challenges of such a destiny. Thus with a final literary flourish, the writer viscerally summarized the doom awaiting the uninsured household: "The poverty which comes suddenly after ease and affluence, not only blisters, but eats deeply into the flesh. It is a chronic smart, which too often gradually wears away the health both of body and mind."[49] As a result of the dominant economic role of fathers within the urban household, it was now their additional duty to shelter their families from the consequences (not only economic, but also psychological and physical) of an untimely death.

The Failure of Life Insurance to Fully
Protect Widows and Orphans

The anxiety created by the unpredictability of death was only compounded by the credit foundations of the economy and fluctuating economic fortunes. The antebellum economy was heavily dependent on credit networks. Businesses of all types and sizes relied on borrowing not only in the initial creation or later expansion of their firms but for day-to-day transactions as well; in Edward Balleisen's words, "they took on debt as purchasers and extended credit as sellers."[50] While this system operated reasonably well under normal circumstances, if debts were called in at inopportune times—such as during an economic panic or in the settlement of an estate—the effect on businessmen and their families could be devastating. In *Debtors and Creditors in America,* Peter Coleman estimates that "by the early nineteenth century one householder in every five would, during his working lifetime, fail outright rather than merely default on a particular debt."[51] In particular, the Panic of 1837 and the depression of 1839–43 had a significant long-term impact on middle-income urbanites, as the nominal value of commodities, land, and other assets fell by 40% under the deflationary pressures of the period.[52] "With these turns in the business cycle," historian Mary P. Ryan concludes, "many a loyal wife watched her economic security disintegrate in some financial wizardry that she scarcely understood."[53]

Whereas Americans had once assumed that failure was the result of a character flaw, this general economic downturn caused many Americans to question their personal responsibility in light of circumstances beyond their control. As Scott Sandage points out in *Born Losers: A History of Failure in America,* at a time when even honest, hardworking men were going into bankruptcy, some people began to place blame on the apparent shortcomings of the capitalist system itself. This changing attitude helped the new Whig majority in Congress win passage of the short-lived Bankruptcy Act of 1841, which enabled many American debtors to break free from their overwhelming debts and start their economic lives anew.[54]

In addition, numerous states enacted valuation and stay laws during periods of economic crisis to protect the property of debtors from being sold in distress sales. While colonial law had traditionally exempted certain items such as "essential clothing, bedding, furniture, eating utensils, and tools" from attachment by creditors in order to prevent the debtor and his family from being reduced to complete squalor (and thus becoming a burden on the community), early-nineteenth-century legislators began debating more general exemptions. In 1842, for example, the New York legislature enacted a bill that permitted families to select up to $150 worth of property to be exempt from the claims of creditors, in addition to the already existing list of enumerated household goods.[55]

Even these remedies left middle-income families vulnerable if the head of household died. What if death intervened before the bankruptcy proceedings were completed or before the person was able to reestablish himself in business? As one 1837 article on life insurance concluded, "The late and present pecuniary embarrassments of the mercantile world, and the consequent derangement in every thing connected with it, . . . show conclusively the necessity of making provision for dependents that shall be beyond the control of reverses in trade or commerce." In particular, this provision needed to take into account the possibility of death, "a contingency which, when it happens is irremediable—beyond which no recovery of disastrous step can be made."[56] The negative economic impact of death was always present, but panics and depressions served to underscore middle-class fears of failure and socioeconomic decline—the same fears that life insurance advertisements continued to highlight.

Unfortunately, an insurance policy could not always deliver the promised shelter from hardship. While their advertising literature touted the protection offered by an insurance policy for widows and orphans, a father could not guarantee that his family would benefit, since insurance payments were considered part of the deceased's estate. (This was in direct contrast to the law of dower, whereby—with the distinct exception of Pennsylvania—the rights of a woman to her dower came before the claims of any creditors.)[57] If the person named in a life insurance policy died in debt, creditors could claim the proceeds of the policy and leave the widow and children penniless.[58] This predicament might be avoided if a wife could take out a policy on the life of her husband, but women were legally barred from this remedy because of their inability to enter into legal contracts and the insurance industry's strict interpretation of the idea of insurable interest. Particularly during the depression years of 1839–43, policyholders became acutely aware of this problem, and the life insurance industry—led by NYL&T—spearheaded a legislative campaign to patch the holes in the insurance safety net.

The Changing Place of Women in the Household

As in colonial times, during the first half of the nineteenth century marriage fundamentally altered the legal status of a woman. Under the married condition of coverture, a woman sacrificed the rights and privileges she had enjoyed as an individual or *feme sole* in order to gain the protective cover of her husband as a *feme covert*. In its purest form, the woman "could neither sue nor be sued in her own name, she was limited in making contracts and wills, and all of her personal property as well as the management of her real property went to her husband."[59] In return, common law required that the husband provide adequate support for his wife and not leave her penniless when he died.[60] As Edward D. Mansfield outlined in his 1845 treatise *The Legal Rights, Liabilities and Duties of Women:* "As a general rule, the maintenance of the wife and of the entire family devolves upon the husband as head of the family. It is his *duty* legal and moral; and it is the corresponding *right* of the wife to demand it . . . The general rule is, that the husband is bound to provide his wife with necessaries *suitable to her situation and his condition in life.*"[61] Thus the husband was bound to provide a comfortable living for his wife during his lifetime and upon his death.

Yet both families and the court system also recognized that the ideal of coverture did not always reflect the reality of married life in early America; a woman sometimes needed additional protection against husbands who either intentionally shirked these duties or unintentionally placed the financial security of their families at risk. As early as the seventeenth century in England, courts recognized the right of a woman to protect property—either brought into the marriage or acquired through gift or inheritance during the marriage—through marriage settlements (antenuptial or postnuptial contracts) or trusts. In his *Commentaries on American Law,* Chancellor James Kent of the New York Court of Chancery noted that the purpose of these legal mechanisms was to shield a woman from "being overwhelmed by the misfortunes, or unkindness, or vices of her husband" and that trusts "usually proceed from the foresight of friends" or from "the warm and anxious affection of parents."[62]

These devices enabled the wife to maintain property separate from her husband's, which she could then use (depending on the terms of the contract) at her own discretion during the marriage, at the discretion of a trustee (who might or might not be her husband), or upon the death of her husband. Most important, this property was usually free from the claims of the husband's creditors. Thus some husbands actively sought to create marriage settlements to protect certain family assets from being used to pay off debts. However, most women did not take advantage of these legal loopholes because they were predicated on a woman's coming into possession of property independent of her husband. As historian Norma Basch concludes, the majority of women were "neither . . . sufficiently wealthy [n]or legally sophisticated to create a separate estate. Most wives continued to live with the harsh disabilities and limited rights of coverture."[63] Although Mississippi would pass the first married women's property act in 1839, it was not until 1848 with the passage of the married women's property act in New York that the property of married women was automatically kept separate from that of their husbands.[64] Yet even married women's property acts largely benefited wealthier women who were in possession of property when they entered into marriage.

Historians of married women's property acts trace their origins not to the emerging women's rights movement of the mid-nineteenth century but to changing economic conditions that created the ideal of separate spheres for men and women and simultaneously challenged the ability of middle-class families to maintain this ideal. With the family and home shifting from primarily being units of production to ones of consumption, the entire family economy was becoming dependent on the income of the principal male breadwinner.[65] This shift outside of the home did not merely represent an economic reorganization; rather, it allowed the creation of two separate spheres, one domestic (and female) and the other public (and male). Although always ultimately subject to the authority of her husband, the ideal middle-class woman was expected to exercise executive control over all matters relating to the home, while minimizing her contact with the public sphere.[66] Mid-nineteenth-century advice manuals often described what historians now call the resulting cult of domesticity:

> Woman is the presiding genius of home. These words, woman and home, are almost synonymous . . . Home should form the centre of a wife's affections, plans, and thoughts. She should view it as a little kingdom, in the ruling and managing of which, she must act the most important part, and assume the greatest responsibility—a kingdom which will altogether the most sensibly feel *her* influence, and which will exhibit such characteristics as she pleases to enstamp upon it. Home is the sphere in which woman can exhibit all the valuable traits of her nature . . . Is a wife economical, industrious, and tasty? In what place can she more visibly or more successfully display these qualities than at home? Is she ambitious? There is no ambition so worthy a woman, as that which prompts her to discharge faithfully and efficiently her duties as a wife, a mother, and the mistress of a household! . . . Let no wife despise this ambition . . . Home is the only proper theatre for the display of a wife's ambition.[67]

Thus the middle-class wife was expected to have complete control over all areas related to the governance of the household. The husband was responsible for providing the money necessary to maintain the home, but it was the wife's duty to exercise "industry, frugality, and economy"[68]—while still creating a respectable middle-class environment that adequately reflected their status and "ambition."

But even in its ideal form, the cult of domesticity could not completely remove the woman from the public realm. To fulfill her duties as the "genius of the home," the woman reentered the public sphere as the person who made the primary decisions about the family's consumption. In Mary Ryan's summation: "The female manager of the middle-class home . . . was expected to mediate between the family and the marketplace in a parsimonious but active manner, to consume enough to accommodate a growing commodity production and yet to save enough for the continuing accumulation of capital during this early period of industrialization."[69] In the day-to-day life of the ideal woman, this symbiotic relationship between the public and private spheres created a substantial gray area in which women became the targeted market segment for many businesses. In efficiently managing and maintaining the home, they became the main consumers in the marketplace.[70] Since insurance protected the sanctity of the household in the event of the death of the husband, the decision to procure a life policy likewise fell into this gray zone. Thus at the same time that life insurers were stressing the moral duty of the husband to obtain an insurance policy, they recognized the significant influence that the wife would have in reaching this decision.

Yet the wife still ultimately depended on her husband to make the final contract, and the benefit on the policy would still be liable to the claims of creditors. When one married couple applied to NYL&T for policies on each of their lives in 1833, Bard responded: "Mrs. Starr, a married woman, can not enter into a contract. I have therefore insured Mrs. Starrs Life in the name of her husband. This even is not good unless Mr. Starr has an interest in his wifes life, that is has an interest in property depending on her life. He can then insure her life to the amount of that interest."[71] Even if Mrs. Starr had been legally able to take out a policy on her husband's life, she likewise would have had to demonstrate an insurable interest in her husband's life. This would have required her to prove that she received a specific monetary benefit from his continued existence and that the death claim on the policy would in no way exceed this benefit and render her husband more valuable after his demise. Unfortunately, neither the wife's dependent status within the household nor her marital love and affection for her husband was adequate assurance that she had an interest in maximizing his longevity.

One way around this problem was for a husband to set up a trust for his wife or children whereby a certain sum of money would be deposited with the company (either in one lump sum or repeatedly over time) and held in trust until the occurrence of some specified contingency such as the death of the husband or father, the attainment of a certain age, or the marriage of a child. The main advantage of such a trust was "to afford the means to Parents & Husbands to secure to their Widows & Children the property they may leave without being liable to the debts of their Husbands or to the accidents which may befall them."[72] Almost all early American life insurance companies were chartered to conduct business in both trusts and life insurance (as well as endowments, annuities, etc.), and for many of these companies the trust side of the business far outperformed the insurance side, partially as a result of this advantage over life insurance. But trusts were effectively a type of savings account for the rich; the beneficiaries only received the sum of money deposited plus accumulated interest, furnishing no protection to those who could not afford to make a large initial outlay of money.

Another alternative was for a trustee to take out a life policy on the wife's behalf. One inquirer to Massachusetts Hospital Life was advised: "Making any sum payable to a wife gives her no right to it in case any creditors have a claim, in case of insolvency. This can be secured to her in no other way than having the insurance made by a Trustee for the use of a wife and children."[73] This arrangement proved to be rare, however, since the wife or children would still have to establish a specific pecuniary *risk-avoiding* interest in the life of the husband or father.

A third possibility was for the husband to take out the policy on his own life and assign his wife or children as the beneficiary. Yet this too was flawed, since the policy, being considered "a part of the personal property of the party who insures his life," could be claimed by any creditors of the insured. Bard informed one inquirer in 1834, "If he is . . . not a bankrupt at the time he insures he may assign the Policy as he may any part of his property for the benefit of his Wife, and if he pays down the insurance in one payment, Creditors cannot interfere in future." However, this option contained a substantial caveat: "But if at the time of making the payment he is a Bankrupt the assignment of the insurance is good for nothing. The policy is his Creditors."[74] Thus at the same time that American life insurance companies were trying to establish a reputation for themselves as the protectors of widows and orphans, the majority of women were legally barred from taking full advantage of this protection.

Protecting Widows and Orphans

Public demand for a remedy to this multifaceted dilemma did not pass unnoticed by the presidents of early American life insurance companies; they viewed it as one of the main stumbling blocks to the continued success of the industry. NYL&T thus spearheaded a campaign to pass a state law enabling women to procure life insurance policies protected from the claims of creditors. This episode provides a rare glimpse into the powerful influence of corporate interests on the crafting and passage of economic legislation designed to solve particular bottlenecks to growth.[75]

In early 1840, President Bard wrote to Gulian C. Verplanck, an influential member of the New York state senate (as well as a founding stockholder of NYL&T and a current member of its board of trustees), stressing the importance of passage of such a law—particularly during the ongoing depression. Bard noted, "The above is a draft of a law by Chancellor [*sic*] Kent" (former chief justice of the New York Supreme Court, chancellor of New York State, professor of law at Columbia College, as well as an incorporator and a current member of the board of trustees of NYL&T); he went on to say: "It is certainly a good one and more especially in the present times, where hundreds are ruined who were in good circumstances a few years since, and who now out of a salary or some little income would willingly see their wives and children secured against absolute want in case of their death." Bard was not merely pointing out a hypothetical situation but attempting to address the demands of potential policyholders. "The applications to this Office are frequent, but without a law, the board have lately determined a wife can not insure." A week later, Verplanck introduced the bill in question to the state senate.[76]

The proposed law fit perfectly with the professed image of the Whigs as "the party of commerce and credit, the party of progress, the party of collective striving by a republican body politic for economic growth and the equalization of opportunity."[77] The law would remove a major hurdle that insurance executives believed might dampen growth of this new industry, thus promoting the general economic expansion of the country by aiding an emerging commercial sector. It would also address other issues of importance for the Whigs, including the removal of shackles restraining economic growth. Like the federal Bankruptcy Act of 1841, which, in the words of one historian, "release[ed] the economic energies of honest debtors through legal discharges from past debts,"[78] the proposed law would allow the families of debtors to emerge from the settlement of an estate with adequate means for continued participation in the economy.

Thomas Herttell's argument to the New York state legislature for the passage of a married women's property act in 1837 could just as easily have been in favor of the 1840 life insurance law:

Daughters not being so liable to be empoverished, would not so frequently as now, be thrown back, with their increased and suffering offspring, as paupers depending for subsistence on the charity and benevolence of their sympathizing and sorrowing parents and friends;—and who would in many instances, as a necessary consequence, be exempted from the trouble and expense of such domestic revulsions . . . It would serve or assist to maintain the family;—to keep them together—and to sustain their standing and respectability in society. It would serve or assist to prevent pauperism and save the public from the burden and expense of supporting many unfortunate and distressed females. It would serve or assist to educate the children, to prevent their being reared in gross ignorance, to lessen the chances and inducements to associate with bad company, to acquire vicious habits, and to become thereby irreclaimably debased.[79]

Enabling middle-class families to maintain their respectable status and comfortable livelihood would reduce pauperism and crime, and charitable donations and tax-payer funds could be conserved for more pressing needs. Households could maintain their consumption of goods and services and provide young males with the education necessary to become productive economic actors in the future. Herttell's language was identical to the marketing literature employed by life insurance companies in promoting their product.

Chancellor Kent's proposed law, which smoothly passed the New York state legislature on April 1, 1840,[80] addressed three important issues. First, it established the right of a woman to enter into a contract of insurance on the life of her husband "by herself and in her name, or in the name of any third person, with his assent, as her trustee." Whereas the courts had previously upheld the legality of the contracts of a married woman in specific instances—such as when acting in the name of her husband when he was away on business, or when acquiring necessities for the operation of the household—this was the first time married women were given blanket legal authority to enter into certain contracts without the express authority of their husbands.[81]

Second, it provided that insurance benefits paid to a widow would be "free from the claims of the representatives of her husband, or of any of his creditors" unless the annual premiums on the policy exceeded $300. This clause was very generous for the time. Whereas the New York State Exempted Property Law of 1842 allowed bankrupts to retain just $150 of their property, this law permitted beneficiaries to retain proceeds from as much life insurance as could be purchased with twice that amount. In 1840, a $300 annual premium would purchase a policy worth approximately $12,700 on the life of a person first insured at age 30, $9,375 on the life of a person first insured at age 40, or $6,700 on the life of a person first insured at age 50.[82] This would be more than adequate to sustain most middle-class households for several years.[83] Thus with a life insurance policy, a middle-class husband could support the livelihood of his wife and family—carrying out his legal and moral duty as provider—from beyond the grave. His wife would not be forced into poverty, forced to leave the domestic sphere in search of work, or forced to find a new husband. And by giving preference to wives in taking out such policies, the legislature was in effect empowering women to lay claim to this domestic space. Therefore one of the unintended consequences of the legislation was the greater financial autonomy granted to widows.

Finally, as the law was interpreted, wives were not required to "make proof of interest," legally establishing for the first time an instance of insurable interest independent of a specific pecuniary interest in the life of another. This was upheld by several court rulings in the ensuing decades, culminating in the 1881 case of *Brummer v. Cohn,* which declared: "The pecuniary interest of a wife in her husband's life is incapable of exact measurement. The insurer, by issuing a policy to the wife, agrees that her interest is at least equal to the sum insured, and the policy is in the nature of a valued policy, and the full amount insured is recoverable in case of death, without proof of actual damages."[84] The legislature was thus validating the concept of separate spheres. Wives, by definition, were economic dependents of their husbands, rendering a woman's additional proof of interest in her husband's life unnecessary.

A week after the law's passage, Bard sent a letter to Francis F. Smith, NYL&T's Baltimore agent, informing him of the new legislation and requesting that he advertise the law in some Baltimore papers. By December 1841, Maryland had enacted an identical law—copied word for word from the New York statute. The Massachusetts legislation of 1844 went one step further by protecting from the claims of creditors all policies procured "for the benefit of a married woman, whether effected by her, her husband, or any other person," while the Tennessee act of 1846 affirmatively declared "that any husband may effect a life insurance on his own life, and the same shall in all cases enure to the benefit of his widow and heirs . . . without being in any manner subject to the debts of said husband." The 1851 New Jersey law was the least liberal, limiting annual premiums to only $100.[85]

At the same time that states were passing discriminatory legislation to protect in-state insurers, some of these companies still found themselves at a competitive disadvantage with firms chartered in states permitting women to insure. Thus in states where a general law like New York's did not exist, new companies often had the provisions of the New York law inserted into their charter, and those provisions were upheld by the state courts. For example, the charters of Connecticut Mutual Life (chartered 1846); Pennsylvania Mutual Life (1847); North Carolina Mutual Life (1849); Charter Oak Life of Hartford, Connecticut (1850); United States Life Insurance, Annuity, and Trust of Philadelphia (1850); National Life of Vermont (1850); and Jefferson Life of Cincinnati, Ohio (1850), all included such protections despite the silence of their respective states' legislatures on these issues. As late as 1869, companies were still advertising these advantages as prominent features of their policies. For example, International Life Insurance and Trust of New Jersey (1868) declared that its charter permitted insurance on husbands without the $100 limitation of the New Jersey law.[86]

Widow protection legislation applied to all policies written by companies chartered in the state in which it was passed, even when policyholders resided out of state. Dr. Beverly R. Wellford, agent for Baltimore Life in Fredericksburg, Virginia, wrote to the company in 1842 on behalf of the widow of a policyholder named Fayette Johnston. Although Johnston's policy was made payable to his wife, Wellford "fear[ed]" an effort on the part of some of his creditors to divert the payment from the course provided in the policy." He requested that the company pay the claim as quickly as possible—before the creditors realized the existence of the policy: "These suggestions . . . are made because I am anxious that no difficulty occur not only on Mrs. J[ohnston]'s account, but as others are similarly situated it would of course operate against this mode of making provision for families and to great extent against insurance on lives." Baltimore Life, however, remained unconcerned, as President Donaldson responded: "I do not think that any difficulty can occur respecting the payment of the money to the widow . . . There is an act of our Legislature authorising wives to insure the lives of their husbands. I thought that I had sent you a Copy." Although Johnston's policy "was not made strictly under this act" since the Maryland law only specifically covered policies taken out by the wife or by a trustee for her benefit (in contrast with the Massachusetts or Tennessee legislation, which protected wives as beneficiaries even when the policy was in the husband's name), Baltimore Life remained confident that Mrs. Johnston was protected under the spirit of the law.[87]

These new laws proved to be a boon for companies. NYL&T sold more policies during 1840 than any other year of its existence. On February 1, 1841, Bard wrote to Senator Verplanck thanking him for his help in securing the legislation, and noting: "It has operated most beneficially and been received favorably by the public. We have made between one and two hundred such insurances since the law was passed." Several existing policyholders wrote to the company asking to change their policies to conform with the new law; husbands who had taken out policies on their own lives for the benefit of their wives and children now wanted the policies to be in their wives' names (making the wife the owner of the policy rather than the assignee). And Mrs. Starr, the woman rejected for insurance by NYL&T in 1833 because she was a married woman (along with many other similarly situated women), was now able to secure an $8,000 policy on the life of her husband, commencing September 1, 1840.[88]

Baltimore Life likewise benefited from passage of this new law. Whereas only 0.3% of nonslave[89] policies had been taken out by women on the lives of their husbands between the company's inception in 1831 and the passage of Maryland's law at the end of 1840, over 18% of policies written by the company from 1841 through its closing in 1867 were on the lives of husbands (and in a handful of cases, on the lives of fathers for their children). These policies were generally much more lucrative to the company than other types of policies, in part because wives insured their husbands for a longer period of time than the average policyholder. While one-quarter of Baltimore Life policies taken out by wives between 1841 and 1867 were for the whole term of life (as opposed to cheaper term policies, which were written for a fixed amount of time—usually one or seven years), less than 11% of the remaining policies written were whole life. Even among term policies, the average time insured was 5.2 years for policies on husbands, compared with 4.4 years on other policies. The dollar value of these policies was also much greater than that of other policies. The average Baltimore Life policy taken out by a wife had a death claim of approximately $3,024, 50% higher than the $2,020 average on other nonslave policies.[90]

Approximately one-third of the husbands insured by their wives with Baltimore Life previously held a policy on their own life with the same company, but many of these were cancelled in favor of new policies that specifically met the stipulations of the law. For example, William Price Stewart of Norfolk, Virginia, who had held a $5,000 whole life policy on himself since 1838, wrote to the company in 1845 inquiring how he could guarantee that the payment would be made for the benefit of his wife and children. The company secretary replied that a "better mode for you to secure the proceeds of your Policy to your wife & children will be to have a new policy in the name of your wife which this office is expressly authorized to do by an Act of our Legislature. You can have this policy payable either to your wife and her heirs or assigns or to her and her children or any of them who you may designate."[91] Within a few months, Sarah Stewart had taken out a new $5,000 whole life policy with Baltimore Life, payable upon the death of her husband William.[92]

Since the Massachusetts law shielded wives from the claims of creditors even when the policy was contracted by the husband, wives were less likely to acquire policies from New England Mutual Life. Instead, to invoke the protection of the law, the beneficiary (especially in the case of in-state applicants) would often be listed as either "wife if she survive him, otherwise surviving children and the representatives of any deceased children" or "wife if she survive him, otherwise heirs and representatives." Whereas more than half of all policyholders with New England Mutual resided in Massachusetts, in-state residents only accounted for one-fifth of the policies contracted for by wives. In contrast, it was much more common for out-of-state wives—particularly those from New York, where the law required the policy to be in the name of the wife—to apply themselves for insurance on their spouses. New Yorkers held 12% of all New England Mutual policies but accounted for 43% of the policies taken out by wives.[93]

Companies located in states with widow protection laws promoted the fact in their marketing campaigns. Institutions such as Mutual Life of New York, Nautilus

Insurance Company (later renamed New York Life), and Mutual Life of Baltimore published the text of the applicable law in full in their brochures during the 1840s and 1850s. New England Mutual Life of Massachusetts advertised in 1855, "Insurance may be effected for the benefit of a married woman beyond the reach of her husband's creditors"; the same year Knickerbocker Life of New York declared, "Married Ladies may insure the lives of their husbands according to a Law of this State, beyond the reach of their husband's creditors." Stories of mortgages being foreclosed and widows and orphans being thrown out of their homes upon the death of their breadwinner began to fill the advertising literature. Among examples of families who had benefited from a life policy, Mutual Life of Baltimore recounted the tale of a businessman sailing for Europe. His wife had "advised him to effect an insurance," but he did not perceive "the advantage of such a provision." "Knowing how much their property would suffer by his loss," the wife took it upon herself to apply for the policy. Of course, the husband met his demise on this journey, and the family was saved from "serious inconvenience" thanks to the wife's forethought.[94]

New York and Massachusetts companies in particular tried to use the existence of their states' laws as a competitive edge to extend their business into other states and limit competition from out-of-state companies in their own states. In its 1848 brochure, Nautilus Insurance maintained:

> This liberal law exists but in two or three other States of the Union, and is not to be found on the statute books of any country in Europe. Now, as corporate associations are everywhere subject to local law, it follows, that upon the death of a person, whose life is insured with a company located where no such law exists, any creditor living there or elsewhere, may legally overreach the claims of the family, for whose benefit the insurance was intended, and by intercepting the amount insured, leave them in utter destitution. [95]

New England Mutual stressed that "policies issued for the benefit of widows and orphans" were only "by the Laws of Massachusetts and New York, protected from the Husband's Creditors."[96] Although in practice the assumption of a wife's insurable interest in the life of her husband was upheld by most state courts after passage of the New York law—particularly when it was included in the company's charter provision—companies in states with widow protection legislation continued to tout the legal advantages in their advertising campaigns throughout the 1850s and 1860s.

With these laws, pecuniary interest, which had been at the very heart of insurable interest, became merely a subset of it. And once women were granted the right to insure the lives of their husbands without needing to prove direct monetary interest, it was only a matter of time before other family members sought the same protection. As soon as February 1841, NYL&T was again lobbying the New York state legislature for an expansion of the law to allow children to procure policies. Although the 1840 law included a provision "that in case of the death of the wife before the decease of her husband, the amount of the Insurance may be made payable after her death to her children," the wife (and not the children) was required to initiate the policy. Writing once more to Verplanck, Bard told the story of "a gentleman [who] has been in the Office enquiring whether, he a widower could not be insured by his children for their benefit." Bard was vexed to have had to inform the man that "as the Law stands he cannot." This was only the most recent instance of "the desire that infant children might be authorized to insure their parent" that had "been so frequently expressed," and Bard hoped "that the law might be amended in this particular so warmly urged."[97] While widows who needed to provide for children were the most visible victims of a husband's death, a smaller number of motherless orphans were just as vulnerable to the loss of their fathers.

Although the New York state legislature did not act upon this particular request, in practice companies and courts gradually expanded their interpretation of nonmonetary insurable interest to include the interest of a husband in the life of his wife,[98] a woman in the life of her fiancé,[99] a parent in the life of a child or a child in the life of a parent,[100] and even a woman in the life of her ex-husband (particularly when there existed children for whom she needed to provide).[101] The interest of a sibling in the life of another sibling when one was dependent on the other for support, originally decided in the 1815 case of *Lord v. Dall,* was also reaffirmed.[102]

Companies believed that the expansion of insurable interest to other family members would substantially raise the profile of life insurance in America, establish its reputation as a socially beneficial institution, and consequently, greatly increase the number of policies sold without undermining the basic soundness of the industry. And by providing security for middle-income families, life insurance enabled urban fathers to take greater economic risks; they could now pursue entrepreneurial opportunities without risking the livelihood and status of their families if death intervened before their business aspirations succeeded. Not all supported the liberalization of insurable interest, however. The Insurance Commissioners of Massachusetts, in their Ninth Annual Report (1864), deplored such changes as an "awkward and uncomely piece of gambling," contending that "if the life of a husband or father contributes nothing, in a pecuniary way, to the maintenance of the wife or the children, it is not justly insurable for their benefit, no matter how great the loss of his life might be to them in point of love."[103]

Despite this warning, the courts continued to support the interest of a person in the life of a relative by blood or marriage. All of these instances were affirmed by the Supreme Court of the United States in the 1881 case of *Warnock v. Davis* when Justice Field stated: "It is not necessary that the expectation of advantage or benefit should be always capable of pecuniary estimation . . . The natural affection in cases of this kind is considered as more powerful—as operating more efficaciously—to protect the life of the insured than any other consideration."[104] Whereas "affection" was repeatedly deemed inadequate in demonstrating insurable interest during the 1830s, by the 1880s the courts had ruled that affection was a better determinant of risk-avoiding interest in the life of another than pecuniary dependence. The industry universally accepted this interpretation as providing the best balance between public reputation and actuarial stability.

The Sentimental Novel

Coincident with the development of the modern life insurance industry was the emergence of fiction written for women, by women, and about women. Targeted at a middle-class audience, these works almost invariably tell either the rags-to-riches story of an orphan girl overcoming her economic plight through the superior moral nature of her character or the riches-to-rags story of a woman struggling to regain her position in the middle class after the death or financial failure of her male provider. Although such novels in no way attempt to challenge accepted gender roles, they do portray women as active agents capable of controlling and molding their emotional and economic destinies from within the domestic sphere. Echoing the argument of many moral reformers of the period that class status based on material wealth was fleeting while social standing based on morality was more durable, these works typically culminate with the establishment of a stable, happy middle-class household built on the firm foundation of the honesty, goodness, and ethical forthrightness of its female members.[105]

Life insurance advertising literature adopted this literary movement for its own purposes, tapping into the same very real middle-class fears of economic decline. The growing separation of public and private spheres placed the wife in a position of complete economic dependence but left her long-term monetary security in question. Just as in these works of fiction, women were portrayed in insurance advertising as the innocent victims of the economic failures and shortsightedness of the male heads of household. As the Panic of 1837 and the depression of 1839–43 demonstrated, the income of the main breadwinner could be lost in a general economic downturn through his own personal business failure or by his death. It was the latter contingency that life insurance intended to address. The industry was attempting to establish its product as one of the necessities of life for the emerging middle class, mitigating against this more modern face of death.

While life insurance literature encouraged men to save their families from economic decline through the purchase of a policy—a heroic position that women's fiction never assigned to men—it left open the possibility that wives could play the role of heroine. The lobbying efforts of the life insurance companies for legislation to allow women to purchase policies demonstrated their recognition of the central role played by women in both the consumptive and economic decisions of the household. (Men supported this moderate expansion of the rights of women because it allowed the paternalism of the husband to extend from beyond the grave.) The industry was willing to compromise its strict regulations regarding taking out an insurance policy on someone else's life in order to tap into this market. By expanding the rights of women—giving them the power to contract for insurance on their husband's lives—the industry was helping to preserve this domestic ideal. A woman could now prepare for her own widowhood, ensuring her ability to remain nestled in the private sphere and shielded from the hardships that were unbecoming for a proper middle-class wife. Like the married women's property acts passed later in the decade, the life insurance legislation of 1840 was an attempt to preserve the concept of separate spheres, even as they both revealed chinks in the armor of this ideal.

CHAPTER 6

Targeting the Aspirations of an Emerging Middle Class

The Triumph of Mutual Life Insurance Companies

In all branches of business, whether manufacturing, commercial, or agricultural, success depends upon a variety of contingent circumstances. A man may profit by his investment, or he may lose . . . The caprice of fortune rules despotically over all branches of business . . . All other risks are uncertain, even after many years. But the cessation of life is certain; death is sure to come . . . But there are other considerations in Life Insurance, aside from the stipulated sum for which each one insures, viz: the accumulations. All money paid in, except what is necessary to meet current expenses and losses, is invested . . . These investments, of course, are drawing interest, which interest is again reloaned, making an investment at compound interest. These interests are an accumulation to the benefit of the company, which in a few years, in a successful one, whose expenses are proportionate to their business, amounts to a large sum . . . All accumulations above losses and expenses, in proprietary or stock companies, go to the stockholders; but in the mutual companies, they are divided equally among the life members, in proportion to the amount of their respective premiums . . . Every one . . . should effect an insurance upon his life . . . because they cannot invest their funds in a more sure and profitable manner, with a greater certainty of a safe return, with interest, than in Life Insurance.[1]

All antebellum life insurers recognized that the value of the sentimental appeal was limited. While middle-income fathers feared the fate that would befall their families in the event of their untimely death, many preferred to suppress rather than directly address these anxieties; death, after all, is not a topic upon which most people care to dwell. Additionally, insurance firms recognized that the middle-class *mentalité* comprised not just the fear of failure and the potential for socioeconomic decline. These concerns were coupled with a much more optimistic belief that families could improve upon their economic condition and ultimately send their children into the world with even more secure prospects. Thus New York Life's 1858 lament regarding the horrific plight of widows and orphans upon the death of their uninsured breadwinner ran side by side with a more sedate, businesslike analysis of the benefits of life insurance for an aspiring middle class. Life insurance companies attempted to market themselves as the answer to both sides of this *mentalité:* removing the high risk attendant on premature death as well as providing investment opportunities during a policyholder's lifetime.

The salaried and professional men of the early nineteenth century understood the many "contingent circumstances" upon which their "success depend[ed]." Obtaining an education, setting up a proper middle-class home, or starting a small business required an initial outlay of funds that many did not possess—although they might be confident they could repay these expenses in the future through their vocational exertions. One of President Bard's examples in his 1832 *A Letter to David Evans* was of a man "desirous of entering upon a hazardous enterprise" that had "a fair prospect of improving his circumstances, but . . . require[d] his personal skill and attention."[2] For these men, whose future wealth depended on their own human capital, a life policy provided critical loan collateral as well as protection for their families should they die before achieving their goal. By securing their current class status against the ultimate risk of death, life insurance allowed them to pursue greater risks in the present in hopes of bettering their class status in the future.

Insurance companies considered these "contingent circumstances" when crafting their policy terms. Through flexible payment schedules, reimbursement of cash surrender values, provision of loans against the value of the policy, and acceptance of premium notes (purchasing insurance partially on credit), firms responded to the economic capabilities and needs of their middle-class clientele. As Bard promised in his lengthy letter, a policyholder could surrender his insurance for a "fair" cash payment: "After a number of years, the policy becomes of value to the insured; it is a part of his property."[3]

Likewise, an insurance policy could remove the "caprices of fortune" that rendered investing risky. Bard suggested that debtors should take out policies for use as loan collateral, those with mortgages to protect against foreclosure, creditors on the lives of their debtors "to secure the eventual payment of doubtful debts," and parents to "secure the return of money paid for education, apprenticeship, capital embarked in business, or other advances made for children, in the event of their premature death."[4] In each of these cases, an insurance policy could make the transaction or investment more secure. Even the risks associated with the purchase of slaves could be reduced through life insurance.

But life companies also marketed the insurance policy itself as a "sure and profitable" investment—an idea that was particularly appealing to middle-class Americans. While people in this group relied on a stable income for survival (like the working class), they also possessed some discretionary funds beyond the requirements for mere subsistence (like the upper class). Yet the investment options in antebellum America were largely unavailable to this group. Stocks and bonds were limited to those with significant resources beyond the means of the middle class, while savings banks catered to those hoping to invest extremely small amounts—particularly as states began passing laws to restrict the total dollar amount of deposits and the occupations of depositors. Indeed, throughout the antebellum period, life firms tried to capitalize on the popularity of these latter financial institutions by touting insurance as "the 'Savings Bank' of the middling and more opulent classes of society."[5]

This focus on life insurance as the ultimate middle-class investment only came to full fruition with the advent of the mutual companies in the 1840s. By cleverly employing loaded terms such as *profit, dividend, accumulated interest,* and *investment income,* the mutuals made middle-income Americans feel that they, too, could participate in the elite world of high finance—in effect buying shares in the company with each premium payment. At the same time, mutual firms assured them that this was one investment with "certainty of a safe return." Providing a profitable outlet for their discretionary funds and the opportunity to improve upon their class status (while still protecting their families against the consequences of a premature death), this inducement to insure was extremely attractive to middle-income city dwellers and gave the newly formed mutual companies a marketing edge over their more-established competitors, enabling them to quickly surpass the stock companies in sales by the middle of the 1840s.

Marketing to Middle-Class Needs and Desires

The numerous morality tales that pervaded life insurance literature served as a means of dramatically gaining the attention of potential clients, but it was company strategies and procedures that eventually concentrated sales within the emerging middle class. Initially, firms unintentionally restricted the appeal of insurance to middle-income individuals by limiting the maximum size of policies—a conservative financial decision designed to protect companies from large draws on their reserves. But as the antebellum period progressed, insurers became much more deliberate in their efforts to provide incentives specifically aimed at the middle class. They recognized that while emotional appeals might open the door, practical features ultimately sold the policy.

Limiting Policy Amounts

Before engaging in the sale of life policies in the early 1820s, Massachusetts Hospital Life interviewed officers of competing life companies to determine the best mode of operation. Union Insurance Company of New York had been chartered in 1818 to sell both life and marine policies but soon abandoned its life business. Its former actuary, James Renwick, advised Massachusetts Hospital Life's representative: "The greatest mistake the company made was in their insurance upon lives, taking too much on one risk, $10,000, before the office had got fairly into operation, and particularly in taking such sums on persons bound to sea or to the Southern States."[6] Pennsylvania Company concurred, telling Massachusetts Hospital Life in a similar interview that among the biggest errors made when the firm began business was "taking rather too large sums on assurances on single lives, particularly on those bound on foreign voyages." Whereas Pennsylvania Company had initially insured for sums up to $15,000,[7] by the early 1820s its maximum had been reduced to $7,000,[8] and Mechanic Life Insurance and Coal Company disclosed to Massachusetts Hospital Life that it had lowered its maximum policy size from $5,000 to $3,000.[9] These early companies learned quickly that fiscal soundness depended not only on spreading sales over a wide customer base but also on making sure that the deaths of a few policyholders would not significantly deplete their still-limited reserve funds.

As a result of the negative experiences of these early insurers, most companies restricted the amount permitted on any single policy. Massachusetts Hospital Life and Baltimore Life rarely sold policies over $5,000, but New York Life and Trust, which began business with a similar $5,000 limit, decided in 1833 that it was large enough to safely raise this restriction: "We found so many desirous of insuring $10,000 that as our numbers had increased to 300 and over we determined to go as high as $10,000 in the Northern and Eastern States but in the Southern we decline an Insurance over $5000."[10] To capture the business of wealthier southerners, Baltimore Life and NYL&T agreed in 1835 to insure southerners for up to $10,000 by splitting the risk between them.[11] In 1837 Baltimore Life reached a similar agreement with Girard Life, although the latter company would raise its own maximum to $10,000 by 1860.[12] By the 1840s, most new companies, including Mutual Life of New York, Mutual Life of Baltimore, Nautilus (New York Life), and New England Mutual, were opening their doors with limits of $10,000,[13] though a few, such as Connecticut Mutual and Mutual Benefit of New Jersey, still capped policies at $5,000.[14] The New York branch of Albion Life of London even went as high as $15,000 by 1845.[15]

Despite these accommodations for wealthier customers, small policies remained the most commonly sold during the antebellum period; between half and three-quarters of all policies written by NYL&T, New England Mutual Life, Baltimore Life (excluding slave policies), and Massachusetts Hospital Life were for amounts less than $2,000. Fewer than one-quarter of policyholders chose to maximize their policy at $5,000 or more. Thus even when given the option of purchasing a larger policy, antebellum applicants overwhelming requested more modest protection, reflecting the middle-income status of a clientele for whom larger premium payments would have been too great a strain.

Payment Schedules

In a more conscious effort to appeal to the middle class, companies also discussed changing their contract terms to accommodate this group's ability to pay. As early as 1837, Girard Life allowed premiums to be paid either annually "or in smaller weekly or monthly amounts,"[16] while Baltimore Life accepted semiannual, quarterly, or monthly payments in order "to extend more widely the benefit of Life Insurance."[17] Only about 5% of policyholders with the latter company selected these more lenient terms during the 1830s and 1840s, but by the 1850s approximately 30% of people insured with Baltimore Life paid their premiums semiannually or quarterly.[18]

In an 1842 letter to John Finlaison, actuary of the National Debt Office in Great Britain, William Bard solicited his opinion as to whether more lenient terms for premium payments "would be beneficial to the public, especially to the middle classes." Citing the difficulty of putting aside money for the annual premium among people "who have not firmness enough to save out of their small earnings . . . but who would do so, if the payments were monthly," Bard predicted "it would vastly increase the life insurance part of our business."[19] NYL&T eventually adopted this proposal in 1846, charging an extra 2½% on the premium for the convenience of making payments semiannually and 4% for those made quarterly.[20] Other companies such as New York Life, Philadelphia Life, Mutual of New York, Mutual of Baltimore, and New England Mutual also allowed semiannual or quarterly payments, usually with the addition of an interest charge.[21] As New England Mutual declared, this policy was "for the convenience of Mechanics, Clerks, and men of moderate means."[22]

Life Insurance as Loan Collateral

Life firms also targeted middle-income consumers by marketing insurance as a service that would help them climb the socioeconomic ladder. The most prevalent proposal was the idea of obtaining a life insurance policy for use as collateral on a loan; this was put forth as early as 1832 in William Bard's *A Letter to David E. Evans:* "An individual wishes to go into business. He has friends, who, having confidence in his skill, industry, and integrity, are willing to advance him money, but knowing the uncertainty of life, fear, if he should die, they would lose their money." Neither the honesty, nor the diligence, nor the prospects for success of this individual were in doubt; the only questionable factor was his ultimate longevity. President Bard suggested that a life insurance policy for the amount of the loan—either taken out by the lenders directly or assigned to the lenders by the insured—would remove this last remaining risk.[23]

As the industry matured, companies became more elaborate and specific in their descriptions of the need for such collateral:

> A young man of twenty-one years of age, of good capacity and habits, wishes to complete his professional education, the expense of which will amount to $600 . . . An enterprising young merchant, of the age of twenty-five years, without capital, depends upon a credit of $5,000 for the means of commencing business with favorable prospects, and the main obstacle to his obtaining that credit, is the uncertainty of life . . . a skillful, industrious mechanic, of the age of twenty-five years, needs a stock of tools or materials, to the amount of $400, to commence business, which he can obtain only on credit . . . a farmer, of the age of twenty-three, wishes to settle upon a tract of wild land, which he can convert into a valuable, cultivated farm, in the course of seven years, but needs an addition of $200 to his capital for this purpose.[24]

The suggested solution for each of these dilemmas was the use of a life insurance policy to remove the risk of the loan. The people described were all aspiring young men with solid prospects and only the highest chances of success—if only they could acquire some crucial seed money. With the exception of the merchant, the sums required were small yet still unobtainable for a young upstart lacking collateral. The most valuable asset of these social climbers was their own human capital, which they could tap only through the use of an insurance policy.

Some companies took this idea further, agreeing to issue the policy and then to act as the creditor providing a loan to the insured (using the policy as collateral). Baltimore Life found that this business plan was especially attractive among the burgeoning military and bureaucratic workforce of the nation's capital. In the autumn of 1831, the company began mailing advertising literature to potential customers in Washington stating that "a person having an estate for his own life may borrow money on such estate by having his life insured . . . A salaried officer may affect a loan in the same manner."[25] Several individuals immediately wrote to Baltimore Life requesting additional information on this type of loan. Thomas Mustin, for example, explained that he was a salaried officer seeking to borrow $1,500, "including the interest at the rate of $400," to pay off his debts. Secured by a life insurance policy, he intended to repay the loan "in instalments, either quarterly or semi annually as may be preferred, out of my salary as a clerk in one of the public offices here, on drafts duly accepted by the Paymaster of the Office in which I am employed."[26] In another letter Mustin went on to suggest that there were numerous "officers of the government, who are obliged to borrow money from month to month, on their salaries for which they pay a heavy interest who would rejoice to make an arrangement similar to the one I propose in order to be relieved."[27] Analogous to modern debt consolidation loans, Mustin's suggestion would have allowed salaried men to pay off their existing high-interest obligations with a much lower-interest loan from Baltimore Life—using their own life as collateral.

Although Mustin did take out several life insurance policies with the company, he never received his desired loan; he was not the type of salaried officer to whom Baltimore Life sought to provide this service. To limit its own risk in advancing such money, the company would only make such loans to bureaucrats with a high degree of job security—those whose positions were "not Dependent upon political or other contingencies."[28] Since regular payment of the insurance premiums, loan interest, and principal would only be guaranteed through the direct garnishment of wages by the paymaster, solely those men with solid long-term employment prospects would qualify.

While this initial attempt to provide loans through life insurance never took off, the idea was reproposed by James H. Causten in 1833. Less than a month after being appointed the company's agent in Washington, he was furnishing Baltimore Life's president with ideas on how to increase sales to federal employees through the creation of a loan program. Causten had been "requested by several officers of the Departments, who are desirous to obtain loans on policies on their own lives," to ask if the company would underwrite such claims—using the "policy as collateral security." To facilitate the payment of these loans, Causten suggested (as Mustin had previously) that they would endorse "drafts upon the paymaster of their Department . . . payable quarterly out of their serving salary"—meaning that their wages would be garnished by Baltimore Life to automatically pay back the loan. "If the Company would do business of this kind," Causten suggested, "I have reason to believe that from fifty to one hundred applications would be made almost forthwith."[29] With his office located "directly opposite to the Department of State," Causten was uniquely positioned to tap into this potential market.[30]

Baltimore Life initially accepted this payment system for loans to their life insurance customers, making arrangements with a variety of federal departments for direct deductions from the salaries of the debtors on a monthly basis. In this system, the person insured would fill out a series of monthly allotment tickets—signed, dated, and made out to Baltimore Life Insurance Company or its Washington agent—for the amount of life insurance premium, principal, and interest agreed upon. The entire series of these tickets would then be recorded with the applicant's paying department and presented to Baltimore Life's Washington agent to guarantee payment.[31] Causten believed that these "drafts in anticipation" were a crucial means of preventing defaults on the loans, particularly since he viewed the officers most interested in taking out such loans as potentially "improvident and reckless of consequences."[32]

The Navy Department agreed to this program, and naval officers of all ranks—including department clerks, midshipmen, pursers, lieutenants, commanders, colonels, captains, and navy surgeons—acquired life insurance policies and loans in this manner.[33] The compliance of the navy paymasters in the allotment system was essential because officers serving on ships for months or years at a time would have no other means of making monthly premium and loan payments. Although naval officers were the main solicitors of life insurance loans from Baltimore Life, federal employees from throughout the bureaucracy applied to the firm for this privilege. While other departments were less liberal in allowing such payroll deductions, the military code of conduct was assumed to provide some measure of assurance. For example, when Lieutenant Charles B. Chalmers requested a loan, Causten wrote that "the War Dept does not accept or record such tickets" but that Chalmers could present the company with his own personal "accounts receipted, which are duly paid when presented monthly, as a false step of the officer issuing such a ticket would forfeit his commission, so there is safety in taking it."[34] In practice, the company preferred military personnel over other bureaucrats for such loans not only because of the code of conduct but also because their terms of employment were the most predictable.

By the 1840s, Baltimore Life had begun reconsidering these loans through life insurance policies, as some loopholes began appearing for debtors to renege on their obligations. The main incident involved a naval lieutenant named Richard W. Meade. Meade had initially obtained an insurance policy and loan from Baltimore Life in 1839, using allotment tickets to pay it off by 1841, at which time the company agreed to a new two-year loan under similar terms. However, by 1842 Meade was seeking protection from his creditors under the 1841 bankruptcy law "and immediately wrote a letter to the Navy agent to stop the allotment under the pretence that the Bankrupt Law operates as an assignment on all his effects." Disappointed in its reliance "upon what we thought the honor of an officer of the Navy," Baltimore Life fought this decision, although the firm was eventually forced to drop its case and abandon the claim.[35] The company then temporarily suspended such sales, informing one naval officer: "The decision of the Auditor that they [allotment tickets] may be cancelled at pleasure, and the conduct of some members of your profession in taking advantage of that decission [*sic*], are sufficient reasons for our course."[36] Although it would continue selling these policies for several more years, the firm was much more cautious in accepting applicants; most later policies of this sort were on officers who had successfully conducted business with Baltimore Life in the past and merely wished to renew their policies. By the end of the 1840s, the company would cease this program altogether.

While Baltimore Life sales certainly benefited from this practice (with loans through life insurance packages accounting for approximately 5% of nonslave policy sales between 1834 and 1848), it was undoubtedly a risky undertaking. When a life insurance policy was used as collateral in a normal debtor/creditor relationship, the risks were balanced between three different parties. The insurance policy provided the debtor with a source of collateral that he would not otherwise have possessed, guaranteeing the payment of the obligation to the creditor (through the death claim) should the debtor die before fulfilling his contract. Of course, this did not remove all risk for the creditor. If the debtor held the policy on himself, with the creditor as the beneficiary, the debtor could theoretically allow that policy to lapse at any time—thereby rendering the collateral useless. On the other hand, if the creditor purchased the policy on the life of the debtor, the former would be required to continue paying premiums for as long as the debt was outstanding; if the debtor was delinquent in paying his obligations—and yet lived for a long time—the premium payments might surpass the value of the debt itself. As the third party in this relationship, the insurance firm incurred the risk of the debtor dying young, but it would benefit from either a long-lived debtor or one who was prompt in repaying his obligation (which would terminate the policy without the payment of a death claim).

In the plan adopted by Baltimore Life, this three-party relationship was reduced to a traditional debtor/creditor relationship. While the firm gained a policyholder, the insurance did nothing to secure the debt. If the debtor died young, the company lost both the principal and interest on the loan as well as the continued revenue stream of the premiums. (By paying the death claim to itself, Baltimore Life would neither gain nor lose on the insurance portion of the transaction.) If the debtor quit or was fired from his job (or filed for bankruptcy)—thereby ending the wage garnishment—the company would have no means of forcing payment of the debt. And again, the insurance policy provided no true collateral because, upon death, the company would merely pay itself the death claim.

As a marketing tool to attract the attention of the growing white-collar bureaucracy, these loans through life insurance policies also proved to be of little value. Very few loan recipients ever returned to the company seeking a normal insurance policy, and there is no evidence from the company correspondence that this plan aroused interest in the company from those who did not receive loans. Baltimore Life would find much greater success in extending sales and differentiating itself from competitors during the 1850s, when it would begin to actively market insurance policies on the lives of slaves (discussed in chapter 7).

Surrender Values

One common argument against taking out a life insurance policy (and in favor of other types of investments such as savings bank deposits) was that a policyholder who ran into financial difficulties and could not pay the premium would be forced to forfeit the policy, sacrificing not only the benefits of the insurance but all the accumulated premiums paid in. On the other hand, a person who outlived his life expectancy and the need for an insurance policy would discover that if he had annually deposited the equivalent of his premium payments in a savings bank, he would have earned much more than the face value of his policy. As one savings bank entrepreneur characterized the industry: "Life insurance is promoted by the same artifice as lotteries,—the publication of every case where an adventurer dies soon after the commencement of his insurance; while nothing is said where the insured abandons his policy in disgust, or from sickness, poverty, or inadvertence, after having distressed himself for years, by annual premiums;—nor where a person pays much more than his heirs are to receive back on his death."[37] The association with lotteries was especially vexing for life insurance executives, but it was indeed true that life insurance advertising was filled with stories of people who met their demise after the payment of only a handful of premiums or delayed procurement of a policy and then died unexpectedly (with little mention of people who outlived their predicted life expectancy).[38]

The promise of a cash surrender on policies was one way for firms to answer these arguments. As early as 1832, New York Life and Trust advertised that it would buy back policies from those who were no longer willing or able to pay their premiums: "The office fairly calculates what is the value of the risk it has run, and pays back to the insured all he has paid over this sum, and which went to make up the consideration for the risk to be run in future." As part of its appeal to potential middle-class customers, NYL&T depicted whole life contracts as an asset under the control of the policyholder: "After a number of years, the policy becomes of value to the insured; it is a part of his property; if he thinks proper to use it during his life, he receives back from the office no inconsiderable part of what has been paid, for the comfort of feeling secure and at ease during the previous years."[39]

Of course, this rosy picture did not disclose the terms under which a policy could be surrendered or the amount a policyholder would actually receive in return. Determining a "fair" payment was as much an art as a science for these early companies. When the secretary of American Life and Trust of Maryland inquired about NYL&T's procedure for determining surrender values, he was informed that President Bard (who was also an accomplished actuary) personally calculated each one: "He has no fix'd rule by which he is govern'd in ascertaining the am[oun]t to be paid in purchasing Life Policies . . . in each case he has made what he considered a fair allowance according to circumstances."[40] Thus while Bard had touted insurance policies as being "part of [the] property" of the insured, the actual value of that property was a mystery to the policyholder and could only be determined at the discretion of the company.

While few companies loaned money on policies to the extent Baltimore Life did, most (including NYL&T, Massachusetts Hospital Life, Girard Life, and American Life and Trust of Maryland) began business in the 1830s with the understanding that they would pay cash surrender values if the insured chose to forfeit the policy to the company. During the early years of life insurance, this benefit was not an official part of the policy contract and would only be honored upon formal forfeiture of the policy to the company if the policy was still in good standing (i.e., had not lapsed due to nonpayment of premiums).[41] Additionally, cash surrenders were only permitted on policies taken out for the whole term of life and that had been in effect for a minimum number of years—usually five.[42]

In its brochure of 1837, Girard Life stated that it would "repurchase, at an equitable rate, the policies of persons, who, from unforeseen misfortune, find their payments onerous."[43] However, by 1840 it had removed this statement from its brochures. Although the company was still willing to pay cash surrenders on long-standing policies, it did not feel compelled to do so in all cases: "Where a policy has been standing for a considerable <u>term of years</u> and parties find the premiums so onerous as to require their discontinuance, & ask an allowance, the company are disposed to consider the application with a view to a reasonable allowance and return."[44] Girard feared that surrenders would become too common and reduce the wide client base it sought to maintain.

One of the few early firms not to allow cash surrenders was Baltimore Life, although it was eventually forced to do so to remain competitive. In 1840, a Washington, DC, clerk by the name of Jacob Nollner wrote to Baltimore Life requesting that it purchase back all six life policies he held with the company, citing the brochure of American Life and Trust of Maryland as support for his request. The policies—taken out between 1833 and 1835—had a total death benefit of $5,650.30, and Nollner had paid $1,018.28 in premiums.[45] Baltimore Life was perplexed by his request, stating: "Your proposition, is (we suppose) that we should buy [the policies]. The extract you give from the prospectus of another Comp[an]y, is no guide to us. We never made a provision of that nature . . . No one before has ever made such a claim . . . The amount Insured on Lives, is too small to make the business profitable."[46] While it is somewhat surprising that this 10-year-old firm would have no knowledge of the surrender terms of other companies, Baltimore Life appeared to be genuinely unacquainted with the idea.

Nollner, however, continued to press his case with the insurer, citing the more favorable attitudes of other companies with whom he held policies. While Girard Life refused to pay a cash surrender on his $2,500 policy since it had been in place for only two years, NYL&T promptly paid him $199.85 for three polices (upon which he had paid about $571 in premiums), and it appears that American Life and Trust also paid him a cash surrender on his policy with that company.[47] In September, he again wrote Baltimore Life, this time stressing "the advantages to be reaped, & the disadvantages which must necessarily follow, by adopting & pursuing a régime so materially different from other like Institutions." Nollner went on to provide the recent example of a clerk in the General Land Office "who is well known to Mr. Causten" (the Washington agent for Baltimore Life) who chose to take out a $5,000 policy with American Life and Trust rather than Baltimore Life "from the single fact of the [American Life and Trust of] Maryland having the provision relatively to the refunding."[48] Even Causten felt it necessary to point out to the head office that while "the decision of the New York Co is directly the reverse of yours, the facts are precisely parallel."[49]

Facing the competitive pressure of other companies attempting to enter its lucrative mid-Atlantic market, Baltimore Life was loath to swim against the tide of the industry. By the end of September, the insurer had conceded to Nollner's request, agreeing to pay him $196.98 (of a total $613.20 paid in premiums) upon the surrender of three policies with a total face value of $3,000.[50] (Consistent with the practice of the other companies, Baltimore Life refused to consider the remaining three policies, worth $2,650, which Nollner had permitted to lapse two to three months prior to requesting the surrender of his policies.)[51] This incident also forced Baltimore Life to reconsider its views on buying back policies in general. By 1845, it was stating to customers: "Our Company is always disposed to purchase their life policies where five years premiums have been paid upon them."[52] And by the eve of the Civil War, it was willing to offer cash surrenders after the payment of only three annual premiums.[53]

But while the protection of a cash surrender was held out as an inducement to insure—and in particular to encourage clients to take out whole life policies rather than shorter term policies—companies were wary of encouraging surrenders. As John James, actuary of Girard Life, warned Henry F. Thompson, secretary of Baltimore Life, in 1854: "As a general rule it is not the sickly members or insured, those who believe that they will soon die, [who] offer to sell and surrender, but on the contrary they are generally the best cases and consequently by the means of surrender make selection against the office, by the good cases leaving and the defective ones remaining."[54] Thus companies had to balance offering the option of a future surrender as an inducement for middle-income Americans to insure against the negative effect of not retaining healthy policyholders for the whole course of their contracts.

One means of encouraging policyholders to continue paying premiums rather than surrendering their policies was by limiting the generosity of their cash surrender payments. The company needed to be remunerated for the risk it had incurred while the policy had remained in force. Yet what was a "fair" calculation in the eyes of the company was often far less than what the insured expected to collect. Policyholders often ignored the fact that they had received a nonmonetary benefit during the life of the policy—namely, peace of mind—while the company had incurred the risk of the person's dying prematurely. In 1848, Edwin Croswell of Albany requested a valuation of his $10,000 whole life policy from NYL&T taken out in 1833. Croswell had paid $4,000-$5,000 in premiums over the fifteen-year period and now expected to get back a large proportion of those payments in light of the fact that his life had not cost the company any money. NYL&T offered to pay him $2,349.88 upon surrender of the policy, explaining, "This may appear to you a small sum as compared with the amount paid by you, but it is to be borne in mind that your life has been insured for $10,000. since 1833, for which the company is entitled to a fair compensation."[55] While Croswell may have remained healthy during those fifteen years, his premium payments needed to cover the death claims of numerous others who died younger than the mortality tables had predicted.

In several cases, policyholders chose to continue their premium payments rather than receive a surrender value that they considered insufficient. For example, the New Hampshire Bank took out a policy in 1830 worth $1,500 on the life of William Hill with Massachusetts Hospital Life. In 1842, after paying $823.80 in premiums, the bank inquired as to the surrender value of the policy and was offered $340.50. It chose instead to continue the policy, inquiring about the value once again in 1847. The bank having then paid $1,133.55, the insurer quoted a cash value of $419.00. The bank again continued making payments, which totaled $1,247.45 upon Hill's death in 1849, when it finally received the face value of the policy.[56] In another case, Charles Norton of Maine held two policies with Massachusetts Hospital Life, worth $500 each, which he took out in 1839 and 1844. In 1847, the company offered to pay him a total of $60.33 for the surrender of both policies. Ten years later, the surrender value calculated by the company was $500. It appears Norton accepted this offer.[57]

In a few rare cases, companies attempted to offer more lucrative surrenders as a means of eliminating potentially costly claims from their books. In one such instance from 1845, the home office of NYL&T wrote to its agent in Montreal regarding a policyholder whose health had declined precipitously: "As you represent Mr. Esson to be in miserable health, and also advise that the Company should make him a liberal offer for his policy, we have under those circumstances thought it best to go beyond our usual calculation, of what would justly be his due, and we accordingly authorize you to make him an offer of $350."[58] While such a proposition may appear insensitive and even immoral, the company had no means of coercing a policyholder to accept the offer; NYL&T was bound by the policy contract unless Esson chose to surrender the policy. And depending on his circumstances, that $350 (received immediately) might have been worth more to him than the face value of the policy paid to his beneficiaries in the future. The company was still taking a gamble, since Esson was obviously not on his deathbed and could potentially live for several more years—and continue to pay premiums—despite his "miserable health."

A second means of discouraging surrenders was to offer the insured a loan on his policy up to the amount of the surrender value. As early as 1845, NYL&T's president spoke of an insurance policy that had run for several years being "good security for the amount of its value."[59] Throughout the 1840s, the company's response to any request for a surrender valuation included a statement such as "This sum the Co would be willing to pay you for a surrender of your policy or they would loan you the whole or any part of the amount at seven per cent interest, holding your policy and note as security."[60] Other companies also adopted this approach; for example, Philadelphia Life (established in 1848) advertised "loans advanced on policies of the [surrender] value of $100 or upwards."[61] Differing substantially from the insurance and loan program offered by Baltimore Life (in which loans were granted prior to the payment of any premiums), this new strategy created a win-win situation for both parties. While firms retained the business of a valuable policyholder, customers could tap into their policies for temporary loans without having to put up additional collateral. If the policyholder died before the repayment of the loan, the principal and interest still due were merely deducted from the final insurance claim paid to the beneficiaries. In this way, an insurance policy truly did become of value to the policyholder in the present.

A Middle-Class Savings Bank

Coinciding with the organization of the first life insurance companies open to the general public was the creation of the first American savings banks. Although the industrious poor were their target market, there is evidence that many middle-income people were attracted to these institutions. Almost every state passed regulations during the nineteenth century to ensure that middle- and upper-income individuals were not taking advantage of the benefits of savings banks, which included a guaranteed return on deposits and liquidity. For example, from 1828 to 1869 deposits in the Philadelphia Savings Fund were limited to $200 per year to avoid "abuse of the bank by the rich."[62] The Savings Bank of Baltimore periodically reviewed the occupations of its depositors and the size of their accounts, liquidating the accounts of those who were not its intended clientele. It conducted at least five of these examinations, returning 8% of deposits in 1828, 12% in 1839, and 2% in 1854.[63] In 1834, the Massachusetts legislature passed a law capping savings bank accounts at $1,000,[64] while in New York the cap was set at $3,000. Several banks paid lower interest on accounts above a certain size (often $500), thus penalizing large savers.[65] Each of these efforts indicates that savings banks were capturing the interest of individuals beyond the working poor.

Savings banks were attractive because middle-class savers faced problems similar to low-income savers: they had few outlets for their money beyond hoarding. Commercial banks rarely accepted small deposits, and few outside of the wealthiest individuals had the information and assets necessary to purchase government or private securities. Jay Cooke would prove the efficacy of selling bonds in smaller denominations to the middle-class during the Civil War, but no similar outlets existed during the antebellum period. The unmet investing desire of the middle class was the niche market segment upon which life insurance companies sought to capitalize.

Almost every company brochure of the antebellum period mentioned the similarities between life insurance and savings banks. William Bard's *A Letter to David E. Evans* stated that "an insurance office becomes a savings bank with a peculiar advantage, in which the smallest annual savings may safely be deposited for the benefit of a family."[66] New England Mutual, Mutual of New York, Pennsylvania Mutual Life, National Life Insurance of Vermont, Ohio Life and Trust, and Nautilus Insurance all described themselves as a type of savings bank as well,[67] while Connecticut Mutual, Girard Life, Mutual of New York, and New York Life and Trust stressed the advantages of life insurance over savings banks. As several brochures noted, "It would take clergymen, physicians, mechanics, clerks, and all those whose income depends upon their personal exertions, a long time to accumulate a competency for their families, out of the small proportion of their earnings, which could be devoted for that purpose" in a savings bank, whereas the same funds could be invested in an insurance policy with a guaranteed payment "received at death even if but *one* premium had been paid."[68] By highlighting the uncertainty of life, the precariousness of a middle-class family's social status, and the difficulty of accumulating adequate savings in the short term, life insurers were able to promote their product as the superior solution for addressing middle-class anxieties and aspirations.

Perhaps fearing that insurance would siphon off their own clientele, savings bank entrepreneurs responded venomously to life insurers. They countered that insurance policies were only of value after a person died—and mainly if the person died young—while a bank deposit could be liquidated at any time and retained its value regardless of the depositor's longevity. But more generally, bank promoters accused the industry of engaging in gambling contracts and encouraging people to commit heinous crimes (see chapter 8), charges that life insurers could ill afford to let stand. Despite the rancor between the two industries, this image of life insurance as a middle-class savings bank was extremely powerful and enduring, recurring throughout the advertising literature of the period.

A Middle-Class Investment: The Emerging Competition from Mutual Life Insurance Companies

Most histories of life insurance regard 1843—the year Mutual of New York became the first purely mutual company actively to engage in the sale of life insurance—as the turning point in the development of the industry. However, as the data on life insurance sales clearly indicate (see figure in the introduction), the advent of the mutual form had little effect on the trend in policy sales; the amount of life insurance in force increased steadily throughout the second quarter of the nineteenth century. And yet it is likewise clear that, given the choice between a mutual and stock company, midcentury Americans overwhelming preferred mutuals.

J. Owen Stalson (the main proponent of the idea of the "Revolution of 1843") correctly asserts in his 1942 book *Marketing Life Insurance* that the success of the mutual companies was not a matter of "mere mutuality";[69] the lackluster performance of Girard Life during the 1830s (which operated as a mixed company—part stock and part mutual) and the inability of stock companies to successfully imitate the mutual form during the 1840s give substantial support to this view. Rather, Stalson credits the mutuals with the development of the first aggressive marketing campaigns within the industry. Stalson dismisses the innovative efforts of earlier companies such as NYL&T and Baltimore Life in devising marketing plans with wide appeal for an emerging middle class "as simple and nonaggressive; volume of life sales was relatively unimportant to them." In Stalson's estimation, the industry was floundering until "the advent of the mutuals," which instigated "an immediate expansion in the range of life insurance marketing activities and an increase in the intensity with which sales efforts were prosecuted."[70] He erroneously claims that earlier companies "do not once mention the idea 'Duty to Insure'" in their sales brochures: "No one is urged to buy, no mention is made of 'avoiding delay,' a phrase so often repeated in the sales booklets of the mutuals."[71] And he asserts that only with the emergence of mutuals did "sales through agents become 'normal.'"[72]

The stark dichotomy Stalson presents between the interests and methods of stock and mutual companies does not conform to the evidence. Stock companies throughout the 1830s and 1840s continually sought ways to increase their sales volume, often employing hard-hitting marketing techniques in the process. What enabled mutual companies to dominate the industry by the late 1840s was neither mere mutuality nor mere marketing. Rather, the significance of mutualization lay in the manner in which mutuals actively differentiated their product from the life insurance sold by stock companies by marketing it as a long-term investment with particular appeal for the middle class. In their attempts to cater to the needs and ambitions of middle-income Americans through their policy terms and marketing literature, stock companies fell short of marketing life insurance as an investment in and of itself. The mutuals, on the other hand, focused on the aspirations of a middle class that sought low-risk opportunities to improve its economic status.[73] Stock companies would not successfully answer this challenge until the postbellum era with the development of their own investment policies.

Without statistical knowledge of American mortality, early life insurers were unwilling to reduce premium rates for fear that the lower rates would not cover their risks. Companies thus competed based on service and reliability rather than on price. Mutualization was a means of indirectly cutting premium rates—returning to policyholders a percentage of their payments only when firms felt confident in their ability to pay anticipated death claims. This return payment was cleverly labeled a "dividend" (rather than a price reduction or rebate) in order to exploit the idea that the policy was an investment. Dividends, when declared, were redistributed to the policyholders either as an increase in the face value of the policy (the amount to be paid the beneficiaries upon death) or in the form of lower future premium payments. In either case, the rate ultimately paid per $1,000 of insurance was reduced. But these dividends were not guaranteed, and the published rates of mutual companies initially remained the same as those of the stock companies. What attracted applicants to the mutual companies and away from older stock companies was not the potential for lower insurance rates but the way in which the new firms marketed *mutual* life policies as long-term investment goods with little risk.

In its 1845 brochure, Mutual of New York predicted that the first dividend to be distributed to policyholders in 1848 would amount to between 70% and 80% on the amount of premium paid.[74] Such dividends, which would be added to the face value of the policy, meant that "on an insurance of long standing with a Mutual Company, the sum payable at death, will, with the accumulation thereon, amount to twice, thrice, and quadruple that of the insurance."[75] Exactly the opposite was true with a stock company, where the policy "is strikingly beneficial only in the event of early and premature death, as in no case can the sum payable at death exceed the amount of the insurance."[76] The mutual companies, in presenting themselves as "a savings institution of the best kind," thus adopted a critique of stock firms similar to that proffered by savings banks against the industry as a whole.[77]

The example given by Mutual of New York clearly illustrated this point. If a 25-year-old man took out a $5,000 policy with a stock company, paid premiums for 34 years, and died at the age of 59, he would have paid $8,382 in premiums, but his beneficiaries would only receive the $5,000 face value of the policy. Those same premiums, when paid to a mutual company, would have been invested and (the company predicted) have resulted in accrued profits of $11,250 for the insured; upon his death this man's beneficiaries would thus receive $16,250.[78]

Mutual of New York provided four sources for this large profit margin—expired policies (term policies that did not result in a death claim), cancelled (lapsed) policies, careful selection of lives resulting in lower than predicted mortality rates, and shrewd investment of funds by company executives.[79] Furthermore, rather than returning dividends as cash payments or allowing them to be used to reduce future premium payments (as was the policy of several other mutuals), Mutual of New York placed them in long-term investments and then added these dividends to the ultimate death benefit. "This . . . is decidedly one of its best features," one brochure noted. Cash payments and premium reductions, the company asserted, "are highly objectionable, and defeat, to a very considerable extent, the chief object of the institution, which is, that of a safe depository for the annual savings of the members, sacredly pledged for the benefit of their widows and children."[80] And like most marketing ploys of the antebellum industry, these inducements and arguments were copied liberally by other mutual insurers.[81]

Mutual companies thus solved the dilemma of choosing between life insurance and savings banks—the former holding the advantage if one died prematurely, and the latter if one outlived the expectancy tables. New England Mutual summed this point up well in its 1846 brochure: "The premiums paid . . . are similar to deposits in a savings-bank, and in case of [the policyholder's] living the average age, will come back to his family with interest; and in a well[-]constituted, well-conducted and successful company, with more than interest; and during his life his policy will always be of value." Not merely akin to savings banks, mutual policies were far superior because "by undertaking comparatively very small annual payments, a person makes himself certain of the full amount of his proposed future savings from the beginning."[82] A mutual life policy doubled as both protection against untimely death (the advantage of life insurance in general) and a low-risk, high-return investment (the advantage of savings banks).

As Mutual of New York indicated, however, not all mutual companies reinvested dividends for the life of the policy. While few companies allowed dividends to be claimed directly as cash payments (unless upon surrender of the policy), several did permit them to be used toward future premium payments. But by far the most controversial practice was accepting notes in partial payment (up to 50%) of premiums in *anticipation* that future dividends would pay off these notes. These methods of reducing the cash outlay for a policy were all very attractive to the middle class. Proponents of these systems argued that mandatory reinvestment of dividends eliminated the benefits of mutual policies during the lifetime of the insured and exposed policyholders to potential fraud by unscrupulous companies. Yet by reducing the funds held in reserve and accumulated through investment, these alternatives exposed companies to greater risk of failure and limited the long-term investment advantage for policyholders. The acceptance of premium notes was considered the riskiest of these practices and thus created the most debate. Whereas the amount and timing of dividends was determined at the discretion of the company—allowing it to declare lower or no dividends if death claims were draining their reserves—premium notes were accepted on anticipated dividends; companies thus had no recourse but to call in these notes if claims outpaced paid-in funds.

The appeal of premium notes spread quickly among the middle class, the major advantage being that they allowed a person to purchase twice as much insurance for the same out-of-pocket price: "The payment of one-half of the premium in notes, while it affords adequate security, is at the same time the most economical mode of investment, as no time is lost, and interest is at once accruing."[83] Companies required that interest on these notes be paid annually but anticipated that "the principal will not be called for, unless the exigencies of the Company require it, when the assessments will be made *pro rata,* and only to the extent required to meet the engagements of the Company."[84] While any remaining amount due on these notes would be deducted from the final death claim, companies espousing this plan argued that annual profits of at least 40% ("which is below the rate assumed by most other offices") would quickly cover the amount owed on the notes, leaving the insured with the face value of the policy plus any accrual above and beyond these notes.[85] Nautilus Insurance (the future New York Life) took this one step farther, promising in 1848 that "the profits or dividends will *probably* be greater than the amount of premium notes, and *cannot* in any year be less" (emphasis added).[86]

Both insurance executives and pundits questioned the safety of this system. Two of the most vehement critics were also two of the largest antebellum insurance companies, Mutual of New York and New England Mutual. In a section of its 1845 brochure entitled "The Credit Plan of Mutual Life Insurance Considered, and its Unsatisfactory and Dangerous Tendencies Exposed," Mutual of New York asserted that "substituting the notes of the assured instead of cash, weakens the institution, and diminishes the benefits in proportion to the extent which the principle is carried out." While the examples of the premium-note companies only extended out seven to ten years—just long enough to demonstrate how profits would outpace dividends—note critics such as Mutual of New York carried their examples out thirty-one years. By this point, the annual interest due on the accumulated premium notes would dwarf the table premium rates; the cash and interest due in their advertising example amounted to $220 in year 31, although the actual premium due was only $137.50. Mutual of New York then summed up its objections in three points: "1st, it creates no sufficient fund to establish such a Company upon a stable foundation, to secure it against liability to be overthrown by any unfavorable turn of risks; 2dly, it makes those who are able liable for the deficiencies of those who are unable to pay; lastly, it defeats in a great measure the chief object of such institutions, which is that of a great savings bank for the benefit of widows and orphans."[87]

New England Life was even more dramatic in its indictment: "The person insured provides, not subsistence, but disappointment and chagrin, for his surviving family . . . in case of his death, the Company will deliver his promissory notes to his widow and children. They ask for bread, and he gives them waste-paper."[88] Premium notes thus undermined the two main benefits of life insurance. On one hand, the protection offered to widows and orphans was compromised, as the death benefit would be reduced to pay off any outstanding notes and interests. On the other, the policy changed from a low-risk investment to a speculative one, as policyholders were gambling on the probable dividend to be declared each year for decades into the future.

Despite this controversy, the premium-note system rapidly gained popularity during the 1840s. Premium notes accounted for less than 1% of industry assets in 1843, rising to 3% by 1845. But the system then caught on quickly, ballooning from 12% of assets the following year (1846) to 23% by 1851 (even as life insurance in force continued to grow at the astounding rate of 37% per annum during the 1840s) and then holding more or less steady at this proportion until the late 1850s. At this point the popularity of premium notes temporarily waned, declining gradually to 15% during the Civil War years before returning to a second peak of 26% in 1867–68. The system would finally be destroyed only by the wave of failures that swept the industry beginning in 1870.[89]

Regardless of which repayment system a mutual company chose to adopt, the marketing of mutual insurance as a middle-class investment good was highly successful, and as a result, the mutual form completely re-created the industry in a remarkably short time. Mutual Life of New York (chartered 1842) began operation in February 1843, underwriting $1.5 million of life insurance during its first eleven months and almost $3 million by the end of 1844; by 1845 it would surpass NYL&T as the largest life underwriter in the country. New England Mutual Life (1835) issued its first policy in February 1844 and underwrote $1 million of insurance during that year.[90] (In contrast, the mixed-form Girard—incorporated in 1836—was in business almost ten years before it could boast $1 million of life insurance in force, despite its offering of mutual policies.) At least fifteen more mutuals were chartered by 1849. In 1850, the ten largest life insurance companies all operated on a mutual basis; only Hartford Life and Health (the seventh largest) sold policies on both the stock and mutual plans.[91] Since the growth rate of life insurance sales did not change significantly during the second half of the 1840s, this rapid expansion among the mutuals came only by shifting the interest of applicants away from stock firms (as opposed to ratcheting up interest in insuring beyond the prevailing trend).

As early as 1844, William Bard recognized the sudden, intense threat presented by Mutual Life of New York, which he noted was "making such progress and so far outstripping us in business." While Bard immediately realized the attraction of the mutuals in "meet[ing] what appears to be the wishes of the public," he was not entirely convinced that they were operating on a sound financial footing. Writing to the president of Girard Life, Bard stated his "opinion that the public is misled by hopes of profit, which have no foundation, and that if the Mutual Co. in New York is conducted on the principles their charter authorizes, it will prove neither profitable or safe." Despite his uncertainty about the future of the mutual form, he believed the threat was strong enough to force NYL&T "to consider whether some change may not be necessary . . . either to adopt some plan of insuring those who prefer it on the Mutual principle, or to reduce [our] rates of insurance."[92] The stock companies would attempt to fight back against these newcomers in each of the ways initially outlined by Bard: by questioning the fiscal soundness of the mutual model, by diversifying into mutual insurance themselves, and by lowering their premium rates on proprietary policies. Failing to recognize that the key to the success of the mutuals was their marketing strategy, the one response the stock companies neglected to make (until the late 1850s) was to realign their own marketing techniques along the model of the mutuals.

By far the easiest response, particularly in the short term, was to challenge the safety of mutual insurance policies. In a letter to John Finlaison in London, Bard predicted: "For several years, business [for the mutuals] will look very profitable. Those who die first will receive a considerable addition, but as the Society advances, the profits will be less and less, and will finally vanish, if not do worse, if the view I take is correct."[93] President John J. Donaldson of Baltimore Life advised potential policyholders in 1844 that "the mutual principle is certainly more attractive in theory" but "how it will operate in practice is another matter."[94] By 1845 stock company prospectuses had been revised to disparage the mutual model. Emphasizing the long-term nature of the insurance contract and the consequent necessity of insuring with a stable, well-capitalized company, the New York branch of Albion Life of London asserted that "in a Mutual Insurance Office no security of the kind exists." It then proceeded to scare potential applicants with a list of the likely pitfalls of insuring with a mutual: "The premiums are always liable to be raised, or the sum insured diminished, according to the exigencies of the Society; and if at any time, whether from misconduct or misfortune, the affairs of the Society should become irreparably involved, there exists no capital to fall back upon to mitigate the distress to which such an event must necessarily give rise."[95] Thus stock companies portrayed insuring with a mutual company as an unscientific gamble; ironically, this was the same argument leveled against the industry as a whole by insurance critics.

The mutual companies defended their plan by citing the profits of the stock companies as adequate evidence of the safety of such a system: "if the stock system is profitable, the mutual system must, at least, be safe; for premiums that yield fund enough to pay interest on capital stock, must, of course, yield fund enough to cover risks."[96] As long as mutual firms were merely refunding to members the excess reserves that stock companies were paying out as dividends to stockholders, then the mutuals made a good point. And the mutual firms that reinvested these excesses (rather than paying them out as cash rebates, premium reductions, or stock dividends) were arguably even safer than the stock companies.

Perhaps the best argument stock companies could make was to point out the mutuals' lack of capital stock as an extra reserve. As President David Thompson of NYL&T explained to one potential applicant in 1847, the possibility that the insurance might continue for decades rendered the careful selection of a financially sound company particularly important. "Certainly this is best done," he argued, "where the security offered is not only the moderate profit which may be made by the Company but a large and well secured capital responsible for all its engagements. In this Company a capital of $1,000,000 is pledged w[h]ere the Insurance is on the proprietary [i.e., stock] system and $50,000 temporarily where the Insurance is on the Mutual. I should prefer the former."[97] Some stock proponents even implied that policyholders on mutual plans would be liable for future assessments beyond their premium payments if death claims outpaced receipts, since these companies lacked the protection of paid-in capital or the ability to raise additional capital through the sale of stock. This prompted the mutuals to include in their brochures a statement declaring that while "each person insuring becomes a member of the company, and shares in its profits . . . [i]n no case is the person insuring liable beyond the amount of premium paid."[98] However, mutual policies were selling rapidly enough to mitigate even the need for this argument, allowing mutual firms to build up substantial reserves, well beyond the protection offered by the minimal capital paid into most stock companies.

But NYL&T and other stock companies did not merely engage in a negative advertising campaign against the mutuals. As early as 1844 (as soon as the problem was recognized), President Hyman Gratz of Pennsylvania Company was writing to Massachusetts Hospital Life to obtain any information he could on mutuality: "This Company finding new Mutual offices springing up around them have determined on offering a participation of profits on all whole Life policies."[99] While Massachusetts Hospital Life had no interest in expanding into this line, Pennsylvania Company did develop a mutual plan later in the decade. Likewise in 1844, Bard began consultations with the British actuary John Finlaison to determine whether it would be feasible for NYL&T to diversify into mutual insurance.[100] However, it took the company a full two years to develop a plan of mutual insurance and revise its premium rates for those remaining on the proprietary (stock) plan.[101]

The plan finally adopted by NYL&T in 1846 allowed policyholders to choose between insuring on the mutual plan at the regular premium rates or remaining on the proprietary plan with a 10% reduction in rates, so that "those on the Mutual [plan] must receive an annual profit of 10 pr ct on their premiums before they are on a par with those on the proprietary system."[102] By 1851, every American stock company was quoting rates at least 5% lower than the mutuals' and several quoted rates between 23% and 35% cheaper.[103] Yet despite these lower rates and the availability of the mutual option, stock companies could not compete with the mutuals. The attractions of the mutual plan clearly were not based on price alone.

None of the older stock companies put their whole weight behind their mutual plans. Potential NYL&T customers were warned of the weaknesses of the mutual plan and encouraged to take out proprietary policies instead.[104] At the same time, the company reduced its advertising budget in an attempt to cut costs[105]—in direct contrast to the continued heavy marketing of the mutual companies. Existing customers desiring to convert to mutual policies were required to go through the cumbersome process of selling back their old policies for a cash surrender value and completely reapplying—filing new paperwork, undergoing a new medical exam, and paying the higher premium rates associated with their more advanced age.[106] By 1849, having sold only twenty policies on the mutual plan, NYL&T abandoned this line of insurance altogether.[107]

The old stock companies all recognized the threat posed by the emergence of mutual companies relatively quickly, but they took too long to respond (the life insurance in force of Mutual Life was more than double that of NYL&T before the latter company had even introduced its new plan) and they misunderstood the nature of the threat altogether—treating it as a pricing challenge rather than a marketing challenge. Unique marketing was the crucial factor in the success of mutual plans, and NYL&T readily admitted that "no exertions were ever made to increase the business on the mutual plan."[108]

To regain ground from the mutual companies, stock companies needed to create their own "investment" policies. The pioneer in this area was the Equitable Life Assurance Society of New York (chartered 1859), which began issuing tontine or deferred dividend policies in 1868. This unique arrangement combined the protection of an insurance policy with the risk of an investment. While a portion of each premium payment went directly toward a standard insurance policy, another portion was deposited in an investment fund with a set maturity date (usually ten, fifteen, or twenty years) and a restricted group of participants. The beneficiaries of deceased policyholders received only the face value of the standard life component, and participants who allowed their policy to lapse received nothing or only a small cash surrender value. At the end of the stipulated period, the dividends that had accumulated in the fund were divided among the remaining participants. Economic historians estimate that only about 40% of the initial policyholders received dividends at the end of the period; of the remainder, approximately 10% had died and

90% had allowed their policies to lapse. Deferred dividend policies, therefore, could be extremely lucrative to the surviving participants, since they received not only their own dividends but also a share in those of the high percentage of deceased and lapsed policyholders.[109] Companies also benefited from this policy form; the long maturity period gave them discretionary control over huge amounts of investment funds for which they were guaranteed not to be held responsible until the end of the period.[110] These "investment" policies proved to be extremely popular, allowing stock companies to reemerge as strong industry competitors in the postbellum era. Estimates indicate that approximately two-thirds of all life insurance policies in force in 1905—the year this policy form was banned by most state legislatures— were deferred dividend plans.[111]

A Middle-Class Clientele

By playing on both the fears and the aspirations of the middle class, the marketing campaigns of antebellum companies were successful in spreading sales to urban middle-class households. The most complete information on policyholders for the period 1830 to 1850 comes from the records of New York Life and Trust. Its policy books include the name, place of residence, occupation, age, length of policy, and amount of insurance for most policyholders underwritten from its inception in 1830 through its suspension of insurance sales in the 1860s.[112] Data for policyholders of New England Mutual—the fifth-largest company during the late 1840s and 1850s— contains similar information beginning with its first policy in 1844, although occupations were available for only about one-third of the insured.[113] Information for policyholders of Baltimore Life—the second-largest insurer behind NYL&T during the 1830s—includes only place of residence and policy length and amount. Although Massachusetts Hospital Life kept meticulous records on its policyholders from 1823 through mid-1832, only policy length and amount were recorded for the remainder of the 1830s, and even that information becomes sporadic beginning in 1839.

With only slight variation by region or occupation, the average policyholder was a male in his mid-thirties. Initially, merchants and financiers held the dominant occupations of NYL&T policyholders within New York City. While they accounted for only 3% of the city's population in 1855 (table 1), almost half of new policyholders during the 1830s and early 1840s belonged to this category, before their proportion declined sharply to one-third after the depression (still ten times greater than their percentage of the population). Small proprietors and professionals such as grocers, hotelkeepers, doctors, lawyers, clergymen, and teachers made up only 13%

of the population but represented about one-fifth of new policyholders before and during the depression, increasing to one-third by the mid-1840s. And whereas only 8% of adult males declared themselves to be salaried, clerical, or government employees, they made up a constant one-quarter of new policyholders. In contrast, artisans made up two-fifths of the population in 1855 but accounted for less than 10% of new policyholders by the late 1840s.

Among policyholders outside of New York City (table 2), small proprietors and professionals initially dominated sales. By the 1840s, one-third of new policyholders were professionals, and another third were merchants or financiers. Clerical workers and artisans each accounted for 13% of sales. It is more difficult to estimate how these proportions compare with the occupation breakdown of the entire adult male population, especially because the policyholders resided in a large number of different locales with varying occupation mixes. But comparison with Mary Ryan's distribution for Utica in 1845 reveals that the proportion of insured merchants and small proprietors/professionals was similar to that found in New York City (respectively about ten times and two times greater than their representation in the population as a whole), while that for salaried employees was only slightly larger than their population share. Compared with Paul Johnson's mix for Rochester in 1827, insured merchants were on par or slightly above their share of the population, while small proprietors were five to seven times more likely to be insured, and salaried workers were three times more likely. Artisans, again, were grossly underrepresented among policyholders with NYL&T.

Other companies demonstrated similar occupational breakdowns. Merchants were the most common single occupation across almost all companies, which should not be surprising because they were the most familiar with the older lines of marine and fire insurance. But virtually the entire spectrum of moderate- and high-income occupations was represented among the antebellum insured, ranging from physicians, lawyers, clergymen, and farmers to blacksmiths, carpenters, shoemakers, and mariners.

Clerks held the most commonly insured occupation among the more moderate-income group. As historian Stuart Blumin has documented, clerks represented the aspirational middle class—those who anticipated climbing up the social ladder despite their limited current incomes: "At any given moment there were large numbers of young clerks (or 'apprentice merchants') who made less money than most skilled workers. But the clerks, unlike the manual workers, had good reason to believe that their incomes would soon rise, and that even as employees they would earn enough money to support themselves and their families."[114] While many clerks were probably familiar with life insurance through their work for merchants—and may even have been aspiring merchants themselves—clerks also worked in a variety

New NYL&T Policyholders, New York City Only

	Merchants and financiers	Small proprietors or professionals	Salaried, clerical, or government	Artisans or skilled manual	Unskilled	Female	All NYC
% of policyholders							
1830–36	44	23	25	2	2	4	
1837–43	47	17	26	5	1	4	
1844–50	31	31	24	9	1	5	
% of NYC population, 1855	3	13	8	42	34	no data	
Average policy amount ($)							
1830–36	5,485	3,840	4,384	*	*	*	4,309
1837–43	5,347	3,637	3,787	4,486	*	5,422	4,389
1844–50	3,606	2,192	2,498	1,375	*	2,985	2,528
% of policies ≤$1,000							
1830–36	8	27	26	*	*	*	18
1837–43	8	38	28	14	*	22	19
1844–50	29	48	52	78	*	25	47
% of policies ≥$5,000							
1830–36	74	47	63	*	*	*	51
1837–43	64	36	40	50	*	67	50
1844–50	40	21	25	6	*	15	25
No. of NYC policyholders in sample							
1830–36	291						
1837–43	562						
1844–50	462						

Sources: New policies written in January and July, Register of Life Insurance, EB-1, New York Life Insurance and Trust Company, Baker Library Historical Collections, Harvard Business School. Occupation statistics were compiled based on the New York State Census of 1855 figures in Robert Ernst, *Immigrant Life in New York City, 1825–1863* (Syracuse: Syracuse University Press, 1994), 206–17.
*Insufficient data.

TABLE 2.
New NYL&T Policyholders Outside New York City

	Merchants and financiers	Small proprietors or professionals	Salaried, clerical, or government	Artisans or skilled manual	Unskilled	Female	All non-NYC
% of policyholders							
1830–36	26	45	16	10	<1	3	
1837–43	30	39	15	10	2	4	
1844–50	36	33	13	13	<1	4	
% of population							
% Utica population, 1845	3	19	10	45	20	not available	
% Rochester population, 1827	26	7	5	50	12	not available	
% Utica converts, 1838	28	37	15	6	0	12	
Average policy amount ($)							
1830–36	4,305	2,464	2,335	2,357	*	3,089	2,760
1837–43	4,546	2,235	2,997	2,941	*	3,385	3,213
1844–50	3,306	2,106	2,840	2,218	*	4,531	2,667
% of policies ≤ $1,000							
1830–36	23	37	48	40	*	43	40
1837–43	15	48	23	35	*	55	30
1844–50	18	51	31	52	*	25	38
% of policies ≥$5,000							
1830–36	51	23	17	20	*	29	27
1837–43	61	16	27	35	*	35	33
1844–50	37	19	25	17	*	44	26
No. of non-NYC policy holders in sample							
1830–36	525						
1837–43	1,087						
1844–50	667						

Sources: New policies written in January and July, Register of Life Insurance, New York Life Insurance and Trust Company, Baker Library Historical Collections, Harvard Business School; Mary P. Ryan, *Cradle of the Middle Class: The Family in Oneida County, New York, 1790–1865* (Cambridge: Cambridge University Press, 1981), 253; and Paul E. Johnson, *A Shopkeeper's Millennium: Society and Revivals in Rochester, New York, 1815–1837* (New York: Farrar, Straus, & Giroux, 1978), 143.
*Insufficient data.

of other areas. Massachusetts Hospital Life insured clerks in banks, the court, the customhouse, and public offices in addition to dry goods, brokers' and merchants' clerks. New England Mutual similarly underwrote clerks working for banks, railroads and steamboats, stores, courts, towns, and customhouses. Baltimore Life insured clerks in a wide array of government offices, including the State Department, treasury, circuit court, solicitor's office, post office, land office, and office of the army paymaster. Approximately 10% of Massachusetts Hospital Life policyholders were theological, medical, law, or other college students (presumably at Harvard). Members of this group were probably using their policies as collateral for education loans. Student policies ranged from $50 to $1,000 and averaged about $440—well below both the average and modal size of policies in the company.

The data indicate that policyholders initially came from the wealthier segments of each occupational category but that insurance soon attracted the attention of less well-to-do members within these groups. While the average New York City policy paid a death benefit of just over $4,300 throughout the 1830s and early 1840s, this amount dropped significantly to only $2,500 after the depression (table 1).[115] Similar dramatic reductions in policy size occurred for each employment group. In reality, policies were not distributed evenly across the whole range of possible amounts. Most clients purchased either the maximum policy (usually limited to $5,000 but sometimes permitted to go higher) or a small policy worth $1,000 or less. Through 1843, about half of all policies were valued at $5,000 or more, with less than one-fifth worth $1,000 or less. The maximum policy was purchased by two-thirds to three-quarters of merchants, one-third to one-half of professionals, two-fifths to two-thirds of salaried workers, and one-half of artisans. Considering that a $5,000 policy would cost the average 35-year-old policyholder $137.50 per year, the small proprietor, artisan, or salaried worker earning a modest annual income of less than $1,000 was clearly not the client for such policies.

After 1843, the maximum policy was purchased by only one-quarter of all new policyholders. By that time nearly half were small policies of $1,000 or less (costing $27.50 or less per year). Three-quarters of artisans opted for this policy size, as did half of salaried workers, small proprietors, and professionals and more than a quarter of merchants. (Outside of New York City, the average policy was about $2,700 throughout the period; approximately two-fifths of policies were worth $1,000 or less, with only one-quarter valued at $5,000 or more.) Assuming that customers bought the maximum protection they could afford, NYL&T was increasingly drawing policyholders from more moderate-income segments within each occupation group. A similar pattern emerges from the records of New England Mutual. Between the inception of sales in 1844 and 1853, the average policy paid a death benefit of just over $2,000. More than half of these policies were written for $1,000 or less, while only 14% of policyholders opted to maximize their coverage at $5,000 or more (table 3).

In addition to their occupations and income levels, the conduct of policyholders indicates that they were drawn from the emerging middle class. Historians have uncovered several characteristics of people who made up this sometimes elusive group. Although Mary Ryan and Paul Johnson differ about the reasons for greater evangelical fervor during the Second Great Awakening, they agree that revivals were particularly attractive to the people they describe as middle class. Ryan provides occupation data for converts during the 1838 revival in Oneida, New York (table 2). Her employment breakdown is almost identical to that of NYL&T policyholders outside of New York City. Only 3% of the population were merchants or financiers, one-fifth were small proprietors or professionals, and one-tenth were salaried, clerical, or government employees, but just under one-third of both converts and the insured were from the merchant class, almost two-fifths were small proprietors, and 15% were salaried. Thus purchasers of life insurance and revival converts were being drawn from the same mix of people.

Another marker of middle-class conduct—and an extension of the Second Great Awakening—was an intense interest in moral reform movements. While the moneyed elite often headed reform organizations, historian Paul Boyer estimates that the volunteers or "urban-morality foot soldiers were often first-generation urbanites active in evangelical churches and holding what would later be called white-collar jobs—clerks, accountants, bank tellers—on the lower rungs of the business or professional ladder." Boyer goes on to assert that these moral reform societies "enabled members of this still inchoate middle class to seek each other out, join together in purposeful common effort, and submit to the oversight of others who shared their aspirations."[116] As indicated in chapter 2, there was significant interest in the temperance movement among the original incorporators of the early insurance companies as well as many of the policyholders who cited their teetotalism as a positive attribute when applying for insurance.

Becoming Middle Class

In his seminal work *The Emergence of the Middle Class: Social Experience in the American City, 1760–1900,* Stuart Blumin discusses the five markers that defined the antebellum middle class—their occupations, their consumption patterns, where they lived, their involvement in voluntary associations, and their family structures—concluding that these "seem to encompass nearly all relevant aspects of an emerging

TABLE 3.
New England Mutual Life Insurance Company Policyholders

	All policy-holders	Merchants and financiers	Small proprietors or professionals	Salaried, clerical, or government	Artisans or skilled manual	Unskilled	Female
% of policyholders, 1844–50		33	33	14	17	0	2
Average policy amount ($), 1844–53	2,035						
% of policies ≤$1,000, 1844–53	54						
% of policies ≥$5,000, 1844–53	14						
No. of policyholders in sample, 1844–50 525							

Source: New policies written in January and July, Policy Books, New England Mutual Life Insurance Company, Baker Library Historical Collections, Harvard Business School.

middle-class 'way of life.'"[117] The spread of life insurance paralleled the growth of this emerging class, with the average policyholder sharing these same characteristics. Life insurance attracted the interest of merchants, small proprietors, professionals, and the growing ranks of salaried, clerical, and government workers in America's cities. It appealed to the same people who were participating in the revivals of the Second Great Awakening, who were becoming active members of reform societies such as the temperance movement, and who were experiencing a reordering of gender relations within the household. In short, life insurance began as a middle-class phenomenon; it increasingly came to represent a means of protecting middle-class households from a precipitous decline in class status upon the death of the main breadwinner. A life insurance policy was the investment of funds by a father during his lifetime to provide for the needs of his family upon his death.

But those in the middle class did not merely seek to preserve the status quo, employing insurance for security and as a means of maintaining respectability. Life insurance encouraged them to engage in socially productive risk taking, facilitating their attempts to climb further up the social ladder. Thus a sixth key trait of this emerging middle class was its growing financial sophistication. Recognizing both the advantages and risks of taking part in the speculative game of investing, the middle class discovered in life insurance (particularly in mutual life insurance) a financial instrument allegedly capable of exploiting the advantages of the capitalist system while mitigating the risks. To assist themselves in this endeavor, policyholders demanded greater flexibility in their payment terms, the option to take out loans on their policies, and cash surrenders if they chose to forfeit their policies. Companies responded by marketing life insurance both as a middle-class savings bank and as a high-return, low-risk investment that appealed to their status consciousness. By the postbellum era, ownership of a life insurance policy was one of the defining characteristics of membership in the middle class. But during the antebellum period, it was a tool to help people become part of that emerging class.

CHAPTER 7

Securing Human Property

Slavery, Industrialization, and Urbanization
in the Upper South

In the fall of 1835, John Day of Chuckatuck, Virginia, inquired with the Baltimore Life agent in nearby Norfolk regarding insurance on one of his slaves, "very likely a good Carpenter sober and steady." For Day, a farmer and the postmaster of that sleepy rural town, ownership of this slave represented an investment in capital from which he could earn a regular income. Although he had been offered $1,200 to sell the man, he had refused "because if he lives he is good property or rather would pay me 12 or 15 pr Cent at that valuation which will well justify me in paying an insurance."[1] Day was among a growing group of southerners, particularly in the Upper South, who viewed slaveholding as a capitalist endeavor, the risks of which could be minimized through the purchase of a life insurance policy.

As life insurance companies diversified into the South, the mainly northern-based industry expected to generate a clientele among the southern middle class. Yet while southern whites were much less likely to seek insurance on their own lives (probably reflecting the more rural makeup of the region), the proportion of insurance policies on the lives of urban slaves in the Upper South approximated that of white male northeasterners by the mid-1850s. Reflecting the paradox of slaves being simultaneously human beings and property, fire insurance companies also began underwriting slave lives. Indeed by the Civil War several major life and fire companies of the Upper South were devoting the majority of their sales efforts to such policies. Life insurance was steadily spreading among the American populace, and slaveholders were on the forefront of southerners who embraced this new product.

Historians of slavery have generally only mentioned life insurance in passing.[2] By focusing on the relatively small number of policies, they fail to recognize that the demand for policies on slaves was growing rapidly during the 1850s and paralleled the growth in policies on northeastern whites. Even Todd Savitt's article "Slave Insurance in Virginia and North Carolina" examines not the rise of slave insurance but the resistance of small farmers and plantation owners to buying these policies. While slaves formed a central portion of the personal property holdings of the wealthiest southerners, life insurance was not viewed as a general means of protecting this investment in the same way that a fire or marine insurance policy would be purchased on a building or a shipment of goods. Indeed, Savitt is correct that insurance was rarely requested for those slaves deemed most valuable: prime male field hands and young, fertile females with a high reproductive potential.[3] Rather, as in the northeast, the life insurance industry established its firmest foothold in southern cities, where the nature of slavery was changing rapidly.

As the center of demand for slave labor shifted during the first decades of the nineteenth century from the tobacco-growing regions of the Upper South to the crescent-shaped cotton belt running from South Carolina to eastern Texas, the states of Maryland, Virginia, and North Carolina were forced to reconsider their economic focus.[4] With slavery confined to growth through natural increase after Congress legally banned the importation of new slaves in 1808, the strong demand for slave labor in the cotton South drove up prices on all bondspeople. This rise in labor costs interacted with declining tobacco profits (caused in part by increased competition from emerging tobacco-producing areas such as Kentucky), compelling Upper South slaveholders to find new ways to profit from their slave population. One option was to hire out surplus slaves (in contracts ranging from one day to a full year); this added a greater degree of flexibility to the system by allowing the supply of slaves to be matched more efficiently to demand within the region. On the eve of the Civil War, approximately 6% of rural and 31% of urban slaves were hired out. In some Upper South cities such as Richmond and Lynchburg, Virginia, hiring arrangements employed one-half to two-thirds of male slaves. A vibrant internal slave trade also emerged, providing the Upper South with a new "crop" in human lives. According to Robert Fogel, more than 700,000 slaves of Maryland, Virginia, and the Carolinas were sold to the Lower South between 1790 and 1860, reducing the potential slave population of the former states by 60%.[5]

A third possible option was to employ the slaves in the nascent industries of the Upper South. The coal mining and iron manufacturing regions near Richmond and throughout the Appalachian Mountains had been active during the first half of the nineteenth century. Cotton mills began appearing in the towns along the fall line of the east coast—particularly during the 1840s—while tobacco factories became prominent in Virginia and North Carolina by the 1850s, before extending into Kentucky and Missouri. Other southern industries included hemp manufacturing, sugar refining, turpentine distilling, rice and flour milling, lead and salt mining, and lumbering. Southern industrial production nearly doubled in the 1850s, accounting for about 15% of the nation's total industrial capacity by the eve of the Civil War. And each of these industries relied heavily on slave labor.[6]

As a direct response to the novel risks associated with the evolving labor system of the Upper South, slaveholders like John Day sought policies on skilled urban slaves employed as trusted house servants and talented artisans, hired out to work in tobacco factories and brickyards, or engaged in especially dangerous industrial occupations such as mining, railroad construction, and steamboat employment. Jonathan Martin's recent work on slave hiring cites life insurance as one means of "protecting the long-term value of a slave" when in the possession of the hirer, while Ronald L. Lewis asserts that "by the 1840s, insurance for slave miners was common-place."[7] Life insurance thus provided a crucial level of protection for slaveholders employing their bondspeople under conditions of new entrepreneurial risk. The growth of life insurance on slaves directly coincides with the extension of slavery into the industries of the Upper South, particularly during the 1850s. As Robert Starobin concludes in *Industrial Slavery in the Old South,* "if slavery had survived past the 1860's, life insurance would have tended further to stabilize slave-based industries."[8] The slaveholders who embraced insurance were probably the same people at the core of Jonathan Daniel Wells's *The Origins of the Southern Middle Class*—people who envisioned a modern, industrialized, *slaveholding* South to com-pete with the mills, mines, and factories of the North.[9]

Insurance also became a means of raising capital for the purchase and manumis-sion of individual slaves, particularly in cases where a bondsperson was about to be taken away from his or her family and sold in the Lower South. Judges, mayors, and professors, as well as free blacks and ex-slaves, all solicited policies on recently pur-chased slaves whom they intended to free. The insurance was to serve as a type of loan collateral until the slave was able to earn his or her own purchase price. While life policies for the purpose of manumission only account for a small percentage of all slave insurance, they represent a novel attempt to prevent the family breakups commonly associated with the slave trade.

The Baltimore Life Insurance Company

The most successful life insurer to operate extensively in the antebellum South was Baltimore Life Insurance Company (1830–67). As is evident from the company's incorporation papers, its advertising literature, and its letters to agents, the organiz-ers and executives of the firm intended to concentrate on underwriting white lives; they did not initially seek slave risks. Yet this was the first life insurance institution in the United States to insure a slave on behalf of the owner (a $100 policy on the life of an enslaved man named Jacob in 1831). Baltimore Life would enjoy a virtual monopoly in slave insurance until the late 1840s and 1850s, when growing demand for such policies spawned competition from a small number of northern life institutions, from newly established southern life companies—particularly North Carolina Mutual (1849–62) and Greensboro Mutual (1853–65)—and from various southern fire insurance firms.[10] By the eve of the Civil War, slave insurance would account for more than two-thirds of new policies underwritten by Baltimore Life.[11]

Soon after its inception in 1830, Baltimore Life began receiving numerous inquiries from southerners regarding its willingness to insure the lives of slaves or animals: "Frequent applications are made for Ins[uranc]e. on valuable Horses and on Slaves . . . It is thought by well informed persons here [in Richmond] that these would be profitable subjects of Ins[uranc]e."[12] Solicitation of a *life* policy on a slave might initially appear to signify a slave's humanity in the eyes of the owner, but the combination of such requests with those on "valuable" animals indicates a more capitalistic concern to protect an investment. Indeed, it was not uncommon for a slave on the auction block to be examined much like an animal: as one former slave explained, "They look at your teeth, and pull your eyelids back and look at your eyes, and feel you just like you was a horse."[13] But for Baltimore Life, slaves and animals represented very different types of risks. The firm universally declined to insure the lives of animals—stating that these risks were "not at all connected with the objects of the institution which are principally to extend to the families of deceased persons the support they would otherwise be destitute of."[14] Company executives were likewise skeptical of insuring bondspeople; as the Fredericksburg, Virginia, agent commented in a letter to the company president in 1836, "I have frequent applications for insurance on slaves which I have declined in obedience to former instructions."[15] Nevertheless, the firm agreed to underwrite a handful of slaves almost every year during the 1830s and 1840s, even as executives opined that these were "not desirable risks."[16]

Baltimore Life had three main concerns about undertaking slave risks. First, the industry had very little information about the mortality of slaves by age, occupation, or geographic location, turning premium tables into mere guesswork. And even if the mortality of the slave population as a whole could be known, the tables would only apply if a large number of slaves were insured and applications were not biased toward the most at-risk bondspeople (such as those employed in dangerous occupations). Second, the company was concerned that the market value of slaves in general might decrease or that the value of an individual slave might deteriorate more rapidly than anticipated. (As John Day of Chuckatuck inquired, "If negroes should decline in value would it make a difference hereafter in the sum at which he is insured?")[17] Such policies would create a problem of moral hazard in which the potential insurance claim would render the slave more valuable dead than alive—

similar to the problem of buildings being insured for more than their market value. A final, related issue was that a slave's master, overseer, renter, or new buyer might mistreat the slave, diminishing his market value and possibly causing an untimely death. While these objections did not lead Baltimore Life to ban the sale of slave insurance, company executives put into place several strategies to limit the company's risk—strategies that greatly curbed the number of slave policies sold during the 1830s and 1840s despite growing requests by slaveholders.

To guarantee that premium payments adequately covered death claims on slave policies, Baltimore Life routinely charged double the rate quoted on white lives of the same age; for example, the premium on a 25-year-old slave was $2 per $100 of insurance (versus $1 on the corresponding white life).[18] Climate premiums of $1 to $2 per $100 of insurance for residence in or travel beyond the southern border of Virginia or Kentucky—identical to those charged on white lives—were also added to policies.[19] And while the company initially was unwilling to insure slaves "employed in dangerous service,"[20] by the second half of the 1830s it underwrote slaves engaged on steamboats for an additional $1 per $100 of insurance and those employed in Richmond coal mines for $3 more.[21]

Writing in 1849 on behalf of Thomas B. Barton—a prominent Fredericksburg lawyer seeking insurance on four servants—agent Dr. Beverly R. Wellford objected to these high rates: "The slaves . . . are well clothed and fed, are subject to far less exposure than [Barton] is in most instances, and if sick have the immediate attendance of the family physician . . . really I cannot perceive any peculiar hazard about our house servants for charging double rate."[22] The company, however, remained firm in its judgment regarding slave risks, even insisting on double rates in the case of "some <u>Free Negroes</u>, whose habits & general conduct are as <u>whites</u>."[23] While Thomas Barton reluctantly acquiesced to the premiums quoted, other potential customers concluded "the premium on the Negros is considered too high."[24] As long as Baltimore Life remained uninterested in promoting the sale of slave policies, this conservative rate structure protected the company's interests.

A second mechanism for reducing the risk of underwriting slaves was to confine policies to amounts "not exceeding 2/3 of actual value."[25] As the company advised Petersburg, Virginia, agent W. F. Davis in 1839, "The value of Slaves is fluctuating, besides we like to leave no room for fraud. For these reasons we seldom (indeed never) take the full value of Slaves."[26] Since slaveholders could bypass this regulation and insure a slave for his full value (or more) by taking out policies with more than one company, Baltimore Life stipulated that "there must be no other insurance on the same life."[27] Finally, although the firm initially quoted rates for slave risks covering their whole term of life, with only two exceptions it refused to insure slaves for more than seven years.[28] This allowed the company to regularly reexamine both market conditions and the health of the individual slave.

The company was especially concerned that mistreatment of slaves could result in an untimely death. Baltimore Life was "particular as to their masters,"[29] reminding its agents on several occasions, "We have insured Negroes where their masters were known as persons of respectability,"[30] and "it is important that the owner of a slave shall have a good reputation."[31] The company relied on its local agents to vouch for the treatment of a slave by the master. Regarding one request for insurance, the Petersburg, Virginia, agent stipulated: "I can say with much confidence (as I have been intimate in his family from a boy) [the treatment] is such as few servants meet with from the most humane masters . . . It is with Mr. S. [Thomas Shire] a step of <u>prudence</u>, and not for the <u>gain</u>, as I know he would <u>much</u> rather they should live."[32] Similarly, the Fredericksburg agent wrote that Thomas Barton was "a gentleman of the first respectability, who of course treats them kindly and provides liberally comforts for them of every sort,"[33] while the Richmond agent could attest: "Mr. W. [William Walthall] is known to me personally as a kind & humane master and a highly respectable man."[34]

While southerners publicly embraced the idea that no rational slaveholder would willingly destroy his own property, various attempts to legislate the humane treatment of enslaved people exposed the darker side of the system. By 1821, for example, slaveholders in every southern state could potentially face murder charges for the gratuitous killing of a slave or for a death directly resulting from the infliction of punishment.[35] Baltimore Life's Petersburg agent was perhaps more blunt than most when he declared, "There are many persons in this place who might wish to insure their servants, but there are only a very few whom I could say any thing in favor of, being as well acquainted as I am with the avariciousness of mankind <u>generally</u>."[36] Thus personal testimonies on the part of the agents were not merely epistolary flourishes but helped to minimize the company's risk when underwriting such lives.

Baltimore Life was also wary of slaveholders' selling or hiring out their insured slaves to another master. As Jonathan Martin argues in *Divided Mastery,* hiring especially threatened to undermine the paternalism at the core of the slave system by replacing "mutual duties and responsibilities" with impersonal market relations and thus divorcing the slave from the "natural discretion and prudence" of the owner.[37] In light of this problem, Baltimore Life approved one policy with the caveat that the slaves "remain in the service of their present master. We should not like to be answerable for them should they be sold & dispersed in different directions & owned by men that we know nothing of."[38] And it repeatedly stipulated: "The Policy [is] not transferable without our consent, that we may have confidence in the master."[39]

"Redeemed by his labor": Life Insurance as a Vehicle for Manumission

Some of the earliest requests to the company for slave insurance policies came from southerners who sought to use life insurance as a means of manumitting individual slaves. In September 1833, for example, the Washington, DC, agent wrote the company regarding a special request for life insurance from a free black government employee, "a very respectable and intelligent Negro man, the under Messenger of the Secretary of State." He had recently paid $600 for a slave "who was about to be carried to Georgia . . . and wishes to insure to that amount on the life of the latter. He is to remain here and to redeem himself by his labor."[40] In effect, the under-messenger entered into an indenture agreement with the slave. He purchased him with the express intent of allowing the slave to earn his own freedom over a seven-year period; the $600 purchase price was in reality a loan to the slave. The life insurance policy was a means of protecting this loan, much as a creditor might insure the life of a debtor until the debt was paid.

Just as middle-class northerners were encouraged to use their life insurance policies as collateral for a loan, free blacks sought the same privilege in order to purchase enslaved family members. In 1852, ex-slave John P. Cox wished to take out a life policy on himself to use as collateral for a loan to purchase his wife; if he died before resolving the debt, his creditors would be compensated. Former Maryland state senator Richard Potts of Frederick solicited Baltimore Life on behalf of Cox, "a colored man . . . of good habits & character, and sound health."[41] The company complied with this request, issuing Cox a $250 policy for seven years, which he then assigned to Potts as one of his creditors.[42] A similar case involved Baltimore resident Noah Davis. In his 1859 autobiography, *A Narrative of the Life of Rev. Noah Davis, A Colored Man,* he recounted three separate instances in which he needed immediate funds to purchase the freedom of his family who were still enslaved in Virginia. In 1851, he borrowed several hundred dollars for the purchase of his wife and two youngest children, using an insurance policy on his own life as collateral for the loan. Just four years later, he learned that his eldest "boy was in one of the trader's jails in Richmond, and for sale. The dealer knew me, and was disposed to let me have him, if I could get any one to purchase him." This time, he convinced a "friend" in Baltimore to advance him the money, insuring his son's life as collateral. Finally, in 1857, his daughter was on the auction block in Fredericksburg. Davis convinced two gentlemen to purchase her and allow her to work off the price, securing this loan with a $1,000 policy on her life.[43]

Free blacks were not the only people to engage in this type of manumission. In

1835 Judge Buckner Thruston of the U.S. Court of Appeals for the DC Circuit inquired about obtaining a life insurance policy worth $600 on a slave he had recently bought. Agent James H. Causten wrote to the company: "The motive is purely benevolent, to prevent the sale from his family of the man, who the Judge has known for many years & is willing to advance the money to save him. The Judge speaks in the highest terms of the slave, who is a bricklayer, robust & healthy and particularly abstemious."[44] In a rare abatement of company policy, Baltimore Life even offered to compromise with Thruston on the rate of premium when he complained of being charged double the rate on white lives.[45] The following year, china and glass merchant Hugh C. Smith of Alexandria, Virginia, also paid $600 to prevent the breakup of a local slave family. The slave wife and her infant son had been sold to the infamous Washington-area slave trader John Armfield. Smith wrote to the company, "My only object in insuring is to secure myself against all risks until the money is repaid me."[46] Fourteen years later, the formerly enslaved family resided together as free citizens of the District of Columbia, along with an additional six children. They had even managed to accumulate a respectable $350 in real estate wealth by 1850.[47]

Requests of this type continued during the 1840s and 1850s. George Lawry of Georgetown, Virginia, solicited insurance on his recently purchased slave "for five or six years, as it is my intention]t to free him as soon as he earns the am[oun]t I have paid for him."[48] Charles Herndon, a young lawyer from Fredericksburg, bought Thomas Gibbs "for the purpose of allowing him to buy his freedom but wishe[d] to protect himself from loss & therefore insure[d] his life."[49] And Richard Swann—a librarian at the Annapolis Naval Academy—wrote the company in 1859 on behalf of "Some of the Professors at Naval Academy & myself," who had "enabled a very worthy Servant man who has been employed for years in one of [the] Departments to purchase himself Knowing if he lives he will refund the Money."[50]

It is impossible to know the full extent of these types of policies, but other companies also underwrote the lives of slaves during their transition to freedom. In 1857, merchant John R. Thornton purchased a 30-year-old slave named Ephraim Delany Cannon, whom he then transported to his home in New Bedford, Massachusetts. Thornton intended to "employ him as a servant in his family" but wished to guarantee that Cannon did not die before earning back his purchase price by insuring him with New England Mutual for "one thousand dollars on his life for seven years, by which time he expects to save out of his wages the sum he has cost."[51]

The majority of these cases involved slaves who were in danger of being sold to distant locations. William H. Miller of Alexandria, Virginia, purchased a $500 slave policy in 1836. The agent noted: "He represents that the Slave was about to be sold to the South, when Mr. Miller, who knew his good habits & faithfulness, and to prevent his separation from his family, paid the residue of the purchase money, which the policy is intended to secure. The motive is represented to be purely benevolent."[52] In 1852, Mayor Henry Addison of Georgetown intervened on behalf of a 30-year-old "good Mechanic" named William Hurd who was being sold away from his family: "His Master . . . agreed to sell him to an owner in Georgetown (where the boy has always lived) for $700, but this person not having the funds, the Mayor of the Town agreed to advance the amount from the town Treasury provided the boys life was insured to the same extent."[53] The mayor received a one-year policy to cover the risk until the new owner could repay the city.[54]

As Michael Tadman demonstrates in *Speculators and Slaves*, the domestic slave trade was the greatest fear of enslaved people of the Upper South, and southerners were highly conflicted regarding this trade. On one hand, the existence of the trade appeared to undermine the paternalistic relationship that was at the heart of most defenses of slavery. Indeed, abolitionist propaganda such as Harriet Beecher Stowe's *Uncle Tom's Cabin* often focused on the dislocations wrought by the slave trade in highlighting the evils of the system. On the other hand, the interregional slave trade was highly active and crucial to the ongoing stability of slavery. Some southerners denied the existence or extent of the trade, others disparaged the slave traders even while employing their services, and still others rationalized that the effects of family separations on the "less-developed" emotions of the enslaved were minimal.[55] The people seeking manumission policies with Baltimore Life formed a fourth group. These were southerners who believed that the breakup of slave families weakened the paternalistic nature of the system by violating the unwritten code of behavior to which slaveholders were expected to adhere. While slaves were obliged to demonstrate loyalty and subservience toward their masters, the owners had a reciprocal obligation to provide for the lifetime needs of their bondspeople as dependent family members. The use of excessive or unjustified force, sexual assault, and familial breakups were all considered flagrant breaches of this code.

The people purchasing the insurance policies had an individual, paternalistic relationship with the slaves they bought, making statements such as "He has been in my employ for some six or eight years a man of steady habits,"[56] and calling them "very orderly and estimable"[57] or "very worthy,"[58] witnessing to their "good habits & faithfulness,"[59] or vouching for them "in the highest terms."[60] In short, each of these enslaved people was properly performing his or her assigned role in the slave system, making the breach of good faith by the master all the more abhorrent. Judge Thruston was "willing to advance the money *to save*" the slave from being separated from his family (emphasis added).[61] Charles Herndon sought to free Thomas Gibbs despite "the declension" of Fredericksburg—one of the cities active in the slave trade.[62] None of these insurance cases was motivated by abolitionist sentiments, nor did they belie any underlying disapproval of slavery as a whole. Each of these slave purchasers simply felt that it was his duty as an upstanding member of the community to intervene and correct a perceived abuse of the system.

Underwriting Urban Slavery

Manumission policies were only a small portion of slave insurance in Baltimore Life; a greater percentage of policies were taken out by slaveholders to protect their investment in slaves. Although very little information on either the slaves insured or their owners exists for the 1830s and 1840s, the available facts clearly indicate that this insurance was an urban phenomenon. Between 1831 and 1836 at least 71% of slave policies with Baltimore Life were purchased by urban residents, two-thirds of whom lived in Baltimore itself. Even as sales spread from the company's home base, urban slaveholders—including a manufacturer, a postmaster, a newspaper publisher, an agent at a copper works, a jeweler, a messenger, a clerk, a German Reformed clergyman, and numerous merchants—accounted for more than three-quarters of slave policies written by the company between 1837 and 1848.[63] The high percentage of urban residents among owners of policies on slaves combined with the letters from inquirers provides strong evidence that few rural slaveholders desired policies on their farm laborers.

Many insured slaves were skilled artisans and house servants. For example, John Day of Chuckatuck and B. W. Green of Richmond both sought policies on carpenters; Green described the man he wanted to insure as working "in my own Shop with only two other whites and one Slave." Green's 1836 letter also inquired into the rates for a "valuable House Servant employed in my own Family" and "4 or 5 others who are employed in driving Carts and Wagons on the Street."[64] During the late 1830s, numerous requests for insurance on slaves being shipped to the Lower South began to arrive at Baltimore Life offices as well. But reflecting a belief shared by the entire industry that the living environment was much less healthy beyond the southern border of Virginia and Kentucky, the company was only willing to underwrite the risk of the journey: "we shou'd not like to continue the Insurance on them after their arrival."[65] While a small number of slaveholders solicited policies on their entire workforce—for example William Walthall of Jefferson, Virginia, on his fifteen to twenty workers who were "House Servants, some of them employed at . . . his Store & Mill perhaps some in the field"—these inquiries were exceptional.[66] By the 1840s a slaveholder rarely purchased policies with Baltimore Life on more than one or two slaves. In all likelihood, these slaveholders only owned a handful of people, in which case the loss of any one could result in a significant blow to their investment portfolio.

Far more common were inquiries for insurance on slaves engaged in dangerous occupations such as mining, railroad construction, or work on steamboats. In the late 1830s Richard Bagnal of Norfolk sought to insure a carpenter and a barber employed on the steamship *South Carolina*,[67] Samuel Wilson of Washington, DC, wanted coverage "against <u>being drowned exclusively</u>" on a teenage boy he had hired out as a cook on a Potomac River trading schooner;[68] and Wilson Winfree of Chesterfield, Virginia, wished to insure two slaves working in the coal pits of Swan & Gwathmey.[69] Baltimore Life initially complied with these requests, yet increasing numbers of steamboat and mining accidents (such as the explosion at Cox's Pit near Richmond in 1850) led to a temporary moratorium on such risks by mid-century.[70] "We have no objection to insure Negroes working in the construction of Rail Roads, but w[oul]d. decline those working in Coal pits," wrote one company correspondent.[71]

The popularity of slave policies—and the willingness of Baltimore Life to issue them—grew significantly during the late 1840s and early 1850s, more than doubling from 4% of new policies in the 1830s and 1840s to 9% at midcentury (see appendix, table A.5). In addition to increasing numbers of direct inquiries from slaveholders, Baltimore Life also began to hear from people wishing to open agencies dedicated to slave policies. For example, Gwathmey Pine of St. Louis wrote in 1844: "I am the agent of the New York Mutual Life Insurance Co . . . and they <u>do not</u> Insure the Lives of <u>Slaves</u>, or Black persons. I have had numerous applications to insure the lives of Slaves . . . and understanding that your company do that kind of business, I beg leave to solicit your Agency."[72] When Baltimore Life hesitated to open an agency that "will include only part of our risks,"[73] Pine resigned his agency with New York Mutual and again solicited Baltimore Life to open a St. Louis agency, writing, "I could do a very large business by insuring the Lives of Slaves, and probably some on white persons. I have, even now, almost daily applications for Slave insurance."[74] Unfortunately, Baltimore Life was less confident that slave insurance—"and probably some on white persons"—would generate enough business to make the agency worthwhile and therefore, once again, declined Pine's offer.[75] The company remained focused on its sales to white southerners and never anticipated that slave policies would come to dominate its business.

Requests for slave agencies continued to arrive in the early 1850s, including solicitations from county clerk Frederick Johnston of Roanoke, Virginia, insurance agent Franklin Slaughter of Fredericksburg, and farmer and merchant Charles E.

Beynroth of Louisville, Kentucky. Each wrote that he served as an agent for various fire, marine, and life insurance companies who refused to underwrite slaves, but each believed he could do a profitable business in that line.[76] Slaughter, for example, already had "a very large number of applications . . . which I am not authorized to take by any of the Companies for which I am agent."[77] Baltimore Life executives declined the appeals of both Slaughter and Johnston and only offered Beynroth an agency in Louisville on half commission, which he refused.[78]

Even though Baltimore Life continued to turn down new agencies dedicated to slave insurance, its executives could not possibly ignore the increase in sales of such policies or the growing competition in this area. The company was almost alone in underwriting such risks during the 1830s and 1840s, but with the increasing demand of the late 1840s and 1850s—particularly in the urban, industrialized areas of the Upper South—more companies were willing to provide slave policies. It is nearly impossible to determine the full extent to which slaveholders sought to insure their slaves, but the extant evidence indicates that Baltimore Life (1830–67), North Carolina Mutual Life (1849–64), Mutual Benefit Life and Fire of Louisiana (1849–53), Greensboro Mutual Life (1853–65), and Virginia Life of Richmond (1860–63) all underwrote a significant number of slave risks.[79] The 1851 edition of *Affleck's Southern Rural Almanack* indicated that most southern insurance companies (though few in number) were willing to insure slaves.[80] By the late 1850s, slave insurance accounted for more than three-quarters of North Carolina Mutual's policies, declining to two-thirds during the war years before ceasing altogether. This heavy reliance on slave policies—combined with the economic difficulties wrought by the Civil War—accounted for the company's failure by 1864. Most other southern companies likewise went out of business in the aftermath of the war.[81]

Reflecting the dual designation of slaves as both persons and property, competition for slave risks during the 1850s also came from southern fire insurance companies including Georgia Insurance and Trust Company of Baltimore, Richmond Fire Association of Virginia, Asheville Mutual Insurance Company of North Carolina, and Lynchburg Hose and Fire Insurance Company of Virginia.[82] In 1853, the secretary of Lynchburg Hose and Fire inquired of his agent in Staunton, Virginia, "What is the prospect for that kind of business with you? It is increasing here [in Lynchburg] very rapidly." Indeed, by that year Richmond Fire Association had written over 1,700 slave policies within the commonwealth of Virginia.[83] However, the records of defunct fire insurance companies are even harder to locate than those of life companies.

It is less clear how common slave policies were among the larger insurance institutions of the Northeast, although many are known to have at least temporarily accepted slave risks. For example, when Franklin A. Slaughter solicited a slave agency from Baltimore Life in the early 1850s, he stated: "The Life riskes [*sic*] taken by me for account of the Mutual Benefit Life Ins. co . . . until recently embraced all Classes of Life riskes. That Company however does not now take riskes on the lives of Slaves."[84] Some northern companies such as New York Life and Trust, Girard Life of Philadelphia, and Mutual Life of New York appear to have refused to insure slaves—with NYL&T and Mutual Life even declining to underwrite the lives of free blacks. But many others at one time accepted these risks, including New York Life, United States Life of New York, Aetna Life of Hartford, Hartford Life, Charter Oak of Hartford, National Safety Life and Trust of Philadelphia, Mutual Benefit of New Jersey, North American Life, Knickerbocker Life of New York, British Commercial Life of London, and National Loan Fund Life of London (New York office). Extant insurance contracts include 338 slave policies written by National Safety as of 1853, but only 24 written by Charter Oak as of 1858.[85]

One particularly valuable source, the Slavery Era Insurance Registry released by the California Department of Insurance in May 2002, required all companies actively doing business within that state in the year 2000—or their predecessor companies—to search their records for evidence of slave policies. Of approximately eighty-two antebellum life companies, only nineteen underwrote policies in California at the end of the twentieth century. Of these, three found evidence of slave policies in their records (see appendix, table A.6). A similar requirement in Illinois, effective January 1, 2004, produced identical results.[86]

New York Life (chartered in 1841 as Nautilus Insurance Company), was doing a relatively slow business in white northeastern lives when, in February 1846, several southern agents of the company started selling policies on the lives of slaves. Slave policies accounted for 339 of the firm's first 1,000 policies. According to New York Life historian Lawrence Abbott, the trustees voted on April 19, 1848, to discontinue this line because "the Company soon discovered that the acceptance of slave risks was indeed a risky business." Over that short two-year period, the company had sold policies to approximately 235 slaveholders covering 488 slaves. But by then New York Life was also doing a brisk business in nonslave policies, becoming the fourth-largest insurer by 1850; slave risks were no longer essential to its survival and could be discontinued.[87]

The slaves most commonly insured by New York Life (almost one-quarter of all policies) were employed on boats as firemen, engineers, cabin boys, waiters, penmen, cooks, and ships carpenters. Miners and coal pit employees accounted for 17% of policies. Without question, these were some of the most dangerous occupations for whites or blacks during the mid-nineteenth century, so it is hardly surprising that slaveholders sought insurance on these people. But other occupations listed reveal that owners bought insurance not only to protect against a greater probability of loss but also to cover especially skilled or valued slaves. Approximately 17% of policies insured artisans, particularly carpenters but also a variety of other craftsmen including brickmakers, masons, blacksmiths, bakers, and barbers; another 12% of policies covered house servants (see appendix, table A.7).[88] As historian Jonathan Martin indicates, these were the same slave employments most likely to be filled through hiring contracts.[89]

The distribution of occupations for slaves underwritten by Baltimore Life from 1849 to 1853 demonstrates a similar pattern, although the firm's cautiousness toward underwriting slaves engaged on steamboats or in coal pits during this time period is readily apparent. As in prior years, at least 80% of those who held policies on slaves with Baltimore Life were urban residents, many of whom sought policies on blacksmiths, clerks, butchers, shoemakers, and brickyard workers.[90] In 1852, Richmond bricklayer Peter Glinn obtained a seven-year policy worth $1,000 on the life of his assistant bricklayer, whom he referred to as "a very valuable hand."[91] Two years later, Richmond boot- and shoemaker David B. Franklin purchased a policy on his assistant Edward, who "would sell in the market for 11 or 1200 dollars. He is very Valuable on that account they hire for 200 dollars good boot makers."[92] Ranging in age from 17 to 45 (and averaging 29), these slaves were a vital part of their owners' businesses, but—unlike field hands—their skills made them both difficult to replace and highly valuable at older ages.[93]

By far the largest number of mid-century Baltimore Life policies was written on urban house servants (see appendix, table A.7). The practice of insuring house servants reflects the significance of slaves within the household economy; the knowledge, experience, and trust that many house servants possessed made them prime candidates for insuring. While life insurance could never replace a valued servant, knowledge and experience could be purchased with the proceeds of a policy. These Baltimore Life solicitations (as well as the company's instructions to agents concerning masters) indicate that most of the slaves insured with that firm remained in the direct employment of their masters through midcentury.[94]

As other companies began selling slave insurance, the types of checks set by Baltimore Life during the 1830s to mitigate risks became the standard of the industry. Slave policies were confined to one year with Richmond Fire Association, four years with Virginia Life of Richmond, five years with North Carolina Mutual and National Loan Fund, and seven years with National Safety Life. North Carolina Mutual and Virginia Life policies could be taken for up to two-thirds the value of the slave, while National Loan Fund, National Safety, and Lynchburg Hose and Fire permitted policies for three-quarters of slaves' market value. All companies charged additional premiums of $0.50 to $2.00 per $100 of insurance for slaves engaged in hazardous occupations such as on boats, on railroads, in coal pits or mines, or as engineers or firemen. Further, both National Safety and National Loan Fund voided the policy in cases where the employment of the slave was changed without written consent of the company.[95]

Like Baltimore Life, National Loan Fund specifically stipulated that "there must be no other insurance on the same life," while Charter Oak, North Carolina Mutual, and Greensboro Mutual insurance contracts all declared that the existence of multiple policies would cancel the claim on the company. Similarly, new companies shared Baltimore Life's concern about the treatment of the slaves. Charter Oak slave policies were void if the slave died "by the hands of a mob—or by a foreign invasion—or by an insurrection—or by the neglect, abuse, or maltreatment of the owner or any one to whom he shall be entrusted," or in cases where the slave "shall be forced, permitted or entreated by his owner, or by the agent of the owner, to engage in any combat causing his death—or shall abscond or be kidnapped." Similar contracts from North Carolina Mutual and Greensboro Mutual also specifically voided the policy if the slave died "for want of proper medical or personal attendance." Only National Loan Fund and National Safety appear to have permitted the assignment of policies "without first obtaining the consent of the Company."[96]

Like Baltimore Life, each of these companies was aware of the potential for fluctuations in the value of a slave and the resulting moral hazard inherent in such insurance. In the November 1847 edition of *De Bow's Commercial Review,* Dr. Josiah Clark Nott—a well-known racial theorist and a medical examiner for several insurance companies in Mobile, Alabama—warned:

> Life insurance on negroes offers strong temptations to be feared . . . As long as the negro is sound, and worth more than the amount insured, self-interest will prompt the owner to preserve the life of the slave; but, if the slave become unsound and there is little prospect of perfect recovery, the underwriters cannot expect fair play—the insurance money is worth more than the slave . . . Any man who will drive a horse cruelly, will drive a negro or operative to death, if he can gain anything by so doing.

But Dr. Nott's main concern in this article was that the rates insurance companies charged on slaves were not adequate to cover the risk. He opined, "Insurance companies are going into this branch of their business pell-mell, without knowing anything of the probabilities," and believed "there are yet no data by which the value of these lives can be fixed with sufficient accuracy to justify the thoughtless procedure of some companies."[97] Ironically, the only area in which new entrants chose to deviate widely from Baltimore Life's restrictions was with regard to the premium rates. Although in all cases they remained higher than the standard premiums on white lives, few companies followed Baltimore Life's lead in charging double the rate on white lives (see appendix, table A.8). As adequate statistics on the mortality rate of slaves were not available, the premium tables were, at best, educated guesses as to what was actuarially sound; at worst, they were blatant attempts to undercut the competition.

Underwriting Industrial Slavery

Despite growing demand for slave insurance and increasing competition from other life and fire companies, at midcentury Baltimore Life was still wary of underwriting too many of these risks. But in 1854—in response to the persistent solicitations of two entrepreneurial slaveholders from Richmond—the company for the first time decided to actively pursue slave policies in that city and to allow policies on hired out slaves. In stark contrast to the company's prior history, approximately 59% of all Baltimore Life policies written between 1854 and 1860 underwrote slaves, peaking at about 70% of all new policies by the eve of the Civil War (see appendix, table A.5). More than 80% of these slave policies were sold through the new Richmond office—mostly on slaves employed in the city's growing industrial enterprises.

Although still lagging far behind the North, at midcentury Richmond was the most heavily industrialized city in the South. More than half of its adult males (white and black) were employed in manufacturing by 1860. According to the census returns, capital investment in Richmond manufacturing increased by 260% during the 1850s, with slaves dominating the labor force of both the tobacco factories and iron foundries of the urban center as well as the coal pits of the periphery. Even if industrial slaves comprised only 5% of the total slave population of the South, they were crucial to the economies of Richmond, Lynchburg, Petersburg, Fredericksburg, and Norfolk, Virginia.[98]

In a letter almost identical to those sent by potential agents of the 1840s and early 1850s, John Darracott of Richmond wrote Baltimore Life in March 1853 regarding the establishment of a slave insurance agency. Although "the office that [he] was ag[en]t for ha[d] declined insurance on Slaves," he saw great potential in this line of insurance: "I think a good business could be done."[99] Later that year, Darracott was joined by Thomas Pollard, a Richmond physician and slaveholder, who believed "that the prospects of business in the way of life Insurance particularly for Servants, were at this time good." Pollard informed the firm that there were only two companies underwriting slaves in Richmond, "the Richmond Fire Association . . . which insures for only one year, and seems indifferent about this kind of Insurance" and an unnamed Philadelphia-based company. Pollard was confident that the changing composition of the Richmond economy made it particularly conducive to slave insurance: "The Negro population is increasing here rapidly, and we think an agency of a Southern Co. would be more in favour with our people than one from a free state."[100]

Although Baltimore Life had closed its Richmond office only a year earlier—with the local agent declaring that "the public did not seem to regard the inducements sufficient for investment"[101]—new secretary Henry F. Thompson decided to reopen the agency on a trial basis. The firm's only stipulation was that the agents guarantee adequate premiums to pay the steep Virginia state and Richmond city taxes on agencies of out-of-state insurance companies.[102] Pollard and Darracott immediately joined the efforts of Franklin Slaughter of Fredericksburg in challenging the constitutionality of the Virginia tax law.[103] Thirty-eight Richmond citizens—among them doctors, lawyers, and merchants—sent a petition to the state legislature in 1854 stating that there was "a growing demand for Insurance on the Lives of Slaves" but the taxes imposed were "almost prohibitory." They also noted that at least six life agencies operating in Richmond had closed their doors since the law was first passed in 1842.[104] The petition was successful, with the legislature voting in 1856 to significantly reduce the tax.[105]

Even as they were negotiating with the home office and petitioning the Virginia state legislature, Darracott and Pollard lost no time in proving to Baltimore Life executives the value of focusing on Richmond slaveholders. During 1854, slave policies accounted for over 60% of Baltimore Life sales (mostly through the Richmond office) and were equivalent to the total number of slaves underwritten by the company since 1836. The Richmond agents initially targeted their friends and families ("What insurances we have effected has [*sic*] been entirely among our acquaintances"),[106] and more than half of the policies in the first year were purchased by Darracott, Pollard, or their relatives.[107] But beyond tapping into their kinship networks, the pair believed that with proper advertising they could possibly underwrite "100 or 150 slaves in 12 months."[108] However, their ideas quickly came in conflict with the risk-reducing restrictions set by the home office, particularly with regard to insuring coal pit hands or slaves hired out for railroad construction and in tobacco factories. They sought to place Baltimore Life on a better footing vis-à-vis its emerging competition in the slave insurance field by relaxing the limits on policy amounts and bringing slave premiums more in line with other companies and endeavored to extend sales by targeting traders in the active Richmond slave market.

By the 1850s, court cases in several southern states had established the responsibility of the hirer to compensate the owner of a slave in cases of injury or death, thus alleviating some of the moral hazard associated with hiring out insured slaves.[109] Given this legal change, Baltimore Life executives silently acquiesced on the issue of insuring slaves hired out from their owners to work in railroad construction and tobacco factories. Southern railroads—including the Southside in Petersburg (built 1849–54), the Richmond and Danville (1847–56), and the Virginia and Tennessee connecting Lynchburg, Virginia, with Bristol, Tennessee (1850–56)—depended heavily on slave laborers in their construction.[110] While Baltimore Life had permitted few policies on bondspeople employed on railroads during the early years of construction, more than one-third of the policies sold through the Richmond office in 1854 were on the lives of slaves hired out to railroads. Likewise, the laborers in the tobacco factories of Richmond, Petersburg, Lynchburg, and Danville, Virginia, were "almost exclusively" slaves, yet no tobacco factory hands were underwritten by Baltimore Life until 1854; factory slaves would account for one-quarter of all policies during the second half of the decade (see appendix, table A.9).[111]

As railroad construction diminished, Pollard and Darracott sought to target another major industry that engaged slave labor: the coal mines of central Virginia. Although the firm had placed a complete moratorium on insuring mine workers during the early 1850s and still did "not like the risks of coal pit hands at present rates," it was willing to defer to the opinion of the agency, being "glad to receive from Dr. Pollard his ideas in full, as regards the additional risk."[112] After inquiring into accident and death rates at the Midlothian Coal Pits, Black Heath pits, the pits on the north side of the James River, and those in Kanawha, Virginia, Pollard concluded: "I have thought for a long time that coal pits are more healthy places for negroes than factories or R. Roads. They have sufficiently active labour there without Exposure to the vicissitudes of weather. To negroes predisposed to consumption & of this disease a great many die in Va., I think the location is particularly favourable."[113] Despite the strong possibility that Pollard's opinion was biased (historians note that "insufficient ventilation and carelessness in safety procedures meant that slave miners were particularly vulnerable to industrial accidents"),[114] the firm accepted his advice to underwrite coal pit hands with the moderate addition of $1 per $100 of insurance.[115] But after several coal pit explosions in the mid-1850s led to a higher number of claims than predicted, Baltimore Life issued temporary freezes on such policies during 1856 and again in the summer of 1857, in the end relenting only to underwrite coal pit hands at much higher premium rates (see appendix, table A.9).[116]

Increasing competition from emerging southern life and fire companies—as well as nagging agents—led Baltimore Life to reconsider other conservative elements of its slave policies. In the mid-1850s, most companies (Baltimore Life included) were only willing to insure between two-thirds and three-quarters of the value of a slave, with an absolute insurance limit of $800 on males and $500 on females—although North Carolina Mutual underwrote a greater amount if "the slave to be insured is a first rate Mechanic and a No 1 risk"[117] and National Safety "when the valuation is $1,500, or upwards."[118] But the market value of slaves was rising rapidly at midcentury, placing pressure on these limits. According to the reports of Richmond slave traders compiled by Michael Tadman, prices of "No. 1 men (19–25 yrs)" increased from between $550 and $725 in 1846 to between $1,400 and $1,650 by 1860. "No. 1 women (16–20 yrs)" sold for $425–$475 in 1846, but their price almost tripled to $1,300–$1,525 by 1860.[119]

In light of these escalating market valuations, several companies began relaxing their insurance limits. In 1860 the newly chartered Virginia Life Insurance Company set virtually no upper bound for the amount of insurance: "In the case of negro mechanics, worth at least $2,000, insurance may be effected for the amount of $1,500."[120] Baltimore Life was willing to increase its insurance caps to $1,000 for males and $800 for females but was reluctant to allow policy amounts to follow the market trend.[121] By early 1860, agents like P. B. Price of Richmond were complaining: "It seems inexpedient to fix the limit on men at $1000. Other Companies do not do it & I think we shall lose patronage by making this limit invariable . . . Negro men are now selling at about $1600 & women in the same proportion; necessarily therefore, upon the ¾ principle, much higher risks will be demanded then formerly."[122] Yet only in a small number of cases did the firm permit policies on males for $1,200 and on females for $1,000 during 1859 and 1860.[123]

The risk to insurers of fluctuating slave prices was further complicated by the increasing popularity of longer policies. Although Baltimore Life had always permitted slaves to be insured for up to seven years, the average policy length during the 1830s and 1840s was only two and a half years (see appendix, table A.5). This allowed the company to reassess its risks on a relatively frequent basis. Policy lengths increased moderately to three and a half years at midcentury before jumping to five and a half years by the late 1850s. Slaveholders increasingly were purchasing the more expensive seven-year policies on their enslaved people, demonstrating their faith in the future of the slave system and in the growing importance of slavery within southern industries. Baltimore Life was thus being tied into longer contract terms just as slave values were skyrocketing, but it very wisely refused to undertake the additional risk of larger policy amounts. Yet even the firm's relatively conservative approach to slave valuations proved too liberal as the threat of war loomed.

According to Tadman, the maximum amount asked for slaves in 1861 had declined to $900–$1,000 on males and $750–$850 on females.[124] Writing to the Richmond agent Price in October 1860, Secretary M. M. Coulter expressed the company's concern: "I notice by the paper that the value of Slaves is rapidly depreciating in the Richmond market. If this is so, do you think it will increase the risk of insurance? We do not wish to exceed three fourths of their value in any case, nor estimate them at too low a figure."[125]

Despite this concern with declining slave values, it was ironically in the final months before the Civil War that Baltimore Life started to actively promote slave insurance as a priority of the firm. Although the company had faced competition from several life and fire insurance companies during the 1850s, it was only in 1860 that the first major *life* insurance competitor opened its doors in Richmond, the Virginia Life Insurance Company. In its inaugural brochure, Virginia Life stated that "this Company will also give special attention to the insurance of SLAVE PROP-ERTY" and that it hoped "after sufficient observation and experience therein, the Companies will be able to afford better terms to the insurers of slaves." The com-pany also emphasized its local pedigree, encouraging slaveholders to "INSURE . . . AT HOME" rather than with "Yankee Companies."[126] Baltimore Life recognized the direct threat posed by Virginia Life to its most successful agency. In light of the fact that slave policies now dominated its portfolio, by the fall of 1860 it began to reex-amine its conservative rules in order to remain competitive in this line.

Both Pollard and Darracott had expressed their belief that it would be profitable to target domestic slave traders, the latter stating in 1854 that "we should get a good many [policies] this fall when the traders start south by advertising and at good rates."[127] But Baltimore Life, North Carolina Mutual, and Greensboro Mutual all refused to insure a large number of slaves outside of the Upper South because of the allegedly unhealthy climate farther south. The latter two firms forbade insured slaves to "pass beyond the limits of the State of North Carolina" without the writ-ten consent of the company,[128] while as late as 1853 Baltimore Life still stipulated that it was "willing to take risks on slaves conveyed out of the state for the journey only."[129] But by the end of the decade, it had relaxed this rule to allow underwriting of slaves in the northern and central parts of Mississippi, Alabama, Georgia, and the Carolinas.[130]

In October 1860, Pollard recommended Lucien Lewis as the firm's new Rich-mond agent precisely because he was an "agent for hiring Negroes, and is Establish-ing a good business in this line."[131] Upon accepting the agency, Lewis suggested that the company aggressively market slave insurance policies by placing advertise-ments in Virginia newspapers in towns where large numbers of slaves were hired out[132] and putting up placards "in the Auction Houses, Hirers Offices, tobacco factories, Tobacco Exchange &c, and send[ing] some to be hung in the principal Depots on the roads leading into the City."[133] Lewis felt that this would be a highly prosperous avenue for the company to explore because "there are one or two sections of the state from which large numbers of negroes are sent to this city to be hired out, and where I am quite well known."[134] The company encouraged its other Virginia agents to start soliciting slave traders as well. On Christmas Eve Secretary Coulter wrote to R. F. Lester of Petersburg, "I believe this is the season for hiring Negroes and with some effort you might succeed in insuring many of them,"[135] and to Charles L. Mosby of Lynchburg he wrote, "We are informed that it is customary for owners to send their Negroes from the adjacent Counties to the City to be hired out during the winter. We have taken many risks of this character & think you might be able to secure some by applying to those agents who attend to the hiring business exclusively."[136]

In addition to targeting slave traders and hirers, Pollard wrote a series of letters to the company in 1855 in which he lobbied Baltimore Life executives to "reduce . . . rates on Slave Insurance to the rates of the Co's with whom we have to compete in this city . . . it would put us on an Equality with these companies, and obviate an objection with which we are frequently met that we charge more than they do."[137] In another letter, Pollard attached the published rate tables from several companies underwriting slaves in Richmond, including Richmond Fire Association, National Safety Life Insurance and Trust Company of Philadelphia, and National Loan Fund Life Assurance of London (see appendix, table A.8).[138] But the company ignored Pollard's requests and did not lower its rates on slaves until November 1860.[139]

By late 1860, the company was upholding the success of the Richmond agency as a model for other cities and strongly encouraged all agents to improve sales through better advertising.[140] Even as sectional tensions worsened, the company exhorted its Petersburg agent on Christmas Eve, "We wish if possible to increase the number of Slave risks this year, & have to beg that you will make every effort to secure them,"[141] and advised the Lynchburg agent, "In view of the financial pressure & general distress pervading the Country we are anxious to make this Co more useful if possible to southern insurers."[142] The focus of the company had shifted to such an extent that new Richmond agent Lucien Lewis did not even know what the company charged on white lives, but this was not a problem, since he did "not anticipate doing much, if anything, in that line."[143] Baltimore Life had come to realize that the demand for insurance on slaves among urban slaveholders was more than sufficient to support a thriving, profitable business.[144]

However, despite the energy and ideas of Lewis in Richmond and the home office's encouragement of other Virginia agents, the economic conditions were already looking "gloomy" by December 1860, owing to the "unsettled state of the country" and the "existing political troubles."[145] Lewis stated that "servants will not hire, it is believed, for much over one half of the prices obtained this year, and every body is so pressed for money besides."[146] The war arrived before Baltimore Life could fully implement its new marketing campaign, but not before it had fatefully reorganized as a company primarily dedicated to underwriting slaves. Emancipation would render the majority of its policies void, and although company executives would make a desperate attempt to refocus the company on white lives during the 1860s,[147] by the summer of 1867 it would have to reinsure its remaining policies with Equitable Life Assurance Society of New York and close its doors.[148]

Southern Capitalists

Historians of slavery have long debated whether the slave system could have survived in an industrializing, urbanizing South. Some (ranging from John Elliott Cairnes and Ulrich B. Phillips to Eugene Genovese and Richard Wade) argue that masters were unwilling to diversify their investments into manufacturing, that slaves would make poor factory operatives, and that the existence of large numbers of industrial slaves in the cities would discourage the in-migration of free white laborers and potentially lead to a greater risk of slave insurrections. For these historians, slavery was necessarily a rural, agricultural system that could not be adapted to an urban, industrial world. On the other side of the debate are many economic historians including Robert Fogel, Stanley Engerman, Gavin Wright, and Claudia Goldin who assert that the low level of industrialization in the South reflected the region's comparative advantage in agriculture (not a retardation because of the existence of slavery), that industrial methods *were* adopted in areas where it made sense economically, and that in those industries that did emerge slaveholders were successfully adapting slavery to the peculiarities of a manufacturing and urban environment.[149]

A full resolution of this debate depends on a prediction of how the southern economy *would* have developed in the absence of the Civil War, but the attitude of urban slaveholders toward insurance on their bondspeople indicates that they, at least, had confidence in the compatibility of slavery and industrialization. Demonstrating a sophisticated grasp of the capitalist system, creative southerners of both races adopted insurance to alleviate some of the most evil consequences of the slave trade, while urbanites of the South promoted insurance as a means of mitigating the untimely loss of their slave property. By the 1850s, the industry was firmly established in Richmond—underwriting the lives of slaves engaged in dangerous occupations, valued as artisans or house slaves, or hired out for work in factories and railroads—and was expanding rapidly into the other industrialized areas of Virginia. Indeed, life insurance was fast becoming a key component of industrialization in the Upper South. With the purchase of insurance, urban slaveholders demonstrated their confidence in both the longevity of the slave system itself and the value of slavery for the future of southern industrialization.

CHAPTER 8

Acting "in defiance of Providence"?
The Public Perception of Life Insurance

In December 1851, A. B. Johnson published an article in *Hunt's Merchants' Magazine* entitled "The Relative Merits of Life Insurance and Savings Banks." Attempting to tarnish the image of the American life industry (to the benefit of savings banks), this seven-page diatribe accused life insurers of engaging in gambling contracts and encouraging people to commit heinous crimes. Beginning with a section labeled "Life Insurance Possesses Many of the Elements of Gambling," Johnson declared: "The characteristic of gambling consists in the absence of mutual benefit to the players. So in life insurance, no party thereto will usually gain, except at the loss of the correlative party." He then went on to liken life insurance to a lottery (an unfavorable comparison by the 1850s)[1] and to illustrate with specific cases the ways in which life insurance undermined thrift, domestic purity, responsibility, and general morality—the very ideals that life insurance companies were working so hard to promote.

The article ended with a list of alleged crimes associated with life insurance, such as some British mothers being "convicted of murdering their infants," or the poisoning by a London man of his sister-in-law "after having induced her to insure her life largely for the benefit of his wife." Finally, there was the New York man who was on his deathbed as his next premium payment came due. For his wife, "conjugal duty and pecuniary interest were in demoralizing conflict," as she had no funds to maintain the insurance: "He died before the hour at which his policy was to expire, and though charity may hope the result was produced by Providence, against the best efforts of the widow, the less human nature is thus tempted, the purer will be our domestic relations."[2] While Johnson's baseless suspicions about the actions of this recent widow wandered outside the bounds of propriety, they echoed many Americans' fear of the potentially corrupting influence of money.

Unwilling to allow these accusations to sully the reputation of the industry, life insurance promoters attempted to counter Johnson's arguments by drawing parallels between insurance and banking or by trying to turn the tables on their accuser by discrediting banks in favor of life insurance. One reply to Johnson's article appeared on the front page of the December 26, 1851, issue of the *New York Times*. It asserted: "Gaming. Nearly all commercial and financial dealing, in the sense assumed by Mr. Johnson, may be said to partake of this element. Life Insurance really has less of it than Banking." The writer went on to define life insurance as a science, detailing the accuracy of mortality tables, which he asserted were "more reliable than the chances of Banking in the United States." He then concluded by revealing the true identity of Johnson, who was president of the Ontario Branch Bank of Utica.[3] Johnson had only signed his name and not his occupation to his article, and the anonymous author of this response obviously sought to further discredit Johnson's opinions by exposing his conflict of interest.

A second reply came from Joseph B. Collins, president of the Mutual Life Insurance Company of New York, and appeared in the February 1852 issue of *Hunt's Merchants' Magazine*. Like the first respondent, he also attempted to downplay the association with gambling by presenting life insurance as a science: "The application of the law of average, so far from giving it the character of a gambling transaction, in reality goes far to equalize among all connected with it, a participation in all the chances of life, whether fortunate or adverse." But to a greater degree than the first respondent, Collins then went on the offensive by linking banking directly with gambling: "In gambling no man can win unless another loses. Just so in banking: a bank cannot make large gains by discounts unless taken from the pockets of those that pay. What the bank gains the individual loses." In contrast, he argued, "In life insurance all pay in, and all draw out. Those that die early are greatly benefited—those that live longer in a less ratio." Collins concluded by reasserting the industry's favorite image of the policyholder as a "reflecting, prudent husband and father, the affectionate care-taker of his dependent family."[4]

While moral hazard and accusations of gambling were certainly a problem for the industry, an association between life insurance and murder in the public mind would be even more devastating. Thus both of these authors treated the banker's anecdotes of crimes committed for the sake of an insurance policy with an air of shock and disbelief, calling them "improbable" and attempting to demonstrate the dubious nature of Johnson's argument. Collins tried to shift the blame away from the financial instrument itself and back to the depraved individuals who might commit such acts, asserting: "It may be urged on the same principle that fire insurance is immoral, because the selfish unprincipled policy holder says, 'Let the house or goods burn, I am insured.' Why provide hospitals and other benevolent institutions, as a resource in case of inevitable sickness, or other misfortune, 'Let each party look out for himself.'"[5] With the same sense of horror at the banker's accusations, the *New York Times* author sought to stress the difference in conduct between those insuring in the United States and elsewhere: "We are pleased for his own credit's sake that he has gone to Europe for the diabolical illustrations which he has employed to *enforce* the argument. Certainly nothing of the sort ever occurred in this country that we are aware of."[6]

For the growing life insurance industry, allegations such as these were particularly troublesome. The American people were becoming increasingly familiar with the concept of life insurance through conversations in the public realm in addition to official company brochures and advertisements. As the product slowly spread from its roots in the urban Northeast to the rest of the country, life insurance began making an appearance in the print culture of the nation. Popular magazines featured nonfiction articles that discussed the methods and merits of insuring, and insurance policies or sales agents began appearing as minor (and occasionally major) features of fictional literature. Whereas few Americans in the second decade of the century would have understood a passing reference to a life insurance agent, by the late 1830s authors could confidently use such allusions as metaphors for larger concepts. Even religious leaders found in life insurance a trope they could employ to demonstrate higher truths.

During the critical early years of the industry—through the mid- to late 1840s—these discussions were overwhelmingly positive, with both the secular and religious press often mimicking the language and arguments of the industry itself. Just as life insurance quietly became an essential safety net for the middle class during the antebellum period, its presence was increasingly apparent and taken for granted in the print culture of that same class. Yet while American industry executives had worked hard to craft a positive image for life insurance—particularly by maintaining a strict adherence to the idea of insurable interest in order to avert crimes committed for the proceeds of an insurance policy—they could not control reports of gambling policies or murder that continued to emerge from Europe. Nor could they prevent life insurance from being portrayed in a pejorative fashion in fictional works. Thus the industry was careful to address all accusations leveled against it, using company brochures and general articles on life insurance to respond to repeated allegations or ongoing misapprehensions and swiftly countering direct attacks with their own aggressive offense.

The Fallacy of a Religious Condemnation of Life Insurance

In her 1979 book *Morals and Markets: The Development of Life Insurance in the United States,* Viviana A. Rotman Zelizer takes for granted the premise that "after the 1840s there was a drastic reversal of trends and life insurance began its fantastic history of financial success. Its sudden prosperity has puzzled insurance historians as much as the initial failure of the industry." But although Zelizer accepts this er-roneous industry growth model (largely based on the work of J. Owen Stalson), she believes that the "failure" of the life insurance industry prior to 1843 and then its rousing success subsequent to that date cannot be explained by the advent of mu-tual companies and the vigorous marketing campaigns touted by Stalson. Rather, she primarily credits "the struggle between fundamentalist and modernist religious outlooks," arguing that some clergymen "denounced life insurance to their congre-gations as a secular and sacrilegious device that competed against God in caring for the welfare of widows and orphans." Zelizer concedes that "many clergymen not only insured their own lives but became leading spokesmen for the growing indus-try," but she nonetheless asserts, "The cultural incompatibility of life insurance with literalist and fundamentalist beliefs hindered its development during the first part of the century."[7]

However, just as the historical record fails to support Stalson's analysis of the failure and success of life insurance, it provides little substantiation for Zelizer's thesis that life insurance sales were hindered by religious concerns that it under-mined trust in God. A close examination of the sources cited by Zelizer reveals that the majority of her evidence consists of inferences drawn from Europeans' experi-ence with life insurance (where life insurance had a much longer and more colorful history), indirect comparisons with American attitudes toward similar topics (death, lotteries, gambling, etc.), and comments made about antebellum life insurance dur-ing the postbellum period. Given her thesis, remarkably few of her sources are from the first four decades of the nineteenth century, and even fewer of these directly support her argument. For example, her statements that before 1843 people consid-ered life insurance sacrilegious, that they criticized it as being "a mere commercial transaction" or "a speculation repugnant to the laws of God and man," and that women viewed the receipt of a death claim as "blood money" are based on sources from 1869, 1870, 1877, 1897, and a twentieth-century article in a Mennonite ency-clopedia.[8] She draws the majority of her supporting anecdotes from *Truth in a Nutshell* (written in favor of insuring by Rev. Henry Ward Beecher in 1869), *The Evils of Life Insurance* (1870), and *Life Insurance Sayings* (1895).

Of course, Zelizer's thin source base does not necessarily impugn the validity of her thesis. In many ways, her argument and chronology conform to that of *The Market Revolution: Jacksonian America, 1815–1846,* in which Charles Sellers presents two competing views of Protestantism: as an antinomian strain that fought the encroachments of the market into all aspects of American life, and as an Arminian strain that "sanctioned competitive individualism and the market's rewards of wealth and status."[9] Yet more recent works on the topic—including *God and Mammon:*

Protestants, Money, and the Market, 1790–1860 and *Friends of the Unrighteous Mammon: Northern Christians and Market Capitalism*—place much greater emphasis on the attempt by religious leaders of the early republic to reconcile Christianity with market capitalism. These two works both conclude that while greed and excessive accumulation were uniformly denounced, only a few fringe groups condemned capitalism outright and refused to engage in the emerging market economy. The main point of contention for the majority of theologians who questioned the compatibility of Christianity with the market system was that it largely ignored the fate of individuals in society—both those who suffered as a result of free-market capitalism (the poor, laborers, etc.) and those who allowed the capitalist spirit of unbridled competition and selfish acquisitiveness to supplant their love of neighbor.[10] In contrast, a general concern that participation in the market demonstrated a lack of faith in Providence rarely appeared. As Mark Noll concludes in his introductory essay in *God and Mammon,* "Most Protestants were at ease with the burgeoning markets of early American history, but never unequivocally so."[11]

In accord with these more recent histories, the contemporary evidence from sermons and religious periodicals overwhelmingly denies a religious proscription on life insurance, while actual policy sales only further undermine Zelizer's argument. Not only do the roots of the American industry extend back to eighteenth-century societies for the protection of the families of ministers, but the sale of insurance to men of the cloth remained high throughout the 1830s and 1840s. Indeed, insurance sales boomed in the burned-over district of New York State during the Second Great Awakening. Whereas "prejudices, mostly of a religious nature" may have "greatly retarded the introduction of the system" in seventeenth- or eighteenth-century Europe,[12] and some minor sects such as the Mennonites certainly may have preached against life insurance during the nineteenth century (just as they preached against the evils of the market as a whole), the antebellum American evidence indicates that practicing Christians across the spectrum of mainstream denominations were much more likely to embrace life insurance as a positive good than to reject it as sacrilegious.

The Religious Roots of Life Insurance

Although companies dedicated to the sale of life insurance for the general public did not begin operation until the incorporation of Pennsylvania Company in 1814, the first American life insurance corporations actually were formed in the late colonial period. The Presbyterian synods in Philadelphia and New York set up the Corporation for Relief of Poor and Distressed Widows and Children of Presbyterian Ministers in 1759,[13] the colonial branch of the Anglican (later Episcopal) Church organized a similar fund in 1769,[14] and the Congregational churches of Massachusetts made a short-lived attempt at their own society in 1786.[15] The hierarchies of these denominations recognized that the remuneration received by clergy did not permit them adequate means of providing for their families in the event of their death. As the charter of the Anglican corporation explained, "The clergy of the church of England in the American colonies, and especially the missionaries in the service of the Society for the propagation of the Gospel in foreign parts, are, with great difficulty, able to provide for their families, so that their widows and children are often left in great distress."[16] Thus the crisis of providing for ministers' families during the second half of the eighteenth century mirrored the problems that would emerge with urbanization and the greater reliance on a single family breadwinner at the beginning of the nineteenth century.

Both the Presbyterian Ministers' Fund and the Episcopal Corporation were designed as partially subsidized insurance plans—hybrids between purely charitable societies and actuarially based insurance companies. The charter of the Episcopal Corporation "constitute[d] a corporation for receiving, managing, and disposing such sums of money as might be subscribed and paid in from time to time by the clergy and missionaries themselves, and such benefactions as might be given by charitable and well-disposed persons, as a fund towards the support and relief of those widows and children."[17] The church hierarchy and corporate trustees repeatedly deliberated about whether to apply the charitable contributions for the relief of the families of *all* clergy, regardless of their formal participation in the insurance plan. But from the corporation's establishment through the middle of the nineteenth century, they always concluded that the fund should be "limited in point of object to the widows and children of *contributing* clergymen only."[18] Whereas the Episcopal bishops felt "charitably disposed to families *other than those of deceased contributors*" and sought alternative measures for providing them relief, the bishops felt strongly that they could "not bestow on them relief from this fund."[19] Ministers were thus expected to take some initiative to provide for the needs of their families.

Despite the firm endorsement of the corporation by the church hierarchy, Episcopal clergymen did not take advantage of this protection in large numbers. One of the reasons the bishops regularly reconsidered how to disburse the charitable portion of the fund was that they continuously ran a surplus. In the minutes of their annual conventions, the bishops repeatedly bemoaned the lack of interest in the corporation. As one bishop declared in 1826: "I have still reason to lament that a greater number of my brethren of the clergy, are so indifferent to the advantages which their families may derive from the fund for widows and children."[20] Clearly, the church hierarchy perceived no conflict between trust in Providence and a life insurance plan, nor did it think that such a perception constrained the interest of its ministers. Rather, they believed the clergy to be merely indifferent to or ignorant of the advantages. In response, the Pennsylvania branch of the corporation amended its charter in the 1830s to permit congregations or individual parishioners to purchase policies in the name of a particular minister; if the clergyman himself was not concerned for the welfare of his family, perhaps his congregation would be.[21]

While the insurance policies offered by these funds may not have been popular among the clergy, many ministers did buy policies with for-profit companies. For example, Rev. Alonzo Potter—Episcopal preacher, Union College professor, and future bishop of the Diocese of Pennsylvania—purchased a $10,000 policy with New York Life and Trust in 1833.[22] During the 1830s, approximately 12% of all NYL&T policies were written on the lives of clergymen. About half of these were affiliated with the Anglican or Episcopal faiths, although Presbyterian, Congregational, and Reformed Dutch ministers also owned policies.[23] In 1844, President Bard even attempted to hire the Episcopal minister John Brown of Newburgh, New York, as a local NYL&T agent, writing to him: "I think you would find the duties, if you have time, rather pleasant to you, the subject is an interesting one." Having personally inquired of the bishop "whether there would be anything in such an Agency, incompatible with your Office and its duties," Bard happily reported that the bishop "said he thought far from it. He views Life Insurance as a benevolent practice."[24] While there is no evidence that Rev. Brown ever accepted this position, his absence from subsequent agency lists was not likely the result of any religious scruples.

Clergymen were also popular clients of other companies. Massachusetts Hospital Life sold about 6% of its policies during the 1820s and 3% during the 1830s and 1840s to ministers or theological students. While the New England–based company attracted some Episcopalian ministers, it is hardly surprising that almost three-quarters of its policies on clergymen covered Congregationalists—with sales evenly split between traditional Trinitarian/Calvinists and the growing Unitarian sect. Even Rev. George Ripley, the famous transcendentalist and future founder of Brook Farm, purchased a seven-year policy on his life in 1829.[25] Although Baltimore Life sold only a handful of policies to clergy during the 1830s, sales to ministers increased significantly during the 1840s and 1850s. Most of its ministerial clients were Episcopalians, but a handful of Methodist, Presbyterian, and Reformed German ministers also purchased policies.[26] Clergymen accounted for about 6% of policyholders with New England Mutual between 1844 and 1850; although few of these indicated their denomination, those who did were Congregationalists (including an "orthodox

Congregational"), Freewill Baptists, or Methodist Episcopalians. Among the most notable of New England Mutual's policyholders was the Reverend Charles Beecher, the son of the famed preacher Lyman Beecher.[27]

Sermons

During the antebellum period, ministers regularly delivered sermons on topics that could potentially elicit a commentary on life insurance, including homilies on domestic issues (such as the duties of a husband toward his wife), those preached before charitable organizations for the relief of widows or orphans, discourses on wealth and poverty, and funeral orations. Sermons discussing the pitfalls of materialism became increasingly common during the early decades of the nineteenth century.[28] Yet an examination of over 150 religious tracts on these topics—written and delivered between 1801 and 1859 by more than 100 different ministers representing most major Protestant denominations[29]—finds neither direct condemnations of the sale of life insurance nor indirect suggestions that the purchase of a life policy demonstrated a lack of faith in a higher being.

To comfort widows and orphans, preachers commonly emphasized how the Bible specifically singles these groups out for protection from above. For example, at the funeral of Dr. George Holcombe in 1828, Presbyterian minister Henry Perkins of Allentown, New Jersey, reminded the congregation that "His language is—'Leave thy fatherless children and I will preserve them alive, and let thy widows trust in me.' *Jeremiah* 49:11.—'The Lord preserveth the stranger, he relieveth the fatherless and the widow.' *Ps.* 146:9. 'A father of the fatherless, and a judge of the widows, is God, in his holy habitation.' *Ps.* 68:5." Rev. Perkins encouraged Holcombe's family to find "consolation" in these words, and to feel "gratitude to God, for the protection and the mercies which he brings for your support."[30] Listeners were to have faith that God would provide both material and spiritual comfort to those left destitute after the death of their main breadwinner.

The postbellum sources that mentioned an incompatibility between faith and life insurance often quoted these same Bible passages, implying that a husband who sought to provide a subsistence for his family in the event of his untimely death demonstrated a lack of trust in the promises of the Lord. But trusting that God would look after the widow and the orphan did not preclude the head of household from attempting to provide for them himself. Frequently quoting St. Paul's first letter to Timothy ("But if any provide not for his own, and especially for those of his own house, he hath denied the faith, and is worse than an infidel"),[31] ministers continually stressed the right—indeed the duty—of a husband and father to take care of the needs of his wife and children.

Citing this verse, the Presbyterian minister and famous temperance lecturer Thomas P. Hunt proclaimed in 1836: "From the whole scope of this passage, it is evident that men cannot, without sin, willingly leave their families dependent on the charities of the church. But that they are bound to diminish rather than to increase the miseries of the world. We must provide for our own families, not only for their present wants, but future support."[32] In an 1805 address before the Massachusetts Humane Society, Unitarian minister Thomas Gray of Roxbury, Massachusetts, admonished his listeners not to overlook their "own household or kindred . . . country or state . . . town or church" when seeking charitable outlets. "It has been said a thousand times, and it shall be repeated here, that true charity must begin at home, and her first fruits be tasted by those, over whom providence has more immediately placed us the guardians, and protectors."[33] Similar sentiments were expressed in 1803 by Episcopal minister John Sylvester John Gardiner of Philadelphia, in 1827 by Congregationalist Leonard Woods of Andover Theological Seminary, and as late as the 1850s by Methodist minister Daniel Wise of Boston and Baptist preacher Stephen Remington of New York.[34] While each of these ministers lectured to varying degrees against the accumulation of excessive wealth and in favor of charitable giving, they also emphasized the sinfulness of ignoring the spiritual and economic needs of one's own family when providing charity to strangers.

Even when not specifically citing St. Paul's first letter to Timothy, ministers throughout the antebellum years stressed men's obligation to provide for their families' needs. Comparing the relationship between Christ and the church to marriage, the evangelist Charles Grandison Finney declared in an 1836 oration: "The woman naturally looks to her husband to preserve her from injury, from insult, and from want. She hangs her happiness on him, and expects he will protect her; and he is bound to do it."[35] An 1845 marriage manual (first published in the late eighteenth century by Rev. Dr. James Foster) listed among husbands' duties "taking care of the family substance, in which the wife has a common right." Given the absolute dependence of a married woman on her husband, the manual logically concluded that "it can never be imagined that any woman in her senses would voluntarily surrender herself up, so entirely to the power and will of a husband, as that, whenever he pleased, he might throw all affairs into confusion, and reduce her and her children to want and misery."[36] In accentuating the traditionally subordinate role of the wife within the marriage, these preachers recognized that such submission necessitated an assurance that a woman's economic needs would be met by her husband.

This obligation of a man to provide for his family continued even after his death. Citing the statement of Proverbs 13 that "a good man leaveth an inheritance to his children's children,"[37] an 1839 funeral oration by Unitarian minister Francis William Pitt Greenwood began by discussing the "good man['s] . . . temporal inheritance," which "in all probability . . . will be sufficient to the children's need."[38] Universalist John Mather Austin likewise stressed the long-term responsibility of the husband toward his spouse: "Where he has a will to make, and a faithful wife to leave behind him, it is his first duty to provide for her future well-being, to the utmost of his power."[39] In all of these cases, trusting that the Lord would provide for the future needs of widows and orphans did not preclude the obligation of a husband to meet those needs himself whenever possible. In fact, each implied that it would be sinful for husbands deliberately to shirk this duty.

Other sermons highlighted the negative impacts—both emotional and economic—that the death of a loved one might have on his or her family. Presbyterian preacher and Union College president Eliphalet Nott cautioned a gathering of the Ladies' Society for the Relief of Distressed Women and Children in Albany: "Hearer-father-mother of a family, God only knows how soon this may be your lot! Mutable is the world! Misfortune may soon dissipate the riches you possess, death may suddenly cut off the life which you enjoy, and your children, left dependent orphans, may be fed from the charity which you now bestow."[40] At midcentury, Old School Presbyterian Archibald Alexander continued this strain: "We are surrounded by dear relatives, with whom we are naturally unwilling to part; a feeble, helpless wife, it may be, and young, dependent children. These also may, as we suppose, need our assistance, and we cannot see how they can be provided for, and rendered comfortable, if we should be taken away from them. We naturally ask, What will become of them? Who will take care of them, when we are gone?"[41] For many ministers, the answer to this question was the local charitable society for the protection of women and orphans. But for some, life insurance was not an unreasonable possibility. By the 1860s, Rev. Alexander was one of several ministers quoted in insurance brochures as directly advocating the purchase of life policies.[42]

Among this collection of consulted sermons, the first indirect reference to life insurance occurred during an 1832 discourse by Congregationalist James William Thompson of Salem, Massachusetts. Warning that "the sun which arose upon our reputation and riches and health, may go down upon our dishonor and poverty and death," he counseled the audience "to endeavor to secure one another, by a sort of mutual insurance, against the evils which naturally result from these changes and disasters; or, in the words of an apostle, 'That one man's abundance should supply another man's want, that there may be an equality.'"[43] While Rev. Thompson was not directly promoting the purchase of insurance policies, the general idea of insuring was a recognizable concept that he effectively employed to help illustrate his point.

A more explicit reference to life insurance was made in 1844 by German Reformed minister John Williamson Nevin. Rev. Nevin was a professor of theology and president of Marshall College in Mercersburg, a small town in southern Pennsylvania about midway between Philadelphia and Pittsburgh. Preaching a funeral oration after the sudden death of a 21-year-old student, Rev. Nevin stressed to his young listeners "the extreme UNCERTAINTY of life." To demonstrate this point, he alerted them to the "wholesome instruction to be drawn on this subject, from bills of mortality and tables of life-insurance. These last are constructed on the basis of long and extensive observations, and determine generally with great accuracy, the measure of life's uncertainty at any given age, as compared with the possibility of its being extended to its longest term."[44] Several things are interesting about this statement. First, it neither promoted nor condemned life insurance but blandly referenced life tables as if everyone in the young audience were familiar with the concept—even if few of these college students owned a policy themselves. Second, the funeral took place in a rural location, indicating that knowledge of life insurance had spread well beyond the confines of urban centers by the early 1840s. And finally, the timing of this sermon is a key element. Stalson argues that life insurance remained a virtually unknown product until Mutual Life of New York began selling policies in 1843. It hardly seems possible that such a novel concept would so rapidly diffuse that a minister in rural Pennsylvania could reference life insurance tables in 1844, confident that his audience would understand his point. Clearly, life insurance had pervaded American culture prior to the establishment of the mutual companies. Even if only a small percentage of the total population owned policies, the concept was already well understood, widespread, and free of moral condemnation.

Fourteen years later, in a sermon entitled "Timely Preparation," Episcopal Bishop Alfred Lee of Wilmington, Delaware, likewise sought to emphasize the uncertainty of life: "Death, with very few exceptions, is a surprise. It comes upon men at a time when they are least thinking of it." For Bishop Lee, the best way to illustrate that point was through the example of "statistical tables," with which "we may learn how large a proportion of the human family die at a given age. Life insurance companies calculate with a degree of exactness upon the ratio of general mortality. But the case of each individual is shrouded in impenetrable mystery. 'The living know that they shall die.' But when? or how?"[45] Once again, life insurance tables were presented as a concept familiar to the audience, which Bishop Lee employed to demonstrate the need of Christians to remain vigilant lest death sneak up on them unexpectedly. And once again, he made no value judgment as to the morality of insuring.

The Religious Press

An extensive examination of religious newspapers and magazines published between 1800 and 1846 further undermines Zelizer's thesis.[46] As was the case with sermons, no condemnations of life insurance appeared in any of these sources. While most of the periodicals never mentioned the product at all (especially during the first three decades of the century), those that did were overwhelmingly positive regarding the idea of insuring. Publications put out by the growing populist sects of Baptists, Methodists, Unitarians, and Universalists actively promoted the benefits of life insurance, but similar encouragements also appeared in the pages of Presbyterian, Congregationalist, and Catholic magazines of the period. While the older denominations of Presbyterians, Congregationalists, Anglicans, and Episcopalians directly advocated life insurance less frequently, they repeatedly employed the popularity of this product in arguing for conversion to Christianity or advocating temperance. Many of these periodicals also allowed life insurance companies to directly advertise within their pages.[47]

When New York Life and Trust was first chartered in 1830, the editor of the *New York Evangelist*, a Congregationalist and Presbyterian weekly, published an open letter to President Bard calling the new institution "an honor to this city" and "advantageous to the public." Although the author's ultimate purpose was to push NYL&T (as well as Massachusetts Hospital Life) to place more emphasis on temperance in their applicants, he still "wish[ed] abundant success to the enterprising and meritorious individuals who have founded it."[48] By the end of that decade, the same publication was lauding the life insurance offices for "rescuing . . . from actual poverty in almost every instance the families of the insured."[49] Thus, far from condemning life insurance, this periodical repeatedly applauded the positive work it performed within the community.

As life insurance sales steadily spread during the 1830s, articles that explained and promoted the new product appeared regularly in the secular press; it was not uncommon for religious periodicals to reproduce these items in their entirety for the benefit of their readers. For example, in 1836 the *Christian Register and Boston Observer*, a Unitarian publication, included one such article reprinted from the *Pennsylvania Inquirer*. The piece sought to demonstrate "the great advantages" of insuring for people from all walks of life and concluded that "we would gladly see every individual in the community in possession of life insurance."[50] An 1836 article in the *Trumpet and Universalist Magazine* referenced the obituary of Colonel Heile-man, which had appeared in the *Army and Navy Chronicle*. As Heileman had in-sured his life for $6,000 with Baltimore Life, the *Trumpet* writer editorialized that "by the judicious appropriation of a small annual sum, this gallant officer has thus been enabled to make provision to the amount stated, for his otherwise destitute widow and six children."[51] The Baptist *Christian Secretary* reprinted the death no-tice of a man holding policies with both New York Life and Trust and Baltimore Life, who "by this timely act of prudence" ensured that his family would "be put in possession of $10,000."[52]

The *Catholic Telegraph* copied the full text of the 1840 New York law allowing women to take out insurance on the lives of their husbands, along with the remarks of the *Cincinnati Gazette* and the *New York Commercial Advertiser* regarding "this most excellent law." The editor prefaced the reprint by stating: "Among the various laws which have lately fallen under our notice, we do not recollect one with which we were more pleased than with the follwing [*sic*]." These religious periodicals found no contradiction between the Christian values promoted within their pages and the positive attributes of life insurance highlighted by the secular press.

In fact the religious press went beyond merely parroting the praise of their secu-lar compatriots, finding in life insurance much to celebrate that was specific to Christianity. After a particularly devastating fire took the lives of several people in 1841, the Baptist *Christian Watchman* printed excerpts of a sermon that reflected, "If life is so uncertain, every thing should be done for others within our power; we should endeavor to render them happy after we die. How much misery has resulted from the want or neglect of insurance!" Echoing the exhortations of the life insur-ance companies themselves, the Reverend James Sherman proclaimed it to be the "duty" of every man "to preserve . . . his family, at his death, from the want and the woe, the pauperism and the beggary, which are often the result of this lamen-table and destructive negligence" through the purchase of a life insurance policy; not to do so was an "inexcusable . . . neglect and folly."[53]

In the few instances where faith in Providence was expressed as an issue, the idea of insuring one's life was judged favorably. For example, in 1835 the Unitarian *Christian Register* discussed the chartering of New England Mutual Life by con-trasting it with "gaming and lotteries." Referring to the "idol" of the gambler as "chance, in defiance of Providence," the author viewed a life insurance policy in exactly the opposite light, calling it "a humble and submissive recognition of Provi-dence" that "induces the prudent and industrious man to lay by a portion of his subsistence . . . which may prove first for the benefit of his own family, or, it may be for the benefit of his neighbor."[54] More than a decade later, the Methodist *Christian*

Advocate and Journal took up the issue, similarly concluding that to buy life insurance "was no more distrusting Providence than to lay up enough to provide a house to shelter one's family, or to purchase a farm to settle them upon, or to put a few dollars in a Saving's Bank . . . The system is not *selfish,* for the insurer seeks not his own, but the benefit of his family."[55] For each of these writers, the purchase of a life insurance policy was an essential part of one's Christian duty to provide for his family; it was a demonstration of faith rather than a failure to trust in God.

Other articles used life insurance as a rhetorical device to encourage Christian conversion but still refrained from criticizing the product. For example, in a lengthy 1831 letter to the editor of the Anglican *Christian Observer,* the writer considered the moral obligations of a physician toward a dangerously ill patient. He concluded that, beyond the best medical care, the patient also deserved to be given hope for the state of his soul and adequate preparation for the possibility of death. Drawing on the emerging popularity of insurance ("we insure our houses from fire; we protect our families by life insurance, from the present pecuniary evils involved in the loss of active life"), the author asserted, "Surely death is not the only evil from the consequences of which we should not seek a safeguard." He exhorted his readers to insure their souls as well through a life of faith: "Is it not equally, nay, more, imperative to protect ourselves from the moral evils involved in the loss of life, 'by laying up treasures in heaven, where neither moth nor rust doth corrupt?'"[56]

The Baptist *Christian Secretary* concurred with this premise. While the author believed it to be "*wise* and *prudent*" for people to be "*insuring* their houses, furniture, and lives," he lamentingly asked, "How few in comparison, insure their souls and their eternal all in the office of God's mercy?"[57] The *Western Christian Advocate* was even more assertive in drawing this parallel, declaring in an 1838 article, "We have heard of 'Fire Insurance Companies,' of 'Life Insurance Companies,' but the art of insuring souls belongs to the latter-day Universalists!"[58] All writing during the early years of life insurance in the 1830s, these authors recognized the growing familiarity of the public with insuring and used its popularity to draw a parallel to the need for Christian conversion.

In addition to the spiritual necessity of conversion, life insurance was also used to demonstrate the temporal benefits of becoming a Christian. In an 1835 sermon published in the *Baltimore Literary and Religious Magazine* (a Presbyterian monthly), the Reverend John Miller Dickey listed the many blessings God would grant to his faithful followers, including "diminish[ing] disease and prolong[ing] life." To highlight this point, he provided the example of two men applying for insurance. The first was "a believer in God, and in the duty of observing his laws." As a direct result of this faith, the man "endeavors to regulate [his] passions, to exercise patience in adverse circumstance, keep [his] mind in peace, and let [his] day pass in industry and cheerfulness." The second applicant, while possessing "a constitution as good" as the first, was nonetheless "a man of the world." The reverend exhorted his readers to place themselves in the shoes of the life insurance actuary, who would inevitably conclude that the Christian man was likely "to support his family the longest" and was thus the better risk of the two.[59] Far from condemning the purchase of life insurance policies, this minister adapted the public's knowledge of insurance for the benefit of his own argument.

Underwriting the Ministry

Early for-profit companies viewed the nation's clergy as prime candidates for life insurance. For example, the 1835 brochure of Ohio Life and Trust listed "the salaried officer, men in public offices, the clergy, clerks, and every other person whose family is dependent on his personal services for support" as the types of people most likely to benefit from a policy.[60] And in the 1848 annual report of Nautilus Insurance, President A. M. Merchant reported, "In some instances, worshipping congregations, are insuring their pastors' lives, and making their annual donations, from year to year, in the shape of a life policy, as a *new year's gift.*"[61] A decade later, the same company (renamed New York Life) stressed that the purchase of life insurance was "particularly obligatory upon *clergymen,* who, with a limited salary and closest economy are only enabled to sustain themselves respectably, with scarce a thought or possibility of providing a future competency for their families, when they shall have been called to render up an account of their stewardship." And like the Corporation for the Relief of the Widows and Children of Clergymen of the Protestant Episcopal Church, New York Life encouraged congregations to provide this protection when the minister himself would not: "Indeed, we hold it to be a duty of every church to provide a life policy for their pastor, or at least to add to his salary beyond his immediate wants a sum enabling him to do it."[62] By 1861, Guardian Life was specifically advertising "Policies granted to Churches on the Life of their Minister, for the benefit of his Family,"[63] while the Equitable Life Assurance Society of New York "grant[ed] policies to clergymen upon a new plan, with special advantages."[64]

Beyond the benefits accruing for Christian families in general, the religious press also readily pointed out how life insurance could help to promote the education and upkeep of the ministry. Addressing students at the Oneida Conference Seminary in 1835, Principal William C. Larrabee discussed the "want of funds" experienced by many theological students. Larrabee suggested that they borrow money from their friends, taking out an insurance policy on their lives to secure the loan.[65] The same month, the *Religious Intelligencer* (a publication of various Bible and missionary societies) similarly recommended that young men seeking a college degree should use a life insurance policy as collateral for an education loan. This journal also reproduced the explanation of life insurance commonly employed in life company brochures but replaced the standard 30-year-old, middle-income man with "a minister 40 years old having a family and no property but his salary." Comparing insurance to other means of providing for the widows and orphans of ministers—such as "a fund raised by the pastoral association" in Massachusetts, or "a sort of savings bank" that was set up in Connecticut—the author concluded that "the same object may be accomplished through the Life Insurance Company with more certainty and ease."[66] *Zion's Herald and the Wesleyan Journal* and the *Christian Advocate and Journal* (both Methodist publications) concurred. In the late 1840s, the former provided a full explanation of the benefits of mutual insurance for "the many ministers, as well as others" who "have little or no means of providing for the support of those whom they best love, after their decease," while the latter declared that "in the Methodist Church this subject is worthy of consideration, by the ministry particularly."[67]

It was not until the late 1840s—well after the establishment and spread of mutual life companies—that some minority voices began to question the piety of encouraging ministers to purchase insurance. In 1847, a debate on this topic ensued in the Baptist *Christian Secretary* after one article opined that "every minister should receive such a salary as would enable him to pay the premium himself, or else his society should be required to do it for his benefit" lest they be guilty of "neglecting the prominent duty of providing for their own household."[68] This article elicited two responses criticizing the idea. In the first, the writer objected as "a question of *conscience*," arguing that it was "acting in contravention of the divinely appointed arrangement concerning their support; or their families' support." The author asserted that, rather than demonstrating a lack of faith in Providence, purchasing insurance showed dissatisfaction with the burden ministers willingly assumed as "Jesus Christ's ambassadors." God intended for ministers to "live and die comparatively poor," and they should thus be "contented with their general lot" rather than pursuing earthly wealth. In this case, the editors of the journal felt it necessary to defend the original article, denying any "disposition to encourage on the part of our ministers a desire for wealth" and chastising the opponent for encouraging a minister to "wholly neglect the interest of his family and in case of his own sudden death, leave them to the world's cold charities."[69] In contrast, the second critic had no qualms about the idea of insuring but objected to charging ministers the normal premium rates when "statistics . . . show, that of all professions, ministers have the longest lives."[70]

In 1848 and 1849 a similar debate erupted in the Methodist *Christian Advocate and Journal.* The controversy began with an article calling for the Methodist Church to throw its support behind the charter for a new specialized life insurance company, "the object of which was to enlist the influence of the ministry and membership in the promotion of the business of life insurance, more especially for the benefit of the families of the former, who, without a provision of this sort, would be generally left without resources in the event of the demise of the head of the family."[71] One respondent reacted vehemently that such a company went against the will of God as defined in the Bible: "The only Scriptural method of insuring our lives is by conforming to the laws of God." This opponent asserted that life insurance demonstrated "fear that at some future time [God] will not provide for us" and that such a lack of faith was deserving of divine "condemnation."[72]

However, this response was overshadowed by a second critic, who objected not based on questions of faith but because he viewed life insurance as a "lottery speculation."[73] While the second commentator had "no objection to . . . convincing ministers that life-insurance would be profitable to them, if such be the fact,"[74] he believed that the only people to truly benefit from life insurance were the company stockholders: "No person in his senses, can doubt that the object of Life Insurance Companies is to make money for their founders and stockholders; in other words, to get from insurers more money than they pay out."[75] Thus the relevant question was whether life insurance provided the best means of protecting the families of ministers, not its religious propriety.

These debates were more than outweighed by the overwhelming advocacy of life insurance in the religious press of the late 1840s—particularly in Unitarian, Universalist, Episcopalian, Baptist, and Methodist publications. In articles variously referring to life insurance as "wise and benevolent,"[76] "on the side of justice, as well as that of humanity,"[77] "an incalculable aid, and an unspeakable relief,"[78] "a thoughtful and worthy example,"[79] "necessary to man's best interests both for time and eternity,"[80] and "judicious and just,"[81] insurance was promoted as the best way to protect the families of congregants and ministers alike against the uncertainty of death.[82]

Religion from the Perspective of Life Insurance Companies

During the first decades of life insurance in America, company executives expressed little concern that religious scruples would slow the sale of life policies. In the complete outgoing correspondence for Massachusetts Hospital Life, New York Life and Trust, and Baltimore Life, as well as the incoming letters to Baltimore Life, only two letters (out of several hundred) mentioned religious opposition to life insurance before 1843; both were in 1837 correspondence between local Virginia agents and the head office of Baltimore Life. In the first letter, company president John Donaldson advised a new Lynchburg agent of his responsibility for educating the public regarding this new product: "People generally are ignorant and prejudic'd as to Life Ins. We found in the beginning that we were oblig'd to explain even to men of education and liberality. This was easier than removing prejudices from religious scruples, however they are disappearing."[83] In the second letter, Richmond agent John O. Lay commented on the recent application "from a leading member of the Presbyterian Church many of whom have heretofore entertained conscientious scruples as to the propriety of Insuring their <u>Lives</u>. The Door being opened probably many others may 'enter in.'"[84]

While Baltimore Life obviously found these "religious scruples" irritating, it treated them as little more than a nuisance, and the topic was never mentioned again. Donaldson's statement to the Lynchburg agent was a departure from his normal introductory comments to new agents, which generally consisted of instructions on remitting applications and premium payments to the main office, the terms of employment, and directions to advertise the agency.[85] But both Donaldson and Lay believed that this antipathy was receding by 1837. Other major Baltimore Life agents, including Dr. Beverly Wellford of Fredericksburg, Virginia, never complained of any resistance to insurance on religious grounds. On the contrary, when Samuel B. Wilson applied for a $1,000 policy on the life of his son John in the fall of 1836, Wellford vouched for Samuel as "a Presbyterian clergyman, of very high character"; the religious nature of his profession merely served as testament to the quality of the applicant.[86]

In his numerous commentaries on the progress of American insurance, on how to increase sales, and on resistance to life insurance, President William Bard of NYL&T never once mentioned religious qualms. The topic only appears briefly in his famous 1832 advertising brochure, *A Letter to David E. Evans.* In comparing life insurance to its fire and marine cousins, Bard stated, "In neither case is there, as there has been supposed by some to be in Life Insurance, an impious attempt to prevent the will of Providence; but a wise and prudent endeavor to tender such events as are beyond our control, less calamitous, than without such caution they would be."[87] He then proceeded to describe the details of the insurance contract, and this issue was never mentioned again in his seventeen-page monograph. Thus like President Donaldson of Baltimore Life, Bard did not find religious concerns a major barrier to the success of the industry.

The marketing literature of the remainder of the industry likewise indicates only a passing concern on the part of companies for a prejudice against insuring based on religious grounds. While a small number of pre-1842 brochures referenced religion or God in general, none were alluding to or arguing against religious criticisms of insurance. In their 1818 prospectus, for example, the Union Insurance Company of New York attempted to counter the perception that an insurance policy was "of a nature purely speculative" and "a mere gambling contract," but the company felt no need to make a similar argument against religious proscriptions.[88] And while an extensive article on life insurance in the 1840 *Merchants' Magazine and Commercial Review* briefly mentioned "the prejudices which exist against it, on the grounds that it trifles with the decrees of Providence," this critique was summarily dismissed as "hardly deserv[ing] to be seriously considered" and arising "from want of due reflection" and "ignorance."[89]

Other than in Bard's *A Letter to David E. Evans,* little attempt was made to address religious opposition to life insurance until the mid-1840s. In a passage buried on page 30 of its 1846 brochure, Mutual Life of New York observed: "An absurd notion has prevailed to some extent, and we know not but that it may exist at the present day; that life insurance implies a distrust in Providence, and is an impious attempt to prevent or control [God's] will." Dismissing this accusation as illogical "fanaticism," the brochure continued: "To forego the advantages of life insurance for such reasons would be as unwise as to fold ones arms in listless inactivity, expecting to be fed, clothed and cared for by supernatural aid, unassisted by any effort of our own."[90] An even terser reference to such opposition appeared in the 1849 brochure of North Carolina Mutual. In a slight variation of the argument that an insurance policy represented a lack of trust in God's promise to provide for the widow and the orphan, North Carolina Mutual indicated that some believed the insured was actually trying to gamble with his own fate. Discussing the origins of the American industry, the company remarked: "The first attempt to establish such companies in this country was regarded as an infringement upon the decrees of that Superintending Providence which hath 'appointed unto all men once to die.' Many supposed, that, being unwilling to confide our destinies to the Supreme Ruler of the Universe, we were about to transfer the safety of human life to the keeping of our fellow men."[91] Neither Mutual Life nor North Carolina Mutual took these arguments very seriously; both referred to them as vestiges of a bygone past and dismissed the idea—almost flippantly—as evidence of backwardness and "fanaticism." No other extant brochures from the first half of the century made any mention whatsoever of a religious bias against insuring.

Interestingly, while concern over a potential conflict between religious principles and life insurance remained minor during the 1850s and early 1860s, references to this issue actually increased in company brochures. Seven of seventeen pamphlets written between 1850 and 1862 mentioned this conflict, compared with only two of twenty-four in the first half of the century and two of seventeen between 1862 and 1870. For example, Connecticut Mutual brochures of 1846 and 1847 made no reference to distrust in Providence,[92] but by 1851 it felt the need to insert two paragraphs countering this idea, concluding:

> To embrace the provisions of life insurance, therefore, is far from implying a distrust of, or trifling with, the dispensations of Providence, as many once imagined; on the contrary, it implies a firm trust in the unchangeableness of the Divine laws, regulating life, and an intelligent *perception and use* of the means which Providence has put into our hands, to be benefited thereby. No man can with sincerity commend his family to that Source for support, when he has neglected this most obvious *means,* which that same Providence has presented for him to adopt.[93]

New York Life did not discuss this issue in its 1848 or 1851 pamphlets,[94] but its 1856, 1858, and 1861 literature listed religious biases as one of several concerns encountered in the sale of insurance. In a section entitled "Objections to Life Insurance Answered," the company responded first to the argument that savings banks were a better investment, second to the comparison between insurance and gambling, third to the idea that wives profited from the death of their spouse, and lastly that insuring demonstrated a lack of trust in Providence.[95]

In contrast to the dismissive references from the late 1840s, comments in later Connecticut Mutual and New York Life brochures treated religious opposition seriously, offering pointed counterarguments and enlisting the vocal support of various religious authorities. For example, New York Life's 1861 pamphlet included an extended extract from the 1856 address by the Episcopal bishop of Missouri that specifically argued against the idea "that Life Insurance is an attempt to control the will and purposes of Heaven—to fix the allotted period of our lives—and, at best, that it is a game of hazard." Echoing the sentiments of St. Paul's letter to Timothy, Bishop C. S. Hawkes declared: "If it is a man's duty in life, 'to provide for his own household,' it is hardly a violation of duty, by a prudent and wise foresight to provide for them after death, when he can protect them no longer."[96] Similarly, an 1862 tract from American Life and Trust included pro-insurance sentiments by Congregationalist preacher R. S. Storrs of Boston, Reformed German minister Elias Heiner of Baltimore, and Old School Presbyterians Nicholas Murray of Elizabethtown, New Jersey, and Archibald Alexander of the Princeton Theological Seminary.[97]

The evidence from antebellum sermons, the religious press, and life insurance literature leads to similar conclusions. First, while pockets of bias against obtaining insurance on religious grounds may have existed among some individuals, most insurance companies did not take this opposition seriously. They were much more worried that insurance would become associated with gambling, lotteries, murder, or suicide than that it represented a lack of trust in Providence. Second, industry concern was almost nonexistent before the late 1840s, peaked during the mid- to late 1850s, and quickly dissipated during and after the Civil War. The few allusions to an anti-insuring strain among religious leaders in the 1830s and 1840s indicated that this sentiment existed at some unspecified time in the past. For example, the president of Baltimore Life believed that by 1837 "prejudices from religious scruples" were "disappearing";[98] Mutual Life of New York spoke in 1846 of "an absurd notion" that "has prevailed to some extent, and we know not but that it may exist at the present day";[99] North Carolina Mutual stated in 1849 that religious objection to insurance was present "until within a very few years past";[100] and Connecticut Mutual observed in 1851 that "many once imagined" it to be a problem.[101] Yet later in the 1850s, companies concerned about this type of opposition addressed it as a current dilemma. In 1856 and 1858, New York Life used the present tense when cataloging religious opposition to life insurance: "*Fourthly,* and lastly. It is objected to on the grounds that it is distrusting the goodness of *Providence.*"[102] Finally, the counterarguments presented in brochures became more detailed and less flippant. Thus religious arguments against life insurance seem to have made a brief appearance in the decade immediately prior to the Civil War, as policy sales were spreading deeper into the middle class and further out of the urban Northeast, and as mutual companies were becoming increasingly popular. This opposition appears to have been temporary and limited in its effects.

The Literary Depiction of Life Insurance

Just as ministers recognized the rhetorical benefits of alluding to the emerging life insurance industry, American fiction writers also began incorporating life insurance into their novels and short stories as early as the late 1830s. Paralleling the types of references employed by ministers, for the most part these writers did not focus on life insurance as a major theme or plot device. Instead, they mentioned life insurance in a comparative manner, using it as a familiar concept that would help readers better understand the actions, motives, or feelings of a character. For example, in Joseph Holt Ingraham's 1839 short story "The Romance of Broadway," the narrator is spying on the courtship between a wealthy gentleman and the beautiful woman who resides in a neighboring building. When the narrator discerns that they are about to leave the apartment and elope, he decides to follow them in order to witness the event: "I descended, as if I carried a policy of insurance upon my life in my pocket."[103] Feeling that no further explanation was necessary, Ingraham assumed that his readers fully understood the implications of this statement. The narrator is racing down the stairs with no concern for his own bodily safety, in a manner similar to a man who feels confident that his family will be adequately protected by his insurance policy.

Similarly, in *The Adventures of Harry Franco* by Charles Frederick Briggs (a novel in the Horatio Alger vein), the title character greets his potential benefactor "with as much solemnity as though [he] had an insurance upon his life" and asks, "How is your health?"[104] Again, the author uses the idea of life insurance metaphorically, in this case to describe the tenor of the conversation. The allusion to life insurance shows Franco's genuine concern for the stranger, as if he actually has a monetary stake in the answer. Both of these examples from 1839 indicate the great extent to which life insurance was familiar to American readers by that early date. Authors such as Ingraham and Briggs could feel confident that both the concept of insuring life and the emotional implications of owning a policy were readily familiar to their target audience. Rather than needing to explain life insurance, these authors could refer to it as a succinct means of conveying other ideas.

This shorthand use of life insurance also appeared during the 1840s and 1850s in the prose of Nathaniel Parker Willis, James Russell Lowell, and George Lippard[105] but nowhere more frequently than in the writing of the great American author Herman Melville. In at least three different works from the 1850s, Melville sought to provide his readers a better understanding of the experiences of his characters by drawing parallels to their own acquaintance with life insurance. In the partially autobiographical novel *White-Jacket* from 1850, Melville describes the hazards of being shaved by a barber upon the high seas: "As I looked upon the practitioner and patient at such times, I could not help thinking that, if the sailor had any insurance on his life, it would certainly be deemed forfeited should the president of the company chance to lounge by and behold him in that imminent peril."[106] In this case, Melville alludes to the caution of life insurers against underwriting people engaged in risky activities to stress the dangers of a barber holding a razor at the neck of a sailor while the ship is tossed about on the ocean.

Five years later, Melville published the short story "I and My Chimney," in which a man stubbornly defends the continued existence of his old, crumbling chimney against the machinations of his family to have it removed. "Inveterately bent upon the extirpation of that noble old chimney," his wife continually taps upon it with a geological hammer, "holding her ear against it, as I have seen the physicians of life insurance companies tap a man's chest."[107] Here Melville renders the unusual scene of a woman listening for irregularities in a chimney much more familiar by drawing on the reader's experience with medical exams for life insurance.

The concept of insuring life served a more philosophical purpose for Melville in *Moby Dick*. Before embarking on his voyage, Ishmael enters the Whaleman's Chapel in New Bedford and contemplates the fortunes of the many men who have perished while undertaking similar journeys. As he views the memorial plaques that decorate the interior of the chapel, Ishmael ponders the fate of the dead who have been immortalized in the "unceasing grief" and "unhealing hearts" of their widows and the "immovable inscriptions" on the "black-bordered marbles which cover no ashes," and asks "why the Life Insurance Companies pay death-forfeitures upon immortals."[108] Melville uses this reference to the for-profit life insurance industry to set up a sharp dichotomy between the stark practicality of death (i.e., the insured dies and his beneficiaries receive a monetary death benefit) and the emotional reality of loved ones who keep the dead alive through their memories, rituals, and permanent inscriptions.

American writers much more rarely employed life insurance as an element of the plot in their stories. In most such instances, the existence of a policy on a husband or father enables a widow or orphan to lead a comfortable life after his death. The 1841 short story "Ruth Fairfax" by F. A. Durivage recounts a mother's efforts to raise her young daughter after her military husband has been killed on "the north-western frontier." The reader is told that, thanks to the father's prudence in taking out a life insurance policy, "the circumstances of the widow and orphan were therefore easy; perhaps, considering their frugal habits, even affluent."[109] While not crucial to the remainder of the story, this small fact frees the author from having to explain how this single mother is able to support herself and her daughter without recourse to a job, charity, or remarriage. Similarly, the 1860 novel *Little by Little* by William Taylor Adams tells the story of a family trying to make ends meet following the death of the father. Paul, the teenage son, is determined "to supply the place of his father in a pecuniary point of view," enabling his mother to avoid seeking work or falling upon charity. As the young boy bemoans his inability to earn an adequate support for his family, his mother informs him that his "father had his life insured for a thousand dollars."[110] While not enough to cover all the family's expenses in the long term, this sum is sufficient to cover the gap between the boy's earnings and what his father had provided on a weekly basis. This plot development renders the heroic efforts of the son to become the main breadwinner much more credible, as the reader understands that his meager earnings are being supplemented by the proceeds of the policy.

In the 1844 story "Ella Winship," the beautiful, pious Ella is courted by George De Witt, who leads her on with insinuations of marriage in hopes of sullying her purity but never intends to follow through with the betrothal because of Ella's modest financial circumstances. Her father "is but a clerk in one of our houses here. What patrimony can he leave from this for Ella's dowry?" George asks his best friend, Charles (who adores Ella from afar and repeatedly chastises George for his dishonorable scheme). Ella is devastated when she realizes George's detestable intentions but consoles herself that she never gave in to the temptation. When her father later dies, Charles is there to comfort her and they soon fall in love. In the dramatic climax of the story, the young lovers discover that Ella's father had insured his life for $10,000: "And for this, her father had denied himself and her all luxuries! This he had struggled so hard to purchase from his yearly salary!" George must now jealously watch as his best friend marries the beautiful (and now rich) Ella.[111] Once again, the life insurance policy is not essential to the plot—Ella could have suddenly attained wealth in any number of ways—yet it adds a degree of justice to the denouement of the story.

Finally, in a much more tongue-and-cheek reference from 1845, an aunt advises her young niece on selecting the proper husband in "Marrying a Fool." Describing the mistakes she made in her own three marriages, the aunt declares that "the only real satisfaction" she acquired from her second marriage "was in receiving the ten thousand dollars paid me as his life insurance."[112] All of these references reflect a benign attitude toward life insurance among antebellum American fiction writers. Authors recognized life insurance as a concept with which their readers would be familiar, but most presented it either in a purely nonjudgmental fashion or as exactly the type of support for widows and orphans that the companies themselves sought to promote.

However, the American literary scene also encompassed the writings of numerous non-Americans—particularly British authors—who often viewed life insurance in much more dubious terms. While several British writers employed the notion of life insurance as a means of drawing comparisons or explaining other concepts[113]—similar to the methods of their American colleagues—many others directly associated life insurance with speculative ventures, gambling, fraud, or even murder.

One popular British story of the 1820s and 1830s (reprinted in several American newspapers and journals of the period) was "Insurance and Assurance." First published in the *London New Monthly Magazine,* this humorous tale revolved around the exploits of a young man in London trying to make his way in the world. In the first scene, he approaches his deceased father's attorney, "a little grizzled, sardonic animal" who is familiar with "all the speculations of the age," seeking advice on how to make his fortune. The attorney determines that the young man "was fit for nothing on earth" and convinces him to take out a life insurance policy instead, signing it over in exchange for cash to the attorney, who remarks: "From my knowledge of your rattle-pated habits, and the various chances against you, I will give you a handsome sum for the insurance." Thus from the outset of the story, the author draws a direct parallel between life insurance and speculation.

In the next scene, the two are waiting in line for a medical examination at the insurance office. In front of them are "several more speculators waiting ruefully for the oracle to pronounce sentence." The author recounts a handful of these examinations, mocking both the detailed physical inspection of the applicants as well as the ridiculous questions put forth by the board of directors. In the meantime, a beautiful young widow arrives to collect the death claim on her late husband. After being approved for his own policy, the young man offers to up the ante with his attorney, proposing that "if you choose to bet the insurance which you have bought of me against the purchase money, I will take you that [the young widow] makes me a sedate married man in less than two months." In the ensuing scenes, the young man successfully woos the widow (who turns out to be exceedingly rich as well), simultaneously winning the bet and marrying into a fortune.[114] Although the story was intended as a lighthearted piece, the depiction of life insurance as a speculative tool and the derisive tone adopted toward the process of applying for insurance painted a less than flattering portrait of the industry.

Charles Dickens mocked the industry in several of his novels. In *The Life and Adventures of Martin Chuzzlewit* (published in serial form from 1843–44), one of the main plot lines revolves around the creation of the fraudulent Anglo-Bengalee Disinterested Loan and Life Assurance Company. Dickens's creation of this company, essentially a pyramid scheme, exploited the prevailing critique of British life insurers as being merely speculative, gambling ventures.[115] Life insurance appears again in Dickens's 1860–61 novel *Great Expectations* as Pip (the main protagonist) becomes reacquainted with his childhood companion Herbert Pocket. In describing his current occupation, Pocket asserts that he is a capitalist who primarily insures ships. However, he is hoping to expand his portfolio by engaging in other speculative endeavors, including "buy[ing] up some good Life Assurance shares . . . do[ing] a little in the mining way . . . [and] trad[ing] . . . to the East Indies, for silks, shawls, spices, dyes, drugs, and precious woods."[116] Although the author does not present the industry in quite the same harsh light as he does in *Martin Chuzzlewit,* life insurance is still portrayed as a moneymaking venture for the investor rather than as a service to the public in protecting the future of widows and orphans.

Although American insurers disliked these associations with speculation and gambling, their greatest fear was to be tainted by murder. In the popular 1846–47 work *Vanity Fair: A Novel without a Hero,* British author William Makepeace Thackeray uses a life insurance policy as motive for murder. The shady Becky Sharpe seduces the naïve, moderately wealthy Joseph Sedley and convinces him to list her as a beneficiary on his insurance. Even though his friends warn him "to break off a connexion which might have the most fatal consequences to him," Sedley refuses; he dies within three months under suspicious circumstances.[117] While she is never directly incriminated in his death, Becky Sharpe is implicated in an illustration of her hiding behind a curtain with a vial in her hand. Bearing the caption "Becky's second appearance in the character of Clytemnestra," the illustration draws a parallel between Sharpe and the figure from Greek mythology who murders her husband.[118]

A scandalous connection between life insurance and the commission of murder is even more apparent in Dickens's 1861 detective story "Hunted Down." The narrator (former chief manager of an insurance agency) reminds the reader that "a Life Assurance Office is at all times exposed to be practised upon by the most crafty and cruel of the human race" before recounting the tale of a man who repeatedly killed or attempted to kill innocent acquaintances (including his own niece) after acquiring policies on their lives.[119] Although the heroes of the story are the narrator himself and the actuary from another office who first suspected the series of crimes, the mere possibility that murders were committed to obtain the proceeds of life insurance policies surely sent shivers down the spines of both the insuring public and the growing American industry.

Life Insurance in the Secular Press

Despite the industry's adherence to a more or less strict interpretation of insurable interest, actual accounts of gambling policies and—even worse—murder flowed freely into American newspapers and journals, threatening to seriously constrain the popularity of life insurance in the United States. Because of the close cultural ties between the two countries, the American press abounded with accounts of British misdeeds performed in the name of life insurance. In one instance, a woman in Durham, England, was charged with poisoning three husbands, six of her own children, eight stepchildren, and a lodger. The *Insurance Monitor* reported: "It would appear that all this horrid catalogue of murders, to which is added that of her own mother, was prompted by a desire to secure insurances and other pecuniary benefits."[120] In another case, a woman canvassed various companies to obtain large policies on the lives of numerous friends and family members. According to the *Insurance Monitor*'s account, "Whenever this woman had effected an insurance, within three months the person insured has died. There was scarcely an office in town where she had not appeared, and scarcely an institution which had not paid her various sums of money on lives which had suddenly fallen." When British authorities discovered that the same doctor had signed the death certificates of every single person insured by the woman, they determined to arrest and try her and the doctor for murder, but she escaped to France before being captured.[121]

Throughout the antebellum period, similar instances of British gambling and murder cases were recounted in the pages of popular American periodicals, some of which carried provocative titles such as "Life Insurance—Or How to Make a Dead Man."[122] In reporting upon one of these cases where a doctor was found guilty of slowly poisoning his mistress, the editor concluded, "It is people whose lives are insured who are in most danger of poison. Their deaths have a specific money value to some one or another." Drawing on the lengthy experience of the British industry, he continued that "the cases are not infrequent in which actuaries feel a moral certainty that there has been foul play." However, these crimes often went unreported, since companies were not "desirous to brand the offices which they represent with the stigma of litigation."[123] Thus beyond merely highlighting the occasional horrific crime committed in the name of life insurance, the editor actually attempted to heighten the fears of the insuring public that their chances of becoming a victim were much greater than they would care to believe.

In another article of 1856 entitled "Does a Man Shorten his Life by Insuring It?" the editors of *Hunt's Merchants' Magazine* published the results of an inquiry made by the well-known British journalist and novelist Henry Mayhew. Mayhew visited thirteen of the largest life insurance offices in London, investigating the occurrence of suspicious deaths of those insured by these companies. At the first office, the secretary stated that "although he could call to mind no recent well-authenticated case of poisoning for the sake of the insurance money, it was quite certain that the lives of persons insured were frequently tampered." The secretary at the second office declared that "more gambling in lives had taken place during the last two years than had ever been known before," while another remarked that "sometimes rich men would insure the lives of mere paupers merely as a speculation." Three other offices complained that policies taken by Irishmen or Germans were often fraudulent, involving the insurer's faking the death of the insured or a man on his deathbed having a healthy man stand in for him at the medical exam in order to procure the policy. Another secretary complained of German Jews who had "learned the trick of insuring failing lives," and at still another office the secretary spoke of people committing suicide in order for their families to claim the insurance money rather than having to forfeit a policy for lack of payment.

Two other offices affirmed that they regularly refused to insure the life of a wife, particularly the wife of a surgeon, and one stated that "it was certainly true that the mortality among insured females was greater than among insured males." Others described healthy men who died suddenly having policies for the benefit of adulterous wives, and serial killers who obtained numerous policies on people who died suspiciously soon afterward. All thirteen London offices were able to provide anecdotes of crimes committed for the sake of a life insurance policy. The article ended with the editor challenging the American companies: "Such are the facts derived from a careful examination of some of the most important London life insurance offices. The question now naturally arises—What has been the experience of American companies? Can any one give us the facts?"[124]

The response of American life insurance promoters to reports such as these was immediate. The retort in the *Insurance Gazette* began by accusing Mayhew and the editors who published the article of "calculat[ing] seriously to damage the interest of the Life Insurance business in this country, by prejudicing the minds of the commercial and mercantile classes against the system as now established and practiced in the United States." The author then went on to recount the remarkably low occurrence of fraud among the American companies, asserting that "not more than five or six cases out of thousands of policy holders, can be made out, and some of those cannot be very clearly established, although suspicions exist." This defender of the industry then equated life insurance with other well-known, well-respected financial intermediaries whose products were also occasionally found to be the motive for heinous crimes: "Altogether the impositions have been few compared with the amount of injury inflicted by evil-disposed persons, against their relatives and friends, who possess real-estate, bank, and railroad stock, or any other description of property upon the result of whose death they anticipate to become heirs, or assignees." The article ended by asserting that even when frauds against American life companies had occurred, they had not involved murder but "false statements with regard to the state of the health of the applicant or his habits; or the parties have been sent out of the country, and the dead bodies of other parties claimed in their stead." All in all, the author maintained that "there is no analogy to be drawn between . . . the British and American Life Insurance impositions, and certainly nothing whatever to create alarm or uneasiness on the part of policy holders in these noble institutions."[125]

The promotional literature for life insurance companies regularly addressed the issue of insurance and longevity, attempting to counter the few instances in which policyholders fell victim to murder with the many more instances in which policies had served to extend their lives. As early as the 1830s, companies were touting the positive effect on life expectancy of owning life insurance: "Every one is sensible that longevity is dependent upon health, and that health is dependent in a very great degree upon tranquility of mind."[126] The very act of worrying about the potential fate of his wife and children should he die too soon might negatively affect a man's health and drive him into an early grave, but the possession of a life insurance policy would relieve his anxieties and lower his stress.

This issue would not be laid to rest easily, however, and life insurers would continue to promote the health benefits of life insurance well into the postbellum era. An 1866 brochure of Economical Mutual Life of Rhode Island proclaimed, "Facts Prove—That the man who insures his life is more likely to live to an advanced age, than he who neglects to do so."[127] Another article from 1868 asserted, "The insured father sleeps soundly, and does not waste his hours and thoughts in unavailing imagination what is to become of his wife and children in the event of his death . . . [the policy] not only maintains the equanimity of the insured, but by its reflected contentment wonderfully preserves the health, enhances the happiness, and prolongs the lives of wives, children, and creditors."[128] Thus rather than making the insured vulnerable to crimes, insurance actually extended his life by furnishing peace of mind that his beneficiaries would be provided for upon his death.

Notwithstanding the best efforts of industry executives and agents to disassociate life insurance from murder in the public's consciousness, several American cases in which an insurance policy was the motive for murder did emerge. That these cases resembled all but the most heinous accusations of the industry's detractors did little to help its image. One incident involved the poisoning of a woman by her husband with the aid of a man named David Wickham:

> According to the testimony, there is to be little doubt that she was deliberately murdered by Wickham for the sake of the insurance on her life. He has fled; but the husband, who is also implicated by the verdict, is in prison. Report has it that Wickham holds a policy for several thousands of dollars on the life of another woman at Port Jervis. The affair has caused a general feeling of uneasiness among the life-insured, especially ladies, and other cases are spoken of as likely to have been of a similar nature.[129]

Other cases involved the kidnapping and subsequent murder in rural New York of a young girl whose life was insured as the kidnapper's "daughter,"[130] the conspiracy of a wife and her lover to kill her husband and split the proceeds of the policy,[131] creditors taking out policies on the lives of debtors for a greater sum than the debt and then murdering them,[132] speculation on the lives of tramps who then turned up dead,[133] and the murder of a person for the purpose of providing a body to substantiate a life insurance claim (while the actual person insured remained alive but in hiding).[134] Unfortunately for the life insurance industry, real and fictional cases of murder by insurance beneficiaries on both sides of the Atlantic would continue to taint the industry throughout its history. But to the industry's credit, confirmed instances of life insurance as the motive for murder were remarkably rare in nineteenth-century America, appearing much more frequently as the plot in fictional stories.

In Search of a Corporate Soul

In his groundbreaking book *Creating the Corporate Soul: The Rise of Public Relations and Corporate Imagery in American Big Business,* Roland Marchand details the careful efforts of late-nineteenth- and twentieth-century firms to create distinctive, personable, compassionate images with the consuming public. Faced with accusations of "amoral conduct, impersonal size, . . . lack of a humanizing personality, . . . intense secrecy and zealous autonomy," Gilded Age corporations pioneered the development of modern marketing techniques and advertising campaigns to counter these outward indications of soullessness.[135] For life insurers, an ornate skyscraper standing out on an urban skyline as a secular cathedral safeguarding the material salvation of its policyholders connoted the crucial ideas of permanence and fiscal soundness.[136] Turn-of-the-century insurance companies used such massive edifices to literally set in stone (and reinforced steel) a longstanding, self-promoted image as quasi-public entities dedicated to protecting the weakest members of society.

During the antebellum period, references to life insurance in both religious and secular works precisely mirrored the growing familiarity of middle-class Americans with this new product and directly reflected many of the positive, "soulful" attributes marketed by early insurers. By the mid- to late 1830s, writers were confident in the ability of their audience to recognize metaphors and subtle allusions to various aspects of the life insurance industry: its statistically backed foundations, the security it offered to middle-class families, the recklessness of fathers who failed to insure their lives, etc. Not only were Americans well acquainted with the idea of insuring several years before J. Owen Stalson's "revolution of 1843," but they generally felt none of Viviana Zelizer's alleged religious qualms about procuring a policy.

Yet life insurers' active cultivation of the image of having a corporate soul, consistent from the antebellum era through the twentieth century, was repeatedly challenged by popular literature and the public press. The association of life insurance with both fictional and factual instances of crime, murder, or speculative pursuits such as lotteries and gambling threatened to paint the industry as an amoral, soulless enterprise. Lacking the tools of Marchand's modern marketing firms and advertising copy, antebellum insurance companies were forced to address this public relations conundrum using the only means at their disposal: pamphlet literature, explanatory articles on life insurance in popular periodicals, and an aggressive editorial response to direct attacks. While they could not always control the public image of life insurance, they recognized the benefits of trying to promote the image of a corporate soul long before the business behemoths of the late-nineteenth and twentieth centuries transformed this pursuit into an art form.

PART III

COOPERATION, COMPETITION, AND THE QUEST FOR STABILITY

LIFE INSURANCE IN NEW-YORK.

Cheerful Ostler. —" Pass along, ma'rm—it ain't nothing only oats and play."

As heightened competition led to a relaxation in rate structure, selection criteria, and policy restrictions during the 1850s and 1860s, some people began to question the soundness of the life insurance industry as a whole. In this 1861 cartoon, the industry is represented as a horse with potentially crippling tumors on its legs (known as "splints and windgalls"). While the unruliness of the horse belies its obvious pain, the hostler tries to pass its actions off as high-spiritedness ("oats and play"). Similarly, the lenient policies of some life insurers were potentially undermining the long-term fiscal soundness of the industry. As long as most policyholders were young, these cut-rate companies appeared to be operating with adequate reserves. But as these policyholders aged, companies could be bankrupted by the inherent flaws in their business model (their own "splints and windgalls"). This cartoonist believed that the public, represented by the passing woman (one of the intended beneficiaries of life insurance), was being sold a defective product, whose weaknesses might manifest themselves at any moment. *Vanity Fair,* July 6, 1861: 10. Courtesy of the University of Michigan Library's Making of America digital collection, http://moa.umdl.umich.edu. A special thanks to Dr. Susanna Lee for her help in interpreting this cartoon.

CHAPTER 9

Seeking Stability in an Increasingly Competitive Industry

The Creation of the American Life Underwriters' Convention

On May 25 and 26, 1859, at the Astor House on Broadway in New York City, the first meeting of the American Life Underwriters' Convention (ALUC) was held. In attendance were presidents, vice presidents, secretaries, actuaries, medical examiners, and agents representing nineteen (out of approximately thirty-nine) life insurance companies, including sixteen of the twenty largest.[1] (Three of the remaining four top companies expressed their support for the convention despite not sending representatives.)[2] The central purpose of the meeting was twofold. First, companies sought to shore up confidence in the safety of the industry by (finally) creating an accurate, indisputable table of mortality for the United States. Second, the convention was intended as a forum for devising model state laws to be uniformly adopted across the country—replacing the multiplicity of competing state regulations that served as a major frustration and expense for the industry.

Convention organizers were aware that the success of the meeting, first proposed in the fall of 1858 by Gilbert Currie, editor of the *United States Insurance Gazette and Magazine of Useful Knowledge,* depended upon active participation of the majority of the industry, so they repeatedly stressed the voluntary, congenial, mutually beneficial nature of the convention. In his original advertisement, Currie promoted the gathering "as a FRIENDLY, SOCIAL MEETING FOR INTERCHANGE OF SENTIMENTS, MUTUAL CONSULTATION, AND CONFIDENTIAL ADVICE, . . . *to promote, as far as practicable, the common cause they have each in view—the success, security, and extension of the practice of Life Insurance among all classes of the community.*" To this end, Currie emphasized that all matters of major contention between companies—including the debate over the use of premium notes and the rivalry between stock and mutual companies—would be expressly excluded from the conversation.[3]

In his initial remarks to the convention, Frederick S. Winston—president of both Mutual Life of New York (the largest life insurer in 1860) and the ALUC—stressed that the purpose of the meeting was "only in the nature of inquiry, and not intended to bind any institution." Winston deemed it "generally understood" that any decisions reached by the assembled executives would leave all "free, each to conduct the business of Life Insurance according to his own views." Morris Franklin, president of New York Life (fourth-largest company in 1860) and vice president of the convention, reiterated Winston's point: "It was, he hoped, understood, that this was not an assemblage in the nature of a caucus, or a dictatorial body, but a meeting of friends interested in the business of Life Insurance, to exchange views and experience. They met as brothers, and as brothers they would depart."[4] Yet despite these lofty pronouncements, if the convention succeeded in either of its stated purposes, then binding the industry—to the main benefit of the larger, more-established firms—would be the inevitable result.

The success of life insurers in the 1830s and 1840s at creating a solid corporate model and promoting their product among the middle class had resulted in a thriving business by midcentury; between 1825 and 1850 life insurance in force had increased at the astonishing rate of 30% per annum. But this rapid growth would come to a screeching halt by 1850. And from what once had been a highly concentrated oligopolistic industry emerged a competitive field mainly comprising newly formed mutual companies. Whereas the top four firms underwrote 80% of all life insurance in force in 1845 and the top eight accounted for 98%, by the eve of the Civil War the market share of the top four had been reduced to 53% and that of the top eight to 70%. Mutual Life alone saw its share drop from 31% to 20% over the same fifteen years.

As the rate of new policy applications slowed during the 1850s, the number of incorporations increased at a more rapid pace than life insurance sales; new entrants thus had to find ways of tapping into the profitable client base of the older companies. While a few attempted to differentiate their product by offering novel plans targeting specific subsets of the population—such as the teetotaler plan offered by American Temperance Life or the plan for "medical gentlemen" of Boston Equitable Life[5]—the majority of these newcomers were modeled in the image of their elder competitors. To gain a foothold in the industry and a greater share of the sluggish market, most of the new firms either cut premium rates or sought charters in states with strong protective legislation against outside companies. But whether as a result of the intense competitiveness of the insurance market or of the lax practices of some of these newcomers, a large percentage failed to survive long. Of the forty-two new life firms incorporated between 1847 and 1859, twenty-four would shortly fail. Although most policyholders were accommodated when their policies were reinsured with other companies, the demise of any firm tarnished the entire industry's reputation for safety and longevity.[6]

The ALUC was designed to undercut the benefits of reduced premiums and protective legislation and thus to keep the new companies at a competitive disadvantage against firms with greater name recognition and a proven record of service and fiscal stability. Stricter standards on the entire industry, limiting practices that could lead to company failure, would also be a boon to established companies. The compilation of an American mortality table would, for the first time, create a benchmark against which all premium rates could be compared. If the industry could convince the public of the scientific accuracy of such a table, it could virtually eliminate risky price competition by painting price-cutters as irresponsible, reckless, and unsound. And by successfully lobbying for uniform state laws, the industry could eliminate the competitive edge of in-state firms over their out-of-state rivals. Such laws could help restrict new entrants to the field on a national (rather than state-by-state) level. Although the ALUC fell short of achieving these results, it gave the industry valuable experience in collaborating, which it would then build on during the postbellum era in its attempts to replace the cacophony of state laws with federal regulation.

Historians of life insurance have dismissed these early collaborative efforts as failures. R. Carlyle Buley, author of *The American Life Convention, 1906–1952: A Study in the History of Life Insurance,* writes: "In view of the large-scale development of life insurance in the United States, it is interesting to note that almost three quarters of a century elapsed before any important cooperative efforts were made among the companies."[7] Although Buley does mention several nineteenth-century collaborative endeavors between companies, he quickly rejects these organizations as short-lived or demonstrating a "lack of sufficient mutual interest on the part of the companies."[8] While he is correct that none of these attempts to organize the industry survived into the twentieth century, both formal and informal discussions of pressing issues occurred between insurance executives throughout the nineteenth century, playing a crucial role in the evolution of the industry.

The Problem of Price-Cutting in an Increasingly Competitive Industry

Despite the decade-long effort of President Bard of New York Life and Trust to create a safe, accurate, and profitable table of mortality for the United States, the emerging mutual companies of the 1840s were still forced to base their pricing decisions on a combination of British tables and educated guesses. While the Carlisle Table remained the industry standard for mutual companies at midcentury, a handful of firms had significantly cut their rates, threatening the rate structure of the entire industry. Kentucky Mutual Life (chartered 1850) charged rates 14% to 22%

cheaper for all ages through 55, and State Mutual Life of Worcester, Massachusetts (1844), advertised premiums 28% to 30% less than the Carlisle Table.[9] Yet in his 1851 edition of *Practical Remarks on the Present State of Life Insurance in the United States,* Harvey Tuckett reserved special criticism for American Mutual Life of New Haven, Connecticut (1847): "This company was started with the intent of selling cheaper than other companies; and, without any fixed principle, or any calculation, they 'reduced their premiums twenty-five per cent. below the usual charge.'"[10] American Mutual justified this reduction by stating that it was "under a firm conviction" that claims on other companies (most of which had been in existence only a handful of years) "seldom exceed and never require *one half* of the annual premium now charged."[11] By 1860, both American Mutual and State Mutual had moderated their price reductions (the former to 15%–16% and the latter to 20%–21% less than the Carlisle Table),[12] but their rates remained out of sync with the rest of the industry.[13]

While it was certainly possible that these lower rates more accurately represented true mortality in the United States, the more conservative firms feared that these new companies were actually engaging in a pyramid scheme that would eventually bring down the entire industry. In the short term, as long as a company was attracting large numbers of new, young, healthy lives—which enjoyed both a selection advantage and the high premium-to-risk ratio of whole life policies—the incoming premium payments would probably outweigh the death claims regardless of the accuracy of the table employed. But if its premiums were calculated at too low a rate, as these policyholders matured and began to die the company could only remain solvent if it continued to bring in ever greater numbers of new applicants. Eventually, such a firm would collapse under the weight of its death claims. This disequilibrium between cost of service and price charged would only be resolved at some unknown future point, when the potential for large numbers of company failures might destroy public confidence in the long-term stability and soundness of the entire industry. In the meantime, the predatory pricing of new entrants would continue to eat away at the business of the more conservative (and arguably safer) companies.

By 1845, when Mutual Life of New York had replaced NYL&T as the largest firm in the industry, this new leader also took upon itself the role of creating a more accurate mortality table. Like NYL&T, Mutual of New York recognized the importance of understanding the long-term costs facing the industry. But Mutual realized that the industry was now facing the very real threat of price competition through rate cutting. The firm understood that the only way to prevent smaller mutual companies from gaining market share through price cuts would be to establish a price floor below which rates could not be reduced; the ideal mechanism to prevent price cuts would be scientific data backed by public opinion. If the industry could develop a new standard based on American mortality rates that would convince the public of both the accuracy of the table employed and the safety of the rates resulting from it, potential price-cutting firms would have a difficult time persuading customers to ignore it. And the removal of price competition from the industry would most benefit companies with established reputations for fiscal soundness and service.

The first attempt came in 1852 when Charles Gill, actuary of Mutual Life, compared the nine-year mortality experience of the company against the existing life tables to create a new table based on American mortality. Gill made both internal comparisons of mortality between geographical areas of the United States and external comparisons with the experience of British life insurance companies.[14] Interestingly, despite the substantial dividend of 52% declared by Mutual Life in 1848 (indicating that premium income had been significantly higher than death claims),[15] the resulting table itself was only a slight variant on the Carlisle rates, reducing premiums by 2% to 3% for policyholders 35 or younger (a savings of only 58 cents on a $1,000 policy for a 30-year-old) and raising them 1% to 2% for those aged 45 to 50.[16] Nonetheless, this table was still not an accurate reflection of the overall mortality rate of the United States, since it was based on medically selected lives (hence making it a "select table"). While Gill's table was purported to represent the actual experience of Mutual Life through 1852, it could only depict future risks if they were selected on exactly the same basis.

However, industry experts were also slowly realizing that the selection advantage based on health and family history was short lived. By 1860 actuaries had determined that this advantage only existed for the first five years of the policy, after which the mortality rate of carefully selected policyholders coincided with that of the overall population.[17] The 1862 report of the Massachusetts Board of Insurance Commissioners asserted that this advantage vanished after a mere three years.[18] As it included the large percentage of policies written within the past three to five years, the Gill Table could only accurately reflect the future mortality experience of the company if it maintained the same ratio of new, medically selected lives as its existing policies matured (a situation similar to the problem of price-cutting firms).

This erosion of the selection advantage over time became particularly important as the length of policy contracts increased, especially with the growing popularity of whole life policies beginning in the mid-1840s. While the length of contract for policies could be set for any period of time—from as little as one month to the whole term of life—the most common increments of policies were for one year, seven years, or life.[19] Before the 1840s, whole life policies were rare; they accounted for fewer than 10% of the policies issued by either Massachusetts Hospital Life or Baltimore Life and only 13% of NYL&T's. Thus during this period, a careful selection of lives could indeed have a major impact on the mortality experience of the company. But the popularity of whole life policies increased substantially in the decades before the Civil War, amounting to almost one-fifth of nonslave Baltimore Life policies during the 1850s, more than one-quarter of NYL&T policies from 1846 to 1854, two-fifths of New England Mutual policies from 1844 to 1852, and close to half of NYL&T policies from 1855 to 1862. The length of nonlife policies was also increasing, averaging between 5 and 5.5 years per policy by the eve of the war, with two-thirds to three-quarters of all policies issued for periods of 7 years or more (see appendix, table A.10). Therefore, the advantage enjoyed by companies through a strict medical selection of lives disappeared before the majority of policy contracts were completed.

This selection advantage was additionally undermined by policy surrenders and lapses. John James, actuary of Girard Life, was concerned about "the power of selection exerted by the insured against the Company." At the 1860 American Life Underwriters' Convention, he warned his fellow insurers: "We all know that a Company selects from among the applicants those only who are of good health and constitution, or whom they believe possess such." Unfortunately for the companies, not all of those carefully selected lives remained policyholders: "After a time, however, the case is very different; many of the insured drop or surrender their policies, and it is natural that the good lives rather than the defective ones would do so." Yet as long as the industry was rapidly expanding—with more incoming policies (upon whom careful selection would have an effect) than existing risks (upon whom this advantage had expired)—actuaries might not immediately recognize that the composite risk profile of the company's policyholders was increasing over time. In James's estimation, "The effects of this process of deterioration may not be immediately perceived, by reason of the constant infusion of new lives selected as others originally were, but it behooves the Company not to be deceived by the deferred effects of the process."[20]

Despite these potential problems with its select life table, Mutual Life charged premium rates based on the Gill Table from 1853 to 1868.[21] But where Mutual led, few followed. By 1860, only United States Life of New York had adopted Mutual's modified rates, and Knickerbocker Life was using a slight variant of the table. But the majority of mutual companies, including five of the top ten, still charged rates based on the Carlisle Table adopted by NYL&T in 1832,[22] with the remaining three top companies using some combination of these two tables.[23] As late as 1867 only eight of seventy companies surveyed were using the Gill Table, thirteen remained on the Carlisle, and the majority of the mutual field adhered to a number of other tables that were variations on the Gill or Carlisle tables. A handful were still quoting cut-rate premiums of 10% to 16% less than the Carlisle Table.[24]

This widespread discrepancy in premium rates between companies directly contradicted the industry's continued public assertions of the scientific basis for its product. In a typical statement, one 1863 article positively declared that "the problem [of calculating life expectancy] may be regarded as solved . . . for an immense body of information has been collected, and statisticians and mathematicians have been employed in working over the data thus obtained for more than half a century." Assuring the reading public that life insurance was in no way akin to gambling or speculating, the author insisted that "the question is so far settled, that it may be said to have ceased to be a problem in science, and to have become only a matter of book-keeping. With the facilities that have been furnished, an ordinary clerk is able to make all the necessary calculations, and to acquire a thorough understanding of them."[25] Cut-rate companies would claim that their lower premiums reflected their superior selection criteria or lower operating costs, an argument that older, more conservative firms found threatening. Yet even the higher-priced firms persisted in making the fallacious assertion that mortality rates were statistically understood in order to avoid providing industry opponents with fodder for their critiques.

Life insurers were apparently confident that neither the insuring public nor insurance detractors were reading any industry publications, where what allegedly had "ceased to be a problem" continued to be discussed as one. In an effort to resolve this nagging issue, other top companies of the 1850s and 1860s similarly promoted the compilation of vital information from their own records in an effort to create an accurate American life table. In each of its annual reports, New England Mutual Life, the fifth-largest company throughout most of the antebellum years, reported the number of deaths for the previous year broken down by cause of death, age, and type of beneficiary (whether dependents or creditors). It also included the occupations and area of residence (New England or middle, western, or southern states) for new policyholders.[26]

In the winter of 1856–57, the editor of the *Insurance Gazette* praised New England Life for publishing its mortality statistics: "It is gratifying to observe that this Company, from its commencement, has taken care to preserve the statistics of such risks in a form so as to be conveniently used, when occasion requires. There can not be too much importance attached to the collection of valuable statistics as relating to the practice of life insurance. We hope that other companies will follow, in this respect, the example of the New England."[27] Other companies did follow suit. For example, State Mutual Life of Worcester, Massachusetts (fifteenth largest), regularly reported the occupations and ages of its deceased members, and New York Life (fourth largest) published the occupations, causes of death, and place of death of its policyholders.[28] In 1858, Mutual Benefit of New Jersey (third largest) published its complete mortality experience from its formation in 1845.[29] Yet all of these data still fell short of the information necessary to create an American mortality table.

The failure of Mutual Life of New York unilaterally to develop a widely accepted industry standard for premium rates during the 1850s, along with the ever-increasing competitiveness of the industry, led the company to seek a more collaborative—even collusive—solution to the problem. William Bard had hoped that the development of state birth and death registries, combined with the mortality statistics of the federal census, would enable the government to create an accurate mortality table, but life insurance promoters (including executives of Mutual Life) remained dissatisfied with the dearth of mortality statistics for the United States and became increasingly frustrated during the 1850s and 1860s with the lack of progress made on the state and federal level in the collection of such data. At the first American Life Underwriters' Convention in 1859, the Committee on Legislation called for the enactment of more state laws (modeled on those passed between 1842 and 1852) to "furnish vital statistics, . . . which, if regularly collected, would benefit, not only Life Insurance Companies, but the public at large."[30] Despite this plea, by 1867 there were still only eight states that required the registration of vital information. During the 1850s, New York and New Hampshire actually rescinded registration laws passed in the 1840s, and Rhode Island and Vermont were the only additional states to pass such laws between 1852 and 1860.[31] Even where state-level statistics were available, life underwriters criticized them as "unreliable" and "mostly taken and collated by careless or incompetent persons."[32]

The insurance press was disdainful of the efforts of the federal government to collect mortality data. In response to the official statement of the superintendent of the 1860 census that "the proportions of the deaths reported in 1850 and 1860 vary so widely—from over two per cent. to less than one-half of one per cent.—that not even the amount of the deficiency can be estimated," the *Insurance Monitor* declared that the census results were "humiliating . . . positively shameful, and altogether inexcusable."[33] While a portion of the problem lay with the census marshals, several of whom considered the mortality schedule to be "merely incidental" to the information regarding the living population and only "to be attended to if convenient and agreeable to both parties concerned,"[34] part of the problem lay in the nature of the mortality schedule itself. Respondents were asked only if anyone *within their household* had died *within the past twelve months.* Not only was it difficult for some to remember if a death had occurred within the year in question (running from June 1 to May 31), but if the death resulted in the dissolution of the household, that death would go unrecorded. As a result, the demise of persons aged 5–19 were the most likely to be counted, while deaths among the elderly, unmarried males, and adult heads of household (when this ended in the disintegration of that household) were the least likely to be reported.[35] Although the life insurance industry would continue to support efforts by the state and federal government to collect mortality statistics, it had grown impatient by 1859 and decided to take matters into its own hands.

The Development of an Industry Standard through Formal Organization

While the small fraternity of life insurance executives had always informally collaborated with each other, the desire to create an industry standard and persuade all firms to accept that standard inspired the formation of the American Life Underwriters' Convention in 1859. To that end, on the agenda for the first meeting was the creation of a committee for "devising and adopting a method of securing correct and uniform Statistics, deduced from the experience of the various Companies."[36] Although the agenda also called for the creation of committees to review state laws regarding life insurance, to examine ways to detect and prevent insurance fraud, and to promote the sale of life insurance in general, the creation of a new mortality table was the "*chief aim* of the Convention to consider . . . The great desideratum— insurance statistics, and a combined experience table, constructed from the records of the several Life Insurance offices doing business in this country, is what is required, and to secure this, is the grand object of the American Life Underwriters' Convention!"[37]

For the largest life insurers, the convention could serve as a means of disciplining the smaller companies engaging in price-cutting. But even the smaller firms recognized the prospective benefits of industry collaboration. Without higher barriers to entry, they would probably suffer most from additional new firms entering the stagnant industry. And unlike the large companies like Mutual of New York that could create mortality tables based on their own experience, the smaller firms lacked adequate data. Thus the convention could serve the purposes of the majority of the industry by pooling statistics for the compilation of a combined experience table to be accepted and adopted by the industry as a whole. Reflecting the diversity of interests, the Committee on Vital Statistics was made up not only of Sheppard

Homans, who replaced Charles Gill as actuary of Mutual of New York upon his death in 1855, but also Lewis Merrill, actuary of Penn Mutual Life (seventh largest), and John Eadie, secretary of United States Life of New York (eighth largest)—two much smaller firms that each accounted for only about 3.5% of the life insurance in force in 1860.

In the committee's initial report to the convention, the British tables still in use in the United States were declared "defective," and the industry as a whole was criticized for "adopt[ing] rates of premium and rules of valuation based upon observations made three thousand miles away" and because "with upwards of *one hundred and fifty* millions of dollars at risk on the lives of more than fifty thousand American citizens, no united effort should have been made by American Life Companies for deducing the prevailing rate of mortality."[38] This indictment of the existing mortality tables, including the still predominant Carlisle Table, shocked none of the convention representatives; despite their public pronouncements in support of the tables, insurance executives had been skeptical of them for decades.

Nor did the proposed solution surprise those present. The committee suggested the creation of a table based on the combined experience of American life insurance companies, to be modeled on the English Combined Experience Table of 1843 (also known as the Actuaries Table or Seventeen Life Assurance Officers' Table),[39] which had been compiled by a committee of British actuaries based on 62,537 observations from 17 companies.[40] Like the Gill Table, the Combined Experience Table was criticized for being a select life table, since the average policy duration was only 8.5 years.[41] Any table derived from the experience of the American companies would also be based largely on policy pools still benefiting from medical selection; nevertheless such a table would be an immense improvement over the existing options. The convention unanimously adopted the report of the Committee on Vital Statistics and appointed Homans, Eadie, and Thomas Russell (vice president of Charter Oak Life, ninth largest, with a 3% market share) as the committee in charge of gathering, combining, and analyzing the data.[42]

The representatives at the convention gave every indication of supporting the project. Several executives spoke resolutely in favor of the proposed table. For instance, E. A. Bulkeley, president of Aetna Life Insurance (fifteenth largest, with a 1% share), asserted: "No Company would refuse to contribute its experience to accomplish this desirable result, the formation of an American table of mortality. It was a great national work, in which every institution could feel the highest interest."[43] Benjamin Chickering, secretary of Berkshire Life (twentieth largest, with a 1% share) "deemed the collection of the proposed statistics to be altogether practicable; all the material is in possession of the Companies, and only requires systematic effort, in the form proposed by the Committee, to achieve a great practical result."[44] The convention as a whole resolved "that it is very desirable that each of the Companies in the United States should unite in a contribution towards the determination of the general experience of the rate of mortality among assured lives in the United States."[45]

Over the course of the next year, the Committee on Vital Statistics solicited policy records of all thirty-nine life insurance companies operating in the United States. To protect the reputations of individual companies, the convention agreed that all statements would be kept "strictly confidential, and to make public only the combined experience ascertained as the result of such statements."[46] By the second convention in May 1860, twenty-three of the thirty-nine companies (including eighteen of the top twenty-five) had agreed to contribute their data, and thirteen of these had already submitted them to the committee.[47] With the lowest published rates in the industry, State Mutual of Life of Worcester, Massachusetts, ignored the request for data and declined to send a representative to the convention. The other major low-premium company (American Mutual) responded negatively to the committee's request, "declining to furnish the *data,* but offering to furnish *results* deduced by themselves."[48]

Agreeing that "a table of mortality may be called the keystone of the arch upon which the vast superstructure of Life Insurance is based, and upon the accuracy of our tables depend, in a great measure, the stability and safety of the great institution,"[49] those present at the 1860 convention unanimously voted to entrust the existing Committee on Vital Statistics with the task of processing the data, as well as any future data received, into an appropriate form for the use of the contributing companies as a mortality table. The convention also authorized the committee to spend whatever funds necessary—to be contributed by the member companies—in the computation of this new table. Although the actuary of Mutual Benefit of New Jersey anticipated that such a task would take at least five years to complete, the convention was confident of the committee's success.[50]

The Failure of Collaboration

Despite Mutual Benefit's warning, members of the convention were impatient to receive the results of the endeavor. By the fall of 1861, with many of the contributing companies clamoring for information on the proposed table, the editor of the *Insurance Gazette* reported that Homans had "the entire control and supervision of the matter in question" and that the other committee members "have not had, for the last eighteen months, anything to do with it, nor are we aware that the Chairman of the Committee [Homans] has asked or solicited any advice or assistance at their hands." Gilbert Currie, as the original proponent of both the convention and the combined mortality table, went on to express his sorrow in observing "in consequence of the protracted delay, and as yet non-appearance of this long-expected 'Combined Experience' document, that so many of the Life Underwriters have become disheartened, cold, and indifferent to the whole affair, and regret that they ever had any thing to do with the matter."[51] In the winter of 1861–62, Currie reported more positively on the progress of the committee. Citing the lack of adequate funding as the reason for the delay, the committee thought it inadvisable to solicit additional moneys during the war. Mutual Life, however, allegedly stepped up to provide the remaining support needed to "carry forward the work to a satisfactory conclusion."[52] But the industry soon became distracted by the Civil War, and the much-anticipated table never materialized.

In 1864, one of the committee members (John Eadie of United States Life) wrote to Elizur Wright, former secretary of the Massachusetts Board of Insurance Commissioners and a well-respected actuary then working on his own mortality table. After complimenting Wright on his substantial progress despite having much more limited data, Eadie lamented the fate of the ALUC table: "I only wish now we had given you half the money for an experience table from your data. It would have paid you well and given us results. As it is, I suppose, we shall have to abandon it."[53] Wright commented several years later that the companies "contributed two or three thousand dollars to get the experience digested; and the work was partially done; but the whole thing failed, for the want, I believe, of the necessary funds."[54] Whether owing to the stress of the war years, frustration with the lack of progress on the combined mortality table, or changes within the industry itself, the convention never met again after 1862.

In 1868 Mutual Life made one more attempt to assert its industry dominance, unilaterally adopting a new table of rates based on the experience of the company from 1843 to 1858.[55] Developed by Sheppard Homans, the American Experience Table undoubtedly employed the data originally contributed by Mutual Life to the Committee on Vital Statistics in 1859. The table itself could not represent overall American mortality, since it was based on medically selected lives and not the general population, but Homans did exclude policies that were in existence for less than five years because the table was "intended to represent the death rate among insured lives residing in healthful districts after the effects of medical selection were eliminated."[56] Celebrated as the first mortality table to be based on widespread American observations, the table predicted life expectancies slightly greater than the Carlisle estimations for those aged 20 to 40 and slightly lower for those aged 50 and above.

This resulted in a minor tweaking of the premium rates.[57] The table was immediately adopted as the standard for policy valuations by the insurance department of the State of New York,[58] which undoubtedly influenced numerous companies to adopt it for their premium rates as well.

The relationship between Homans's American Experience Table and the Combined Experience Table commissioned by the ALUC is unclear. In his 1946 history of Mutual Life, Shepard Clough places the blame for the failure of the latter squarely on the shoulders of the other companies, which, he asserts, were "loath to make known what the rate of mortality among their insured was, for fear that their record, if poorer than that of other companies, would injure them. Thus, except for a little information obtained from the Mutual Benefit of New Jersey [published in 1858], Homans had to rely upon the mortality experience of The Mutual Life."[59] But this assessment does not conform to the fact that at least twelve other companies did furnish their data as of the May 1860 meeting of the ALUC. It is certainly possible that the companies refused to continue contributing financially to the project after 1860, but there is no evidence to suggest that the committee ever solicited additional funds from the member firms. In fact, as Currie's editorial from the fall of 1861 suggested, it appeared that the committee had been disbanded altogether as Homans attempted to compile the data without input from the executives assigned for his support.

One possibility is that Homans and Mutual Life, in light of the increasing and rapidly encroaching competition of the early 1860s, chose to abandon the proposed Combined Experience Table and act solely on their own behalf—pilfering the data and setting the quest for an American life table back another decade. As the largest of the companies, Mutual Life clearly stood to benefit the most from a new mortality table. It had also contributed the most data and funds to the project, sufficient data to form a table separate from the other companies. However, this scenario seems unlikely, since there is no evidence (after about 1862) of firms bemoaning the failure of the ALUC committee. Nor did any of the twelve other companies that supplied data complain that their contributions had been snubbed. The more likely explanation is that the need for an accurate mortality table—at least in the opinion of the majority of the industry—had passed.

By the time the nation emerged from the war, the structure of the life insurance industry had again shifted substantially. With the slow growth rates of the 1850s, companies were most concerned about maintaining their market shares and profit margins in the face of new companies that threatened to undercut their client base with predatory premium rates. A related fear was that the maturation of policies would prove the premium rates to be inadequate for the long-term fiscal soundness of the industry. The establishment of an industry-standard mortality table would thus stabilize the industry—guaranteeing profits to existing companies and removing the threat of potentially devastating price competition. But as sales surged during and following the Civil War, the leading firms would prove unable to stem the floodtide of new entrants in the now booming life insurance industry. The market share of the top four firms would drop to 35% and of the top eight to 52% (from 53% and 70%, respectively, in 1860). In this period of rapid growth, the largest companies would no longer wield the same degree of power and influence over their smaller competitors, and their window of opportunity for creating an industry-standard mortality table would close. When life insurance executives attempted to create a new industry association in 1866—the Chamber of Life Insurance—the main focus of the industry had shifted toward state and federal regulation of life insurance, with the collection and analysis of mortality data a distant second.

Uniform Legislation: The Massachusetts Model

While the primary goal of the initial meeting of the American Life Underwriters' Convention was to prevent predatory pricing through the creation of an industry-standard life table, insurance firms recognized that this forum could also serve as an opportunity for them to address the multiplicity of often conflicting state laws that had developed by midcentury. Some of these laws were designed to regulate the fiscal soundness of life insurers operating within the state for the protection of its citizens. The companies necessarily expended a great deal of time and resources deciphering and complying with these laws, but they continued to face problems associated with "the frequent modification of these laws, and the severe enactments which are added, and the complications which grow out of the various forms for making returns adopted by the officers which these laws create."[60] As the mandates for compliance with these laws varied widely from state to state, multistate companies had to employ an army of bureaucrats to compile the necessary information for each state report—an expensive and time-consuming process.

Other state laws were specifically aimed at promoting the growth and success of in-state companies, serving a protectionist purpose but in some cases undermining industry safety to the detriment of life-insuring citizens. Company executives believed that the retaliatory measures passed in most states were damaging the industry as a whole: "The laws of the States which relate to Life Insurance Companies and their agencies, are found to be very dissimilar, and in many instances, not only conflicting, but retaliatory in their origin and character."[61] As the industry became increasingly competitive, such protectionist legislation handicapped the spread of more-established companies seeking new market opportunities while shielding newcomers from full competitive pressure. By lobbying state lawmakers for uniform legislation, the ALUC hoped both to streamline reporting requirements and establish de facto barriers to entry for new firms. Their model for such legislation would begin with the Massachusetts Board of Insurance Commissioners and the work of its powerful head, Elizur Wright.

An accomplished mathematician and actuary, Elizur Wright was the most vocal proponent of and vehement lobbyist for state oversight of the life insurance industry in the mid-nineteenth century. From the 1840s forward, Wright had championed the virtues of life insurance and criticized practices he deemed unsafe. For example, he labeled the premium-note system "financial quackery" and "moonshine life insurance," persuading at least one major company to overhaul its system.[62] He also believed that most companies did not have a sufficient understanding of how to determine the premium reserve necessary to maintain solvency. To address this problem, Wright (and several of his equally mathematically adept children) completed tens of thousands of calculations to produce his *Valuation Tables,* published in 1853. These tables enabled a life insurer to easily determine what percentage of each premium payment was required for the reserve in order to stay solvent.[63]

By the early 1850s, Wright also began calling for greater state oversight of insurance company operations, lobbying the Massachusetts legislature to pass a law requiring firms to value their policies annually (according to his tables) and report their status to the state. But when Massachusetts created an insurance department in 1855, it merely shifted the responsibility of enforcing existing legislation from the state comptroller to this new agency.[64] Wright's bill, "An Act for the Better Establishment of the Board of Insurance Commissioners," was repeatedly defeated until a sympathetic senator snuck it through in 1858. The renovated department would place a value on all insurance policies underwriting citizens of Massachusetts (for which companies would be taxed 0.01% of their life insurance in force) and report their findings annually to the public. Policyholders could thus easily determine whether their company was operating on a solvent basis. As the person with the greatest knowledge of valuation, Elizur Wright was appointed one of the two commissioners, a position he held from 1858 to 1867.

Because of their relation to valuation, Wright was immensely concerned about lapsed and surrendered policies. Upon witnessing an English auction in 1844 during which impoverished persons sold their life policies to the highest bidder, he commented: "What I saw at that sublime center of trade was a sale at auction of several old policies on very aged men to speculators . . . to be kept up by them by their paying annual premiums to the company till the decease. This was done, I was told, because the companies made it a rule '*never to buy their own policies.*' A poor rule, it seemed to me! I had seen slave auctions at home. I could hardly see more justice in this British practice."[65] As a result of this experience, Wright determined that all companies should be obligated to refund policyholders the unused portion of their policies or to convert whole life policies to cheaper, term policies if payments ceased. New York insurance superintendent William Barnes agreed with Wright's assessment, condemning "the impolicy, if not the injustice of this provision." Barnes even believed that this practice might explain the stagnant state of the industry at midcentury: "The entire forfeiture of policies by the non-payment of premiums at a certain specified date has long been a serious obstacle to the increase of life insurance."[66]

Under the level premium system of insurance, a person's premium remained constant over time. Thus young people paid a higher amount than their initial risk level would require. As they aged, their premium remained static while their level of risk increased, until they were paying less than their actual risk level. Since each Massachusetts insurance policy that passed through his office was individually logged and valued, Wright encouraged policyholders to come to his office and see the value of their policy at any given point—what would be a fair surrender value to receive from the company, and what they would lose if they allowed the policy to lapse.[67]

But beyond merely educating the public, both Wright and Barnes believed that policyholders who forfeited their protection (regardless of reason) should receive back that value of their premium payments paid in anticipation of the greater risks of middle and old age. Rather than requiring a cash surrender value for lapsed or lapsing policies, Wright proposed continuing the insurance under the conditions of term policies; if premium payments on a whole life policy ceased for any reason (except, of course, death), those policies would be valued and then converted to cheaper term life policies. Thus the policyholder would receive the full value of his premium payments even if he chose to stop making them.

Meeting with company representatives at the 1860 ALUC, Wright presented his arguments in favor of a nonforfeiture law. Most of those present were opposed. Actuary Sheppard Homans of Mutual Life, for example, argued that most policyholders desiring to end their contract arrangements would prefer a cash surrender rather than the continuation of a term policy: "I think that the public is now being educated on this subject, and every day the evil is more and more correcting itself. Persons know that their policies have a value, and they will come and claim it, and I have no doubt will get it in every instance."[68] But although companies commonly paid customers a cash surrender value for their policies upon request, it was not required, companies were not obligated to return a set amount (the surrender value was entirely at their discretion), and they would not comply if the policy had already lapsed for nonpayment.

Despite opposition from the industry, both Wright and Barnes promoted the adoption of nonforfeiture provisions, either voluntarily by the life insurance industry or by state mandate. In the fall of 1860, New York Life would become the first company to guarantee nonforfeiture when it "issued a table of rates of premium for life policies expressly stipulating that after the receipt of two or more annual premiums, if further payments are discontinued, a new policy will be issued to the original holder, if living, for a specified proportion of the sum insured, or, if deceased, an equitable sum will be paid to his family or legal representatives." This unilateral shift received the accolades of Barnes, who "regard[ed] it . . . as a matter of public congratulation."[69] The following spring, Massachusetts became the first state to pass a mandatory nonforfeiture law, one of the most significant reforms of the period. Although New York would not pass a similar law until 1879, most companies selling insurance in that market followed the lead of New York Life in guaranteeing nonforfeiture on all policies.[70]

Even though insurance executives at the ALUC meeting opposed Wright's nonforfeiture act, they largely respected his other regulatory efforts in Massachusetts. Antebellum insurers understood that the overall stability of the industry benefited everyone and that fly-by-night companies that were unable to fulfill their obligations to policyholders would hurt the reputation of all firms. Although there had been as yet few outright failures among life firms (failures in which policyholders were not transferred to other companies or given adequate compensation for their accumulated premium payments), many industry leaders were concerned that rapid expansion and intensifying competition from companies employing questionable business practices would lead to widespread closures. They feared that the public, unable to differentiate between sound and unsound practices, would lose confidence in the industry as a whole. According to Vice President Thomas Russell of Charter Oak Life, the most fundamental purpose for state legislation was to inform people "whether the Insurance Company with which they transact business is a solvent one."[71]

However, while they supported the adoption of state regulations that would minimize or eliminate unsound practices, industry executives were highly critical of most current regulations on the books. The company representatives strongly believed that neither deposit requirements nor taxation accomplished the task of ensuring solvency. As President Julius Dewey of National Life of Vermont opined: "I do not think that the deposit for Life Insurance Companies with the Comptroller, the State Legislature, or the State Treasurer, in other States, is worth a fig. It is only an annoyance to the Companies, without being of any security to the people."[72] The actuary of Mutual Benefit of New Jersey agreed, saying, "What is $100,000, for example, to our Company, as a matter of security to the insured lives residing in the State of New-York, that are members of our Company? I suppose that we have millions of insurance effected in New-York. What is $100,000 as security to them? None whatever."[73] According to industry leaders, the existing system of ad hoc regulatory and protectionist measures did little to protect the public from unsavory business practices but exposed the entire industry to competitive pressures from the unsound actions of some newcomers to the field.

The ALUC Committee on Legislation, made up of the president of Aetna Life, the secretary of American Mutual of New Haven, and an agent of Royal Life of Liverpool, concluded that the only acceptable resolution would be to make "the legislation of all the States, relating to Life Insurance Companies, incorporated by other States . . . uniform and simple, and of such a character as to secure the public against Companies not organized according to law."[74] The convention as a whole accepted the report of the committee and resolved to draft a general law (to be presented at its next meeting in 1860) that they would then use as the basis for lobbying efforts in their state legislatures.[75] Companies thus sought to replace the current patchwork of legislation with a more uniform system of laws that would set up more effective barriers to entry for questionable upstarts.

But when the committee met to draft such a general law, it encountered numerous problems. First, the state official charged with oversight of the laws varied from state to state, ranging from insurance superintendents and state comptrollers to auditors and treasurers. The diverse and often conflicting nature of stipulations regarding such things as investments and deposit requirements further confounded the committee. Thus rather than drafting a specific law or set of laws, it decided to focus on eliminating what it deemed the greatest legislative problem: protectionist measures designed to "prevent competition from other sources."[76] While the committee conceded that states retained the right to determine which companies could compete within their borders, it called for states to allow all companies that could demonstrate "satisfactory evidence of ability faithfully to perform their obligations now and in the future" to operate on an equal footing. It asserted "that competition upon this subject among the people should be the real test" of a company's soundness.[77] This free-trade proposal would, in effect, eliminate the many discriminatory laws (such as taxes upon out-of-state agencies) and retaliatory legislation, but it would not touch on the problem of the diverse requirements for investing and reporting.

Many of the representatives were disappointed that, after a year of discussion, this minimalist statement was the best the Committee on Legislation could do. As one frustrated delegate, President Julius Dewey of National Life of Vermont, responded to the report: "I do not suppose that every thing can be done in a single year; but yet, it is not best to sit down and say there cannot be any thing done." Yet Dewey did agree with the basic premise of the report, opining that "if you could satisfy Insurance men, agents and officers, that free trade was better for the whole— that no one suffered by letting others have a chance to come in—then all difficulty would be done away with." This, he asserted, had been accomplished most successfully in Massachusetts, where "the people . . . know what they should trust, and what they should not."[78] Others agreed, suggesting that the Massachusetts insurance laws, as designed and implemented by Elizur Wright, would provide the ideal balance of safety and sanity for the industry.[79]

Upon President Dewey's suggestion, the convention shifted its discussion to the valuation law of Massachusetts and the desirability of employing that as the model for the country as a whole. The Massachusetts law was, in effect, a sunshine law requiring each company to make a full report of its condition, which would then be published "so that the public may know the amount of its capital, accumulations and surplus, and how the same are invested, and such other facts as are necessary to a proper understanding of the condition of the Company . . . the public, aided by the information which honorable competition disseminates, would judge for themselves, and act accordingly."[80] Of course, the publication of raw balance sheets would be relatively useless for the average applicant lacking the knowledge to make judgments upon those numbers. So the Massachusetts Board of Insurance Commissioners processed this information for the purpose of answering one basic question: if the company decided to close its doors and had to purchase new policies for each of its current customers (at their current ages) in another company, would they have enough money to do so? In Dewey's assessment, "The amount of its [the company's] assets does not tell its strength. The strength depends upon the proportion of its assets to the liabilities; and in that respect the law of Massachusetts probes the Companies to the bottom. In the State of Massachusetts a Company must have enough to re-insure their risks." This was in direct contrast to the laws in most states, which merely required a minimum deposit of funds that, depending on the number and age of the company's policyholders, might or might not be adequate protection and gave customers no way of determining the firm's ultimate soundness.[81]

Unfortunately the convention's efforts to reform state insurance laws would have to be put aside the following year as the Civil War broke out. Although it would meet two more times—in 1861 to discuss war risks and in 1862 to discuss federal war taxation—the disruptions of the war years ended the American Life Underwriters' Convention. And, as has been noted, the composition of the industry dramatically changed during the 1860s. Whereas the more-established firms in the industry viewed the strict Massachusetts legislation as an acceptable alternative to the multiplicity of often contradictory state laws (as well as an effective barrier to entry for new firms), the new entrants of the 1860s supported laissez-faire options. During the second half of the 1860s, a much stronger movement for federal oversight of the industry would emerge.

Self-Regulation in the Banking Industry

These cooperative attempts by life insurers to control their competitive environment were hardly unique. Antebellum bankers faced similar challenges to their survival and legitimacy as they tried to rein in rogue banks. Like the newer life companies that placed the long-term viability of the industry at risk by undercutting premium rates, many banks located far from the city centers issued bank notes well in excess of their assets, gambling that the relatively high expense of redeeming their notes meant that they would remain in circulation (even if they traded at a steep discount). The questionable quality of the notes and the high rate of bank failure resulting from this practice left even the most conservative banks suspect.

Beginning in 1818, the Boston banking community successfully addressed this problem by collaborating in the creation of an unofficial central bank. Much as the Second Bank of the United States would later try to do nationwide, the Suffolk Bank stabilized currency throughout New England by holding all banks accountable for their notes. The Suffolk served as a central clearinghouse for banknotes from the surrounding area; it would regularly return these notes to the issuing banks in large numbers for redemption, thus forcing banks to hold adequate reserves to cover their liabilities. With the stability created under the Suffolk system, the notes of most New England banks traded at or close to par—a feat unmatched in the rest of the country.[82]

During the late 1850s, increased competition within a stagnating market likewise forced life insurers to seek collaborative solutions to their shared problems. By attempting to establish an industrywide mortality table, more conservative firms sought to expose the allegedly unsound practices of their cut-rate competitors. And by lobbying for the passage of uniform state legislation, they hoped to unravel the multiplicity of state requirements and protective regulations that prevented the more-established companies from spreading their risks and shielded newer companies from full competitive pressure. But unlike the Suffolk Bank, the American Life Underwriters' Convention failed in its endeavors. While the contingencies of war distracted the industry from its goals, the rapidly evolving market for life insurance ultimately outpaced the efforts of industry leaders to rein in and manage their upstart competitors.

CHAPTER 10

Insuring Soldiers, Insuring Civilians

The Civil War as a Watershed for the Life Insurance Industry

Less than a month after South Carolina seceded from the Union (but before any other southern states joined her rebellion), agent C. B. Wellford of Fredericksburg, Virginia, was already asking the home office of Baltimore Life for clarification regarding their military clause. While most policies (including those of Baltimore Life) contained stipulations that voided them in the case of active military service, the company secretary assured Wellford that "when hostilities shall commence, our Co. will fix 'war risks' on policies already issued and on applications to be made."[1] Although Wellford would press the company for more specifics regarding this proposed "war rate,"[2] Baltimore Life was "not desirous of anticipating a necessity which may never exist" and refused to adopt a specific guideline without understanding "the character and prospects of any contest on which they may be based."[3] It was Secretary F. M. Colston's "hope that the necessity for these applications may never exist, until Virginia with all her sister States, may have to meet a common enemy of our Whole country."[4] Recognizing that life insurance companies had spent decades carefully crafting an image as protector of the widow and the orphan, executives such as Colston understood that invoking these clauses to void policies at a time of national crisis would risk shattering that image. As tensions between the North and South increased during the early months of 1861, life insurers had to weigh their responses to the crisis extremely carefully.

Unlike the companies farther north that dominated the industry, Baltimore Life did not know whether it would eventually be headquartered in a Union or Confederate state. A large proportion of its policyholders resided in Virginia, and since the mid-1850s, slave policies had formed the most important segment of its business. In some cases, this uncertain relationship between Baltimore Life and the emerging Confederacy strained policyholder allegiance. Dr. Thomas Pollard, medical examiner and acting agent for the company in Richmond, complained in February 1861: "Policy holders too in some instances have declined to renew insurance for fear of the position of Maryland in the Event of Virginias secession from the Union."[5]

Regardless of Maryland's ultimate allegiance in the conflict, the company was getting caught in the middle and could not afford to discriminate against war risks.

By early May, agent Wellford's theoretical question had become a practical one, as his cousin Lieutenant P. A. Wellford sought a $5,000 policy that would cover him in case of war. Although Virginia would not secede until later in the month, there was "a settled impression" among the men in Lieutenant Wellford's Richmond regiment "that hostilities may soon be inaugurated," and he wished to protect his family against that contingency.[6] Presuming the lieutenant less than forty years old, the company agreed to insure the risk for one year (despite his request for a seven-year policy) under the relatively generous terms of a 5% premium ($50 per $1,000 of insurance) "which rate will cover all risks, including ordinary, war and climate." With the premium for an ordinary one-year policy (for a man aged 35–40) costing about 1.5% ($15 per $1,000), this translated into an additional 3.5% to cover the risks of war and climate.[7] To establish that this surcharge was not "excessive"—as well as to demonstrate that its "sympathy with your cause takes a practical turn"—Colston quoted the recently published rates of New York Life, which included a 5% surcharge for war risks (*over and above* the initial policy premium), with another 5% added for travel below 34° north latitude.[8] As Wellford anticipated that "several additional war Risks will be wanted,"[9] the company gave him permission to "grant war risks on any of our policies now in force at four per cent (4%) extra."[10] Baltimore Life wanted to assure its southern policyholders of its continued commitment to serving them, regardless of the status of the war.

Yet Baltimore Life still needed to balance loyalty to its southern clientele with the reality of its own continued domicile within a Union state. The role of the agent would become more critical, with the company relying heavily on the agent's judgment in approving war risks. Soon after Virginia's secession, Colston strongly reminded Wellford that his primary duty as agent continued to be acting as the eyes and ears of Baltimore Life in Fredericksburg, only permitting war risks "when you and our medical examiner are satisfied that it is judicious and to the interest of our Company."[11] With the company's ability to screen policyholders limited by the conditions of war, it would need to grant southern agents much greater autonomy in decision making—or be forced to abandon all business in the South.

Dependence on the agent would only increase as both the Union and the Confederacy put into place regulations solidifying the state of war. In May 1861, a Confederate act sequestered the debts of southerners owed to northerners; this law was extended in August when all property ownership by northerners in the South was declared illegal under the Sequestration Act, and the government began to seize

northern assets, including bank deposits, stock and bond certificates, and debt contracts.[12] Also in May, mail service between the sections was halted by order of the
United States Postmaster General.[13] Abraham Lincoln issued a presidential procla-
mation forbidding all commercial interaction between northern companies and
southern states, commonly known as the Non-Intercourse Act, to take effect August
26, 1861.[14] Meanwhile, Mississippi actively expelled northern life insurance companies from its borders, stating that the conditions necessary for renewing their li-
censes in that state were vitiated with the dissolution of the Union.[15]

As the northern company with the most at stake in the South, Baltimore Life did
everything in its power to bypass these obstacles to continuing its southern business. Agent Wellford expressed his concern about underwriting new policies while
communication was "so uncertain . . . unless some arrangement can be made by
which risks can be made binding here."[16] The company agreed that underwriting
new lives would not be advisable, but it did not want to alienate existing policyholders. Colston thus empowered Wellford with unprecedented discretion: "You
are hereby authorized to use your own judgment and any latitude of power necessary, in regard to the old business, the retention of risks, the re-insurance of policies
now in force but which may expire." Baltimore Life was clearly trying to focus on
the interests of the company in the long term; it hoped that by demonstrating an
unwavering commitment to its current clientele, it would maintain a solid foundation upon which to construct a strong postwar organization: "When business shall
again resume . . . we hope to be more in favor than ever in your State, and your own
attention to our interest will be only rewarded."[17]

Baltimore Life was also confronted with the interrelated problems of dealing
with southern sequestration acts, the federal Non-Intercourse Act, and currency
discrepancies between the warring sides. While it initially demanded that "premium[s] be paid us in funds current in Baltimore,"[18] the company later agreed to
accept payments in any form—including Confederate notes—"with the understanding that should a loss occur during the continuance of this State of affairs that
the amount shall be paid in the same funds in which the premiums are now paid."[19]
The firm then consolidated its Virginia operations into the Richmond agency,
where Dr. Thomas Pollard was instructed to serve as the nexus for the collection of
premium payments and the dispersal of death claims for all Virginia agencies.[20]
Although Pollard would legally be bound (under the Confederate Sequestration
Act) to turn over all premium payments made to the Union-based company, the
company hoped to remain outside the reach of the law by holding these funds expressly for the purpose of paying southern claims.[21] However, the insurer would not
have any more contact with Dr. Pollard either during or after the war; it would

never know if he had complied with its instructions, shut down the agency, collected premium payments and absconded with its funds, or turned over premium payments to the Confederacy.[22]

Beginning in early 1862, contact between Baltimore Life headquarters and all of its southern agents ceased for the remainder of the war, and the firm would not be able to evaluate its financial position until the end of hostilities in 1865. With the emancipation of slaves, the most lucrative segment of its business was completely eliminated.[23] The majority of nonslave premiums during the war had been paid to the agents in currency that was now worthless.[24] Although the company attempted to deal liberally with these customers (out of "simple justice")[25] by reinstating their policies despite the lost of premium payments during the war,[26] the physical and economic devastation of the war (including the emancipation of the slaves) left its southern business in shambles.

By November 1866, the company was considering the feasibility of continuing to underwrite risks, soliciting the advice of consulting actuary Sheppard Homans on several occasions regarding the valuation of its remaining policies and its future prospects.[27] By February 1867, the board of directors and stockholders had determined that the best course would be to reinsure the remaining risks with another company.[28] The firm reached an agreement in May with Equitable Life Assurance Society of New York to take over these risks, paying cash surrender values to any policyholders not wishing to have their policies transferred to New York.[29] With this final transaction, one of the oldest life insurance companies in the country—and the longest-serving in the southern market—ceased to exist.

Although Baltimore Life was the only Union-based company with significant operations within the Confederacy, the remainder of the industry faced similar dilemmas during the war years. The Civil War occurred at a critical point in the history of life insurance. While the amount of insurance in force had been growing at an average real rate of about 30% per annum from 1825 to 1850, this rate had slowed considerably to just over 3.5% per annum for the period from 1850 to 1862. With the rapid entrance of new firms to the industry in the late 1840s (bringing the total number from eighteen in 1845 to fifty in 1851),[30] companies faced stiffening competition for new policyholders, and the life insurance in force of four of the top ten firms in 1850 either stagnated or declined during the 1850s. State regulation of insurance through taxation, deposit laws, investment restrictions, and insurance departments exacerbated the tightening conditions of the 1850s. The Civil War would thus test the stability and resilience of an industry still fighting to prove its indispensability for the average American family.

The Civil War was the first national catastrophe with the capacity to introduce true chaos into the insurance system, for which understanding and controlling risk was so crucial. The 1860s began with the industry still lacking an accurate American mortality table, a problem that could devastate firms if they experienced higher than expected claims. American life insurance companies had no experience with mortality during war—particularly a war on American soil—where the young and healthy would be sent from their homes to face the very real possibility of engaging in combat on the battlefield or contracting diseases in camp.[31] While the industry had prepared for this type of contingency by inserting clauses to void policies in case of military service, it had also spent half a century carefully crafting a public image as the protector of widows and orphans. If it shirked that duty now—when the need was the greatest—would its reputation ever recover? If companies agreed to underwrite soldiers, would the increased mortality burden damage or even destroy their fiscal soundness? This was the dilemma of 1861. The industry thus had to address two separate issues related to the war: how to treat existing policyholders in the southern states and whether to insure northern war risks.

The industry adopted both approaches. Companies almost universally used every possible means of legally voiding policies on southerners. Some went beyond merely weeding out war risks, and the exigencies of the four-year conflict forced most to take a hard line with respect to lapsing policies. With the prominent exception of Baltimore Life, most northern companies had hardly penetrated the southern market by the eve of the Civil War and thus could afford to sacrifice those policies. Accounting for less than 7% of all life insurance in force in 1860, the southern market was of only minor importance to the industry as the war began.[32] The industry might have greatly benefited in the postbellum period from a more forgiving approach toward the region, but that was a risk firms were unwilling to take.

In the North, the industry embraced its public duty—or at least wrapped itself in the image of doing so. In the decades before the war, life insurers had realized the importance of acting in concert when confronting new challenges. They readily cooperated in all areas where direct competition would have resulted in a net loss for the industry (even if individual companies stood to gain temporarily). Thus their immediate reaction to the dilemma of insuring war risks was to call a meeting of the American Life Underwriters' Convention and create a united front. This allowed them to charge an exorbitant war premium to cover the uncertainties of war while still credibly claiming to be patriotically supporting the Union and defending families from some of the worst consequences of the conflict. In hindsight, their tactics were brilliant. Suffering little loss as a result of its war risk policies, the industry converted this reputation capital into huge gains as northern demand for life insurance skyrocketed during and after the war years.

Northern War Risks

From the inception of the industry in America, the occupation most feared by life insurance companies was active military duty. A standard condition of policies stated that "insurances will be made on the lives of military and naval officers, off or on duty, in time of peace *only,*"[33] and that policies would be rendered void if the insured "enter[ed] into any military or naval service whatsoever, the militia not in actual service excepted."[34] However, with the outbreak of the Civil War, the northern life insurers immediately recognized the need to reconsider this provision for reasons of business expediency and as a sign of their support for the Union. At issue was not only whether to allow existing policyholders to remain insured if they voluntarily or involuntarily joined the war effort but also whether it would be prudent to acquire any new military risks.

The war tested the sincerity of an industry that had always highlighted its role in promoting the public good. In the winter of 1860–61, before any shots had been fired, the press was already goading life underwriters to do their "patriotic duty." An article entitled "Patriotism and Liberality of our Life Insurance Corporations," reprinted in the *Insurance Gazette* from the *New York Evening Post,* recounted the story of "an officer at Fort Moultrie."[35] Citing "the probability that the fort would soon be attacked, and the certainty that 'it would be defended to the last extremity,'" the officer inquired with his life insurer as to the fate of his policy should he be killed. Although the company acknowledged that it "was not legally liable where the assured fell in battle," it still affirmatively declared that "if he should fall now while doing his duty gloriously, and abandoned by the Government, he need have no fear but that the policy would be paid."[36]

When shots did ring out over Fort Sumter in April of 1861, the *New York Herald* praised both Equitable Life Assurance Society of New York and New York Life for "rallying to the support of the constitution" by "unfurl[ing] a large and beautiful American flag" on "their fine marble building." Both companies were "sound for the Union."[37] But beyond mere symbolism, the public expected life insurers to demonstrate their patriotism proactively by underwriting soldiers. As a small article entitled "How to Aid Volunteers" that appeared in the April 24, 1861, edition of the *New York Times* opined, "The best possible way to aid officers and others who are volunteering for the War, is to *insure their lives* . . . The friends of those who are going could render them no better service than this, and it might not be amiss to raise a public fund for that purpose."[38] Of course, such policies would only be valid if the companies chose to waive their military exclusions. This connection between patriotism and life insurance would remain a common theme throughout the war, obliging companies to develop a plan to ensure soldiers without sacrificing the fiscal soundness of the industry.

Following the firing on Fort Sumter, Elizur Wright—secretary of the Massachusetts Board of Insurance Commissioners and a well-respected actuary—issued a letter dated April 21, 1861, to all companies doing business in that state on the topic of war risks. He divided the extra risk owing to war into three parts—"the enhancement of ordinary diseases," "deaths from casualties in action," and reduced life expectancy resulting from "disease or vicious habits contracted in the service." Wright emphasized that the risk added by war varied widely and that "this war has really no precedent in the history of the world, either among foreign, civil or servile wars," which made a mathematically accurate calculation of the risk impossible. Despite this warning, Wright anticipated a short war with few casualties for the North. While his prediction of a swift victory was certainly not unusual among northerners, the opinion of this ardent abolitionist certainly must have been tainted by his disdain for slaveholders, upon whom he blamed the war. In one of the most colorful passages from the letter he stated, "I can liken the war only to that between the enraged bull and the locomotive. The natural brute is sure to get the worst of it, while, with caution and a cow-catcher, the artificial will convert its antagonist into harmless beef with no material damage to itself."[39]

Wright believed that a quick, low-casualty war (at least among northerners) would require insurance companies to charge not more than a 2% additional premium surcharge for war risks ($20 per $1,000 of insurance). Even if this proved inadequate, Wright also believed the industry had a duty to the public in this time of war: "Their position is so strong that I think [the life insurance companies] can shoulder some loss, and their constituents would cheerfully justify them in doing it . . . The flag must be sustained, or our institutions sink into a common ruin."[40] Similarly, Commissioner William Barnes of the New York Insurance Department wrote in his 1862 report that if the war risk premium adopted by the companies proved to be insufficient, "the loss to the Companies will be one of those contingencies, for which it is the obvious duty of all patriotic corporations to provide." For an industry that had always promoted itself as a quasi-public entity beneficial to the common welfare of the people, the war would prove to be the critical moment when companies would either decisively demonstrate this public beneficence or abandon forever that line of rhetoric. However, as Barnes continued, such an embrace of public duty would reciprocally "afford a claim hereafter for governmental aid and protection to the interests of Life Insurance, which will result in mutual benefit to the State and people."[41] Going well beyond the promotional-regulatory understanding of the relationship between businesses and the state, the commissioner reflected an emerging interpretation that the government had a positive obligation to ensure the continued existence of private corporations or industries that served the public good.

At approximately the same time that Commissioner Wright was issuing his war risk recommendations, Mutual Life of New York called an emergency meeting of the American Life Underwriters' Convention to be held in New York on April 19, 1861.[42] The sixteen life insurance companies represented—including Mutual of New York, New York Life, Connecticut Mutual, Manhattan Life, and New England Life—met solely to discuss the issue of war risks. The companies in attendance agreed to allow existing policyholders to enter the military provided they pay a war premium of 5% over and above their existing premium rates. Additionally, they would have to pay a 5% climate premium (for a total surcharge of 10%, or $100 per $1,000 of insurance) if they were sent to areas south of 34° north latitude (falling approximately just south of Columbia, South Carolina). Policyholders choosing not to pay the war risk premium could either surrender their policies and receive a cash surrender value or renew them at the original premium rate upon discharge from the service—provided that they passed a new medical exam. The convention also recommended that any new military policies be accepted according to the same guidelines.[43]

The need to standardize the rules and rates for war risks was twofold. The industry was feeling public pressure to liberalize policy provisions to show support for the northern war effort. But companies did not want to risk their long-term safety by charging premiums that were too low. The ALUC agreement enabled companies to charge an extremely high war premium without sacrificing their reputation for protecting the families of the deceased. With an industry standard in time of war, there would be less temptation for companies to undercut rates in an effort to gain market share. Although the agreement of the convention was in no way binding, most life insurance companies—including those not in attendance—adopted the proposed war risk conditions for existing policyholders (although a few smaller companies, following Wright's recommendations, chose to charge as little as 2%).[44]

At its 1862 meeting, the convention reaffirmed its decision, agreeing "to take war risks upon the rates and rules adopted last spring,"[45] and nine companies reported on their experience with war risks during the previous year. New York Life had permitted war risks on 200 of its policies, with 1 loss of life resulting in a $500 claim; Connecticut Mutual had 174 war risks on its books, 2 of which had resulted in claims totaling $3,500; and Penn Mutual and American Mutual each had 100 risks with no claims.[46]

The industry's liberality in dealing with northern war risks—or at least its rhetoric of liberality—continued throughout the war. Several companies added stories and testimonials involving war risks to their advertising literature. New York Life, for example, inserted the tale of Hugh C. Irish—one of "those gallant men who left their homes at the call of their country"—in its 1863 brochure. Irish held a $2,000 policy on his life but failed to pay the extra war premium because of "a misunderstanding" and thus "departed for the seat of war without having obtained permission from the Company to enter into military service, thereby virtually forfeiting his policy." Although the firm could easily have cancelled his policy in light of his lapse, company executives determined that Irish "inten[ded] . . . to comply" with the war risk provisions and "believed that he had done so." Determined to fulfill their patriotic duty to this brave soldier, the officers and board "unanimously concluded to pay the policy, and a check for the amount was duly handed to his afflicted wife."[47] While instances such as this were undoubtedly rare, they served the purpose of promoting the patriotism and goodwill of a company. New York Life assumed that the new policies sold to people inspired by this story would more than cover the cost of paying the death claim on a legally invalid policy.

While most companies were willing to underwrite war risks for the additional 5% charge, at least one company—the newly chartered Equitable Life Assurance Society of New York (1859)—declined to assume war risks at any premium, even as it was becoming actively involved in the ALUC.[48] In an unsigned letter to the editor of the *Insurance Gazette* dated August 1862, an official representing one of the newer New York companies (perhaps Equitable, although it is impossible to determine from the letter) dissented from the opinion of the ALUC, asserting that "the extra rates in the end will not pay." Echoing Elizur Wright's analysis of the three-pronged increase in mortality caused by war, the author warned: "They may pay in the beginning, but the losses by battle are small in comparison to what they are estimated to be by disease contracted in camp, or by exposure. If this war should end to-day thousands who have been in the army will die in one, two, or three years, from the effect of wounds and disease therein or thereby contracted." Yet this executive was careful to distinguish wartime patriotism from the company's duty to all of its policyholders: "This Company has as much patriotism as any other, and as far as it can go without wronging half a dozen policyholders to benefit one it will go." Thus even while dissenting from the consensus of its competitors, this newcomer still embraced the quasi-public ideal promoted since the industry's inception.[49]

The anonymous executive did not conclude his letter on the issue of patriotism and duty but had two additional objectives. First, he sought to rouse northerners from their optimistic complacency about the war. Demonstrating a remarkable amount of prescience concerning the war's outcome, the author declared: "This war that is upon us, and for ought any one can tell, may be a long and bloody one, and those who calculate otherwise show their ignorance of the enemy we have to deal with. The loss of life by this war when it is ended, end when and how it may, will surprise the world."[50] The jingoism of war had led even the staid, pragmatic Wright to render judgments based on overly patriotic predictions rather than weighing the effects of all the possible outcomes. For the executive of this young company, it would be foolish to risk the financial security of the company's future on the hopes of a quick victory.

Second, the author sought to take the decision of the convention out of the realm of patriotic duty and put it into that of cold, competitive pragmatism—indicting the older companies for manipulating the language of patriotism: "Some of the large Companies may combine and take war risks, but their object is to lead the younger Companies on to do the same, in order that they may be used up, and thus lessen competition."[51] Elimination of price competition was the unstated goal of the ALUC in setting war risk premiums, just as it had been in the convention's efforts to establish a standard American mortality table. This letter of dissent thus foreshadowed the rift that would open up between older, more conservative companies and their less risk-averse rivals, whose numbers would multiply rapidly in the immediate postwar period.

While few other companies were willing to dissent from the ALUC position on existing policyholders, all the companies were much more wary when it came to underwriting new military risks. Some, like Mutual Life Insurance of Wisconsin, were extremely straightforward about their unwillingness to acquire additional war risks, stating unequivocally that "new risks for military or naval service are not desired, and agents will not solicit or encourage them, or in any manner obligate the Company to take them."[52] Other companies were much more circumspect in their attitude toward these risks. New York Life, the fourth-largest life insurer in the country, initially agreed to issue new policies on the lives of soldiers for a maximum of $1,000 for the benefit of their dependents only (not creditors).[53] Declaring that the company was only charging "such a rate as would indemnify the Company against loss, and with no expectation that it would yield a profit," New York Life executives again adopted the language of public duty and patriotic support for the Union: "Persons voluntarily exposing themselves to the deprivations and dangers of the camp and the battle-field were entitled to every facility to enable them to make provision for their families in the event of death."[54] The company's literature for the winter of 1861–62 advertised "war risks taken at usual war rates,"[55] but this statement does not appear to have been included in subsequent advertising.

Despite these public proclamations of willingness to insure northern soldiers,

New York Life was actually extremely conservative regarding new war risks; during the course of the entire conflict, the company would underwrite only 731 war risks, and only about one-quarter of these were for new policyholders.[56] On one occasion the company stressed that "the officers desire it to be expressly understood that they do not consider these as a desirable class of risks," and that it was only underwriting soldiers as part of its patriotic duty: "Our agents are therefore particularly requested not to direct their efforts in canvassing for war risks, and especially, as much as may be, to avoid receiving applications from more than a very limited number in any one company or regiment."[57] Contrary to such guidance to its agents, the company's public pronouncements continued to reinforce its positive role in the war effort. For example, in 1862—New York Life's most successful year to date, when it underwrote more than half of the new policies issued by all New York companies—company executives partially attributed its success to continuing to write new policies on Union soldiers.[58] But given the small number of war policies actually written by the company, this assessment cannot possibly be accurate. Even by the end of the war, the amount of insurance in force on war risks constituted a mere 3% of the total amount in force for the entire company.[59] New York Life was thus using the rhetoric of patriotism to enhance public goodwill toward the company without actually writing a significant number of war policies.

A few companies did actively solicit new war risks, including New England Mutual Life and Eagle and Albion Life Insurance of London and New York.[60] Approximately 20% of all new policies written by New England Life during the second half of 1861 were on war risks.[61] The company reasoned that it would be unfair to allow existing policyholders to keep their protection subject to a war risk premium and not treat new insurers in the same manner. However, like New York Life, it specifically limited such policies to those of which the beneficiary was a dependent of the insured, stating that "Applications on such risks as collateral security to creditors have been declined."[62] Eagle and Albion, on the other hand, added the phrase "WAR RISKS TAKEN" to its advertising during the war years, displaying it prominently on the copy.[63] Given their status as a British company with only a small American market share, this may have been a calculated attempt to more closely associate the firm with the Union cause. Few (if any) other companies chartered before the war advertised their acceptance of war risks so brazenly.

New companies, however, quickly sprouted up to tap into this market. North America Life Insurance of New York began targeting war risks from its organization in 1862. Soon after the passage of the Conscription Act in March 1863—which established a lottery for the drafting of all men aged 20 to 35 and unmarried men under 45—the company developed a plan of insurance against the draft. Designated "war permits," these policies combined a regular life insurance component with a contingency that would "allow the insured to enter, *in the event of being drafted,* the service of the United States for one year, without further payment." But what made this policy truly unique was the clause allowing the policyholder to forfeit the war permit in exchange for $300 "should the holders of these Permits be drafted, and prefer not to enter the army."[64] Since the Conscription Act included a commutation clause that permitted the draftee either to provide a substitute in his place or pay $300 to avoid service, the plan of North America Life was but a thinly veiled effort to attract customers by guaranteeing them the $300 needed in the event they were drafted.[65] In the end, however, the company probably obtained little business in its home base of New York City as a result of this marketing ploy; following the draft riots in July 1863, the city agreed to pay the requisite $300 to any citizen drafted or volunteering for service.[66] And by the summer of 1864, the clause permitting the payment of $300 in lieu of being drafted was rescinded by the government altogether.[67]

National Union Life and Limb Insurance Company was chartered specifically to underwrite war risks by issuing policies on "the lives or limbs of officers, soldiers or sailors in the army or navy of the United States."[68] In order to write both life and casualty insurance—an endeavor banned by the general insurance law of New York State—the organizers required a special charter from the legislature, which they received in April 1863.[69] The following year, after its failure to raise the $100,000 in capital required by law, the charter was amended to permit insurance on civilian lives as well—in exchange for the promise of dropping the casualty line at the next legislative session.[70] Despite the overwhelming success of other new life insurance ventures during the war years, National Union Life and Limb ended 1864 with only seventeen life and fifty-six accident policies in force; the company stood out as being the only one in the state of New York to finish the year in the red.[71]

Based on the little data available, it appears that coverage of war risks accounted for an extremely small percentage of the life insurance in force for the industry as a whole. Few soldiers (relative to the total size of the Union army) benefited from this protection. Yet overall, the experiment in war risk insurance was a positive one, with the industry roughly breaking even on these policies. New York Life paid about $20,000 more in claims than was collected for war risk premiums.[72] Similarly, Mutual Benefit of New Jersey reported paying about $20,000 above the extra premium paid by their 500–700 war risks, but the death claims were still below the total premiums collected on this age group when civilian risks were included.[73] United States Life reported in 1863 that it continued to make a profit on its war risk insurance, and New England Life—with its almost 5,000 war risk policies—likewise turned a small profit on the endeavor.[74] Mutual Life of New York reported collecting $141,000 in war risk premiums in addition to the $64,358 in ordinary premiums required on their approximately 1,200 war risk policies but paid only $129,300 on 74 losses.[75] Connecticut Mutual paid $110,750 on the lives of 64 men killed during the war, for which the war premiums appear to have been more than adequate.[76] Unfortunately, none of these companies tracked the mortality rates of combatants during the postbellum years, so there is no way to tell if diseases and habits acquired during the war affected mortality in the long term as was predicted by Elizur Wright and others.

The true benefit of the war came in the form of new civilian policies; the goodwill and publicity engendered with the payment of each death claim, combined with a generally heightened awareness of mortality, greatly increased interest in life insurance both during and in the immediate aftermath of the war. Many companies tried to emphasize and capitalize on their patriotism, but the entire industry benefited from the experience of the war. Equitable Life of New York, for example, had only been chartered in 1859 and publicly declined underwriting war risks. Yet by 1866 it had grown to become the sixth-largest company in the industry through its superior marketing. For the industry as a whole, life insurance in force (in 1860 dollars) almost doubled in only three years, rising from $159 million in 1862 to $301 million in 1865 before reaching just under $1.3 billion by 1870. From 1864 to 1868, it increased at the incredible rate of 43% per annum.[77]

The war had revealed to Americans the benefits of insurance in general rather than the superiority of any one company, which boosted sales for the entire industry and in turn attracted a host of new competitors to the field. Whereas only 43 companies existed on the eve of the war, the newfound popularity of life insurance would result in the establishment of 13 new companies during the war years and another 107 between 1865 and 1870.[78] By 1870, 1 out of every 3 northeastern males between the ages of 20 and 49 would own a life insurance policy, compared with only 1 in 30 at the start of the war. As one early historian of the industry commented, "Men who witnessed it were puzzled at the rapidity with which the growth took place."[79]

Southern Policyholders

Although only a small percentage of policyholders resided in the South, these customers would prove to be much more problematic for the industry. Companies initially promised to treat their southern members fairly, but after four years of war—during which premiums were sometimes paid in Confederate currency but more often went unpaid or were refused outright by local agents—it became increasingly unclear what "fair" meant. For most policyholders, the reinstatement of their policy in the aftermath of the war was more than sufficient, but for the beneficiaries of those who died between April 1861 and April 1865, recompense would only come after two decades of court cases.

With the outbreak of war, life insurance companies initially anticipated little interruption of their business in the South. Southerners would continue to be protected under the terms of their policies, although the leniency firms would extend to military risks in the North would not be matched by most companies with regard to the Confederates. In the spring of 1861, a letter from Mutual Life of New York was published in the *Richmond Dispatch* reassuring its policyholders that their contracts would continue even if Virginia seceded: "The limits for residence named in our policies are territorial and not governmental limits, and they are paid with equal promptitude to the citizens of our own or any other government."[80] Similarly, New York Life promised a Virginia policyholder on January 29, 1861, that "the fact of war existing between the Federal and State Governments does not vitiate our policy." Differentiating between the policyholder's being "killed while acting in your own defence, or that of your family or property," and his "joining the contending forces," the company pledged that the policy would only be forfeited in the latter instance.[81]

However, the passage of the various southern sequestration acts as well as the federal Non-Intercourse Act in the late spring and summer of 1861 rendered this relationship between companies residing in the Union and Confederate policyholders much more difficult to maintain. With the exception of Baltimore Life, most northern companies assumed that the Non-Intercourse Act either suspended or voided southern policies. Thus Mutual of New York offered to pay its southern policyholders on demand a cash surrender value equivalent to the total premiums paid less the risk assumed by the company during the term for which the policy had been in force. New York Life offered its policyholders the option of taking a cash surrender or renewing the policy at the end of the war—upon paying all back premiums, undergoing a new medical exam, and providing proof that they had not actively participated on the side of the Confederacy. New England Life offered the same two options, although it maintained the right to choose who could exercise the latter one.[82]

A few northern companies attempted to formally disband their southern business altogether. Manhattan Life officially closed all its agencies in the South, although it provided its policyholders with similar options for redeeming or renewing their policies. Noting the problems of continued business with southerners "in consequence of a discontinuance of the mails, and the derangement of the exchanges, as well as the depreciated currency, in which we could not receive our premiums," Secretary C. Y. Wemple informed the company's Richmond agent that his policyholders could either pay their premiums directly at the New York office or suspend their policies "with permission to renew them at present rates at any time within a year, upon satisfactory evidence of good health." Although the company was unwilling to pay a death claim during the suspension period, it would return the surrender value to the policyholder's beneficiaries should the person die before renewal.[83] Repeating these guidelines in a second letter on August 6, 1861, Wemple additionally expressed the company's fear of property seizure by Confederate states and concluded: "You will, therefore, see the impropriety and impossibility of this company receiving its premiums in your city."[84]

While these companies at least maintained the appearance of accommodating southern policyholders, others were more forthright in cutting off this market. The most severe action was taken by Mutual Benefit of New Jersey. In a circular to its southern agents dated August 23, 1861, company secretary B. C. Miller reported the decision of the directors to immediately suspend all agencies in the Confederacy. Existing policyholders were then required "to make their payments at the Principal Office of the Company at Newark, N.J."; those unable or unwilling to do so would void their policies "according to the terms of the contract" with no option for surrender or future renewal.[85] This plan tied the hands of southern policyholders, nullifying the vast majority of Mutual Benefit policies in the South.

Although many companies attempted to reach a fair resolution of their southern business—or at least employed the rhetoric of fairness—not all northern insurance promoters believed that Confederate policyholders retained any contract rights after secession. In one editorial from 1861, the writer chastised those companies who had "already paid out thousands of dollars for surrendered policies, which from the peculiar circumstances of the case must have ultimately relapsed of themselves on the ground of nonpayment." He considered this not only a poor business decision but unpatriotic: "A little patient forbearance on the part of such Directors might have saved to their respective institutions a large amount of money, which has passed directly into the hands of rebellious secessionists." The writer believed that southern policies would lapse naturally as policyholders were unable to pay their annual premiums under the Non-Intercourse Act, relieving the companies of any legal obligation toward policyholders in the Confederacy. The author then concluded by praising the hard line taken by Mutual Benefit as the most prudent.[86]

While the contingencies of war understandably left northern companies with limited options for their southern policyholders, the cessation of hostilities after four long years forced them to address the reality of involuntarily lapsed policies, premium payments in depreciated or defunct currency, and (most problematically) death claims. According to the company-commissioned histories of the largest life insurers, most of these institutions dealt with their southern policyholders in an extremely liberal fashion following the war. For example, the history of Manhattan Life reports that it did a "herculean job . . . in locating its Southern Policyholders and paying claims which occurred during the war years." The company supposedly restored the contract terms of all antebellum policies without requiring new medical examinations and paid any death claims that had resulted in the interim:

> Through the states in which the Company had operated in pre-war days word spread about what The Manhattan Life was doing. Its emissaries were there, in the dark days, seeking claimants to whom, under its extraordinary post-war policy, it owed money, despite the fact that legally it had had no contract with the insured at the time of his death. Where policyholders had died, the Company paid all claims just as if all premiums had been paid. The only deduction was for unpaid premiums during the war years.[87]

The history of Mutual Benefit of New Jersey—the company with the harshest official policy during the war—states that the company president personally went to Richmond and from there sought out all southerners who had possessed policies on the eve of the Civil War, paying "the 'equitable value' of policies lapsed for non-payment of premium, or death claims *if the terms of the contract had not been violated*" (emphasis added). If the policyholder remained healthy, reinstatement of the policy under the original contract terms was also permitted. The company calculated: "Settlements were made on 337 surrendered policies, involving an outlay of $88,000 in case and a cancellation of $110,000 of indebtedness, a total of $198,000. This represented about a million dollars of business, out of a total outstanding at the beginning of the war of about twenty-two millions. In addition death claims of $148,000 were also paid on 34 'Southern policies.'"[88] Of course, the stipulation that death claims would only be paid "if the terms of the contract had not been violated" freed the company of any obligations when premiums remained unpaid, even if this nonpayment was the result of a legal obstacle such as the Non-Intercourse Act or the confiscation threats of the Confederate government.

The liberality claimed by the companies both during the war and in their corporate histories is contradicted by the legal record. Of the ten largest life insurance companies in 1860, at least seven were named as defendants in lawsuits filed in the wake of the war; these seven companies accounted for a full two-thirds of the life insurance in force as of 1860.[89] The vast majority of these cases were brought by the beneficiaries or estate administrators of southern policyholders who had died over the course of the war whose claims were denied on account of failure to pay their annual premiums. There were also a few cases involving living policyholders who wished to have their policies reinstated. These lawsuits—nearly identical to each other in all but the smallest details—were eventually argued before the supreme courts of at least ten different states before being finally settled by the United States Supreme Court more than a decade after the culmination of the war.

At issue in each of these cases was the clause inserted in every policy that stipulated the annual (or semiannual or quarterly) date for the payment of premiums and provided for the forfeiture of the policy upon failure of payment.[90] The companies maintained that this clause protected them from any claim by a policyholder from whom premiums were not received during the war, regardless of the reason for the nonpayment. Arguing for a strict, formalist interpretation of contract law, counsels for the defense repeated the rationale presented in the 1871 case of *Statham v. New York Life* that "it is wholly immaterial what cause operated to prevent the payment of the premium due on the 8th day of December, 1861, as neither a state of war nor non-intercourse acts of congress, nor even the acts of God, had been provided against by the assured as a cause or causes to excuse such default in such payment."[91] However, given the unusual circumstances of the Civil War, the cases did not seem so straightforward to judges or juries.

In most of the suits, the policyholder had actually attempted to pay at least the first premium due after the onset of hostilities, only to have the local agent of the company refuse to accept such payment. The main reason proffered by these agents was that their authority had been revoked by the home office.[92] Several of the companies further argued that although the firms had been responsible for officially rescinding their southern agencies, the blame for violating the contract terms ultimately fell on the policyholders, who were still permitted to maintain their policies by paying premiums directly to the home office. For example, in the cases of *Statham v. New York Life* (1871), *Hillyard v. Mutual Benefit Life* (1872), and *Worthington v. Charter Oak Life* (1874), the companies contended that since it was physically possible for the claimants to relocate their homes to a nonbelligerent state, the forfeiture of the policy was necessarily the fault of the policyholder and could not be blamed on the company or the existence of war.[93] As counsel for New York Life argued, continued residence in the Confederate States was a "voluntary act," and therefore policyholders who insisted on remaining in those states "must suffer any loss which could happen to them as results of such non-intercourse acts of congress."[94] In two other cases, *Robinson v. International Life of London* (1870) and *Sands v. New York Life* (1872), the premiums were paid to and accepted by the agent in Confederate money, which the companies (citing the revocation of the authority of the agencies) subsequently refused to recognize as valid payments.[95]

Other companies argued that regardless of whether they had revoked the authority of the agent, the Non-Intercourse Act automatically voided the policy by making the continued collection of premiums on behalf of a northern company illegal.[96] In the latter cases, company attorneys were careful to differentiate an insurance policy (which required *"continuing performance"* of "commercial intercourse between such antagonist parties") from a straightforward debt contract (which could easily be suspended during the war and remedied by "a single act" once contact resumed).[97]

In several instances, policyholders or their beneficiaries sued even when there had been no attempt to maintain premium payments during the war years. In the cases of *Dillard v. Manhattan* (1871) and *Hillyard v. Mutual Benefit* (1872), beneficiaries of the deceased acknowledged this failure to pay (as a result of the Non-Intercourse Act) but claimed that the policyholder *would have* tendered the premiums with interest at the end of hostilities if he had not died first.[98] The cases of *Cohen v. New York Life* (1872), *Manhattan Life v. LePert* (1880), and *Abell v. Penn Mutual* (1881) dealt with living policyholders who wished to reinstate their policies in the aftermath of the war but had their unpaid premiums refused by the companies.[99]

With the exception of *Dillard v. Manhattan Life* (1871) and *Worthington v. Charter Oak Life* (1874), the state courts rejected the companies' arguments and unanimously found in favor of the policyholders during the 1870s, ruling (or upholding lower court rulings) that companies had to reinstate policies upon payment of back premiums, pay a fair cash surrender value, or (when the policyholder was already deceased) pay the face value of the policy less any premiums that went unpaid during the life of the policyholder. Employing the same argument used by the proponents of nonforfeiture laws, jurists reasoned that by the very nature of the level premium system of rates, policyholders gained vested rights in their policies: "It is sufficient now to say, that on the payment of the first premium a right became vested in the continuance of the contract of insurance."[100] These vested rights having been legally obtained, it would be unfair to void a policy without adequate recompense when the impossibility of payment "was not created by the act or default of the plaintiff but resulted from the acts of the governments of which the respective parties were subjects."[101]

The companies argued that the policy terms left no exceptions open for the nonpayment of premiums, but the courts disagreed. They ruled that southern policyholders had not breached the terms of their contracts but rather that these were incomplete contracts that failed to provide for the contingency of a civil war.[102] As the Kentucky Court of Appeals averred in the 1870 case of *New York Life v. Clopton,* "None of the parties can be presumed to have contemplated such disabling war, or to have intended by the condition of avoidance more than *voluntary* failure to pay, *when there was legal ability to receive* the premiums."[103] Thus instead of voiding such policies, the state of war merely suspended their execution, and the return to peace enabled both sides to resume fulfillment of their contractual obligations.

In reaching these decisions, the courts refuted the claim that life insurance was a contract that relied upon continuing performance—like a partnership—which was automatically dissolved by the existence of war. In the case of *Cohen v. New York Mutual Life* (1872), the judge ruled that a contract for life insurance was unique and thus could not be easily categorized within the existing case law for contracts. Rather than representing a continuing relationship or a reciprocal contract, the policy was "executed by the plaintiff by the payment of the annual premiums from 1849 to and including 1861," with these payments being "in excess of the actual risks . . . paid in advance for the greater risk during the later years in case of a prolonged life." The company, on the other hand, had not yet performed any of its obligation to the policyholder, rendering the policy "wholly executory on the part of the defendant, its undertaking being to pay the amount specified upon the death of the insured."[104]

The courts repeatedly referenced the fairness of the outcome for the parties involved in these judgments. Each jurist seemed appalled at the idea that the policyholders would be the sole losers in policy forfeitures, with the companies clearly gaining. In the 1872 cases of *Hillyard v. Mutual Benefit of New Jersey* and *Cohen v. New York Mutual Life,* the courts specifically likened the avoidance of a policy to an illegal seizure: "This would simply be a confiscation of property after war had ceased, at the instance and for the benefit of individuals."[105] As the Supreme Court of New Jersey stated: "If tangible property and debts are not confiscated by a condition of war for the benefit of the public, how can it be plausibly urged that a vested right, such as arises out of the present policy, is to be forfeited by the operation of the same cause, for the benefit of one of the contracting parties?"[106] Others, such as the Supreme Court of Mississippi, called such an outcome a "gross injustice," asserting that it would be "repugnant to reason that intervening war should destroy the contract, devolving all loss upon one party to the gain of the other."[107] The Supreme Court of Virginia opined, "It would be a monstrous perversion of law, and repugnant to our every sense of justice, to say that this company, after having received more than half the sum assured, could by this act determine the policy, hold on to the money they had received, and to say to their confiding victim, 'you may whistle to the winds for your merited reward, notwithstanding you relied upon our covenant and good faith to pay it.'"[108] In each of these instances, the jurists believed that the companies were being unfaithful to their contract obligations by attempting to evade payment on policies that lapsed by no fault of the policyholder. By construing the policies as incomplete contracts and then determining that the role of the court was to interpret what good-faith execution of that contract would entail, the justices were positively asserting their role in promoting the effective functioning of the market.[109]

When these cases finally began to reach the United States Supreme Court in the mid-1870s, the life insurance companies had already suffered a long string of losses on the state level. However, by this time the companies had appropriated the ideal of a good-faith completion of the contract in their own defense, emphasizing the hardship placed on them as a result of the state court rulings. One of the industry's few state victories came in the case of *Worthington v. Charter Oak Life,* decided by the Connecticut Supreme Court of Errors in 1874. In the court's ruling, Judge Carpenter (probably reflecting an argument presented by counsel for the company) took a more holistic view of the situation, reasoning that the company's operations in the South were severely impaired by the war. While thousands of polices temporarily lapsed during the war, the judge reasoned, "it will probably be found that a few only returned to pay their premiums at the close of the war. Of those, most, if not all, are cases in which the insured either died during the war, or survived it in impaired health." If all southern policyholders were to pay their back premiums and reinstate their policies, "there would be some justice in holding the company liable in those cases where the policies have terminated by the death of the insured."[110] Of course, such a resolution was not possible; most healthy policyholders who wanted to continue their insurance found it cheaper to take out new policies at slightly higher rates (reflecting their increased age) than to pay the four or five years of back premiums and interest necessary to reinstate their old ones. Thus by forcing companies to pay death claims and reinstate contracts for unhealthy policyholders, the courts exposed companies to extremely high levels of risk that were not balanced by healthy policyholders. It was not fair to hold the companies to good-faith execution of a minority of policies when the remaining majority of policyholders could not be held to good-faith execution on their part.

This rationale was presented before the United States Supreme Court in the combined case of *New York Life v. Statham, New York Life v. Seyms, Manhattan Life v. Buck,* decided in October 1876. The counsel for the companies presented the same basic arguments for policy forfeiture as had been presented in the state courts. However, James Garfield, who represented New York Life, offered a compromise solution when he suggested that the payment of cash surrender values would more accurately reflect the vested interests of the policyholders without placing an unfair burden on the companies: "Such an adjustment would not impose on the assured the forfeiture of the premiums paid, or on the company the hardship of paying all lapses, whether voluntary or involuntary."[111] Speaking on behalf of the court, Justice Bradley concurred that the state court rulings had only taken into account the negative impact of voiding policies for the customer, without considering the implications of reinstatement on the firms:

> The average rate of mortality is the basis on which [life insurance] rests. By spreading their risks over a large number of cases, the companies calculate on this average with reasonable certainty and safety. Any thing that interferes with it deranges the security of the business. If every policy lapsed by reason of the war should be revived, and all the back premiums should be paid, the companies would have the benefit of this average amount of risk. But the good risks are never heard from; only the bad are sought to be revived, where the person insured is either dead or dying. Those in health can get new policies cheaper than to pay arrearages on the old. [112]

Consequently, the court ruled that "the equitable value of a policy" was due to the insured, consisting of the total premiums paid, "subject to a deduction for the value of the assurance enjoyed by him whilst the policy was in existence."[113] One year later, the Supreme Court reaffirmed this decision, rendering *New York Life v. Statham et. al.* as the final word on the rights of southern policyholders during the Civil War.[114]

The Good Faith Fulfillment of Contracts

In his recent book *Calculating Promises: The Emergence of Modern American Contract Doctrine*, Roy Kreitner persuasively argues that modern legal scholars are remiss in assuming that the application of the concept of good faith to the completion of incomplete contracts only entered the American court system in the mid-twentieth century. By examining a number of commercial suits from the turn of the century, he finds that even during the classical period of jurisprudence—when courts were most likely to adhere to a rigid, formalist interpretation of contract law—justices repeatedly required a good-faith interpretation of contract obligations lest one party be allowed to opportunistically void the agreement.[115]

An examination of the life insurance cases arising as a result of the Civil War—certainly an event for which most contracts failed to provide—demonstrates that this activist intervention in the marketplace was occurring as early as the immediate postbellum period. Viewing life insurance contracts as incomplete in not providing for the contingency of the contracting parties being on opposing sides during a war, the courts attempted to determine the fairest outcome for both parties. Whether ruling in favor of the policyholder or the company, the justices were not attempting to police or regulate the marketplace. Rather, by applying the doctrine of good faith to incomplete contracts, they were trying to ensure that the market's own logic (or "morality") was being applied uniformly across all market relations.

Whereas the contract terms of southern policies with northern insurance companies during the war were found to be incomplete, the issue of war risks had always been clearly defined by life firms. Although they had no "good-faith" obligation to insure war risks, companies understood that the quasi-public nature of their antebellum advertising campaigns left them with a moral (or at least reputational) obligation to their northern clientele. While strict adherence to contract terms might have maximized profits in the short term, life companies recognized that such a position would have undermined their carefully crafted image of operating for the welfare of the public. They managed to minimize losses resulting from the war while maintaining the appearance of fulfilling their public duty by colluding under the auspices of the American Life Underwriters' Convention. Ironically, the industry's rapid postbellum growth (which can largely be credited to its successful image management during the war) would erode any sense of moral responsibility to the public as new competitors would pursue profit maximization without even the semblance of promoting the public welfare.

CHAPTER II

The Perils of Success during the Postbellum Years

In the fall of 1863, just as sales of life policies were on the verge of skyrocketing, the *North American Review* published a remarkable twenty-three-page article on life insurance. Presented as a neutral assessment of the current state of the industry, the piece was actually an extended defense of insurance as sold by the large, well-established mutual companies. It opened with a short (well-crafted but patently false) history of insuring in the United States, which it claimed could "hardly be said to have existed" before the incorporation of mutual companies in the 1840s. The article then went on to recite the main arguments traditionally offered for insuring and to address the critiques historically leveled against the industry. Among the points covered were

- the quasi-public nature of life insurance ("it is not at all a commercial enterprise undertaken for the purpose of profit");
- the benefits of mutual companies over their stock competitors ("the insured constitute the company, its accumulations are theirs, its success is theirs, and the ostensible managers and directors are only their agents and trustees, empowered to invest and protect the funds for their benefit");
- the numerous advantages of life insurance over savings banks ("for those who can make but moderate savings each year, what security is there that they will live long enough to accumulate a sum sufficient for their purpose?");
- the scientific nature of the business model ("not only the most precise calculations, but actual experience . . . prove [that] there is really no element of uncertainty" in companies' operations);
- the statistical foundations of the industry's tables ("the question is so far settled, that it may be said to have ceased to be a problem of science, and to have become only a matter of book-keeping");
- the people who would most benefit from the product ("persons of fixed incomes, including those who depend upon salaries and wages");
- the hazards of not insuring ("the misery thus caused is incalculable");

- the compatibility of life insurance with religion ("it not only renders men provident, but it shares, though in a humble degree, with religion in extending this providence to a period beyond the life of the individual"); and
- the benefits of life insurance to the economy as a whole ("the large funds accumulated for Life Insurance are in great part a positive addition, which would not otherwise be made, to the available capital of the country").[1]

But by far the bulk of the article was an attempt to manipulate public opinion regarding the new competitors in the industry. In nine distinct sections, the author attacked newer, smaller firms as being less safe, less efficient, and more likely to engage in fraudulent business practices than the older, larger insurers. The writer warned that the statistical basis for life insurance was sound only *"provided the company can obtain business enough."* When contracting with a smaller firm, an applicant ran the risk that the underwriter would be overwhelmed by death claims before it had spread its risks across a large enough pool of policyholders. Thus, *"among equally well-managed Life Insurance Companies, that is the safest, the cheapest, and the most deserving of confidence, which has done, and is doing, the largest amount of business."* In their haste to expand their customer base, newer firms were not only forced to devote a much higher proportion of premium payments to expenses (therefore lowering future dividend payments) but were also more likely to endanger their fiscal soundness further by "endeavor[ing] to attract business by offering to insure at low premiums" and "accept[ing] undue risks, including some that have already been declined by the larger establishments." In ominous tones the author concluded: "Beware what company you enter! Choose not the youngest, nor the one which is ostensibly and for the moment the cheapest, nor that which holds out the most flattering promises, and is pressed most persistently upon your notice."[2]

While in other industries "competition is generally for the public good," the insurance industry's need to spread risks widely meant that too much competition was detrimental to both life insurers and policyholders. The author therefore praised the rigorous regulatory measures of the New York and Massachusetts insurance departments and called for much greater "oversight and restraint by the legislature" with regard to "the establishment and conduct of *new* companies for Life Insurance" (emphasis added). The "large, really solvent, and well-managed companies . . . welcomed" such supervision, particularly "as their tendency is to lessen the number of new and weak offices, and thus to diminish a competition which is all the more injurious to the insured and to the sound institutions, because it is often unprincipled, reckless, and even fraudulent."[3] Just as they had attempted to do with the American Life Underwriters' Convention, industry leaders sought to assert their market power in defining safe market practices, crafting state legislation, and limiting the ability of newcomers to enter the field. Yet these tactics were no more successful in 1863 than they had been in 1859, and the larger insurers could not prevent the onslaught of new competitors. The number of life firms almost tripled in the immediate postbellum period, feeding off of the eight-fold increase in policy sales.

But the very success and profitability of life insurance firms during the 1860s led to the greatest challenge the industry would face. With new companies being chartered at an alarming rate to take advantage of the increasing demand, firms began to undermine the policies, procedures, and regulations that the industry had voluntarily imposed to ensure the reputation and safety of insurers (just as the 1863 *North American Review* article had warned). The fiscal soundness of a life insurance company was based on three elements: the mortality rate of its policyholders, the return on investments, and the expenses of the company for obtaining new business and maintaining existing customers. Antebellum companies took an extremely conservative approach to each of these elements, but during the rapid expansion of the postbellum period new life companies began to push the boundaries of prudence in order to gain a competitive edge over their rivals.

First, companies liberalized policy terms—removing restrictions on travel and occupation, waiving their right to contest questionable claims, and in some instances eliminating medical exams and permitting the payment of claims in cases of suicide. Even the principle of insurable interest was eased, allowing the emergence of (in modern parlance) "key-man insurance." Guardian Life advertised in 1861: "Policies to Mercantile Firms, namely, To the Junior Partners on the Life of the Member who furnishes the Capital, or the one whose business abilities and extended acquaintance is relied upon for the continuance of the business."[4] This relaxation of selection criteria and rule enforcement opened firms to all kinds of adverse selection problems, including murder.

Second, the expenses of postbellum companies quickly ballooned out of control as firms went on the offensive in the face of stiff competition. Commission rates for agents skyrocketed, companies built lavish office buildings and published slick advertising literature to impress the public with their financial stability, and potential clients were enticed to insure through rebates on their first premium payment and a renewed reliance on the credit system for premiums. As long as the industry was expanding and new customers outnumbered old, these practices appeared to be harmless and even to help promote the industry's growth. But as policies began to mature and the proportion of new to existing policies shifted toward the latter, companies quickly found that their premium rates were inadequate to cover the risks they had assumed.

Finally, companies became engaged in the speculative frenzy of the postbellum period in order to increase the return on their investments. Life insurance companies based their premium rates on both the predicted rate of mortality of their policyholders and the expected return from investing these premiums over time. By creating increasingly risky investment portfolios, firms placed the long-term safety of their premium income in jeopardy. With the weakening of the securities markets in the early 1870s, insurance companies watched as their assets quickly fell below the amount required to cover their claims, and one by one they declared bankruptcy or reinsured their risks with other companies.

The Quest for National Oversight

In direct contrast to the participants in the American Life Underwriters' Convention who sought to rationalize the regulatory environment by creating standardized state laws, postbellum insurance firms wanted to escape the confines of strict regulation altogether. Whereas companies threatened to leave—and sometimes did leave—the smaller markets in response to unfriendly legislation, this was not an option for them in the Northeast. And unfortunately for many firms, some of the strictest legislation existed in New York and Massachusetts, where most of the major corporations were headquartered. Since the potential for avoiding state regulation through horizontal escape—by exiting the state and operating elsewhere—was limited, companies attempted to move vertically from state to federal jurisdiction by challenging state legislation in the Supreme Court and seeking more congenial legislation from Congress.[5] During and immediately after the Civil War, companies began pursuing vertical goals on both of these fronts.

The early 1860s was a period of high nationalist sentiment. Passage of the National Bank Act in 1863 and its revision in 1864 elevated industry confidence in the potential for federal legislation regarding insurance. In 1866, the National Board of Fire Underwriters proposed a bill that would have placed the industry under the supervision of the Treasury Department and a national commissioner and stipulated minimum capital and reserve requirements, annual financial reports, limitations on premium taxes, and the prohibition of licensing fees and security deposit requirements.[6] But as would prove true in most of their attempts at national legislation, the life and fire lines of the industry chose to disagree rather than band together. Although the newly formed Chamber of Life Insurance also supported a "National Insurance Act," it never endorsed the Fire Underwriters' bill. Instead, it drafted a new proposal dealing exclusively with life insurance. Its legislation would have established *industry* control over the interstate market—exempting life companies from all state taxation and regulation and requiring only annual financial reporting to Congress.[7]

In November 1866, the executives of seventeen companies met to create the Chamber of Life Insurance of the United States and resolved "that the object of the Association shall be the procuring of national or uniform State legislation; collecting, collating, and publishing vital and other statistics incident to life insurance, and, in general, the promotion of the interests of life insurance in the United States."[8] But the Chamber was much less representative of the industry than the ALUC had been. While half of the companies in existence and 80% of the top twenty had participated in the ALUC, only 22% of companies and six of the top fifteen attended the organizational meeting of the Chamber.[9] Conspicuous among those absent at the 1866 and 1867 meetings were three of the top four companies in 1865: Mutual of New York, Mutual Benefit of New Jersey, and New York Life, which collectively represented one-third of life insurance in force.

Whereas the need for accurate mortality statistics had been the driving purpose of the ALUC, the Chamber was much more concerned with attaining uniform insurance legislation and federal supervision. The Chamber believed "that congress has authority, under the clause of the Constitution authorizing it to regulate commerce, to establish such a Bureau," and one of the goals that emerged from the 1867 meeting was the creation of a National Bureau of Insurance.[10] A bill dealing exclusively with the establishment of such a bureau was proposed to Congress in the winter of 1867–68, receiving the backing of some industry executives as well as Elizur Wright. But many others questioned the propriety of replacing state with federal oversight of life insurance. William Barnes, superintendent of the New York State Insurance Department, strongly objected to the proposal in his 1868 report. In his estimation, only "a small minority" of insurers sought "to wrest from the several States their legitimate and constitutional functions of supervision and control," in the name of "the pretended interests of policy-holders." The true purpose of these proponents, he asserted, was "to aggregate to themselves all supervisory powers and jurisdiction." Barnes was confident that this "system of self-supervision by the corporations themselves . . . however artfully disguised, will not be accepted by the public as a substitute for an independent Government supervision made in the interest of the State and of the whole commonwealth."[11] He was correct; the bill received little support outside of the industry and was left to die in the Committee on Commerce. By the end of the decade, Congress was no longer willing to assume national control over additional industries, and no bill in favor of federal insurance regulation ever reached the floor of Congress in the late 1860s.[12]

At the same time that they were lobbying for national insurance legislation, firms also turned to the judicial branch for relief. The industry sought to escape the stranglehold of state regulations by receiving either of two verdicts. First, they hoped that the court would overrule *Bank of Augusta v. Earle* by placing corporations under the protection of the Privileges and Immunities Clause of the Constitution, thus rendering discriminatory regulation of out-of-state corporations illegal. Even better would be a decision that national companies were engaged in interstate commerce, which would place them under federal jurisdiction and prohibit *all* state regulation of foreign insurance corporations.[13]

Both the Fire Underwriters and the Chamber encouraged their members to bring test cases before the courts. An 1866 Chamber resolution stated that "friendly or other suit should be brought in the Supreme Court of the United States to test the constitutionality of these discriminatory laws, and that the expenses be defrayed from the funds of the Chamber."[14] Although none of the Chamber-sponsored cases reached the highest court, the case of *Paul v. Virginia,* in which a fire insurance agent representing several New York firms refused to pay a Virginia licensing fee, did reach the Supreme Court on appeal in 1869. This test case had been concocted by the New York Association of Underwriters and partially funded (to the tune of $15,000) by the National Association of Fire Underwriters.[15]

Unfortunately for the industry, its challenge in the *Paul* case was unanimously defeated on both grounds.[16] Justice Field upheld the distinction made in *Earle* between natural persons and corporations under Article IV, Section 2, maintaining that states "may exclude the foreign corporation entirely; they may restrict its business to particular localities or they may exact such security or performance of its contracts with their citizens as in their judgment will best promote the public interest."[17] Justice Field further ruled that insurance polices were not commerce and therefore fell outside of the jurisdiction of Article III, Section 2:

> They are not subjects of trade and barter offered in the market as something having an existence and value independent of the parties to them. They are not commodities to be shipped and forwarded from one State to another, and then put up for sale . . . The policies do not take effect—are not executed contracts—until delivered by the agent in Virginia. They are, then, local transactions, and are governed by the local law. They do not constitute a part of the commerce between the States any more than a contract for the purchase and sale of goods in Virginia by a citizen of New York whilst in Virginia would constitute a portion of such commerce.[18]

Over the ensuing decades, this ruling would be upheld in repeated cases designed to overturn *Paul,* including *Liverpool Insurance Company v. Massachusetts* (1870), *Ducat v. Chicago* (1870), *Philadelphia Fire Association v. New York* (1886), *Hooper v. California* (1895), *New York Life Insurance Company v. Cravens* (1900), *Nutting v. Massachusetts* (1902), and *New York Life Insurance Company v. Deer Lodge County* (1913). Each of these cases concerned the constitutionality of state regulation of the insurance industry; all rulings relied upon Justice Field's conclusions in *Paul* without reconsidering that decision.[19] The 1869 decision would stand until the 1944 case of *United States v. South-Eastern Underwriters Association* overturned *Paul*, declaring insurance contracts commerce and opening up the potential for the industry to be placed under federal control. In response to this decision, however, Congress passed the McCarran-Ferguson Act of 1945, which declared continuance of state regulation and taxation of the insurance industry to be in the public's best interest.[20]

The states were happy to maintain a foothold for themselves within an increasingly centralizing system. Both Congress and the Supreme Court had repeatedly reduced their sovereignty, and the states recognized that their control over insurance was not only financially lucrative but remained their last major presence within federalism. They took full advantage of the "judicial accident" of *Paul v. Virginia,* striving to prove their ability to successfully police the industry—in direct contrast to the jumble of discriminatory, retaliatory, and often contradictory legislation of the antebellum era. By coordinating their efforts through the National Convention of Insurance Commissioners beginning in 1871, they ensured that all states did their part.[21] The lack of calls for federal regulation by any groups outside the industry demonstrates their success. As one contemporary observed on the eve of World War I, "While there are perhaps merits to having uniform and systematic insurance statutes, there exists greater merit in having the states administer the insurance business . . . They know what is best and there has been great policyholder satisfaction over the past years with local regulation in most states."[22] Insurance was the only major industry to remain under state control through the twentieth century.

Growing Leniency in an Increasingly Competitive Industry

While a portion of the industry was still willing to work together in seeking national legislation, this cooperative atmosphere no longer extended to discussions of business practices or the maintenance of the safety of the industry as a whole. The immediate postbellum period represented a virtual wildcat era among life insurers. New entrants to the field, intent on capturing a portion of the lucrative market, demonstrated little concern that the flush times might come to an end. Rather than adopting the voluntary measures endorsed by their more-established peers, they radically liberalized their selection process, policy terms, and outlook on insurable interest and moral hazard. Further encouraging this trend was the increasing use of aggressive sales agents. Paid on a commission basis and no longer carefully selected for their respectability and reputation, these agents had little incentive to weed out potentially hazardous applicants.[23]

This shift in attitude between the more conservative firms and their newly incorporated competitors is best illustrated through their treatment of cases of insurance fraud. During the boom period of the 1860s, several companies began brazenly advertising that suicide or fraud would *never* void a policy. In the intensely competitive business environment of the time, companies feared that they would lose hard-earned market share if they developed a reputation for fighting claims, and newly established companies viewed this extreme liberalization of policy terms as a means of breaking into the market. Statements such as "the company has *no losses unpaid*,"[24] "no claims in dispute,"[25] "policies indisputable,"[26] "not a case litigated,"[27] "policies incontestable,"[28] and "never contests a claim"[29] began to appear in the advertising of numerous life companies. As Empire Mutual emphatically advertised in 1870: "ALL POLICIES INCONTESTABLE. *All Restrictions* upon *Travel* and *Residence* removed, and *no Permits required*."[30]

Like the British companies that turned a blind eye to gambling policies earlier in the century, these companies intended to attract those customers who *feared* that the claims of their beneficiaries would be unfairly challenged upon their death: "The great value of indisputability, after all, lies in the assurance which it gives to the policy-holder, whose fears are roused by the reports of litigated cases."[31] Taking out a policy with a company that clearly stated it would not contest claims in the case of misrepresentation or a breach of policy contract diminished this fear. As one article acknowledged, "To be able to affirm so much is worth thousands of dollars to an active and enterprising company."[32] But these companies also opened themselves up to both intentional fraud and suicidal people who obtained policies with the intention of immediately taking their own lives, thus eroding the expectations of death based on mortality tables and placing these companies on a very precarious actuarial footing.

Most of the larger, more-established companies refused to insert incontestability clauses in their policies, but the publicity surrounding disputed claims led most institutions to adopt a policy of settling rather than going to court. When a man attempted to swindle three life insurance companies in 1861 by "procur[ing] a considerable amount of insurance upon certain poor and unsound parties," two of the companies (Equitable Life and United States Life) settled with the claimant, who had effectively employed publicity to break the will of the companies. The editor of the *Insurance Monitor*, dismayed by this result, threw his full support behind the third company, Knickerbocker Life, which "has had the courage and sagacity successfully to ferret out and resist several frauds attempted on it, and we believe the President, Mr. Lyman, does not apprehend any discouraging result from the company's pending contest."[33] But the support of the insurance press was not as important as the opinion of the insuring public, who could choose to penalize Knickerbocker Life for its principled position by taking their business elsewhere.

The emergence of companies willing to state openly that they would not dispute claims only added to the public relations problem of contesting claims for the remaining institutions. One article in the *Insurance Monitor* from 1867 attempted to discourage the practice of *not* contesting claims by demonstrating the destructive consequences:

> Suppose, actuated by their mistaken zeal for the material interest and reputation of the company, they pay the claim, what follows?—It follows that injustice has been done to every stockholder, mutual member, or insurant in the company; that they have all been to a certain amount defrauded; that a great crime has been committed, winked at, encouraged and fostered, and that a successful attempt has been made to introduce a poisonous element into the constitution of Life Insurance, that will corrupt, and may destroy altogether, its usefulness and vitality.[34]

If the real issue was the public's fear of being treated unfairly by life insurers, firms hoped that a few simple statistics might allay these concerns. According to the industry, "down to 1876 the death record of seventy-one companies gives the following facts . . . Less than nine tenths of one per cent of the whole number of policy claims were resisted, and only one and three tenths per cent of the amount of money involved."[35] Yet given the unwillingness of many companies to contest claims in court, this percentage would probably have been much higher if public perception had not been such an important issue.

By the middle of the 1860s, the industry began actively to debate the wisdom of this extreme liberalization with regard to policy claims. At the first annual meeting of the Chamber of Life Insurance in 1867, the issue of companies not contesting fraudulent claims was high on the agenda, since "many Companies paid claims because of the odium that would come upon them if they refused, though the claims were unjust."[36] The Chamber attempted to form an arbitration committee, composed of five New York businessmen, who would review all questionable claims and decide "whether, in their opinion, the claim should be paid without litigation or otherwise."[37] The purpose of this committee was to free companies from the shackles of public opinion. As explained by N. D. Morgan, president of North

American Life and vice president of the Chamber, "If there was a Board of Arbitration to say what claims should be paid, then this trouble might be avoided, as the certificate of that Board would be a sufficient proof that the Company refusing to pay a claim did not do it from a litigious motive."[38] But the arbitration committee never materialized—perhaps dying with the Chamber itself. Two years later, the *Insurance Monitor* continued to lament the state of the industry: "Fraud and incompetency have done their work. What recourse has the company? The law, say you? No sir; juries believe that corporations have no souls, and the direct cost and indirect damage done a company's general business by litigation fully balances all the probabilities of gain by evoking the aid of the law. Some companies make a virtue of necessity and largely advertise the fact that they *never contested a claim*."[39]

While it is impossible to ascertain the frequency of actual crimes committed against the insurance companies, increasing reports of faked deaths provide one crude gauge of the problem. During the antebellum period, extremely few cases of faked deaths were discovered, and most of these were reports from abroad. However, starting in the late 1860s and coinciding with the rapid postbellum growth of life insurance in America and the appearance of incontestability clauses, cases of policyholders attempting to fake their own deaths began to appear regularly in both the popular press and the insurance journals. In the 1878 book *Remarkable Stratagems and Conspiracies: An Authentic Record of Surprising Attempts to Defraud Life Insurance Companies,* two full chapters were devoted to various cases of faked death, another to instances of murder, and another to suicide. While it was necessary for the authors to look to London, Berlin, and France for early examples of this type of fraud, by the late 1860s they could describe cases from throughout the United States.[40]

Because these occurrences were rare in antebellum America, the legal system failed to account for the problem. In one case from 1866, a doctor and another man were arrested on suspicion of murder. When it was discovered that the supposed victim was still alive and that the men in custody were actually accomplices to a scheme to defraud the insurance companies, the authorities were unsure how to proceed: "The charge of murder against these parties will of course have to be withdrawn, as no murdered man can be found, and what crime can be substituted in its place will puzzle the Prosecuting Attorney to determine."[41] While it was clear that the perpetrators were guilty of some crime, the legal system had not yet adapted to address the issue even as late as 1866.

No mention of faked deaths appeared in the issues of the *Insurance Monitor* through 1865, but five separate articles detailing both specific cases and the emergence of this new type of fraud in general were published in 1867 (the 1866 issues are not available). The July issue noted, "In some parts of the West they are burying logs in coffins, and calling them people. The business is said to be thriving. As much as $20,000 upon a single log have been collected from the Life Insurance Companies." In another article from October, the author reported:

> During the past two years, says a Philadelphia paper, many attempts have been made to swindle life insurance companies. In Illinois an insured man sent some other person's dead body as his representative to the grave, while he staid [*sic*] back to collect the policy. In Cincinnati a man buried a lot of willow sticks for the same purpose; and a variety of singular contrivances have been made to this end in different sections of the country, which seems to indicate that a regular systematic organization has been effected to defraud these benevolent institutions.[42]

In both of these cases, the authors alluded to the crime of faking death as a recent problem for the life insurance companies. While it is not possible to determine whether the existence of incontestability clauses caused this increase in crime against insurance companies, it certainly did little to arrest the trend.

Bursting the Bubble and Reinventing the Industry

The combination of high expense ratios, leniency in selecting risks and pursuing frauds, and a competitive drive to lower premium rates and increase dividend payments—compounded by a general economic downturn—pushed the industry into a severe depression during the 1870s. Whereas life insurance in force had increased at the astonishing rate of 43% per annum from 1864 to 1868, this growth ground to a halt during the early 1870s.[43] California's commissioner of insurance and banking declared that the 1870s "were the most trying period in the history of American life insurance."[44] The more-established companies such as Mutual of New York, New York Life, and Equitable Life of New York had refused to liberalize their policy terms and thus were strong enough to weather the depression with few problems, but most of the new companies organized during the 1860s were unable to survive. Fourteen of the fifteen life insurance companies incorporated in New York between 1866 and 1868 failed during the 1870s (the fifteenth was Metropolitan Life Insurance Company of New York, discussed below).[45] All told, ninety-eight life insurance firms went out of business between 1868 and 1877—approximately two-thirds of the companies in the industry.

One might suspect that the severe depression of the 1870s was the underlying cause of these failures, but the majority occurred in the years *before* the bank panic began in September 1873. The industry took much longer to recover from the depression than other industries, only beginning its gradual upturn during the 1880s; it would be the late 1880s before the amount of insurance in force surpassed its peak in 1870. For the few successful life insurance companies organized during the 1860s and 1870s, market innovation in the area of industrial insurance would be the only means of avoiding failure; this would open an entirely new period in the history of the life insurance industry.

Aware that they could not compete with the major companies in a tight market, some emerging companies looked to the example of fraternal benefit societies, whose growth coincided with the rapid expansion of the life insurance industry during the 1860s. Although fraternal societies had existed throughout the history of the United States, it was only during the second half of the nineteenth century that they mushroomed in number and emerged as major providers of life insurance. They took advantage of the depression of the 1870s to promote their benefits over those offered by the collapsing for-profit industry. By the turn of the century, the approximately six hundred fraternal societies in existence provided over $5 billion in life insurance to their members, making them direct competitors of the major stock and mutual companies.[46]

Beginning in the 1870s, for-profit companies such as Metropolitan Life Insurance Company, John Hancock Company, and Prudential Insurance Company of America began issuing industrial life insurance—"insurance for the masses rather than for the classes."[47] Industrial insurance, which began in England in the late 1840s, targeted lower-income families by providing policies in amounts as small as $100. Premiums ranging from $0.05 to $0.65 were collected on a weekly basis, often by agents going door to door.[48]

A liberal interpretation of the concept of insurable interest was crucial to the development of industrial insurance. Based on the premise that every family should be able to provide a proper burial for its members, this innovation furnished coverage for all parts of the family, including infants.[49] As one 1896 advertisement for Prudential Life stated: "A Life Insurance Policy issued by The Prudential is vastly more important to the welfare of a family than is Gibraltar to the British Empire. The Prudential insures men, women, and children."[50] A second ad of the same year announced "Life Insurance for Children, Women and Men. Ages, 1 to 70. Amounts, $15 to $50,000,"[51] while a third declared: "The Prudential policies insure men, women and children, that each life may protect the lives of others."[52] Although the smallest policies (those on infants and young children) merely served to provide a proper burial, larger policies could be obtained on all members contributing monetarily to the survival of the family. In effect, Prudential was promoting a working-class conception of the household where the contributions of every member were required for its survival, as opposed to the middle-class ideal of the wife and children being dependent on one main breadwinner. Insurable interest became vested in the entire family unit rather than one individual member.

With the emergence of industrial insurance in the 1870s, questions about the relationship between insurance and murder reached a fever pitch. Although the legality of obtaining policies on the lives of family members had been upheld in numerous insurable interest cases, never before in the history of life insurance had soliciting agents specifically targeted whole families for insurance. The popularity of industrial insurance quickly produced a debate among progressive reformers, life insurance executives, legislators, and the general public over the prudence of insuring children. Newspaper accounts of parents (almost always in Britain) neglecting or murdering their children in order to claim the insurance benefit only added fuel to the fire. From 1889 to 1895, bills to ban insurance on the lives of children were introduced in the legislatures of Pennsylvania, New York, Ohio, Massachusetts, Connecticut, and Canada. Investigations in each of these (as well as in Illinois and Tennessee) produced no credible evidence to substantiate the claims of murder or neglect, resulting in the failure of the bills.[53] But the accusations themselves were sufficient to taint life insurance in the minds of many, and agents were liable to be interrogated with questions such as "What about these stories on the perils of infantile insurance, for example, 'baby insurance,' as the papers called it. Hadn't the Trenton *True American* stated that insurance on youngsters was actually an inducement to murder? Weren't there stories that mothers and fathers were neglecting their children in sickness or actually 'putting them out of the way?'"[54]

Despite these concerns, sales of industrial policies skyrocketed—particularly as most fraternal benefit societies collapsed under the weight of poor organization. Although industrial insurance remained only a fraction of the dollar amount of life insurance in force through 1929, the number of policies written climbed to more than 81 million. By the Great Depression there were more than 120 million life insurance policies in force—approximately equivalent to one policy for every man, woman, and child in the United States at that time. Life insurance had emerged from virtual obscurity to become an essential component of life for all Americans, pervading the entire fabric of the American experience.

"Have you provided for your Family an Insurance on your Life?"

In 1856, *Harper's Monthly Magazine* published a sixteen-panel cartoon entitled "Life Insurance—A Dream." The protagonist, Mr. Smythe, is sitting in his easy chair in front of the hearth, gently rocking his baby's cradle as he reads about life insurance, an activity which inexplicably puts him to sleep. In his dreams, he heads off to the insurance office, where he is greeted enthusiastically by the upscale gentleman who represents the company; in the absence of soliciting agents, Smythe is obliged to take the initiative in seeking a policy. The directors visually assess him, opining that he is "good for 25 years," before sending him off to be examined by the firm's doctor, who, upon determining that his "brain, lungs, and heart are affected," sets the appropriate premium. Yet for some unnamed reason, Smythe leaves the office (as did so many others) without the proposed policy, perhaps intending to think it over for a couple of days. He quickly realizes the recklessness of delaying completion of this essential task.

While he continues to slumber, Smythe's subconscious (reflected in the ensuing panels) reveals all his concerns about modern living. In the crowded urban metropolis, he might lose his footing on the sidewalk, be run over by a wagon while crossing the street, or be hit by falling debris from a construction project. Accidentally landing in a "Lager Bier Saloon," he perhaps fears the detrimental effects of alcohol on his longevity (the German immigrants in the saloon would probably be turned down for a life policy because of their intemperance). The city is an anonymous world, and Smythe imagines being attacked by someone who mistakes his identity as he walks innocently down the street. When he tries to escape the hazards of urban life by heading to the country, he fears dying in a hunting or fishing accident—his close encounter with drowning reminiscent of the many instances of faked deaths perpetrated against the life insurance companies in this manner. But certainly the highest risks are the result of modern technologies: a camphene lamp blowing up, a railroad crash, or (his greatest fear) a steamboat explosion. Everywhere he turns, his life is in danger, putting his middle-class family at constant risk of losing their only source of support.

Mr. SMYTHE, having read about Life Insurance, dreams thereof, as follows:

He calls at the Insurance Office; whereat the officials rejoice greatly.

On board a Steamer.—Is blown up. What he dreamt became of him.

Awakes.—Finds he is really blown up—by Wife for putting Foot on Baby.

Examines himself.—Finds it was all a Dream; but it might have been true.

Best to be on the safe side. Proceeds to get his Life insured.

"Life Insurance—A Dream," panels 1–2 and 13–16, *Harper's New Monthly Magazine,* January 1856: 284–85. Courtesy of Cornell University Library, Making of America Digital Collection.

In addition to the parlor decor and his clothing, Smythe's middle-class status is indicated by his wife, who is the strong, central presence ruling the domestic sphere (but absent from all the public frames): she admonishes him when he props his feet on the bassinet, has the "presence of mind" to throw water on him when his hair is set aflame in the house, and comforts him while he is treated by a doctor. As she rescues the baby from his carelessness, he recognizes the fragility of their comfortable existence; without his steady income, her middle-class lifestyle would quickly come to an end, and any aspirations he might have for his baby would be shattered. The final panel reads: "Best to be on the safe side. Proceeds to get his Life insured."[1]

Despite the lightheartedness of the etchings, the cartoon was intended to convey a serious message to the reading public: the world is a dangerous place, but life insurance can allay some of the economic consequences of an untimely death. For families dependent on a regular salaried income for survival, life insurance at mid-century was evolving from a novel solution for mitigating one of the greatest risks they faced (the death of the main breadwinner) to a necessity of middle-class life. Whereas life insurance had once been called a wager contract, the father refusing to take out a policy was now accused of gambling with the future of his family. Life insurance had become "indispensable; indeed . . . the only method by which such persons can make any provision for those dependent upon them in case of premature death."[2] By the early 1860s, it was not unreasonable for a company to ask prominently in its advertising, "Have you provided for your Family an Insurance on your Life?"[3]

One of the greatest hurdles facing the earliest for-profit companies was educating the public about their novel product and convincing them of its value in addressing the unique economic circumstances of an urban, salaried middle class. From Pennsylvania Company's 1813 and 1814 advertising pamphlets to William Bard's 1832 *A Letter to David E. Evans,* the first movers in the industry highlighted the numerous ways a life insurance policy protected the emerging middle class from the hazards of death. These efforts were so successful that by 1866 the *Atlantic Monthly* could assert: "Few will deny the advantages which life assurance has conferred upon the public, especially in America, whose middle classes, ambitiously living up to their income, are rich mostly in their labor and their homesteads,—in their earnings rather than their savings." Beyond merely providing a safety net for the status quo, the mutual companies of the 1840s pushed the envelope by promoting life insurance as a low-risk means of climbing further up the class ladder. "In a country like this," the article continued, "no one can estimate the amount of comfort secured by *investment* in life assurance" (emphasis added).[4] By encouraging thousands of middle-income families to "invest" regularly in life insurance, the insurance companies facilitated the pooling and diffusion of capital throughout the economy. With approximately one in every three northeastern families protected by a life policy in 1870, life insurance had indeed become a pillar of modern middle-class life.

TABLE A.I.
Early American Life Insurance Companies, 1759–1843

Company	Year chartered	Year terminated	Insurance in force 1840 ($)
Corp. for the Relief of Poor and Distressed Widows and Children of Presbyterian Ministers (Presbyterian Ministers Fund)	1759	continued into 20th century	negligible
Corporation for the Relief of the Widows and Children of Clergymen in the Communion of the Church of England in America (Episcopal Ministers Fund)	1769	continued into 20th century	negligible
Insurance Company of the State of Pennsylvania	1794	1798	
Insurance Company of North America, PA	1794	1798	
United Insurance Company, NY	1798	1802	
New York Insurance Company	1798	1802	
Pennsylvania Company for Insurances on Lives and Granting Annuities	1812	1872*	691,000
New York Mechanics Life and Fire Insurance Company	1812	1813	
Dutchess County Fire, Marine and Life Insurance Company, NY	1814	1818	
Massachusetts Hospital Life Insurance Company	1818	1867*	342,000
Union Insurance Company, NY	1818	1840	
Aetna Insurance Company (mainly fire insurance; separate life company chartered in 1853)	1820	1853	negligible
Farmers Loan and Trust Company, NY	1822	1843	unknown
Baltimore Life Insurance Company	1830	1867	750,000 (est.)
New York Life Insurance and Trust Company	1830	1865*	2,880,000
Lawrenceburg Insurance Company	1832	1836	
Mississippi Insurance Company	1833	1837	
Protection Insurance Company, Mississippi	1833	1837	

(continued)

TABLE A.I. (*continued*)

Company	Year chartered	Year terminated	Insurance in force 1840 ($)
Ohio Life Insurance and Trust Company (life policies appear to have been reinsured with New York Life and Trust in the late 1840s)	1834	1857	54,000
American Life Insurance and Trust Company, Baltimore, MD	1834	1840	
New England Mutual Life Insurance Company, MA (did not begin issuing policies until 1844)	1835	continued into 20th century	0
Ocean Mutual Insurance Company, LA	1835	1839	
Southern Life and Trust Insurance Company, AL	1836	1840	
Girard Life Insurance, Annuity and Trust Company, PA	1836	1894	723,000
Missouri Life and Trust Insurance Company	1837	1841	negligible
Missouri Mutual Insurance Company	1837	1841	negligible
Globe Life Insurance, Trust and Annuity Company, PA	1837	1857	negligible
Odd Fellow Life Insurance and Trust Company, PA	1840	1857	negligible
National Insurance Company of Pennsylvania	1841	1852	
Nautilus Insurance Company (did not begin issuing policies until 1845; renamed New York Life Insurance Company in 1849)	1841	continued into 20th century	
Mutual Life Insurance Company of New York	1842	continued into 20th century	

Sources: J. Owen Stalson, *Marketing Life Insurance: Its History in America* (Cambridge, MA: Harvard University Press, 1942), 784–85; and Policy Books, Baltimore Life Insurance Collection, MS 175, H. Furlong Baldwin Library, Maryland Historical Society.

*Date company ceased writing life insurance; continued operation as a trust company.

TABLE A.2.
Years of Life Expectancy

Age	British tables of life expectancy				American tables of life expectancy		
	Northampton (1783)	Carlisle (1815)	British government (1829)	Equitable (1829)	Wigglesworth (1789)	Board of Health (1806)	Episcopal Church (c. 1814)
Birth	25.2	25.2			28.2		
10	39.8	48.8			39.2	34.6	37.1
20	33.4	41.5	41.2	41.7	34.2	27	30.6
30	28.3	34.3	35.4	34.3	30.2	21.5	25.5
40	23.1	27.6	29.1	27.4	26	19.2	21.4
50	18	21.1	22.3	20.4	21.2	16.8	17.3
60	13.2	14.3	15.9	13.9	15.4	13.7	13.8
70	8.6	9.2			10.1	9.8	9.4
80	4.8	5.5			5.9	7	6
90	2.4	3.3			3.7	4.7	

Sources: Steven Haberman and Trevor A. Sibbett, eds., *History of Actuarial Science*, vol. 1. (London: William Pickering, 1995), introduction; Richard Price, *Observations on Reversionary Payments; on Schemes for providing Annuities for Widows, and for Persons in Old Age; on the Method of calculating the values of Assurances on Lives*, 4th ed. (London: T. Cadell, 1783), in Haberman and Sibbett, vol. 2; Joshua Milne, *A Treatise on the Valuation of Annuities and Assurances on Lives and Survivorships; on the Construction of Tables of Mortality; and on the Probabilities and Expectation of Life* (London: Longman, Hurst, Rees, Orme, and Brown, 1815), in Haberman and Sibbett, vol. 2, 79–118; Edward Wigglesworth, "A Table shewing Probability of the Duration, the Decrement, and the Expectation of Life, in the States of Massachusetts and New Hampshire, formed from sixty two Bills of Mortality on the files of the American Academy of Arts and Sciences, in the year 1789," *Memoirs of the American Academy of Arts and Sciences*, vol. 2 (Boston: Isaiah Thomas and Ebenezer T. Andrews, 1793), in Haberman and Sibbett, vol. 2, 133–34: *An Address from the President and Directors of the Pennsylvania Company for Insurances on Lives and Granting Annuities, to the Inhabitants of the United States, upon the Subject of the Beneficial Objects of that Institution* (Philadelphia: J. Maxwell, 1814), 22–24; Moses L. Knapp, *Lectures on the Science of Life Insurance* (Philadelphia: E. S. Jones, 1853), 95–96; "Life Insurance in the United States," *Hunt's Merchants' Magazine and Commercial Review*, February 1843: 126; Charles Kelley Knight, *The History of Life Insurance in the United States to 1870* (Philadelphia: University of Pennsylvania, 1920), 79–80; John Gudmundsen, *The Great Provider: The Dramatic Story of Life Insurance in America* (South Norwalk, CT: Industrial Publications, 1959), 30; and R. Carlyle Buley, *The American Life Convention, 1906–1952: A Study in the History of Life Insurance* (New York: Appleton-Century-Crofts, 1953), 32.

TABLE A.3.
Premium Rates per $1,000 of Insurance

Age	Northampton +10% [N+10] (all companies to 1831)	Northampton +1% [N+1] (Penn. Co. 1831)	Carlisle +35% [C] (NYL&T 1832)	Rate difference N+10 to C(%)	Rate difference N+1 to C(%)
15	21.20	19.20	15.30	−28	−20
20	23.90	21.70	17.70	−26	−18
25	26.50	24.10	20.40	−23	−15
30	29.30	26.70	23.60	−19	−12
35	32.80	29.80	27.50	−16	−8
40	37.20	33.90	32.00	−14	−6
45	42.90	39.00	37.30	−13	−4
50	49.90	45.40	46.00	−8	+1
55	58.50	53.20	57.80	−1	+9
60	70.00	63.70	70.00	0	+10

Sources: Moses L. Knapp, *Lectures on the Science of Life Insurance* (Philadelphia: E. S. Jones, 1853), 55; Shepard B. Clough, *A Century of American Life Insurance: A History of the Mutual Life Insurance Company of New York, 1843–1943* (New York: Columbia University Press, 1946), 25; Alexander Mackie, *Facile Princeps: The Story of the Beginning of Life Insurance in America* (Lancaster, PA: Lancaster Press, 1956), 142; Viviana A. Rotman Zelizer, *Morals and Markets: The Development of Life Insurance in the United States* (New York: Columbia University Press, 1979), 14;—*Proposals of the Pennsylvania Company for Insurances on Lives and Granting Annuities* (Philadelphia: James Kay, Jun. & Brother, 1837), 2; Letter Books GA-1, GA-2, and GA-3; New York Life Insurance and Trust Company, Baker Library Historical Collections, Harvard Business School; Letter Books LA-1 and LA-2, Schedule of Insurance, FL-1, and "Notes on the Pennsylvania Life Assurance Company," Unbound Papers Box 1, Massachusetts Hospital Life Insurance Company, Baker Library Historical Collections, Harvard Business School; and Policy Books, Baltimore Life Insurance Collection, MS 175, H. Furlong Baldwin Library, Maryland Historical Society.

TABLE A.4.

State and City Laws Regarding the Taxation of Foreign Companies and Deposit Requirements

State	Year	Requirement	City/County	Additional Requirement
Pennsylvania	by 1840	20% of all premiums paid		
	1856	3% of all premiums paid	Philadelphia	$250 per agent annually
			Alleghany and Lancaster counties	$150 per agent annually
			other counties	$100 per agent annually
Kentucky	1840	2.5% of all premiums paid		
	by 1852	2.5% of all premiums paid	Louisville	$100 per agent annually
Virginia	1842	$100 per agent annually		
	by 1853	$300 per agent annually	Richmond	$50 per agent annually plus 0.75% of all premiums paid
Massachusetts	1856	0.5% of all premiums paid		
Missouri	1844	reciprocal		
Rhode Island	by 1845	$600 per agent annually		
Maryland	1846	3% of all premiums paid		
	1846	$100 per agent annually		
	1858	$250 per agent annually		
Wisconsin	1850	$100,000 deposit		
New York	1851	$100,000 deposit		
	1865	reciprocal		
Vermont	1852	0.5% of all premiums paid		
	by 1856	$50,000 deposit		

(*continued*)

State	Year	Requirement	City/County	Additional Requirement
Iowa	1854	1% of all premiums paid	county tax	additional 1% of all premiums paid
Illinois	1858	$40,000 deposit		
	1855	3% of all premiums paid		
	1869	reciprocal		
Louisiana	1855		New Orleans	$500 per agent annually
Connecticut	by 1852	reciprocal		
New Jersey	by 1857	1% school tax on capital and $20,000–$100,000 deposit		
Georgia	1858	1% on all premiums paid		
Tennessee	1859/60	$20,000 deposit		
	1868	$750 per agent annually, 1.5% of all premiums paid, and $20,000 deposit		
Alabama	1859/60	tax for benefit of medical school in Mobile		

Sources: "Of Statements by Insurance Companies," Hunt's Merchants' Magazine, December 1849: 662–64; "The New Life Insurance Law of New York," Hunt's Merchants' Magazine, June 1851: 755–57; Letters from D. Thompson to Mrs. Margaret Andrews and Peter B. Manchester, Cincinnati, OH, July 19, 1853, Letter Book GA-18, NYL&T; "Illinois Insurance Law," Hunt's Merchants' Magazine, March 1855: 366; "The Insurance Law of Kentucky," Hunt's Merchants' Magazine, September 1855: 374–75; "Law of Kentucky Regulating Agencies of Foreign Insurance Companies," Hunt's Merchants' Magazine, June 1856: 737–38; "Insurance Law of Louisiana," Hunt's Merchants' Magazine, December 1856: 741–42; "Insurance Laws of Connecticut," "Vermont Insurance Law," and "An Act Concerning Insurance Companies," United States Insurance Almanac, 1856 (New York: G. E. Currie, 1856), §6, 68, and 72; Letter from A. B. Coulter, secretary, to Charles W. Pairo, Washington, DC, agent, January 16, 1857, Letter Books, 1852–67, Baltimore Life Insurance Collection, MS 175, H. Furlong Baldwin Library, Maryland Historical Society; United States Insurance Almanac, 1857 (New York: G. E. Currie, 1857), 49–93; "Iowa Insurance Law," Hunt's Merchants' Magazine, August 1858: 238–39; "Maryland Insurance Law," Hunt's Merchants' Magazine, December 1858: 743–45; United States Insurance Almanac, 1859 (New York: G. E. Currie, 1859): 37–65; "Vermont Insurance Law," United States Insurance Gazette and Magazine of Useful Knowledge, November 1859–April 1860: 10–15; "Insurance Law of Georgia," Hunt's Merchants' Magazine, May 1860: 622–24; "Proceedings of the Life Insurance Convention," United States Insurance Gazette and Magazine of Useful Knowledge, August 1860: 224; and "The New Insurance Tax Law of Tennessee," Spectator, May 1868: 89.

TABLE A.5.
Baltimore Life White and Slave Policies

Year	White No.	Slave No.	Percent of all policies	Average amount ($)	Average policy length (years)
1831	23	2	8	300	4
1832	69	5	7	320	1
1833	117	3	3	308	1
1834	119	14	11	625	3
1835	148	18	11	327	1.19
1836	159	9	5	652	2.18
1837	126	3	2	500	5.33
1838	171	0	0	0	0
1839	139	2	1	550	2
1840	108	2	2	450	0.5
1841	86	4	4	306	3
1842	95	3	3	292	3
1843	100	2	2	150	5.5
1844	118	3	2	483	3.33
1845	127	0	0	0	0
1846	92	4	4	388	2.05
1847	113	3	3	300	5.67
1848	94	4	4	238	5
1849	176	14	7	480	4.14
1850	108	9	8	430	2.5
1851	83	12	13	394	2.75
1852	103	16	13	489	3.69
1853	78	6	7	375	3.53
1854	59	91	61	577	6.23
1855	66	74	53	600	6.24
1856	48	33	41	648	5.89
1857	48	70	59	712	5.16
1858	35	32	48	689	5.46
1859	31	79	72	777	4.59
1860	33	75	72	878	4.97
1861	17	17	50	797	4.74
1831–36	635	51	8	463	1.94
1837–48	1,369	30	2	358	3.61
1831–48	2,004	81	4	424	2.56
1849–53	548	57	9	445	3.46
1854–60	320	454	59	699	5.5

Source: Policy Books, Baltimore Life Insurance Collection, MS 175, H. Furlong Baldwin Library, Maryland Historical Society.

TABLE A.6.
Companies Underwriting Slaves from California Slavery Era Insurance Registry

Company	No. of policies	Years sold	Main slaveholding locations
Aetna Life	29	1854–60	MO, SC, VA, AL, LA
New York Life	488	1846–48	KY (26%), VA (21%), NC (19%)
US Life	173	none given	KY (73%), VA (22%)

Source: California Department of Insurance Slavery Era Insurance Registry Report to the California Legislature and Registry by Name of Slaveholder, May 2002.

TABLE A.7.
Employment of Insured Slaves

Occupation	New York Life 1846–48		Baltimore Life 1849–53	
	% of slave policies	No. (488 total)	% of slave policies	No. (54 total)
Artisans (carpenters, coopers, wheelwrights, smiths, masons, bricklayers, tailors, butchers, bakers, shoemakers, etc.)	17 (carpenters 29)	83 (carpenters 24)	16	9
Boat-related employment	24 (firemen 54)	117 (firemen 63)	5–16	3–9
Coal pits and mining	17	83	0	0
Farm work	5	24	12–16	7–9
House servants and cooks	12	59	31	18
Laborers (common, stevedores, draymen, drivers)	11	54	2	1
Mills and distilleries	5	24	0	0
Railroad construction	0	0	3	2
Unknown	9	44	10–24	6–14

Sources: California Department of Insurance Slavery Era Insurance Registry Report to the California Legislature and Registry by Name of Slaveholder, May 2002; and Policy Books and Policy Applications, Baltimore Life Insurance Collection, MS 175, H. Furlong Baldwin Library, Maryland Historical Society.

TABLE A.8.

Premium Rates ($) for 1-Year Policy per $100 of Insurance

Age	White rates (Carlisle Table)	Slave rates, 1850s				
		NC Mutual	National Safety	Richmond Fire and VA Life	Unnamed New Orleans co.	Baltimore Life
15	0.77	1.18	1.28	1.30	2.00	1.54
20	0.91	1.24	1.36	1.38	2.00	1.82
25	1.00	1.32	1.45	1.47	2.00	2.00
30	1.31	1.41	1.57	1.59	2.50	2.62
35	1.36	1.60	1.75	1.77	2.50	2.72
40	1.69	1.77	1.95	1.97	3.00	3.38
45	1.91	2.10	2.31	2.33	3.00	3.82
50	1.96	2.70	2.98	3.00		3.92
55	2.32	3.75	4.15	4.16		4.64
60	4.35	5.10	5.65	5.66		8.70

Sources: Life Insurance: Its Principles, Operations and Benefits, as presented by the North Carolina Mutual Life Insurance Company (Raleigh: Seaton Gales, 1849), 23; Virginia Life Insurance Company 1860 brochure: 63, University of Texas Libraries, Austin; Franklin Slaughter's slave insurance agency advertisement, 1849, in Grinnan Family Papers, MSS 49, Special Collections, University of Virginia Library, Charlottesville, VA; letter from Charles E. Beynroth, Louisville, KY, to Richard B. Dorsey, June 22, 1852, and brochures enclosed with letter from Dr. Thomas Pollard to D. Thompson, January 11, 1855, Correspondence 12, Baltimore Life Insurance Collection, MS 175, H. Furlong Baldwin Library, Maryland Historical Society. Unlike the other circulars accompanying Pollard's letter, National Loan Fund Life quoted rates on slaves for the term of five years.

TABLE A.9.
Employment of Slaves Insured by Baltimore Life (%)

Occupation	1849–53 (54 slaves)	1854 (91 slaves)	1855 (74 slaves)	1856 (33 slaves)	1857 (70 slaves)	4/59–4/60 (88 slaves)
Artisans	16 (9)	10 (9)	8 (6)	15 (5)	10 (7)	14 (12)
Boat-related	5–16 (3–9)	0 (0)	0 (0)	0 (0)	0 (0)	0 (0)
Coal pits/mines	0 (0)	1 (1)	21 (16)	6 (2)	20 (14)	5 (4)
Factory labor	0 (0)	5 (5)	11 (8)	24 (8)	29 (20)	20 (18)
Farm work	12–16 (7–9)	5 (5)	14 (10)	9 (3)	6 (4)	14 (12)
House/cooks	31 (18)	29 (26)	19 (14)	24 (8)	17 (12)	22 (19)
Laborers	2 (1)	10 (9)	16 (12)	3 (1)	7 (5)	7 (6)
Railroad const.	3 (2)	34 (31)	5 (4)	0 (0)	0 (0)	6 (5)
Unknown	10–24 (6–14)	6 (5)	5 (4)	18 (6)	11 (8)	14 (12)

Source: Policy Books and Policy Applications, Baltimore Life Insurance Collection, MS 175, H. Furlong Baldwin Library, Maryland Historical Society.

TABLE A.10.
Length of Policies

Company	Years	% Whole life policies	Average policy length, non-life (years)	% Nonlife policies 7 years or greater
Massachusetts	1823–32	4.32	3.71	33.55
Hospital Life	1833–39	6.02	5.45	76.24
Baltimore Life	1831–50	8.73	4.29	47.25
(nonslave)	1851–62	19.48	5.04	62.80
New York Life	1830–45	12.89	5.37	65.40
and Trust	1846–54	28.71	5.63	71.88
	1855–62	44.48	5.27	68.67
New England Mutual	1844–53	40.99	5.67	68.91

Source: Policy Books, Baltimore Life Insurance Collection, MS 175, H. Furlong Baldwin Library, Maryland Historical Society; Schedule of Insurance, Massachusetts Hospital Life Insurance Company, Baker Library Historical Collections, Harvard Business School; Register of Life Insurance, New York Life Insurance and Trust Company, Baker Library Historical Collections, Harvard Business School; and Policy Books, New England Mutual Life Insurance Company, Baker Library Historical Collections, Harvard Business School.

Abbreviations

BLIC   Baltimore Life Insurance Collection, H. Furlong Baldwin Library, Maryland Historical Society

HCR   Historic Corporate Reports, Baker Library Historical Collections, Harvard Business School

MHL   Massachusetts Hospital Life Insurance Company, Baker Library Historical Collections, Harvard Business School

NEMLIC New England Mutual Life Insurance Company, Baker Library Historical Collections, Harvard Business School

NYL&T   New York Life Insurance and Trust Company, Baker Library Historical Collections, Harvard Business School

UNC   Southern Historical Collection, Wilson Library, University of North Carolina at Chapel Hill

WCP   Elizur Wright Correspondence and Papers, Baker Library Historical Collections, Harvard Business School

Introduction

1. Horace Mather Lippincott, *Early Philadelphia: Its People, Life and Progress* (Philadelphia: J. B. Lippincott, 1917), 234; and *Philadelphia and Popular Philadelphians* (Philadelphia: North American, 1891), 93.

2. Lester W. Zartman and William H. Price, *Yale Readings in Insurance: Property Insurance—Marine and Fire* (New Haven, CT: Yale University Press, 1926); William M. Fowler Jr., "Marine Insurance in Boston: The Early Years of the Boston Marine Insurance Company, 1799–1807," in Conrad Edick Wright and Katheryn P. Viens, eds., *Entrepreneurs: The Boston Business Community, 1700–1850* (Boston: Massachusetts Historical Society, 1997), 165–70; and Alexander Mackie, *Facile Princeps: The Story of the Beginning of Life Insurance in America* (Lancaster, PA: Lancaster Press, 1956), 135, 141–42.

3. Mackie, 64, 127–28; and Corporation for the Relief of the Widows and Children of Clergymen of the Protestant Episcopal Church, *The Charters, with the Laws and the List of Members* (Philadelphia: Hall and Sellers, 1791).

4. David T. Beito, "'This Enormous Army': The Mutual-Aid Tradition of American Fraternal Societies before the Twentieth Century," in David T. Beito, Peter Gordon, and Alexander Tabarrok, eds., *The Voluntary City: Choice, Community, and Civil Society* (Ann Arbor: University of Michigan Press, 2002), 189–94.

5. Mackie, 141–42; "Insurances Upon Lives by the Pelican Life Insurance Company, of London," *New-York Evening Post,* July 3, 1806: 4; "Communications. To the Members of the General Court," *Independent Chronicle,* February 23, 1807; "Insurances Upon Lives by the Pelican Life Insurance Company, of London," *Boston Gazette,* February 23, 1807; "Insurances Upon Lives by the Pelican Life Insurance Company, of London," *Poulson's American Daily Advertiser,* March 3, 1807: 3; and "Life Insurance. To Parents, Guardians, and others, desirous of securing a provision against Sudden Death," *New-York Evening Post,* July 13, 1808: 3. Israel Whelen, one of Pennsylvania Company's original incorporators, had served as the Philadelphia agent for Pelican Life during the second decade of the nineteenth century. See "Insurances Upon Lives by the Pelican Life Insurance Company, of London," *Poulson's American Daily Advertiser,* March 3, 1807: 3; and John Gudmundsen, *The Great Provider: The Dramatic Story of Life Insurance in America* (South Norwalk, CT: Industrial Publications, 1959), 30.

6. *An Address to the Citizens of Pennsylvania, Upon the Subject of a Life Insurance Company* (Philadelphia, 1813), 2–3.

7. Shawn Johansen, *Family Men: Middle-Class Fatherhood in Early Industrializing America* (New York: Routledge, 2001), 23–24.

8. Jack Larkin, *The Reshaping of Everyday Life, 1790–1840* (New York: Harper & Row, 1988), 265.

9. *An Address to the Citizens,* 6.

10. For an extended discussion of this practice, see Naomi R. Lamoreaux, *Insider Lending: Banks, Personal Connections, and Economic Development in Industrial New England* (Cambridge: Cambridge University Press, 1996).

11. *An Address from the President and Directors of the Pennsylvania Company for Insurances on Lives and Granting Annuities, to the Inhabitants of the United States, upon the Subject of the Beneficial Objects of that Institution* (Philadelphia: J. Maxwell, 1814), 4.

12. *An Address to the Citizens,* 7.

13. *An Address to the Citizens,* 7; and *An Address from the President,* 6.

14. *An Address from the President,* 9.

15. *An Address from the President,* 3, 6–7.

16. *Constitution and by-laws of the Orphan Society of Philadelphia* (Philadelphia: William Fry, 1815); *The First Annual Report of the Philadelphia Orphan Society* (Philadelphia: William Fry, 1816); and *An Address from the President.*

17. Robert F. Dalzell Jr., *Enterprising Elite: The Boston Associates and the World They Made* (Cambridge, MA: Harvard University Press, 1987), 105–8, 113–15; N. I. Bowditch, *History of the Massachusetts General Hospital* (Boston: 1872), 10–11; and Peter Dobkin Hall, "What the Merchants Did with Their Money: Charitable and Testamentary Trusts in Massachusetts, 1780–1880," in Wright and Viens, 403.

18. J. Owen Stalson, *Marketing Life Insurance: Its History in America* (Cambridge, MA: Harvard University Press, 1942), 750.

19. Charles Kelley Knight, *The History of Life Insurance in the United States to 1870* (Philadelphia: University of Pennsylvania, 1920), 103–4.

20. Stalson, 103–25; and Viviana A. Rotman Zelizer, *Morals and Markets: The Development of Life Insurance in the United States* (New York: Columbia University Press, 1979), 5–7.

21. Stalson, 748–51.

22. *Historical Statistics of the United States, Colonial Times to 1970* (Washington, DC: Government Printing Office, 1975), 1057.

Chapter One · *Understanding Mortality in Antebellum America*

1. This biographical sketch of William Bard is based on Felix E. Hirsch, "The Bard Family," *Columbia University Quarterly* (October 1941): 222–41; Abraham Ernest Helffenstein, *Pierre Fauconnier and His Descendants; with Some Account of the Allied Valleaux* (Philadelphia: S. H. Burbank, 1911); and The Diary of Arthur Sandys, Bard College Archives.

2. Hirsch, 33.

3. William Bard to George Atkinson, February 25, 1841, GA-9, New York Life Insurance and Trust Company, Baker Library Historical Collections, Harvard Business School (hereafter NYL&T).

4. Frank H. Knight, *Risk, Uncertainty, and Profit* (Boston: Houghton Mifflin, 1921), 241–48.

5. Ansley J. Coale and Paul Demeny, *Regional Model Life Tables and Stable Populations* (New York: Academic Press, 1983), 4.

6. Richard Price, *Observations on Reversionary Payments; on Schemes for providing Annuities for Widows, and for Persons in Old Age; on the Method of calculating the values of Assurances on Lives,* 4th ed. (London: T. Cadell, 1783), in Steven Haberman and Trevor A. Sibbett, eds., *History of Actuarial Science,* vol. 2 (London: William Pickering, 1995), 39–70; and Haberman and Sibbett, vol. 1, xxxv.

7. Haberman and Sibbett, vol. 1, xxvi; and Joshua Milne, *A Treatise on the Valuation of Annuities and Assurances on Lives and Survivorships; on the Construction of Tables of Mortality; and on the Probabilities and Expectations of Life* (London: Longman, Hurst, Rees, Orme, and Brown, 1815), in Haberman and Sibbett, vol. 2, 79–118.

8. Moses L. Knapp, *Lectures on the Science of Life Insurance* (Philadelphia: E. S. Jones, 1853), 91; and Thomas Young, "A Formula for Expressing the Decrement of Human Life" (read before the Royal Society, April 19, 1826), in Haberman and Sibbett, vol. 2, 193–216.

9. R. Carlyle Buley, *The American Life Convention, 1906–1952: A Study in the History of Life Insurance* (New York: Appleton-Century-Crofts, 1953), 23–24; J. Owen Stalson, *Marketing Life Insurance: Its History in America* (Cambridge, MA: Harvard University Press, 1942), 40; Haberman and Sibbett, vol. 1, xxvi–xxvii; and Knapp, 93.

10. Knapp, 95–96; Edward Wigglesworth, "A Table shewing Probability of the Duration, the Decrement, and the Expectation of Life, in the States of Massachusetts and New Hampshire, formed from sixty two Bills of Mortality on the files of the American Academy of Arts and Sciences, in the year 1789," *Memoirs of the American Academy of Arts and Sciences,* vol. 2 (Boston: Isaiah Thomas and Ebenezer T. Andrews, 1793), in Haberman and Sibbett, vol. 2, 133–34; and "Life Insurance in the United States," *Hunt's Merchants' Magazine,* February 1843: 126.

11. Wigglesworth, 73–77; Maris A. Vinovskis, "The 1789 Life Table of Edward Wigglesworth," *Journal of Economic History* 31 (1971): 570–90; Haberman and Sibbett, vol. 1, xxvi; Alexander Mackie, *Facile Princeps: The Story of the Beginning of Life Insurance in America* (Lancaster, PA: Lancaster Press, 1956), 123–24; and Knapp, 86.

12. Knapp, 86.

13. *An Address from the President and Directors of the Pennsylvania Company for Insurances on Lives and Granting Annuities to the Inhabitants of the United States, upon the Subject of the Beneficial Objects of that Institution* (Philadelphia: J. Maxwell, 1814), 22–24; Charles Kelley Knight, *The History of Life Insurance in the United States to 1870* (Philadelphia: University of Pennsylvania, 1920), 79–80; John Gudmundsen, *The Great Provider: The Dramatic Story of Life Insurance in America* (South Norwalk, CT: Industrial Publications, 1959), 30; and Buley, *The American Life Convention*, 32. For an evaluation of the accuracy of these tables, see Maris A. Vinovskis, "The Jacobson Life Table of 1850: A Critical Reexamination from a Massachusetts Perspective," *Journal of Interdisciplinary History* 8 (1978): 721–22.

14. Knight claims that Massachusetts Hospital Life charged much higher rates than Pennsylvania Company, but this was not the case during the 1820s and early 1830s. It was only from 1837 to 1845 or 1846 that the rates of Massachusetts Hospital Life were higher than those of Pennsylvania Company. Knight, 84.

15. Knapp, 55; Shepard B. Clough, *A Century of American Life Insurance: A History of the Mutual Life Insurance Company of New York, 1843–1943* (New York: Columbia University Press, 1946), 25; Mackie, 142; Viviana A. Rotman Zelizer, *Morals and Markets: The Development of Life Insurance in the United States* (New York: Columbia University Press, 1979), 14; "Notes on the Pennsylvania Life Assurance Company," Unbound Papers 1, Massachusetts Hospital Life Insurance Company, Baker Library Historical Collections, Harvard Business School (hereafter MHL); and Bard to T. W. Ludlow, August 16, 1832, GA-2, NYL&T.

16. Bard to Pennsylvania Company, January 8, 1831, GA-1, NYL&T.

17. Bard to Pennsylvania Company, January 8, 1831, GA-1, NYL&T.

18. Bard to T. W. Ludlow, August 16, 1832, GA-2, NYL&T.

19. Bard to Thomas C. Perkins, May 15, 1833, GA-3, NYL&T.

20. Bard to T. W. Ludlow, August 16, 1832, GA-2, NYL&T.

21. It is clear from his correspondence that Bard had read *The Report of the Select Committee on Life Annuities,* published by the House of Commons on June 4, 1829, *The Report of John Finlaison Actuary of the National Debt on the Evidence and Elementary Facts on which the Tables of Life Annuities are Founded* from March 31, 1819, and *A View of the Use and Progress of the Equitable Society,* published by William Morgan in 1829. See Bard to Thomas T. Smiley, July 6, 1831, GA-1, NYL&T.

22. Bard to Pennsylvania Company, January 8, 1831, GA-1, NYL&T.

23. Bard to Thomas T. Smiley, July 6, 1831, and to J. Goodhue, September 27, 1831, GA-1, NYL&T.

24. Bard to Joseph Roberts, April 26, 1831, GA-1, NYL&T.

25. Nathaniel Bowditch to Thomas Smiley, Pennsylvania Company, March 2, 1829, and to Joseph Roberts Jr., Pennsylvania Company, February 27, 1832, LA-1, MHL.

26. Massachusetts Hospital Life to Thomas Sanborn, March 17, 1841, LA-2, MHL.

27. Bard to Thomas C. Perkins, May 15, 1833, GA-3, NYL&T.

28. "Notes on the Pennsylvania Life Assurance Company," Unbound Papers 1, MHL.

29. *Proposals of the Pennsylvania Company for Insurances on Lives and Granting Annuities* (Philadelphia: James Kay, Jun. & Brother, 1837), 2.

30. Bowditch to Joseph Roberts Jr., Pennsylvania Company, February 27, 1832, LA-1, MHL.

31. Bard to T. W. Ludlow, August 16, 1832, GA-2, NYL&T.

32. Bard to Nathaniel Bowditch and Thomas Astley, January 7, 1832, GA-2, NYL&T. Although chartered in 1830, Baltimore Life did not begin issuing policies until May 1831 and only had twenty-five policies on its books by the end of that year. It was thus never included or mentioned (and did not attempt to participate) in these early conversations regarding premium rates.

33. Rates calculated based on Massachusetts Hospital Life Schedule of Insurance, FL-1, MHL; and Baltimore Life Insurance Company Policy Books, Baltimore Life Insurance Collection, MS 175, H. Furlong Baldwin Library, Maryland Historical Society (hereafter BLIC).

34. James H. Causten to John J. Donaldson, April 5, 1833, Correspondence 1, BLIC.

35. Donaldson to James H. Causten, June 19, 1833, Letter Book, and Policy Books, BLIC.

36. Stalson, 789.

37. Bard to Thomas C. Perkins, October 30, 1832, GA-2, May 9, 1833, GA-3, and October 31, 1833, GA-4, NYL&T; List of Life Insurance Agents, GA-4, NYL&T; and Bowditch to Thomas C. Perkins, April 11, 1831, and March 3, 1832, LA-1, MHL.

38. Donaldson to Thomas C. Perkins, April 7, 1835, Letter Book, BLIC.

39. Donaldson to James H. Causten, June 11, 1835, Letter Book, BLIC.

40. *Proposals of the Pennsylvania Company,* 2; and "Life Insurance," *Salem Gazette,* March 24, 1837: 2.

41. B. W. Richards, Girard Life, to Donaldson, May 6, 1837, Correspondence 2, BLIC.

42. "Comparative Rates of Domestic and Foreign Life Insurance," *Hunt's Merchants' Magazine,* November 1859: 612; *Life Insurance: Its Principles, Operations and Benefits, as presented by the North Carolina Mutual Life Insurance Company* (Raleigh: Seaton Gales, 1849), 8, 22; Girard Life 1837 brochure: 3, Historic Corporate Reports, Baker Library Historical Collections, Harvard Business School (hereafter HCR); Mutual Life of Baltimore 1849 brochure: 11, HCR; Mutual Life of New York 1846 brochure: 35, HCR; New York Life 1851 brochure: 14, HCR; James M. Hudnut, *Semi-Centennial History of the New-York Life Insurance Company, 1845–1895* (New York: New York Life Insurance Company, 1895), 21–22; "Mutual Life Insurance," *Hunt's Merchants' Magazine,* October 1844: 344; Mildred F. Stone, *Since 1845: A History of the Mutual Benefit Life Insurance Company* (New Brunswick, NJ: Rutgers University Press, 1957), 189; Edward E. Rhodes, *Recollections of Amzi Dodd and Bloomfield J. Miller* (Newark, NJ: Mutual Benefit Life Insurance Company, 1945), 11–12; and Zelizer, 14. According to Shepard B. Clough, in 1842 "the Mutual adopted the rates and mortality table then employed by the New York Life Insurance and Trust Company," which he states was a combination of the Carlisle and Northampton tables (Clough, 57). However, I have come across no other evidence indicating that either of these companies used such a combined table.

43. Moses L. Hale to Harvey C. Wood, March 16, 1846, LA-3, and Francis C. Lowell to Samuel Lord, September 3, 1847, LA-4, MHL.

44. Gerald T. White, *A History of the Massachusetts Hospital Life Insurance Company* (Cambridge, MA: Harvard University Press, 1955), 27.

45. Harrison S. Morris, *A Sketch of the Pennsylvania Company for Insurances on Lives and Granting Annuities* (Philadelphia: J. B. Lippincott, 1896), 35.

46. "Life Insurance in the United States," *Hunt's Merchants' Magazine*, February 1843: 122.

47. *A Treatise on Life Insurance; together with a Short Account of the Mutual Life Insurance Company of New York* (New York, 1845), reprinted in "Mutual Life Insurance," *Hunt's Merchants' Magazine*, February 1847: 159.

48. "Mutual Life Insurance," *Hunt's Merchants' Magazine*, October 1844: 343. The article attributes this table to the work of Professor J. W. Wright of New York, but the table printed is identical to the Carlisle Table.

49. *North Carolina Mutual Life*, 8. See also *Life Insurance: Its Principles, Operations and Benefits, as presented by the Connecticut Mutual Life Insurance Company* (Hartford: Case, Tiffany & Burnham, 1846), 4; Nautilus Insurance 1848 brochure: 8–9, HCR; and Mutual Life of New York 1846 brochure: 17–18, HCR.

50. Donaldson to John O. Lay, March 29, 1837, Letter Book, BLIC.

51. Bard to T. W. Ludlow, August 16, 1832, GA-2, NYL&T.

52. Haberman and Sibbett, vol. 1, xxvi.

53. Bard to B. F. Butler, July 26, 1832, GA-2, to Frederick H. Smith, October 4, 1834, GA-4, and to T. W. Ludlow, July 12, 1838, GA-6, NYL&T; and "Life Insurance in the United States," *Hunt's Merchants' Magazine*, February 1843: 130. It is unclear whether Bard ever made contact with Babbage, but he did carry on correspondence with Finlaison.

54. Bard to T. W. Ludlow, July 12, 1838, GA-6, NYL&T.

55. Bard to B. F. Butler, July 26, 1832, GA-2, and to Magniac Smith, November 21, 1838, and July 6, 1839, GA-7, and Thomas W. Ludlow to Magniac Smith, March 14, 1839, GA-7, NYL&T.

56. Thomas W. Ludlow to Magniac Smith, March 14, 1839, GA-7, NYL&T.

57. Bard to John Forsyth, September 26, 1839, GA-7, NYL&T.

58. J. D. B. DeBow, *Mortality Statistics of the Seventh Census of the United States, 1850* (Washington, DC: A. O. P. Nicholson, 1855), 8–9; and Carroll D. Wright, *The History and Growth of the United States Census* (Washington, DC: Government Printing Office, 1900), 45.

59. Bard to Frederick H. Smith, October 4, 1834, GA-4, NYL&T.

60. Bard to John Finlaison, February 8, 1840, GA-8, NYL&T. As historian Patricia Cline Cohen has observed, this method of obtaining statistics from leading local gentlemen had become commonplace by the early decades of the nineteenth century. See Patricia Cline Cohen, *A Calculating People: The Spread of Numeracy in Early America* (Chicago: University of Chicago Press, 1982), 152–54.

61. Bard to John Finlaison, February 8, 1840, GA-8, NYL&T.

62. James Mease, M.D., "Observations on Bills of Mortality," *American Journal of Science and Arts*, July–September 1841: 306.

63. "The Mortality of Baltimore," *Hunt's Merchants' Magazine*, January 1850: 35–44; Thomas Walter Reed, *History of the University of Georgia* (Athens, GA, 1949), chapter IX-B; E. J. Moorhead, *Our Yesterdays: the History of the Actuarial Profession in North America, 1809–1979* (Schaumburg, IL: Society of Actuaries, 1989), 20–21; and Knapp, 86.

64. DeBow, 7–8. For a discussion of the Massachusetts law, see Walter F. Willcox, "Lem-

uel Shattuck, Statist, Founder of the American Statistical Association," *Journal of the American Statistical Association* (March 1940): 232–33.

65. "Principles of Life Insurance in Relation to Tables of Mortality in Europe and the United States," *Insurance Gazette*, May–October 1857: 203.

66. DeBow, 8.

67. Bard to George Atkinson, February 25, 1841, GA-9, NYL&T.

68. "The New England Life Insurance Company," *Hunt's Merchants' Magazine*, February 1847: 224; and "Thirteenth Annual Report of the New England Mutual Life Insurance Company of Boston," *Insurance Gazette*, February 1857: 182.

69. Bard to Dr. Marsh, December 24, 1831, GA-1, NYL&T.

70. National Life 1856 brochure: 11, HCR.

71. Bard to G. W. Clinton, February 19, 1835, GA-4, NYL&T.

72. Bard to P. Lythoff, July 9, 1833, GA-3, NYL&T.

73. Bard to Levi Ward, July 9, 1833, GA-3, NYL&T.

74. Policies 296 and 1889, EB-1, NYL&T.

75. Bard to G. W. Clinton, February 19, 1834, GA-4, NYL&T.

76. New policies written in January and July, EB-1, NYL&T.

77. From 1832 to 1937, all immigrants coming into Quebec were placed in quarantine on Grosse Île until their health could be ascertained. Marianna O'Gallagher, *Grosse Île: Gateway to Canada, 1832–1937* (Dublin: Carraig Books, 1984), 13.

78. Bard to William D. Dupont, April 14, 1836, GA-5, NYL&T.

79. For example, see Connecticut Mutual Life 1846 and 1851 brochures: 19, Mutual Life of New York 1847 brochure: 22–23, Albion Life 1845 brochure: 5, and Mutual Life of Baltimore 1849 brochure: 16, HCR.

80. "Life Insurance in the United States," *Hunt's Merchants' Magazine*, March 1843: 231. See also "American Life Insurance Companies Opposed to Granting 'Days of Grace,'" *Insurance Gazette*, May–October 1858: 99; and *North Carolina Mutual Life*, 16.

81. *Rates and Proposals of the New-York Life Insurance and Trust Company, No. 38 Wall-Street, for Insurance on Lives, Granting Annuities, Receiving Money in Trust, and the Management of Trust Estates* (New York: Clayton & Van Norden, 1830), 18.

82. Bard to Henry M. Morfit, March 11, 1835, GA-4, NYL&T.

83. Bard to William F. Hopkins, September 17, 1832, GA-2, NYL&T.

84. D. Thompson to Levi Twigg, May 25, 1846, GA-13, NYL&T.

85. Bard to Henry M. Morfit, March 18, 1835, GA-4, NYL&T.

86. Bard to Henry M. Morfit, March 25, 1835, GA-4, NYL&T.

87. Bard to Henry M. Morfit, March 18, 1835, GA-4, NYL&T.

88. D. Thompson to Prescott Bigelow, January 8, 1850, GA-16, NYL&T.

89. D. Thompson to George K. McGunnegle, May 24, 1852, GA-18, NYL&T.

90. Mutual Life of Baltimore 1849 brochure: 4, HCR.

91. Mutual Life of Baltimore 1849 brochure: 8, HCR.

92. Baltimore Life advertisement, *Army and Navy Chronicle*, March 2, 1837: 144.

93. Policy 542. See also Policies 7, 24, 37, 51, 114, 244, 422, 434, 482, 518, 831, 841, 868, 889, 1149, 1160, 1182, 1260, 1277, 1281, 1282, 1295, 1304, 1325, 1342, 1344, 1348, 1380, 1382, 1385, 1495,

1534, 1566, 1568, 1575, 1581, 1726, 1744, 1758, 1793, 1798, 2159, 2310, and 2317, Policy Books, BLIC.

94. Policy 567. See also Policies 531, 885, 893 [replaces 889 above], 972, 1018, 1035, 1036, 1097, 1160, 1244, 1245, 1253, 1598, 1701, 1715, 1741, 1750, 1753, 1763, 1780, 1781, 1782, 1787, 1797, 1799, 2378, 2385, and 2392, Policy Books, BLIC.

95. "Life Insurance," *Army and Navy Chronicle,* February 2, 1837: 72.

96. Bard to J. Leander Starr, June 24, 1833, GA-3, NYL&T.

97. Bard to B. Davis Noxen, February 26, 1833, GA-3, NYL&T.

98. GA-4, NYL&T.

99. Bard to B. Davis Noxen, February 26, 1833, GA-3, NYL&T.

100. Bard to George Atkinson, March 15, 1834, GA-4, NYL&T.

101. Bard to Levi Ward, May 30, 1834, GA-4, NYL&T.

102. Bard to N. G. Pendleton, May 15, 1833, GA-3, NYL&T.

103. Bard to F. Bronson, Ohio Life and Trust, February 23, 1837, GA-6, NYL&T.

104. In some cases, the first of October or the first of December served as the start date for permissible travel to the South, but November 1 was the most common date given.

105. See National Life 1856 brochure: 11–12, HCR; and Bard to Michael Philips, October 11, 1830, GA-1, to Jacob Leland, December 18, 1832, GA-2, and to T. C. Perkins, October 5, 1833, and October 16, 1833, GA-3, NYL&T.

106. Bard to Henry White, August 23, 1833, GA-3, and to William Atkinson, December 31, 1833, GA-4, NYL&T.

107. Bard to R. W. Montgomery, September 22, 1833, GA-3, NYL&T.

108. Bard to George Atkinson, May 15, 1834, GA-4, NYL&T.

109. Bard to Samuel J. Lymon, April 28, 1835, GA-5, NYL&T.

110. Bard to Gustavus A. Myers, October 10, 1834, and to John G. Gamball, February 24, 1835, GA-4, NYL&T. See also Georgina D. Feldberg, *Disease and Class: Tuberculosis and the Shaping of Modern North American Society* (New Brunswick, NJ: Rutgers University Press, 1995), 19.

111. Bard to William Atkinson, December 31, 1833, GA-4, NYL&T.

112. "Value and Prospects of Life in the United States," *Hunt's Merchants' Magazine,* January 1846: 19–28. For a broader discussion of the problems and controversies involved with the census of 1840, see Cohen, chapter 6.

113. "Life and Death in the United States. Our Climate," *Insurance Gazette,* November 1855–April 1856: 216–18. Other studies (which did not rely on the census returns) came to exactly the opposite conclusion. See "Mortality and Hygiene of New-Orleans. Fenner's Southern Medical Reports," *DeBow's Commercial Review,* October–November 1851: 474–88.

114. "In Relation to Tables of Mortality in Europe and the US," *Insurance Gazette,* May–October 1857: 201–8.

115. Lawrence F. Abbott, *The Story of NYLIC: A History of the Origin and Development of the New York Life Insurance Company from 1845 to 1929* (New York, 1930), 58.

116. Mutual Life of Baltimore 1849 brochure: 15–16, HCR.

117. *North Carolina Mutual Life,* 15.

118. Donaldson to John O. Lay, March 29, 1837, Letter Book, BLIC.

119. Donaldson to J. H. Causten, June 17, 1834, Letter Book, BLIC.

120. Donaldson to William F. Davis, January 9, 1839, Letter Book, BLIC. See also Donaldson to Davis, November 17 and 26, 1838, Letter Book, BLIC.

121. Donaldson to William F. Davis, January 29, 1839, Letter Book, BLIC. See also Donaldson to Davis, January 25, 1839, Letter Book, BLIC.

122. David Thompson to Henry M. Morfit, January 23, 1849, GA-15, NYL&T.

123. P. R. Kearney to Francis H. Smith, February 2, 1849, GA-15, NYL&T.

124. For example, see David Thompson to A. L. Stimson, June 20, 1849, GA-16, NYL&T.

125. R. B. Dorsey to Dr. Beverly Wellford, March 5, 1849, Letter Book, BLIC. See also Henry Stagg to Dorsey, March 17, 1849, and G. R. Phillips, Connecticut Mutual Life, to Dorsey, April 1849, Correspondence 10, BLIC.

126. For example, see David Thompson to W. L. Griswold, November 27, 1849, GA-16, NYL&T.

127. Bard to W. L. Griswold, June 20, 1851, GA-17, NYL&T.

128. R. B. Dorsey to Dr. Beverly Wellford, December 23, 1848, Letter Book, BLIC.

129. R. B. Dorsey to H. Stagg, February 26, 1849, Letter Book, BLIC.

130. R. B. Dorsey to H. Stagg, February 26, 1849, to William H. Dorsey, March 30, 1849, to J. S. Cronise, November 22, 1849, and to Isaac Dillon, March 23, 1850, Letter Book, BLIC.

131. R. B. Dorsey to H. Stagg, May 2, 1850, Letter Book, BLIC.

132. Abbott, 50.

133. New York Life 1851 brochure: 20–21, HCR.

134. Albion Life advertisement, *New York Times,* January 16, 1852: 4; and Albion Life advertisement, *Insurance Gazette,* November 1855–April 1856.

135. British Commercial Life advertisement, *New York Times,* December 16, 1853: 7; and British Commercial Life advertisement, *Insurance Gazette,* November 1855–April 1856.

136. State Mutual Life advertisement, *Insurance Gazette,* November 1855–April 1856.

137. Howard Life advertisement, *New York Times,* November 1, 1854: 7; and Howard Life and Knickerbocker Life advertisements, *Insurance Gazette,* November 1855–April 1856.

138. "Statement of the Connecticut Mutual Life Insurance Company," *Insurance Gazette,* May–October 1859: 45.

139. "Life Insurance in California," *Insurance Monitor,* June 1869: 446.

140. *Rates and Proposals of the New-York Life Insurance and Trust,* 31.

141. Bard to John M. Mann, January 12, 1835, GA-4, NYL&T.

142. Bard to John M. Mann, February 10, 1835, GA-4, NYL&T.

143. Horatio N. Crabb to Donaldson, December 28, 1837, Correspondence 3, BLIC.

144. Walter Smith to Donaldson, January 28, 1841, Correspondence 6, BLIC.

145. Quoted in "Married or Single?" *Insurance Monitor,* November 1880: 587.

146. Quoted in "Married or Single?" *Insurance Monitor,* November 1880: 587. See also "Vital Statistics," *Ladies' Repository: A Monthly Periodical, Devoted to Literature, Arts, and Religion,* August 1867: 509.

147. Editorialists were quick to point out that members of the Church of Latter Day Saints could use this study to their advantage: "Polygamists are delighted with this discovery, and argue that if 1 wife can extend her husband's days 19½ years, 2 wives can prolong it 41 years, and so on. At this rate, Brigham Young, the Mormon prophet, will live for a thousand years to come." "Death Busy among the Bachelors," *Insurance Monitor,* August 1867.

148. Buley, *The American Life Convention,* 22.

149. "Notes on the Pennsylvania Life Assurance Company," Unbound Papers 1, MHL.

150. This conclusion is based on an examination of the policy books for each of these companies. Schedule of Insurance, FL-1, MHL; Register of Life Insurance, EB-1, NYL&T; and Policy Books 1831–55 and 1855–65, BLIC.

151. Bard to J. L. Starr, July 20, 1833, GA-3, NYL&T.

152. Donaldson to George Richards, March 29, 1837, Letter Book, BLIC.

153. Application 6, New England Mutual Life Insurance Company, Baker Library Historical Collections, Harvard Business School (hereafter NEMLIC).

154. Application 776, NEMLIC.

155. Girard Life 1837 brochure: 5, HCR.

156. Knapp, 93. See also "Proportionate Longevity of the Two Sexes," *Journal of Health. Conducted by an Association of Physicians,* October 26, 1831: 53–54.

157. Knapp, 89. See also "Relative Longevity of the Sexes," *Harper's New Monthly Magazine,* February 1874: 457–58.

158. Harvey Tuckett, *Practical Remarks on the Present State of Life Insurance in the United States. Showing the Evils which Exist, and Rules for Improvement* (Philadelphia: published by the author, 1851), 48.

159. National Life of Vermont 1856 brochure: 11, HCR.

160. Application 776, NEMLIC.

161. Application 1505, NEMLIC.

162. "Insurance of Women against Accident," *Insurance Monitor,* August 1869: 616.

163. "The New Experience Tables of Mortality," *Spectator,* August 1869: 80. See also Lucius Adams, actuary, letter to the editor, "Extra Rates for Female Lives," *Spectator,* July 1869: 18.

164. "Assurance of Women," *New York Times,* August 22, 1869: 3.

165. J. L. Halsey, Manhattan Life Insurance, to Elizur Wright, December 15, 1865, Letters, Elizur Wright Correspondence and Papers, Baker Library Historical Collections, Harvard Business School (hereafter WCP).

166. "May Women Insure?" *New York Times,* February 25, 1871: 8.

167. "May Women Insure?" *New York Times,* February 25, 1871: 8.

168. Without information on who was rejected for insurance, it is impossible to discern the rejection rate for women. However, the number of letters written to NYL&T, Massachusetts Hospital Life, and Baltimore Life suggests that the percentage of women writing for information on insuring their own lives was extremely small.

169. A. W. Kellogg, Northwestern Mutual Life, to Elizur Wright, January 31, 1866, Letters, WCP.

170. "Letter from our Special Correspondent," *Spectator,* October 1871: 349.

171. See Theodore M. Porter, *The Rise of Statistical Thinking, 1820–1900* (Princeton, NJ:: Princeton University Press, 1986), chapters 1–3; and Cohen, chapters 4–5.

Chapter Two · *Selecting Risks in an Anonymous World*

1. William Bard to Frederick Whittlesey, July 25, 1832, GA-2, NYL&T.

2. Bard to Pennsylvania Company, January 8, 1831, GA-1, NYL&T.

3. Bard to Frederick Whittlesey, July 25, 1832, GA-2, NYL&T.

4. Bard to Levi A. Ward Jr., July 25, 1832, GA-2, NYL&T.

5. Paul E. Johnson, *A Shopkeeper's Millennium: Society and Revivals in Rochester, New York, 1815–1837* (New York: Farrar, Straus & Giroux, 1978), 74; Joseph W. Barnes, "Rochester's Congressmen, Part I: 1789–1869," *Rochester History* 41 (July 1979): 13; and "Frederick Whittlesey," *American Political Leaders, 1789–2000* (Washington, DC: Congressional Quarterly Books, 2000), 322.

6. J. Owen Stalson, *Marketing Life Insurance: Its History in America* (Cambridge, MA: Harvard University Press, 1942), 103–25, 156. See also R. Carlyle Buley, *The American Life Convention, 1906-1952: A Study in the History of Life Insurance* (New York: Appleton-Century-Crofts, 1953), 48–50; and Viviana A. Rotman Zelizer, *Morals and Markets: The Development of Life Insurance in the United States* (New York: Columbia University Press, 1979), 17–18.

7. Bard to Frederick Whittlesey, July 25, 1832, GA-2, NYL&T.

8. Blake McKelvey, "Civil Medals Awarded Posthumously," *Rochester History* 22 (April 1960): 4; and Johnson, 65.

9. Blake McKelvey, "Rochester Mayors before the Civil War," *Rochester History* 26 (January 1964): 13.

10. GA-4, NYL&T.

11. *Life Insurance History, 1843–1910: Yearly Business of All Active United States Life Insurance Companies from Organization* (New York: Spectator Company, 1911), 84–85, 90–91; and Stalson, 791–95.

12. David Thompson to Charles Augustus Doelter, October 18, 1849, GA-16, NYL&T.

13. "Notes on the Pennsylvania Life Assurance Company," Unbound Papers 1, MHL; *Proposals of the Massachusetts Hospital Life Insurance Company, to Make Insurance on Lives, to Grant Annuities on Lives and in Trust, and Endowments for Children* (Boston: James Loring, 1835), 42; and Applications, BLIC.

14. *Rates and Proposals of the New-York Life Insurance and Trust Company, No. 38 Wall-Street, for Insurance on Lives, Granting Annuities, Receiving Money in Trust, and the Management of Trust Estates* (New York: Clayton and Van Norden, 1830), 31–32.

15. Hervé Bazin, *The Eradication of Smallpox: Edward Jenner and the First and Only Eradication of a Human Infectious Disease* (San Diego: Academic Press, 2000), 6.

16. Buley, *The American Life Convention*, 22; and Bard to J. B. LaForge, January 21, 1834, GA-4, NYL&T.

17. Bard to Levi Ward, September 21, 1833, to Bond Murdock, July 10, 1845, and to Henry Hayes, July 2, 1846, GA-3 and GA-13, NYL&T.

18. Bazin, 7, 40–41. Although doctors initially believed that vaccination provided lifelong immunity, they later discovered that periodic revaccination was necessary. Bazin, 80, 124; and Application 1219, NEMLIC.

19. Bard to W. C. Lord, July 21, 1845, GA-13, NYL&T.

20. Norbert Hirschhorn, "Was It Tuberculosis? Another Glimpse of Emily Dickinson's Health," *New England Quarterly* 72 (March 1999): 103–4; and "Diseased and Doubtful Lives," *Insurance Monitor*, November 1861: 252–53. It would not be until the 1880s—with the emergence of the germ theory of disease—that the medical community would identify the bacteria at the root of tuberculosis, positively demonstrating that consumption was actually an

infectious disease. But historians of the disease contend that even after this discovery, at the end of the nineteenth century "its hereditary, constitutional nature continued to be widely stressed." W. F. Bynum, *Science and the Practice of Medicine in the Nineteenth Century* (Cambridge: Cambridge University Press, 1994), 130.

21. Esmond R. Long, "The Decline of Tuberculosis as the Chief Cause of Death," *Proceedings of the American Philosophical Society* 92 (July 1948): 141; and Georgina D. Feldberg, *Disease and Class: Tuberculosis and the Shaping of Modern North American Society* (New Brunswick, NJ: Rutgers University Press, 1995), 11–12.

22. Bard to Gustavus A. Myers, October 10, 1834, GA-4, NYL&T. Bard's statistics match the results of a twentieth-century study done by Prudential Insurance Company of America on tuberculosis death rates in mid-nineteenth-century New York City. Long, 141; and Bard to Thomas C. Perkins, March 17, 1836, GA-5, NYL&T.

23. Mildred F. Stone, *Since 1845: A History of the Mutual Benefit Life Insurance Company* (New Brunswick, NJ: Rutgers University Press, 1957), 53.

24. United States Life of New York 1873 Annual Report: 22–23, HCR.

25. Stone, 23; Mazyck P. Ravenel, "The Warfare against Tuberculosis," *Proceedings of the American Philosophical Society* 42 (April 1903): 212; Bynum, 23, 130; Feldberg, 14; and Hirschhorn, 103–4.

26. Bard to Thomas C. Perkins, March 17, 1836, GA-5, NYL&T; to Alexis Ward, September 1, 1846, to Pelham W. Warren, September 8, 1846, and to David A. Noble, September 12, 1846, GA-14, NYL&T; and David Thompson to Sanford S. Smith, September 17, 1846, to Thomas T. Davis, December 28, 1846, and to Messieurs Baker and Millerd, February 25, 1847, GA-14, NYL&T.

27. Joseph Tilden to Eccles Gillender, August 14, 1839, and Moses L. Hale to George M. Weston, June 15, 1841, LA-2, MHL.

28. "Notes on the Pennsylvania Life Assurance Company," Unbound Papers 1, MHL; *Proposals of the Massachusetts Hospital Life*, 43; and Applications, BLIC.

29. Bard to Thomas C. Perkins, April 7, 1831, GA-1, and to Ira T. Eastman, February 7, 1832, GA-2, NYL&T.

30. Charles Little to George Carr Grundy, March 17, 1832, Correspondence 1, BLIC.

31. Bard to Mark W. Collet, April 3, 1832, GA-2, NYL&T.

32. Bard to Peter Lythoff, March 12, 1832, GA-2, NYL&T.

33. Stalson, 54, 103–25.

34. Application 6, NEMLIC.

35. Applications 6 and 1513, NEMLIC.

36. Jack S. Blocker Jr., *American Temperance Movements: Cycles of Reform* (Boston: Twayne, 1989), 10; and W. J. Rorabaugh, *The Alcoholic Republic: An American Tradition* (Oxford: Oxford University Press, 1981), 95–100, 232. See also Thomas R. Pegram, *Battling Demon Rum: The Struggle for a Dry America, 1800–1933* (Chicago: Ivan R. Dee, 1998); Ronald G. Walters, *American Reformers: 1815–1860* (New York: Hill and Wang, 1997), chapter 6; and Robert H. Abzug, *Cosmos Crumbling: American Reform and the Religious Imagination* (New York: Oxford University Press, 1994), chapter 4.

37. Benjamin Rush, *An Inquiry into the Effects of Ardent Spirits Upon the Human Body and Mind* (1784), quoted in Blocker, 7.

38. "Notes on the Pennsylvania Life Assurance Company," Unbound Papers 1, MHL; *Proposals of the Massachusetts Hospital Life,* 42; and Applications 1831–65, BLIC.

39. Application 1534, NEMLIC.

40. Bard to Dr. E. J. Marsh, December 31, 1831, GA-1, and to Levi Ward, July 25, 1832, GA-2, NYL&T.

41. Bard to Philip Viele, June 19, 1833, GA-3, NYL&T.

42. John J. Donaldson to J. S. Carson, October 17, 1837, Letter Book, BLIC.

43. Charles Little to George Carr Grundy, March 14, 1832, Correspondence 1, BLIC.

44. Lieutenant George Mason Hove, US Frigate *Columbia,* to Donaldson, February 5, 1842, Correspondence 7, BLIC.

45. Gaines M. Foster, *Moral Reconstruction: Christian Lobbyists and the Federal Legislation of Morality, 1865–1900* (Chapel Hill: University of North Carolina Press, 2002), 14.

46. Blocker, 13.

47. Johnson, 131.

48. Johnson, 79.

49. Robertson & Branda to Donaldson, March 24, 1842, Correspondence 7, BLIC.

50. American Temperance Life advertisement, *Portage County Democrat,* June 7, 1854: 4; and George Larkin Clark, *A History of Connecticut: Its People and Institutions* (New York: Knickerbocker, 1914), 410.

51. Eagle Life and Health advertisement, *New York Times,* September 1, 1852: 4.

52. Nathaniel Bowditch to Ulm [illegible], February 20, 1828, LA-1, MHL.

53. Francis C. Lowell to Samuel H. Mather, December 14, 1846, LA-3, MHL.

54. Samuel H. Mather to Joseph Tilden, September 1, 1846, LB-2, MHL.

55. Francis C. Lowell to Samuel H. Mather, September 7, 1846, LA-3, MHL.

56. MHL secretary to George Rivers, June 27, 1850, LA-4, MHL.

57. NYL&T to Peter Wainwright Jr., Provident Institution for Savings, February 29, 1840, GA-8, NYL&T.

58. These conclusions are based on biographical information on more than three-quarters of the approximately forty New Yorkers who served as life insurance agents for NYL&T during the 1830s and 1840s, as well as more than half of the agents representing the company outside of New York. The agents' names are found in GA-1, GA-2, and GA-3, NYL&T. Biographical information is primarily drawn from *American Political Leaders, 1789–2000* and *Biographical Directory of the American Congress, 1774 to 1961* (Washington, DC: Government Printing Office, 1961). Additional information comes from *American Biographical History of Eminent and Self-Made Men of the State of Michigan* (Cincinnati: Western Biographical Publishing, 1878), 53; Nathaniel Goodwin, *The Foote Family: Or, The Descendants of Nathaniel Foote* (Hartford: Case, Tiffany, 1849), 89; Horace W. Fuller, ed., *The Green Bag: A Useless but Entertaining Magazine for Lawyers* 3 (1891): 428; *Guide to the Archival Collections at the New York University Archives* (New York); *Guide to the Archival Collections at the Missouri Historical Society* (St. Louis); *Guide to the Archival Collections at the William L. Clements Library, The University of Michigan* (Ann Arbor); John P. Downs and Fenwick Y. Hedley, *History of Chautauqua County, New York, and its People* (New York: American Historical Society, 1921); Silas Farmer, *The History of Detroit and Michigan: Or, The Metropolis Illustrated: A Chronological Cyclopaedia of the Past and Present* (Detroit: Silas Farmer, 1884), 785, 865; Francis M. Thomp-

son, *History of Greenfield, Shire Town of Franklin County, Massachusetts* (Greenfield, MA: T. Morey and Son, 1904), 845; *History of Ontario County, NY* (1878), 38–39; George S. Conover, ed., *History of Ontario County, NY* (Syracuse, NY: D. Mason, 1893), 154–79; *History of Saratoga Springs, NY from our County and its People: A Descriptive and Biographical Record of Saratoga Springs, New York* (Boston, 1899); John H. Selkreg, *Landmarks of Tompkins County, New York* (New York: Mason, 1894); William L. Mackenzie, *The Lives and Opinions of Benj'n Franklin Butler, United States District Attorney for the Southern District of New York; and Jesse Hoyt, Counsellor at Law, formerly Collector of Customs for the Port of New York* (Boston: Cook, 1845), 32; and Theodore Corbett, *The Making of American Resorts: Saratoga Springs, Ballston Spa, Lake George* (New Brunswick, NJ: Rutgers University Press, 2001), 66.

59. NYL&T to Millard Fillmore, June 2, 1840, GA-8, NYL&T. Agents earned one dollar for each new policy (paid by the policyholder, in addition to the premium, upon *acceptance* of the application) plus 5% of all initial and subsequent premium payments. If the applicant needed to be examined by the agency physician, the one-dollar fee would be paid to the physician. David Thompson to A. L. Stimson, June 20, 1849, GA-16, NYL&T.

60. "Millard Fillmore" and "Nathan Kelsey Hall," *American Political Leaders, 1789–2000,* 15, 25, 158, 178.

61. "Erastus Corning," *American Political Leaders, 1789–2000,* 133.

62. Bard to Erastus Corning, December 24, 1832, GA-2, NYL&T.

63. Bard to H. Gates, June 21, 1833, GA-3, NYL&T.

64. Bard to B. Davis Noxen, February 26, 1833, GA-3, NYL&T.

65. Bard to Levi Ward, August 16, 1832, GA-2, and to H. Gates, June 21, 1833, GA-3, NYL&T.

66. Bard to Levi Ward, July 25, 1832, GA-2, NYL&T.

67. Bard to Peter Lythoff, February 25, 1832, and 16 March 1832, GA-2, NYL&T.

68. James H. Causten to Donaldson, April 6, 1833, Correspondence 1, BLIC.

69. James H. Causten, to Donaldson, January 7, 1835, Correspondence 1, BLIC.

70. Donaldson to James H. Causten, January 9, 1835, Letter Book, BLIC.

71. Bard to Levi A. Ward Jr., August 19, 1851, GA-17, NYL&T.

72. Bard to Levi A. Ward Jr., November 18, 1851, GA-17, NYL&T.

73. Note from Thomas A. Gold, June 8, 1846, Application 1192, NEMLIC.

74. Bard to John L. Starr, October 8, 1833, GA-3, NYL&T.

75. Bard to Thomas C. Perkins, March 17, 1836, GA-5, NYL&T.

76. Note from A. C. Robbins May 31, 1847, Application 1606, NEMLIC.

77. Dr. Beverly R. Wellford to Donaldson, January 6, 1835, Correspondence 1, BLIC.

78. Note from William H. Taylor, December 29, 1846, Application 1404, NEMLIC.

79. Note from Newton Fitch, August 18, 1847, Application 1720, NEMLIC.

80. Bynum, 51–52.

81. Application 1534, NEMLIC.

82. Bard to M. Collet, November 26, 1831, and to Dr. E. J. Marsh, December 24, 1831, GA-1, NYL&T.

83. Bard to Alexis Ward, September 1, 1846, to Pelham W. Warren, September 8, 1846, and to David A. Noble, September 12, 1846, GA-14, NYL&T; and David Thompson to

Sanford S. Smith, September 17, 1846, to Thomas T. Davis, December 28, 1846, and to Messieurs Baker and Millerd, February 25, 1847, GA-14, NYL&T.

84. Medical form from Robert Brae, M.D., March 1846, Application 1098, and from H. B. Smith, 28 April 1845 [*sic;* 1846], Applications 1143–57, NEMLIC. See also medical forms from Nathaniel B. Shurtlett, March 1853 [*sic;* 1846], Application 1050, and from Theodore Hillredge, M.D., February 22, 1849, Application 2499, NEMLIC.

85. Medical form from A. A. Hobert, M.D., February 25, 1853 [*sic;* 1846], Application 1021, and from Daniel Collins, November 25, 1848, Application 2264, NEMLIC.

86. Medical form from James Jackson, December 30, 1848, Application 2343, NEMLIC.

87. Bard to Francis H. Smith, November 28, 1838, GA-7, NYL&T.

88. Bard to Peter Lythoff, January 1, 1846, GA-13, NYL&T.

89. Bard to Messieurs Hale & Welbasky, June 3, 1846, GA-13, NYL&T.

90. Henry F. Thompson to John Darracott, February 26, 1855, Letter Book, BLIC.

91. Henry F. Thompson to John Darracott, February 26, 1855, Letter Book, BLIC.

92. Donaldson to John Darracott, May 3, 1856, Letter Book, BLIC.

93. Bard to Messrs. Delafield & Burnett, February 19, 1840, GA-8, and to William Weston, October 14, 1846, GA-14, NYL&T; David Thompson to Alexander James, March 3, 1847, GA-14, to Elijah Bond, February 15, 1849, GA-15, and to W. S. Simpson, September 6, 1850, GA-16, NYL&T; Tom Pinkney to Donaldson, January 28, 1834, Correspondence 1, BLIC; and Corydon H. Sutton to Baltimore Life, December 14, 1852, Correspondence 12, BLIC.

94. Donaldson to James H. Causten, November 28, 1838, Letter Book, BLIC.

95. James H. Causten to Donaldson, January 17, 1839, Correspondence 4, BLIC.

96. Donaldson to James H. Causten, January 21, 1839, Letter Book, BLIC.

97. Letter Book and Correspondence 9, BLIC.

98. Blocker, 12, 16, 21.

99. The extant New England Mutual records only contain the questionnaires for those applicants who were accepted. Thus none of the following respondents were denied coverage based on their answers to the temperance question. All responses are from policies issued between 1844 and 1850. Applications, NEMLIC.

100. Application 2090, NEMLIC.

101. Applications 2506 and 2264, NEMLIC.

102. Application 642, NEMLIC.

103. Application 2169, NEMLIC.

104. For a discussion of the debate over which drinks should be excluded from the temperate lifestyle, see Blocker, 21–23.

105. Application 292, NEMLIC.

106. Application 854, NEMLIC.

107. Walters, 149–50.

108. Application 451, NEMLIC.

109. Application 1098, NEMLIC.

110. Application 1656, NEMLIC.

111. Applications 1167 and 1857, NEMLIC.

112. Application 2343, NEMLIC.

113. Application 973, NEMLIC.

114. Applications 1194 and 1790, NEMLIC.

115. Applications 458 and 889, NEMLIC.

116. Application 1513, NEMLIC.

117. Application 200, NEMLIC.

118. United States Life of New York 1873 Annual Report: 36, HCR.

119. Stone, 53.

120. Application 1505, NEMLIC.

121. "Editor's Drawer," *Harper's New Monthly Magazine,* October 1856: 715.

122. Josh Billings, "Josh Billings Insures His Life," *Josh Billings, Hiz Sayings* (New York: Carleton, 1866), 15–16.

123. "The American Popular Life," *Insurance Monitor,* February 1867: 101.

124. James D. Norris, *R. G. Dun & Co., 1841–1900: The Development of Credit-Reporting in the Nineteenth Century* (Westport, CT: Greenwood, 1978), xv. See also Rowena Olegario, *A Culture of Credit: Embedding Trust and Transparency in American Business* (Cambridge, MA: Harvard University Press, 2006), 3, 38–39.

125. Olegario, 49.

126. Olegario, 52.

Chapter Three • Lying, Cheating, and Stealing versus The Court of Public Opinion

1. William Bard to Gardner Lawrence, July 13, 1836, GA-5, NYL&T.

2. Bard to Gardner Lawrence, July 13, 1836, GA-5, NYL&T.

3. James R. Lawrence referenced in Bard to B. Davis Noxen, October 4, 1836, GA-5, NYL&T.

4. Bard to James R. Lawrence, October 17, 1836, GA-5, NYL&T.

5. Bard to B. Davis Noxen, October 4, 1836, GA-5, NYL&T.

6. Insurance Policy 1 on John Minot, September 15, 1823, MHL. A similar clause was inserted in all early life insurance policies.

7. "Subrogation as Applied to Life Policies. Insurance for Suicides and Murders," *Insurance Monitor,* January 1872: 48–50.

8. David Jenkins and Takau Yoneyama, eds., *History of Insurance,* vol. 4, *Life* (London: Pickering & Chatto, 2000), 2.

9. L. B. Proctor, *Lives of Eminent Lawyers and Statesmen of the State of New York, with Notes of Cases Tried by Them, Speeches, Anecdotes, and Incidents in their Lives,* vol. 2 (New York: S. S. Peloubet, 1882), 672–91; and Bard to B. Davis Noxen, February 26, 1833, GA-3, NYL&T. While company records spell this lawyer's name "Noxen," several published references indicate that it may have been correctly spelled "Noxon."

10. Bard to B. Davis Noxen, October 4, 1836, GA-5, NYL&T.

11. Bard to James R. Lawrence, October 17, 1836, GA-5, NYL&T.

12. "Life Insurance," *Merchants' Magazine and Commercial Review,* March 1, 1840: 230; R. Carlyle Buley, *The American Life Convention, 1906–1952: A Study in the History of Life Insurance* (New York: Appleton-Century-Crofts, 1953), 18–19; and Geoffrey Clark, *Betting on*

Lives: The Culture of Life Insurance in England, 1695–1775 (Manchester: Manchester University Press, 1999), 1.

13. Tom Baker, "On the Genealogy of Moral Hazard," *Texas Law Review* (December 1996): 2.

14. Viviana A. Rotman Zelizer, *Morals and Markets: The Development of Life Insurance in the United States* (New York: Columbia University Press, 1979), 36–39; Buley, *The American Life Convention,* 18–19; Morton Keller, *The Life Insurance Enterprise, 1885–1910: A Study in the Limits of Corporate Power* (Cambridge, MA: Belknap, 1963), 4; "Life Insurance in the United States," *Hunt's Merchants' Magazine,* February 1843: 111, 114; and "What is Said Against Life Insurance by its Enemies," *United States Insurance Gazette and Magazine of Useful Knowledge,* April–October 1864: 73–74.

15. Buley, *The American Life Convention,* 18–19; Zelizer, 71; Keller, 4; and Jenkins and Yoneyama, 3.

16. "Life Insurance," *United States Magazine and Democratic Review,* November 1846: 360; and "Insurance: its History, Legal Philosophy, and Morals," *Hunt's Merchants' Magazine,* May 1849: 503.

17. *Deed of Constitution, and Articles and Regulations of the Scottish Widows' Fund and Life Assurance Society* (Edinburgh: Caledonian Mercury, 1814), 16.

18. "Life Insurance," *United States Magazine and Democratic Review,* November 1846: 360.

19. *Godsall v. Boldero* would be officially overturned in the 1855 case of *Dalby v. The India and London Life Assurance Company and St. John v. American Mutual Life Insurance Company. St. John v. American Mutual Life Insurance Company,* 13 N.Y. 31 (1855). See also *Loomis v. Eagle Life and Health Insurance Company,* 72 Mass. 396 (1856).

20. "Sale of British Life Policies," *Insurance Gazette,* April–October 1858: 151.

21. Baker, 7.

22. *An Address from the President and Directors of the Pennsylvania Company for Insurances on Lives and Granting Annuities, to the Inhabitants of the United States, upon the Subject of the Beneficial Objects of that Institution* (Philadelphia: J. Maxwell, 1814), 19.

23. *Prospectus of the Union Insurance Company, Incorporated by the State of New-York, for Making Insurance on Lives, and Granting Annuities* (New York: J. Seymour, 1818), 13; and "Life Insurance in the United States," *Hunt's Merchants' Magazine,* March 1843: 231–32.

24. *Rates and Proposals of the New-York Life Insurance and Trust Company, No. 38 Wall-Street, for Insurance on Lives, Granting Annuities, Receiving Money in Trust, and the Management of Trust Estates* (New York: Clayton & Van Norden, 1830), 17.

25. Nathaniel Bowditch to Thos C. Perkins, April 11, 1831, LA-1, MHL.

26. Bard to Philip Viele, February 19, 1833, GA-3, NYL&T.

27. Bard to J. B. LaForge, September 10, 1834, GA-4, NYL&T.

28. James H. Causten to John J. Donaldson, January 17, 1839, Correspondence 4, BLIC.

29. *Trenton Mutual Life and Fire Insurance Company v. Johnson,* 24 N.J.L. 576 (1854).

30. *Loomis v. Eagle Life and Health* (1856).

31. *Coon v. Swan and Meeker,* 30 Vt. 6 (1856).

32. *Ruse v. Mutual Benefit Life Insurance Company,* 23 N.Y. 516 (1861).

33. "Life Insurance," *United States Magazine and Democratic Review,* November 1846: 360.

34. "Illustrations of Life Insurance," *Hunt's Merchants' Magazine,* October 1846: 424.

35. Bard to J. L. McHenna, July 17, 1830, GA-1, NYL&T.

36. Bard to P. Lythoff, February 3, 1832, GA-2, NYL&T.

37. Bard to P. Lythoff, June 6, 1833, GA-3, NYL&T. See also Bard to James Foley, August 16, 1834, GA-4, and to Henry White, January 25, 1836, GA-5, NYL&T.

38. Bard to J. L. McHenna, October 15, 1830, GA-1, NYL&T.

39. GHH to John T. Coffin, August 25, 1837, LA-2, MHL; and *Lord v. Dall,* 12 Mass. 115 (1815).

40. Bowditch to R. H. Coming, July 18, 1828, LA-1, MHL.

41. *St. John v. American Mutual Life* (1855).

42. *Mutual Life Insurance Company v. Allen & another,* 138 Mass. 24 (1884).

43. Roy Kreitner, *Calculating Promises: The Emergence of Modern American Contract Doctrine* (Stanford, CA: Stanford University Press, 2007), chapter 8.

44. Insurance Policy 1 on John Minot, September 15, 1823, MHL. See also *Rates and Proposals of the New-York Life Insurance and Trust Company,* 31–33.

45. "Life Insurance—Caution," *Christian Advocate and Journal,* November 22, 1849: 186.

46. "Heartless Injustice to the Widow and Orphan by a Life Insurance Company," *Insurance Monitor,* August 1867: 477.

47. Harvey Tuckett, *Practical Remarks on the Present State of Life Insurance in the United States. Showing the Evils which Exist, and Rules for Improvement* (Philadelphia: published by the author, 1851), 28–29.

48. Tuckett, 21.

49. "Life Insurance Companies," *Christian Watchman and Christian Reflector,* November 28, 1850: 191.

50. "Novel Life Insurance Case," *Hunt's Merchants' Magazine,* October 1857: 494–95.

51. See *Monk v. The Union Mutual Life Insurance Company,* in "Life Insurance. Fraudulent Representations," *Insurance Monitor,* May 1869: 386–87.

52. See *M. E. Kibbe, Administratrix, v. Berkshire Life Insurance Company,* in "Insurance Legal Decision. Life Insurance—Important Case," *Insurance Gazette,* November 1861–April 1862: 45–47; and *Smith v. Aetna Life Insurance Company,* 49 N.Y. 211 (1872), in "Warranty in Life Insurance," *Insurance Monitor,* July 1872: 602.

53. "Union Mutual Life Insurance Company of Maine," *Insurance Gazette,* November 1858–April 1859: 331.

54. "Union Mutual Life Insurance Company of Maine," *Insurance Gazette,* November 1858–April 1859: 331.

55. "Union Mutual Life Insurance Co.—Fraudulent Representations," *Insurance Monitor,* February 1869: 118.

56. "Life Insurance," *North American Review,* October 1863: 320.

57. "The Forfeiture of Tweed's Life Insurance," *Insurance Monitor,* July 1879: 334.

58. "Mr. Comstock's Habits," *New York Times,* October 19, 1883: 3; "E. G. Comstock's Life Insurance," *New York Times,* October 23, 1883: 8; and Samuel Breancer to Henry B. Hyde, June 30, 1885, ELAS-New York: 1885–86, Hyde Collection (Equitable Life Assurance Society), Baker Library Historical Collections, Harvard Business School.

59. "Barrett vs. The Conn. Mutual Life. Counsel's Statement of the Case," *Insurance Monitor Supplement,* October 1869: 852.

60. Tamara Plakins Thornton, "'A Great Machine' or a 'Beast of Prey': A Boston Corporation and Its Rural Debtors in an Age of Capitalist Transformation," *Journal of the Early Republic* (Winter 2007): 573–80.

61. *Proposals of the Massachusetts Hospital Life Insurance Company, to Make Insurance on Lives, to Grant Annuities on Lives and in Trust, and Endowments for Children* (Boston: James Loring, 1835), 7–8.

62. "American Life Insurance Companies Opposed to Granting 'Days of Grace,'" *Insurance Gazette*, April–November 1858: 95.

63. "The United States Life Insurance Company of New York—the Withdrawal of the Plea in the Contested Suit," *Insurance Gazette*, November 1858–April 1859: 324–26.

64. "Life Insurance—Caution," *Christian Advocate and Journal*, November 22, 1849: 186.

65. See, for example, Edward J. Balleisen, *Navigating Failure: Bankruptcy and Commercial Society in Antebellum America* (Chapel Hill: University of North Carolina Press, 2001), 124–30; Bruce Mann, *Republic of Debtors: Bankruptcy in the Age of American Independence* (Cambridge, MA: Harvard University Press, 2002), 258–63; and Scott A. Sandage, *Born Losers: A History of Failure in America* (Cambridge, MA: Harvard University Press, 2005), 35–39.

66. Albion Life 1845 brochure: 4, HCR.

67. Tuckett, 53.

68. *Life Insurance: Its Principles, Operations and Benefits, as presented by the North Carolina Mutual Life Insurance Company* (Raleigh: Seaton Gales, 1849), 15–16.

69. "American Life Insurance Companies Opposed to Granting 'Days of Grace,'" *Insurance Gazette*, April–November 1858: 92–103.

70. Girard Life 1860 brochure: 4, 7, HCR.

71. J. Owen Stalson, *Marketing Life Insurance: Its History in America* (Cambridge, MA: Harvard University Press, 1942), 501.

72. Insurance Policy 1 on John Minot, September 15, 1823, MHL. See also *Hartman v. Keystone Insurance Company*, 21 Pa. 466 (1853).

73. J. B. Lewis and C. C. Bombaugh, *Remarkable Stratagems and Conspiracies: An Authentic Record of Surprising Attempts to Defraud Life Insurance Companies* (New York: G. W. Carleton, 1878), 360–61.

74. *Breasted et al., Admrs, etc. v. Farmers' Loan and Trust Company*, 4 Hill 73 (1843). See also "Life Assurance," *Atlantic Monthly*, September 1866: 310–11.

75. "Suicide, when does it Vitiate a Policy of Life Insurance?" *Boston Medical and Surgical Journal*, February 18, 1846: 68.

76. "Suicide and Dueling," *Insurance Monitor*, July 1869: 529; and "Life Assurance," *Atlantic Monthly*, September 1866: 310–11.

77. "Suicide Insurance," *Insurance Monitor*, July 1869: 531.

78. "The Suicide Clause," *Insurance Monitor*, March 1872: 216.

79. *Mutual Life Insurance Company v. Terry*, 82 U.S. 580 (1872). See also "The Suicide Clause," *Insurance Monitor*, March 1872: 216.

80. "Another Case of Suicide Lost by the Company," *Insurance Monitor*, July 1872: 574.

81. *New York Times*, November 7, 1883: 4.

82. "The Suicide Clause," *Insurance Monitor*, March 1872: 216; and *Bigelow v. Berkshire Life Insurance Company*, 93 U.S. 284 (1876).

83. *Bigelow v. Berkshire Life* (1876).

84. "The Mutual Benefit Life Insurance Association," *Insurance Gazette,* November 1859–April 1860.

85. "The National Life Insurance Company," *Insurance Monitor,* January 1872: 21.

86. "The Great Western Mutual Life Insurance Company," *Insurance Monitor,* February 1869: 96. See also "National Travelers Insurance Company," *Insurance Monitor,* June 1867: 345.

87. "North American Life Insurance Company," *Insurance Gazette,* April–November 1864.

88. "Attempt to Swindle a Life Insurance Company," *Insurance Monitor,* January 1867: 36; "The Chicago Life Ins. Swindle," *Insurance Monitor,* March 1867: 161; "Insurance Items," *Insurance Monitor,* July 1867: 395; and "Another Life Insurance Fraud," *Insurance Monitor,* March 1869: 209.

89. "Insurance Items," *Insurance Monitor,* August 1867: 488; "A Philadelphia Life Ins. Fraud. A Singular Story," *Insurance Monitor,* October 1867: 620; and "Life Insurance Fraud," *Insurance Monitor,* February 1869: 123.

90. "Graveyard Insurance. Fraudulent Practices in Operation In Massachusetts," *New York Times,* December 11, 1883: 5; "The Graveyard Insurances. Additional Facts Come to Light in Fall River," *New York Times,* December 13, 1883: 5; John N. Reynolds, *The Twin Hells: A Thrilling Narrative of Life in the Kansas and Missouri Penitentiaries* (Chicago: M. A. Donohue, 1890), 175–76; and "Hillmon Tells his Story: The Murderer Found in the Mountains of Utah," *New York Times,* January 2, 1894: 1.

91. Quoted in Peter Karsten, *Heart versus Head: Judge-Made Law in Nineteenth-Century America* (Chapel Hill: University of North Carolina Press, 1997), 272.

92. Quoted in Valerie P. Hans and Neil Vidmar, *Judging the Jury* (New York: Plenum, 1987), 131.

93. James W. Ely Jr., *Railroads and American Law* (Lawrence: University Press of Kansas, 2002), 124, 216, 221.

Chapter Four • The Public Interest in a Private Industry

1. "The Absconding Secretary of the Trust Company," *Brother Jonathan. A Weekly Compend of Belles Lettres and the Fine Arts, Standard Literature, and General Intelligence,* January 7, 1843: 4.

2. William Bard to George Atkinson, July 13, 1841, GA-9, NYL&T.

3. "The Absconding Secretary."

4. "The Absconding Secretary."

5. Bard to Reuben Walworth, December 24, 1842, and December 26, 1842, GA-11, NYL&T.

6. Bard to Reuben Walworth, December 24, 1842, GA-11, NYL&T.

7. Bard to Reuben Walworth, December 24 and 26, 1842, and January 3, 1843, GA-11, NYL&T.

8. Bard to Reuben Walworth, December 26, 1842, and January 3, 1843, GA-11, and Stephen Allen to Magniac Jardine & Co., January 26, 1843, GA-11, NYL&T.

9. Stephen Allen to Reuben Walworth, January 21, 1843, GA-11, NYL&T.

10. Series of letters to borrowers of NYL&T, January 10, 1843, GA-11, NYL&T.

11. Stephen Allen to Editors of the *Commercial Advertiser, Evening Post, NY Express, Sun Newspaper, Albany Argus, Albany Evening Journal, National Intelligencer, Globe,* and *Madisonian,* January 25, 1843, GA-11, NYL&T.

12. Stephen Allen to Francis W. Edmunds, May 11, 1843, GA-11, NYL&T.

13. "The Absconding Secretary."

14. "Money Market," *New York Herald,* January 6, 1843: 3.

15. Stephen Allen to Magniac Jardine & Co., February 13, 1843, GA-11, NYL&T.

16. Spencer L. Kimball, *Insurance and Public Policy: A Study in the Legal Implementation of Social and Economic Public Policy, Based on Wisconsin Records, 1835–1959* (Madison: University of Wisconsin Press, 1960), 260–62. See also Kimball, 304–5.

17. "An Act to Incorporate the New-York Life Insurance and Trust Company," in *Rates and Proposals of the New-York Life Insurance and Trust Company, No. 38 Wall-Street, for Insurance on Lives, Granting Annuities, Receiving Money in Trust, and the Management of Trust Estates* (New York: Clayton & Van Norden, 1830), 4.

18. "An Act to Incorporate the New-York Life," 7–8.

19. Bard to Reuben Walworth, December 26, 1842, GA-11, NYL&T.

20. Bard to Reuben Walworth, January 3, 1843, GA-11, NYL&T.

21. See Charles W. McCurdy, "Justice Field and the Jurisprudence of Government-Business Relations: Some Parameters of Laissez-Faire Constitutionalism, 1863–1897," *Journal of American History* (March 1975): 970–1005.

22. "Life Insurance," *Hallowell Gazette,* August 2, 1826: 2.

23. "Life Insurance," *Hunt's Merchants' Magazine,* March 1840: 240.

24. Bard to Reuben Walworth, December 26, 1842, GA-11, NYL&T.

25. Stephen Allen to Reuben Walworth, January 21, 1843, GA-11, NYL&T.

26. William J. Novak, *The People's Welfare: Law and Regulation in Nineteenth-Century America* (Chapel Hill: University of North Carolina Press, 1996), 106. See also Ronald E. Seavoy, *The Origins of the American Business Corporation, 1784–1855: Broadening the Concept of Public Service During Industrialization* (Westport, CT: Greenwood, 1982), 4.

27. See Edmund W. Kitch, "Regulation and the American Common Market," in A. Dan Tarlock, ed., *Regulation, Federalism, and Interstate Commerce* (Cambridge, MA: Oelgeschlager, Gunn & Hain, 1981), 24–25; and Herbert Hovenkamp, *Enterprise and American Law, 1836–1937* (Cambridge, MA: Harvard University Press, 1991), 42–48.

28. "An Act to incorporate the Pennsylvania Company," in *An Address from the President and Directors of the Pennsylvania Company for Insurances on Lives and Granting Annuities, to the Inhabitants of the United States, upon the Subject of the Beneficial Objects of that Institution* (Philadelphia: J. Maxwell, 1814), 38.

29. Seavoy, 4.

30. James Willard Hurst, *Law and the Conditions of Freedom in the Nineteenth-Century United States* (Madison: University of Wisconsin Press, 1956), 17.

31. "An Act to incorporate The Massachusetts Hospital Life Insurance Company," in *Proposals of the Massachusetts Hospital Life Insurance Company, to Make Insurance on Lives, to Grant Annuities on Lives and in Trust, and Endowments for Children* (Boston: James Loring, 1835), 30.

32. Hovenkamp, 49–51.

33. "An Act to Incorporate the Baltimore Life Insurance Company," in Jerry M. Hynson, *Genealogical Abstractions from the Baltimore Life Insurance Company* (Westminster, MD: Willow Bend & Heritage Books, 2004), 110.

34. "An Act to Incorporate the New-York Life," 3, and "An Act to Incorporate the Mutual Life Insurance Company of New York," in Mutual Life of New York 1848 brochure: 34, HCR.

35. Hovenkamp, 20.

36. Hovenkamp, 27.

37. "An Act to incorporate the Pennsylvania Company," 45.

38. "An Act to Incorporate the New-York Life," 8; and "An Act to Incorporate the Mutual Life," 36.

39. "An Act to Incorporate the Baltimore Life," 111–12.

40. "An Act to Incorporate a Mutual Life Insurance Company in the State of North Carolina," in *Life Insurance: Its Principles, Operations and Benefits, as presented by the North Carolina Mutual Life Insurance Company* (Raleigh: Seaton Gales, 1849), 21.

41. "An Act to Incorporate the Ohio Life Insurance and Trust Company," in Ohio Life and Trust 1835 brochure: 11–12, HCR.

42. *Massachusetts General Hospital v. State Mutual Life Assurance Company of Worcester,* 70 Mass. 227 (1855).

43. Legislatures and courts often depicted railroads in a similar fashion, referring to them as "a public work" or "public highways" to be used "for accomplishment of a well defined public object." The railroads often exploited this understanding as justification for privileges such as eminent domain. See James W. Ely Jr., *Railroads and American Law* (Lawrence: University Press of Kansas, 2002), 17, 35–26.

44. "An Act to incorporate the Pennsylvania Company," 45.

45. "An Act to incorporate The Massachusetts Hospital Life," 31. See also "An Act to incorporate the Pennsylvania Company," 43.

46. "An Act to Incorporate the Ohio Life," 9. See also "An Act to Incorporate the New-York Life," 7.

47. "An Act to Incorporate the Baltimore Life," 109.

48. "An Act to Incorporate the New-York Life," 8; and "An Act to incorporate the Pennsylvania Company," 43–44.

49. "An Act to Incorporate the Baltimore Life," 109. See also "An Act to incorporate The Massachusetts Hospital Life," 31–32.

50. "An Act to Incorporate the Ohio Life," 11.

51. Bruce Michael Pritchett has conducted the most complete study of life insurance investment portfolios, although his study does not include any data prior to 1843. See Bruce Michael Pritchett, *A Study of Capital Mobilization: The Life Insurance Industry of the Nineteenth Century* (New York: Arno, 1977); and Bruce Michael Pritchett, *Financing Growth: A Financial History of American Life Insurance through 1900* (Philadelphia: S. S. Huebner Foundation for Insurance Education, 1985).

52. Gerald T. White, *A History of the Massachusetts Hospital Life Insurance Company* (Cambridge, MA: Harvard University Press, 1955), 2–3.

53. "An Act to incorporate The Massachusetts Hospital Life," 32.

54. "An Act to incorporate The Massachusetts Hospital Life," 35–36.

55. Abram T. Collier, *A Capital Ship, New England Life: A History of America's First Chartered Mutual Life Insurance Company, 1835–1985* (Boston: New England Mutual Life Insurance Company, 1985), 19–21; and *Massachusetts General Hospital v. State Mutual Life* (1855).

56. *Massachusetts General Hospital v. State Mutual Life* (1855).

57. *Massachusetts General Hospital v. State Mutual Life* (1855).

58. "The Eleventh Annual Report of the State Mutual Life Assurance Co., of Worcester, Mass.," *United States Insurance Gazette and Magazine of Useful Knowledge,* November 1857–April 1858: 102–3.

59. "An Act to Incorporate the Ohio Life," 4–5.

60. "An Act to incorporate The Massachusetts Hospital Life," 32–33.

61. "An Act to Incorporate the Baltimore Life," 110.

62. "An Act to Incorporate the Ohio Life," 11.

63. William Bard, *A Letter to David E. Evans, Esquire, of Batavia, on Life Insurance* (New York: William Van Norden, 1832), 17.

64. Mutual Life of New York 1845 brochure: 29–30, HCR. See also New England Mutual Life brochure: 3, HCR.

65. Mutual Life of New York 1845 brochure: 29–30, and Mutual Life of New York 1847 brochure: 14, HCR. For similar statements, see also New England Mutual Life brochure: 3, HCR; and *Life Insurance: Its Principles, Operations and Benefits, as presented by the Connecticut Mutual Life Insurance Company of Hartford* (Hartford: Case, Tiffany & Burnham, 1846), 6.

66. Nautilus Insurance brochure: 12–13, HCR.

67. New York Life 1858 brochure: 6, HCR.

68. The high point of state regulatory power came in the 1870s and 1880s. Hovenkamp, 126–30.

69. Bard to E. A. Welbasky, September 23, 1840, GA-9, NYL&T.

70. Bard to E. A. Welbasky, September 23, 1840, GA-9, NYL&T.

71. Agents Records, NYL&T.

72. Blakely & Mitchel to John J. Donaldson, December 20, 1844, Correspondence 8, BLIC; and J. Owen Stalson, *Marketing Life Insurance: Its History in America* (Cambridge, MA: Harvard University Press, 1942), 298–99.

73. John J. Myers, North American Insurance, to Donaldson, March 24, 1840, Correspondence 5, BLIC.

74. Donaldson to John Myers, North American Insurance, March 28, 1840, Letter Books, BLIC.

75. Donaldson to Messrs Blakely & Mitchel, December 3, 1844, Letter Books, BLIC.

76. Blakely & Mitchel to Donaldson, December 20, 1844, Correspondence 8, BLIC.

77. Stalson, 299. Licensing fees were a common regulatory tool employed by state and local governments wishing to maintain control of the economic activity within their jurisdictions. See Novak, *The People's Welfare,* 90–94.

78. C. H. Baldwin to Donaldson, May 14, 1842, Correspondence 7, BLIC.

79. Donaldson to R. Ritchie, April 19, 1842, and to Dr. D. M. Little, June 14, 1842, Letter Books, and C. H. Baldwin to Donaldson, May 14, 1842, Correspondence 7, BLIC.

80. Dr. Beverly R. Wellford to Donaldson, May 18, 1843, Correspondence 8, BLIC.

81. Baltimore Life Office to Dr. Beverly R. Wellford, March 22, 1853, Letter Books, BLIC.

82. J. S. Wellford to Donaldson, November 4, 1854, Correspondence 12, BLIC.

83. Donaldson to R. Ritchie, April 19, 1842, Letter Books, BLIC.

84. Donaldson to Charles L. Mosby, December 13, 1842, Letter Books, BLIC.

85. E. H. Williamson to Donaldson, October 26, 1844, Correspondence 8, BLIC.

86. E. H. Williamson to Donaldson, April 9, 1845, Correspondence 9, BLIC.

87. W. E. Hinton to Donaldson, April 15, 1845, Correspondence 9, BLIC.

88. Agents Records, NYL&T.

89. D. Thompson to Richard Riches, February 11, 1851, GA-17, NYL&T.

90. John M. Speed to Donaldson, January 20, 1847, Correspondence 10, BLIC.

91. Donaldson to Dr. Thomas Pollard, December 3, 1853, Letter Book, and Pollard to Baltimore Life Office, December 23, 1853, Correspondence 12, BLIC.

92. Dr. Thomas Pollard to Donaldson, December 23, 1853, Correspondence 12, BLIC.

93. Dr. Thomas Pollard to Donaldson, October 23, 1854, Correspondence 12, BLIC.

94. Dr. Thomas Pollard to Donaldson, October 23, 1854, Correspondence 12, BLIC.

95. J. S. Wellford to Baltimore Life Office, March 29, 1856, Correspondence 13, BLIC; and "Of Foreign Life Insurance Companies in Virginia," *Hunt's Merchants' Magazine*, June 1856: 736–37.

96. "Vermont Insurance Law," *Insurance Gazette*, November 1859–April 1860: 10–15; and "Maryland Insurance Law," *Hunt's Merchants' Magazine*, December 1858: 743–45.

97. "Maryland Insurance Law," *Hunt's Merchants' Magazine*, December 1858: 743–45.

98. "Maryland Insurance Law," *Hunt's Merchants' Magazine*, December 1858: 743–45.

99. "Pennsylvania Insurance Law," *Hunt's Merchants' Magazine*, June 1859: 738.

100. "Foreign Insurance Companies," *Insurance Gazette*, November 1855–April 1856: 171–72.

101. This argument was not unique to the insurance industry. In some states, the quasi-public status of railroads exempted them from the payment of taxes, an exemption upheld by the courts. For example, see Chief Justice Lemuel Shaw's decision in the Massachusetts case of *Inhabitants of Worcester v. Western Rail Road Corporation* (1842), in Ely, 34.

102. "Eighth Annual Statement of the Directors of the Union Mutual Life Insurance Company of Maine," *Insurance Gazette*, November 1857–April 1858: 347.

103. "Taxing Life Insurance Companies," *Hunt's Merchants' Magazine*, June 1, 1862: 566.

104. "The Cincinnati Price Current on Life Insurance," *Hunt's Merchants' Magazine*, September 1851: 390–91.

105. "Incorporation of Insurance Companies in New York," *Hunt's Merchants' Magazine*, August 1849: 225–29.

106. "The New Life Insurance Law of New York," *Hunt's Merchants' Magazine*, June 1851: 755–57.

107. Stalson, 302.

108. "An Act to Incorporate the Ohio Life," 9. See also "An Act to Incorporate the New-York Life," 7.

109. "An Act to Incorporate the Mutual Life," 35.

110. Bard to Philo C. Fuller, May 2, 1851, GA-17, NYL&T.

111. Bard to Philo C. Fuller, May 2, 1851, GA-17, NYL&T.

112. David Thompson to Philo C. Fuller, July 17 and 28, 1851, GA-17, NYL&T.

113. Lucian Bisbee to Richard B. Dorsey, January 31, 1852, Correspondence 11, BLIC.

114. Kenneth J. Meier, *The Political Economy of Regulation: The Case of Insurance* (Albany: State University of New York Press, 1988), 61.

115. "The Proposed Insurance Law for the State of Ohio," *Insurance Gazette,* November 1858–April 1859: 379.

116. *North Carolina Mutual Life,* 6.

117. *Charter and Bylaws of the Virginia Life Insurance Company* (Richmond, VA: H. K. Ellyson, 1860), 7.

118. "An Act Concerning Foreign Insurance Companies," in Gilbert Eggleson Currie, ed., *The United States Insurance Almanac* 1856 (New York: G. E. Currie, 1856), 68.

119. Kimball, 265. See also Harry N. Scheiber, "Federalism and the American Economic Order, 1789–1910," *Law and Society Review* 10 (1975): 114–15.

120. "The Eleventh Annual Report of the State Mutual Life Assurance Co., of Worcester, Mass.," *Insurance Gazette,* November 1857–April 1858: 102–3.

121. William J. Novak, "The American Law of Association: The Legal-Political Construction of Civil Society," *Studies in American Political Development* 15 (2001): 182.

122. Novak, *The People's Welfare,* 9.

Chapter Five • Protecting Women and Children "in the hour of their distress"

1. New York Life 1858 brochure: 19, HCR.

2. James M. Hudnut, *Semi-Centennial History of the New-York Life Insurance Company, 1845–1895* (New York: New York Life Insurance Company, 1895), 1–3.

3. Anne M. Boylan, "Women in Groups: An Analysis of Women's Benevolent Organizations in New York and Boston, 1797–1840," *Journal of American History* (December 1984): 504–5; "Fatherless and Widows' Society," *Boston Recorder,* October 19, 1838: 167; "Boston Fatherless and Widows' Society," *Boston Recorder,* October 30, 1840: 173; and "Fatherless and Widows' Society, Boston," *Christian Inquirer,* November 3, 1849: 2.

4. "The Hospital Life Insurance Company," *Boston Daily Advertiser,* December 6, 1823: 2.

5. "Life Insurance," *Waldie's Literary Omnibus,* April 7, 1837: 8.

6. "Life Insurances," *Poulson's American Daily Advertiser,* October 14, 1816: 3.

7. "Life Insurance," *Poulson's American Daily Advertiser,* November 30, 1819: 3.

8. *An Address from the President and Directors of the Pennsylvania Company for Insurances on Lives and Granting Annuities, to the Inhabitants of the United States, upon the Subject of the Beneficial Objects of that Institution* (Philadelphia: J. Maxwell, 1814), 7.

9. "Life Insurance, &c.," *Commercial Advertiser,* April 14, 1818: 3.

10. Norma Basch, *In the Eyes of the Law: Women, Marriage, and Property in Nineteenth-Century New York* (Ithaca, NY: Cornell University Press, 1982), 97, 104–5; Marylynn Salmon, *Women and the Law of Property in Early America* (Chapel Hill: University of North Carolina Press, 1986), 16, 76; Elizabeth Bowles Warbasse, *The Changing Legal Rights of Married Women, 1800–1861* (New York: Garland, 1987), 10; Joan M. Jensen, *Loosening the Bonds: Mid-Atlantic Farm Women, 1750–1850* (New Haven, CT: Yale University Press, 1986), 19, 141; Christopher Clark, *The Roots of Rural Capitalism: Western Massachusetts, 1780–1860* (Ithaca, NY: Cornell University Press, 1990), 87; Nancy Grey Osterud, *Bonds of Community: The Lives of Farm*

Women in Nineteenth-Century New York (Ithaca, NY: Cornell University Press, 1991), 1–2, 58–65, 134, 167, 277; and Jack Larkin, *The Reshaping of Everyday Life: 1790–1840* (New York: Harper & Row, 1988), 13. For more information on the evolution of the right of dower, see Salmon, chapter 7.

11. Larkin, 13.

12. Shawn Johansen, *Family Men: Middle-Class Fatherhood in Early Industrializing America* (New York: Routledge, 2001), 23–24.

13. Johansen, 23–24; Bruce Dorsey, *Reforming Men and Women: Gender in the Antebellum City* (Ithaca, NY: Cornell University Press, 2002), 75–76, 85–87; Mary P. Ryan, *Cradle of the Middle Class: The Family in Oneida County, New York, 1790–1865* (Cambridge: Cambridge University Press, 1981), 223–24; Amy Gilman, "From Widowhood to Wickedness: The Politics of Class and Gender in New York City Private Charity, 1799–1860," *History of Education Quarterly* 24 (1984): 61; Mary P. Ryan, *Womanhood in America: From Colonial Times to the Present* (New York: Franklin Watts, 1983), 81–82; and Catherine Kelly, "Gender and Class Formations in the Antebellum North," in Nancy A. Hewitt, ed., *A Companion to American Women's History* (Oxford: Blackwell, 2002), 106.

14. Stephen M. Frank, *Life with Father: Parenthood and Masculinity in the Nineteenth-Century American North* (Baltimore: Johns Hopkins University Press, 1998), 153.

15. Ryan, *Womanhood in America,* 110.

16. Annual Report of the Association for Improving the Condition of the Poor (1852), 20–21, quoted in Gilman, 61.

17. "Life Insurance," *Episcopal Reader,* January 2, 1848: 178. See also "Boston Equitable Life Insurance Society," *Boston Medical and Surgical Journal,* August 3, 1842: 416.

18. "Life Insurance," *Merchants' Magazine and Commercial Review,* March 1, 1840: 230.

19. See Scott A. Sandage, *Born Losers: A History of Failure in America* (Cambridge, MA: Harvard University Press, 2005), 249.

20. Nautilus Insurance 1848 brochure: 14, HCR.

21. William Bard to David E. Evans, November 30, 1832, to E. Croswell, November 29, 1832, to Erastus Corning, December 24, 1832, to James Hillhouse, January 10, 1833, and to Ebenezar Seely, January 12, 1833, GA-2 and GA-3, NYL&T.

22. For example, see "Life Insurance," *Vermont State Paper,* August 11, 1835: 1; and "A Letter on Life Insurance," *National Banner and Nashville Whig,* September 14, 1836: 2.

23. William Bard, *A Letter to David E. Evans, Esquire, of Batavia, on Life Insurance* (New York: William Van Norden, 1832), 11.

24. Bard, *A Letter to David E. Evans,* 5.

25. "Proposals and Rates of the Baltimore Life Insurance Company," Baltimore Life 1831 brochure: 6, Historical Society of Pennsylvania; and Ohio Life 1835 brochure: 7, HCR.

26. Girard Life 1837 brochure: 7, HCR.

27. Mutual Life of New York 1846 brochure: 8–9, and Nautilus Insurance 1848 brochure: 26–30, HCR; *Life Insurance: Its Principles, Operations and Benefits, as presented by the Connecticut Mutual Life Insurance Company of Hartford* (Hartford: Case, Tiffany & Burnham, 1846), 23–24; and *Life Insurance: Its Principles, Operations and Benefits, as presented by the North Carolina Mutual Life Insurance Company* (Raleigh: Seaton Gales, 1849), 25–26.

28. Bard, *A Letter to David E. Evans,* 5–6; *Proposals of the Pennsylvania Company for Insur-*

ances on Lives and Granting Annuities (Philadelphia: James Kay, Jun. & Brothers, 1837), 7; and Girard Life 1837 brochure: 7–8, HCR.

29. Quoted in Stuart M. Blumin, *The Emergence of the Middle Class: Social Experience in the American City, 1760–1900* (New York: Cambridge University Press, 1989), 1.

30. Bard, *A Letter to David E. Evans,* 14; and New York Life 1851 brochure: 19, HCR.

31. Connecticut Mutual Life 1851 brochure: 8, HCR.

32. Ohio Life 1835 brochure: 7, HCR.

33. Bard, *A Letter to David E. Evans,* 6; and Girard Life 1837 brochure: 8, HCR.

34. Bard, *A Letter to David E. Evans,* 12.

35. New England Mutual Life 1846 brochure: 4, HCR.

36. New York Life 1858 brochure: 12, 18, HCR.

37. Horace O. Allen to John J. Donaldson, March 28, 1834, Correspondence 1, BLIC.

38. A. B. Spooner to George Carr Grundy, January 28, 1832, Correspondence 1, BLIC.

39. John O. Lay to George Carr Grundy, May 25, 1833, Correspondence 1, BLIC.

40. See Edward J. Balleisen, *Navigating Failure: Bankruptcy and Commercial Society in Antebellum America* (Chapel Hill: University of North Carolina Press, 2001), 3; and Blumin, 115.

41. John P. Trezevant to Donaldson, September 5, 1845, Correspondence 9, BLIC.

42. Col. Michael Nourse to George Carr Grundy, April 11, 1831, Correspondence 1, BLIC.

43. James H. Causten to Donaldson, March 31, 1833, Correspondence 1, BLIC.

44. James H. Causten to Donaldson, February 13, 1839, Correspondence 4, BLIC

45. James H. Causten to Donaldson, February 13, 1839, Correspondence 4, BLIC

46. Donaldson to James H. Causten, February 19, 1839, BLIC.

47. Eagle Life 1848 brochure: 4–5, HCR.

48. Eagle Life 1848 brochure: 5, HCR.

49. Life Insurance," *North American Review,* October 1863: 313.

50. Balleisen, 28.

51. Peter J. Coleman, *Debtors and Creditors in America: Insolvency, Imprisonment for Debt, and Bankruptcy, 1607–1900* (Madison: State Historical Society of Wisconsin, 1974), 287–88.

52. For a summary of the causes and results of the panics of 1837 and 1839, see Balleisen, 32–41.

53. Ryan, *Womanhood in America,* 139.

54. Sandage, 15; Balleisen, 102–8, 206.

55. Coleman, 9, 275; and Charles W. McCurdy, *The Anti-Rent Era in New York Law and Politics, 1839–1865* (Chapel Hill: University of North Carolina Press, 2001), 65–68, 88–89.

56. "Life Insurance," *Waldie's Literary Omnibus,* August 11, 1837: 8.

57. Salmon, 143, 160.

58. In some of its earliest advertisements, Baltimore Life maintained, "These insurances can be made to enure to the benefit of the families without being subject to the claims of creditors." By 1837 Baltimore Life had omitted this sentence from its ads, and it would later be a strong proponent of the legislation permitting such policies. See Baltimore Life advertisements, *Baltimore Patriot,* April 19, 1831: 3, and January 1, 1834: 4; and *Baltimore Gazette and Daily Advertiser,* June 15, 1837: 4.

59. Basch, 17.

60. Basch, 17; Nancy Cott, *The Bonds of Womanhood: "Woman's Sphere" in New England,*

1780–1835 (New Haven, CT: Yale University Press, 1977), 21–23; Salmon, 14–15, 41, 76–77; and Warbasse, 21.

61. Edward D. Mansfield, A.M., *The Legal Rights, Liabilities and Duties of Women* (Salem, MA: John P. Jewett, 1845), 244, 246.

62. Basch, 21, 72; Salmon, 83; and James Kent, *Commentaries on American Law,* quoted in Basch, 63.

63. Basch, 25.

64. Mansfield, 281–83; Richard H. Chused, "Married Women's Property Law: 1800–1850," *Georgetown Law Journal* (June 1983): 19–20; Sandage, 31; Salmon, 83, 88, 93, 101; Basch, 25, 74, 90, 156–60; and Warbasse, 31, 36, 227–28.

65. Basch, 29–41, 121, 124–25; Chused, 20–21; Cott, 43; Warbasse, 180; Larkin, 265; Campbell Gibson, ed., *Population of the 100 Largest Cities and Other Urban Places in the United States: 1790 to 1900* (Washington, DC: U.S. Bureau of the Census, 1998); Johansen, 23–24; Ryan, *Cradle of the Middle Class,* chapter 1; Carroll Smith-Rosenberg, *Disorderly Conduct: Visions of Gender in Victorian America* (New York: Alfred A. Knopf, 1985), 12, 86; E. Anthony Rotundo, *American Manhood: Transformations in Masculinity from the Revolution to the Modern Era* (New York: Basic Books, 1993), 22–24; Jeanne Boydston, *Home and Work: Housework, Wages, and the Ideology of Labor in the Early Republic* (New York: Oxford University Press, 1990), 99.

66. Ryan, *Cradle of the Middle Class,* 146–55.

67. John Mather Austin, *A Voice to the Married; Being a Compendium of Social, Moral, and Religious Duties* (New York: J. Bolles, 1847), 228–29.

68. Austin, 176.

69. Ryan, *Cradle of the Middle Class,* 199–200.

70. Rotundo, 209.

71. Bard to J. L. Starr, August 24, 1833, GA-3, NYL&T.

72. Bard to William P. Sherman, March 18, 1834, GA-4, NYL&T.

73. GHH [George H. Hallett?] to John T. Coffin, August 25, 1837, LA-2, MHL.

74. Bard to William P. Sherman, March 18, 1834, GA-4, NYL&T.

75. See Charles Sellers, *The Market Revolution: Jacksonian America, 1815–1846* (Oxford: Oxford University Press, 1991), 51.

76. *Rates and Proposals of the New-York Life Insurance and Trust Company, No. 38 Wall-Street, for Insurance on Lives, Granting Annuities, Receiving Money in Trust, and the Management of Trust Estates* (New York: Clayton & Van Norden, 1830), 3, 5; "New-York Life Insurance and Trust Company" advertisement, *Daily Albany Argus,* February 20, 1840: 3; Bard to Gulian C. Verplanck, January 13, 1840, GA-8, NYL&T; and "Legislature of New-York. In Senate Thursday, January 16," *Daily Albany Argus,* January 17, 1840: 2.

77. McCurdy, *The Anti-Rent Era,* 9.

78. Balleisen, 103.

79. Thomas Herttell, *Remarks in the House of Assembly of the State of New-York to restore to married women "the Right of Property"* (New York: Henry Durell, 1839), 81–83.

80. If the bill met with any debate in the senate or assembly, such discussions were not recorded by the journalists covering the legislature for the *Albany Evening Journal* or the *Daily Albany Argus.*

81. "Life Insurance," *United States Magazine and Democratic Review,* November 1846: 360; Nautilus Company 1848 brochure, HCR; and Basch, 51–52.

82. In a sample of 750 NYL&T policies from between 1830 and 1866, only 3 exceeded the $300 premium maximum established by the law.

83. Register of Life Insurance, EB-1, NYL&T. In 1840, civil engineers earned between $737 and $2,888, the average American clerk made about $548, and a small-town lawyer about $1,000. See *Historical Statistics of the United States,* vol. 2 (Cambridge: Cambridge University Press, 2006), 261–62; and Boydston, 70.

84. D. Thompson to I. H. Rathbone, October 12, 1849, GA-8, NYL&T; and *Brummer, Respondent v. Cohn, Appellant,* 86 N.Y. 11 (1881).

85. Bard to Francis F. Smith, April 10, 1840, GA-16, NYL&T; Mutual Life of Baltimore 1849 brochure: 5, and New England Mutual Life 1846 brochure: 4, HCR; Abram T. Collier, *A Capital Ship: New England Life, A History of America's First Chartered Mutual Life Insurance Company, 1835–1985* (Boston: New England Mutual Life Insurance Company, 1985), 38–39; Act of 1846, ch. 216, §3, quoted in *Rison v. Wilkerson & Co.,* 35 Tenn. 565 (1856).

86. *Connecticut Mutual,* 12; "Legal Construction of Wife's Policies," *Insurance Monitor,* December 1867: 755; Pennsylvania Mutual Life 1847 brochure: 7, HCR; *North Carolina Mutual,* 12, 20; Charter Oak Life 1865 brochure: 24, HCR; National Life of Vermont 1856 brochure: 11, HCR; Harvey Tuckett, *Practical Remarks on the Present State of Life Insurance in the United States. Showing the Evils which Exist, and Rules for Improvement* (Philadelphia: published by the author, 1851), 49, 58; and *Spectator,* October 1869: 248.

87. Dr. Beverly R. Wellford to Donaldson, September 22, 1842, Correspondence 7, and Donaldson to Dr. Beverly R. Wellford, September 26, 1842, Letter Book, BLIC.

88. Bard to Gulian C. Verplanck, February 1, 1841, to R. D. Searle, May 9, 1840, and to J. L. Starr August 15, 1840, GA-8 and GA-9, NYL&T.

89. Slave policies are not included in any Baltimore Life policy calculations mentioned herein.

90. Policy Book, BLIC.

91. Richard B. Dorsey to William Price Stewart, April 19, 1845, Letter Book, BLIC.

92. Policy Book, BLIC.

93. Policy Books, NEMLIC.

94. Mutual Life of New York 1846 brochure: 33, Nautilus Insurance 1848 brochure: 16, New York Life 1851 brochure: 18, and Mutual Life of Baltimore 1849 brochure: 5–6, HCR; and "Insurance Advertising Sheet," *United States Insurance Gazette and Magazine of Useful Knowledge,* November 1855–April 1856. See also Mutual Life Insurance Company of New York, *Life Insurance Illustrated* (1868): 37; and Economical Mutual Life of Rhode Island 1866 brochure: 35, HCR.

95. Nautilus Insurance 1848 brochure: 16, HCR. The company continued to make an identical statement thirteen years later under its new name, New York Life Insurance Company. New York Life 1861 brochure: 22, HCR.

96. New England Mutual Life 1858 brochure: 2, HCR.

97. Bard to Gulian C. Verplanck, February 1, 1841, GA-9, NYL&T.

98. *Baker, Respondent v. Union Mutual Life Insurance Company, of Maine, Appellant,* 43 N.Y. 283 (1871).

99. *Chisholm, Respondrix v. National Capitol Life Insurance Company, Appellant,* 52 Mo. 213 (1873).

100. *Loomis v. Eagle Life and Health Insurance Company,* 72 Mass. 396 (1856); *Mitchell v. Union Life Insurance Company,* 45 Me. 104 (1858); and *Reserve Mutual Insurance Company v. Kane,* 81 Pa. 154 (1876).

101. *McKee v. Phoenix Insurance Company,* 28 Mo. 383 (1859).

102. *Lord v. Dall,* 12 Mass. 115 (1815).

103. "Abstract of the Ninth Annual Report of the Insurance Commissioners of Massachusetts," *Insurance Gazette,* April–November 1864: 61.

104. *Warnock v. Davis,* 104 U.S. 775 (1881).

105. Nina Baym, *Woman's Fiction: A Guide to Novels by and about Women in America, 1820–1870* (Ithaca, NY: Cornell University Press, 1978), chapters 1–2; Lori Ginzberg, *Women and the Work of Benevolence: Morality, Politics, and Class in the Nineteenth-Century United States* (New Haven, CT: Yale University Press, 1990), 22; and Dorsey, 85–89.

Chapter Six • *Targeting the Aspirations of an Emerging Middle Class*

1. New York Life 1858 brochure: 7–10, HCR.

2. William Bard, *A Letter to David E. Evans, Esquire, of Batavia, on Life Insurance* (New York: William Van Norden, 1832), 8.

3. Bard, *A Letter to David Evans,* 14.

4. Bard, *A Letter to David Evans,* 10–11.

5. "The Hospital Life Insurance Company," *Boston Daily Advertiser,* December 6, 1823: 2.

6. "Notes on the Union Insurance Company New York," Unbound Papers 1, MHL.

7. John Gudmundsen, *The Great Provider: The Dramatic Story of Life Insurance in America* (South Norwalk, CT: Industrial Publications, 1959), 30.

8. "Notes on the Pennsylvania Life Assurance Company," Unbound Papers 1, MHL.

9. "Notes on the Mechanic Life Insurance and Coal Company New York," Unbound Papers 1, MHL.

10. William Bard to William Atkinson, December 31, 1833, GA-4, NYL&T.

11. John J. Donaldson to William Bard, January 13, 1835, Letter Books, , BLIC.

12. B. W. Richards, Girard Life, to Donaldson, February 7, 1837, Correspondence 3, BLIC; and Girard Life 1860 brochure: 4, HCR.

13. Mutual Life of New York 1846 brochure: 32, and Mutual Life of Baltimore 1849 brochure: 15, HCR; and Harvey Tuckett, *Practical Remarks on the Present State of Life Insurance in the United States. Showing the Evils which Exist, and Rules for Improvement* (Philadelphia: published by the author, 1851), 52–53. New England Mutual initially stated it would only underwrite up to $5,000, but within a few months of selling policies, it deemed its business adequate to increase that amount to $10,000. See "Provision for a family by Life-Insurance," *Boston Cultivator,* May 25, 1844: 164.

14. *Life Insurance: Its Principles, Operations and Benefits, as presented by the Connecticut Mutual Life Insurance Company* (Hartford: Case, Tiffany & Burnham, 1846), 12; Connecticut Mutual Life 1851 brochure: 19, HCR; and Mutual Benefit Life of New Jersey advertisement, *Christian Register,* February 20, 1847: 31.

15. Albion Life 1845 brochure: 4, HCR.

16. Girard Life 1837 brochure: 4, HCR.

17. Baltimore Life advertisement, *Baltimore Gazette and Daily Advertiser,* June 15, 1837: 4.

18. Policy Books, BLIC.

19. Bard to John Finlaison, July 16, 1842, GA-10, NYL&T.

20. Bard to Francis H. Smith, June 18, 1846, GA-13, NYL&T; and D. Thompson to Smith, July 9, 1846, GA-13, and to Reverend Thomas Kinton, July 24, 1848, GA-15, NYL&T.

21. Tuckett, 53, 56; and Mutual Life of New York 1846 brochure: 32, Mutual Life of Baltimore 1849 brochure: 15, and New England Mutual Life 1858 brochure: 3, HCR. Other companies such as Connecticut Mutual do not appear to have allowed such payments during the 1840s and early 1850s. Connecticut Mutual Life 1846, 1847, and 1851 brochures, HCR.

22. New England Mutual Life 1858 brochure: 3, HCR.

23. Bard, *A Letter to David E. Evans,* 8.

24. *Connecticut Mutual Life,* 16.

25. Thomas Mustin to George Carr Grundy, May 19, 1831, Correspondence 1, BLIC. Other companies such as Ohio Life and Trust inserted an identical clause into their sales brochures. Ohio Life and Trust 1835 brochure: 7, HCR.

26. Thomas Mustin to George Carr Grundy, May 19, 1831, Correspondence 1, BLIC.

27. Thomas Mustin to George Carr Grundy, August 25, 1831, Correspondence 1, BLIC.

28. George Carr Grundy to Thomas Mustin, August 26, 1831, Correspondence 1, BLIC.

29. James H. Causten to Donaldson, April 18, 1833, Correspondence 1, BLIC.

30. "Agency at Washington," *Huntress,* January 4, 1840: 4.

31. For example, see Marine Corps Captain Augustus A. Nicholson to Donaldson, October 26, 1835, James H. Causten to Donaldson, July 1, 1836, and Captain James Renshaw to Donaldson, January 26, 1838, Correspondence 1–3, BLIC.

32. James H. Causten to Donaldson, April 18, 1833, Correspondence 1, BLIC. See also Causten to Donaldson, April 27, 1833, Correspondence 1, BLIC.

33. See John D. Simms to Donaldson, June 3, 1835, and Marine Corps Captain Augustus A. Nicholson to Donaldson, October 26, 1835, Correspondence 1, BLIC.

34. James H. Causten to Donaldson, December 17, 1836, Correspondence 2, BLIC.

35. Donaldson to John M. Mason, June 7, 1845, Letter Book, BLIC.

36. Donaldson to J. J. B. Walbach, September 13 1842, Letter Book, BLIC.

37. "The Relative Merits of Life Insurance and Savings Banks," *Hunt's Merchants' Magazine,* December 1851: 670.

38. See *Baltimore Patriot,* November 17, 1831: 2; "Life Assurances," *Baltimore Gazette and Daily Advertiser,* May 15, 1833: 2; "Advantages of Life Insurance," *Barre Gazette,* January 22, 1836: 3; "Benefits of Life Insurance," *Trumpet and Universalist Magazine,* September 6, 1845: 47; "The Life Insurance," *New York Illustrated Magazine of Literature and Art,* January 1, 1847: 44; "Life Insurance," *Zion's Herald and Wesleyan Journal,* November 24, 1847: 187; "The Folly of Delay," *New York Evangelist,* November 30, 1848: 1; and "Life Insurance," *Boston Medical and Surgical Journal,* December 27, 1848: 444.

39. Bard, *A Letter to David E. Evans,* 14.

40. Richard Wilson, American Life, to Donaldson, September 16, 1840, Correspondence 5, BLIC.

41. See Donaldson to Jacob Nollner, August 24, 1840, Letter Book, BLIC.

42. See Bard to William Peddie & Co., January 15, 1840, GA-8, NYL&T; D. Thompson to Charles L. Barie, December 3, 1849, GA-16, NYL&T; and Donaldson to P. G. Washington, January 25, 1845, Letter Book, BLIC.

43. Girard Life 1837 brochure: 6, HCR.

44. B. W. Richards, Girard Life, to James H. Causten, February 27, 1840, Correspondence 5, BLIC.

45. Jacob Nollner to Donaldson, August 22, 1840, Correspondence 5, BLIC.

46. Donaldson to Jacob Nollner, August 24, 1840, Letter Book, BLIC.

47. James H. Causten to Donaldson, August 28, 1840, and August 29, 1840, and Richard Wilson, American Life and Trust of Maryland, to Donaldson, September 16, 1840, Correspondence 5, BLIC.

48. Jacob Nollner to Donaldson, September 2, 1840, Correspondence 5, BLIC.

49. James H. Causten to Donaldson, August 29, 1840, Correspondence 5, BLIC.

50. Donaldson to Jacob Nollner, September 26, 1840, Letter Book, and Nollner to Donaldson, October 6, 1840, Correspondence 5, BLIC.

51. Donaldson to Jacob Nollner, August 24, 1840, Letter Book, BLIC.

52. Donaldson to P. G. Washington, January 25, 1845, Letter Book, BLIC.

53. John P. McEldowney, Navy Department, to S. B. Coulter, June 7, 1859, Correspondence 14, BLIC.

54. John James, Girard Life, to Henry F. Thompson, December 1854, Correspondence 12, BLIC.

55. D. Thompson to Edwin Croswell, September 13, 1848, GA-15, NYL&T.

56. Moses L. Hale, to William Haven, April 6, 1842, LA-2, and to D. H. Treadwell, April 17, 1847, LA-3, MHL.

57. Moses L. Hale to Charles E. Norton, January 8, 1847, LA-3, and December 4, 1856, LA-5, MHL.

58. John R. Thompson to William Peddie & Co., July 14, 1845, GA-13, NYL&T.

59. Bard to Bensan Gates, June 16, 1845, GA-13, NYL&T.

60. D. Thompson to Reverend Dr. Author, May 30, 1849, GA-16, NYL&T. See also Bard to John Bradford, January 15, 1846, GA-13, and D. Thompson to Oliver Steele, August 23, 1848, GA-15, NYL&T.

61. Tuckett, 56.

62. Weldon Welfling, *Mutual Savings Banks: The Evolution of a Financial Intermediary* (Cleveland: Press of Case Western Reserve University, 1968), 9.

63. Welfling, 11; and Peter Lester Payne and Lance Edwin Davis, *The Savings Bank of Baltimore, 1818–1866: A Historical and Analytical Study* (Baltimore: John Hopkins Press, 1956), 34–35.

64. Welfling, 29.

65. Alan L. Olmstead, *New York City Mutual Savings Banks, 1819–1861* (Chapel Hill: University of North Carolina Press, 1976), 59.

66. Bard, *A Letter to David E. Evans,* 11.

67. See Ohio Life 1835 brochure: 7, Nautilus Insurance 1848 brochure: 15, Mutual Life of New York 1846 brochure: 5–6, 24, New England Mutual Life 1846 brochure: 3, 6, New En-

gland Mutual Life 1858 brochure: 1, National Life of Vermont 1855 brochure: 4, and Pennsylvania Mutual Life 1857 brochure: 11, HCR.

68. Connecticut Mutual Life 1851 brochure: 14, HCR. See also Girard Life 1837 brochure: 7–8, and Girard Life 1860 brochure: 11–12, HCR; *Are Accumulative Life Policies Superior to Savings Banks in Providing for Families?* (New York: Mutual Life Insurance Company of New York, 1854); and Bard, *A Letter to David E. Evans,* 7–8.

69. J. Owen Stalson, *Marketing Life Insurance: Its History in America* (Cambridge, MA: Harvard University Press, 1942), 105.

70. Stalson, 126.

71. Stalson, 142.

72. Stalson, 135.

73. See, for example, "Life Assurance," *Atlantic Monthly,* September 1866: 314.

74. Mutual Life of New York 1845 brochure: 5, HCR.

75. Mutual Life of New York 1845 brochure: 21–22, HCR. See also Connecticut Mutual Life 1847 brochure: 12, HCR.

76. Mutual Life of New York 1845 brochure: 21, HCR. See also Connecticut Mutual Life 1847 brochure: 12, HCR.

77. Mutual Life of New York 1845 brochure: 24, HCR.

78. Mutual Life of New York 1845 brochure: 19–20, HCR.

79. Mutual Life of New York 1845 brochure: 20–21, HCR.

80. Mutual Life of New York 1845 brochure: 6, HCR.

81. See Connecticut Mutual Life 1846 brochure: 7–10, HCR.

82. New England Mutual Life 1846 brochure: 6, HCR.

83. Connecticut Mutual Life 1846 brochure: 13, HCR.

84. Nautilus Insurance 1848 brochure: 19, HCR.

85. Connecticut Mutual Life 1846 brochure: 14, HCR.

86. Nautilus Insurance 1848 brochure: 19–20, HCR.

87. Mutual Life of New York 1845 brochure: 10–14, HCR.

88. New England Mutual Life 1846 brochure: 11–12, HCR.

89. Premium-note data based on the calculations of Bruce Michael Pritchett, *A Study of Capital Mobilization: The Life Insurance Industry of the Nineteenth Century* (New York: Arno, 1977), 92–93.

90. *Life Insurance History, 1843–1910: Yearly Business of All Active United States Life Insurance Companies from Organization* (New York: Spectator Company, 1911), 84–85, 90–91.

91. Stalson, 321, 791–92.

92. Bard to Girard Life, July 30, 1844, GA-12, NYL&T.

93. Bard to John Finlaison, November 7, 1844, GA-12, NYL&T.

94. Donaldson to Sidney Smith, September 11, 1844, Letter Book, BLIC.

95. Albion Life of London, New York Office, 1845 brochure: 3, HCR.

96. "Mutual Life Insurance," *Hunt's Merchants' Magazine,* February 1847: 159.

97. D. Thompson to William H. Wilson, June 8, 1847, GA-14, NYL&T.

98. See Connecticut Mutual Life 1846 Brochure: 12, and Nautilus Insurance 1848 brochure: 23, HCR; and Mutual Benefit Life of New Jersey advertisement, *Christian Register,* February 20, 1847: 31.

99. Hyman Gratz, Pennsylvania Company, to Joseph Tilden, December 5, 1844, LB-2, MHL.

100. See Bard to John Finlaison, August 15, 1844, and November 7, 1844, GA-12, NYL&T.

101. Bard to William L. Griswold, March 19, 1846, and to Francis H. Smith, June 18, 1846, GA-13, NYL&T.

102. D. Thompson to Edward B. Huntington, June 18, 1847, GA-14, NYL&T.

103. Tuckett, 59–67.

104. See D. Thompson to William H. Wilson, June 8, 1847, GA-14, and Bard to Reverend James C. Cockrane, December 21, 1847, GA-15, NYL&T.

105. Bard to William L. Griswold, March 19, 1846, GA-13, NYL&T.

106. Bard to Francis H. Smith, June 18, 1846, GA-13, NYL&T.

107. Bard to Francis H. Smith, June 11, 1849, GA-16, NYL&T; and J. F. Entz, NYL&T, to William A. Talbott, April 8, 1850, Correspondence 11, BLIC.

108. J. F. Entz, NYL&T, to William A. Talbott, April 8, 1850, Correspondence 11, BLIC.

109. Douglass North, "Capital Accumulation in Life Insurance between the Civil War and the Investigation of 1905," in William Miller, ed., *Men in Business: Essays on the Historical Role of the Entrepreneur* (New York: Harper & Row, 1952), 241–42.

110. See North, 241–43; Morton Keller, *The Life Insurance Enterprise, 1885–1910: A Study in the Limits of Corporate Power* (Cambridge, MA: Belknap, 1963), 192; Spencer L. Kimball, *Insurance and Public Policy: A Study in the Legal Implementation of Social and Economic Public Policy, Based on Wisconsin Records, 1835–1959* (Madison: University of Wisconsin Press, 1960), 165; and H. Roger Grant, *Insurance Reform: Consumer Action in the Progressive Era* (Ames: Iowa State University Press, 1988), 10.

111. Roger L Ransom and Richard Sutch, "Tontine Insurance and the Armstrong Investigation: A Case of Stifled Innovation, 1868–1905," *Journal of Economic History* 47 (1987): 384–85.

112. Given the large number of policyholders, I only collected data on those purchasing policies in January and July.

113. Occupations for New England Mutual policyholders can only be gleaned from their initial applications. Once a policy terminated because of forfeiture or death, the application was removed from the ledger and is no longer extant. I assume that forfeitures and deaths occurred randomly among the different occupational groups and therefore that the policyholders represented form an acceptable random sample of the overall occupational makeup of New England Mutual members. The remaining data on New England Mutual policyholders were taken from the company policy books. As with NYL&T, I only collected data on those purchasing policies in January and July.

114. Stuart M. Blumin, *The Emergence of the Middle Class: Social Experience in the American City, 1760–1900* (New York: Cambridge University Press, 1989), 112–13.

115. Even taking into account deflation (which started in 1840), the drop is significant. If I assume the $2,700 reflects 1843–44 (when prices were at their lowest) and convert it to 1837 dollars (when prices were at their height), the average policy amount for the postdepression period would be $3,200—still a 25% drop off the average from 1830 to 1843.

116. Paul Boyer, *Urban Masses and Moral Order in America: 1820–1920* (Cambridge, MA, 1978), 15, 61.

117. Blumin, 11.

Chapter Seven · Securing Human Property

1. John Day to D. Robertson, September 4, 1835, Correspondence 1, BLIC.

2. See Ulrich Bonnell Phillips, *American Negro Slavery: A Survey of the Supply, Employment and Control of Negro Labor as Determined by the Plantation Regime* (New York: D. Appleton, 1918), 363–64; Frederic Bancroft, *Slave Trading in the Old South* (New York: Frederick Ungar, 1931), 157; Kenneth M. Stampp, *The Peculiar Institution: Slavery in the Ante-Bellum South* (New York: Alfred A. Knopf, 1961), 403; Eugene D. Genovese, "The Medical and Insurance Costs of Slaveholding in the Cotton Belt," *Journal of Negro History* 45 (July 1960): 146; Robert S. Starobin, *Industrial Slavery in the Old South* (London: Oxford University Press, 1970), vii, 71–74; and Claudia Dale Goldin, *Urban Slavery in the American South 1820–1860: A Quantitative History* (Chicago: University of Chicago Press, 1976), 38, 143.

3. Todd L. Savitt, "Slave Life Insurance in Virginia and North Carolina," *Journal of Southern History* 43 (November 1977): 585–86.

4. Robert William Fogel, *Without Consent or Contract: The Rise and Fall of American Slavery* (New York: W. W. Norton, 1989), 29–32, 70; and Gavin Wright, *The Political Economy of the Cotton South: Households, Markets, and Wealth in the Nineteenth Century* (New York: W. W. Norton, 1978), 11–15.

5. Fogel, 32–33, 63, 71; Jonathan D. Martin, *Divided Mastery: Slave Hiring in the American South* (Cambridge, MA: Harvard University Press, 2004), 1–2, 61–62; Charles B. Dew, "Disciplining Slave Iron Workers in the Antebellum South," *American Historical Review* 79 (April 1974): 393–418; Marie Tyler-McGraw and Gregg D. Kimball, *In Bondage and Freedom: Antebellum Black Life in Richmond, Virginia* (Richmond, VA: Valentine Museum, 1988), 21–27; Michael Tadman, *Speculators and Slaves: Masters, Traders, and Slaves in the Old South* (Madison: University of Wisconsin Press, 1989); Peter Kolchin, *American Slavery: 1619–1877* (New York: Hill and Wang, 1993), 109–10; and Goldin, 36.

6. Starobin, 3–34.

7. Martin, *Divided Mastery*, 103; and Ronald L. Lewis, *Coal, Iron, and Slaves: Industrial Slavery in Maryland and Virginia, 1715–1865* (Westport, CT: Greenwood, 1979), 95.

8. Starobin, 72.

9. Jonathan Daniel Wells, *The Origins of the Southern Middle Class, 1800–1861* (Chapel Hill: University of North Carolina Press, 2004).

10. *Life Insurance: Its Principles, Operations and Benefits, as presented by the North Carolina Mutual Life Insurance Company* (Raleigh: Seaton Gales, 1849); Greensboro Mutual Life Insurance and Trust Company policy, Joseph Adolph Linn Papers, Southern Historical Collection, Wilson Library, University of North Carolina at Chapel Hill (hereafter UNC); and Savitt, 587. Over 70% of the southern life insurance companies chartered before 1853 survived less than five years; few records of these companies are extant.

11. Policy Book, BLIC.

12. John O. Lay to Donaldson, June 29, 1833, Correspondence 1, BLIC. See also Levin Lawrence to George Carr Grundy, October 26, 1832, Correspondence 1, BLIC. In one particularly interesting request, President Andrew Jackson donated to three Washington orphan asylums a lion he had received from the emperor of Morocco. The asylums wished to insure the lion until they could sell the animal, but the company refused. James H. Causten to Donaldson, March 18, 1835, Correspondence 1, BLIC; "The Lion," *United States Catholic Miscellany,* March 21, 1835: 302; and "The Leaf-and-Stem-Basket;—Or, Items of News," *Southern Rose Bud,* March 21, 1835: 118.

13. George P. Rawick, *The American Slave: A Composite Autobiography* (Westport, CT: Greenwood, 1972), 262. See also Eugene D. Genovese, *Roll, Jordon, Roll: The World the Slaves Made* (New York: Random House, 1972), 27–30.

14. George Carr Grundy to Thomas J. Read, February 2, 1832, Correspondence 1, BLIC.

15. Donaldson to Robertson & Branda, October 31, 1836, Correspondence 2, BLIC.

16. Dr. Beverly R. Wellford to Donaldson, November 15, 1836, written on Application 604, Policy Book, BLIC.

17. John Day to D. Robertson, September 4, 1835, Correspondence 1, BLIC.

18. See W. F. Davis to Donaldson, January 15, 1839, Correspondence 4, Donaldson to Gwathmey Pine, July 3, 1844, and Richard B. Dorsey to John M. Speed, January 26, 1847, Letter Book, BLIC.

19. Donaldson to Donaldson & Geisendorff, December 7, 1835, Letter Book, BLIC.

20. Donaldson to John O. Lay, February 16, 1835, Letter Book, BLIC.

21. Donaldson to Robertson & Branda, October 7, 1836, and to John O. Lay, July 29, 1839, Letter Book, BLIC.

22. Dr. Beverly R. Wellford to Donaldson, May 23, 1849, Correspondence 11, BLIC.

23. Corydon H. Sutton to Richard B. Dorsey, October 16, 1851, Correspondence 11, BLIC. See also Dorsey to Dr. Beverly R. Wellford, May 24, 1849, and to Corydon H. Sutton, October 20, 1851, Letter Book, BLIC.

24. Robertson & Branda to Donaldson, October 28, 1836, Correspondence 2, BLIC.

25. Donaldson to John O. Lay, July 12, 1839, Letter Book, BLIC. See also Donaldson to Gwathmey Pine, July 3, 1844, Richard B. Dorsey to John M. Speed, January 26, 1847, and Donaldson to Dr. Thomas Pollard, December 3, 1853, Letter Book, BLIC.

26. Donaldson to W. F. Davis, February 21, 1839, Letter Book, BLIC.

27. A. B. Coulter to William Nourse, June 11, 1856, Letter Book, BLIC.

28. See Donaldson to Robertson & Branda, October 7, 1836, and Richard B. Dorsey to Corydon H. Sutton, October 20, 1851, Letter Book, BLIC. The only exceptions were a $200 policy insuring the life of slave Lucy Williams for twelve years, taken out in February 1847 by her owner David Keener of Baltimore, and a policy written in December 1851 for $300 on the whole life of slave Eliza Brogdon, owned by Elizabeth Worthington. See BLIC Policy Book.

29. W. F. Davis to Donaldson, January 15, 1839, Correspondence 4, BLIC.

30. Donaldson to John O. Lay, February 16, 1835, Letter Book, BLIC.

31. Donaldson to Duncan Robertson, May 26, 1835, Letter Book, BLIC.

32. W. F. Davis to Donaldson, January 15, 1839, Correspondence 4, BLIC.

33. Dr. Beverly Wellford to Donaldson, May 15, 1849, Correspondence 11, BLIC.

34. John O. Lay to Donaldson, July 11, 1839, Correspondence 4, BLIC.

35. Kolchin, 130; and Genovese, *Roll, Jordon, Roll,* 37–43.

36. W. F. Davis to Donaldson, January 15, 1839, Correspondence 4, BLIC.

37. Martin, 19, 100.

38. Donaldson to John O. Lay, July 12, 1839, Letter Book, BLIC. See also Donaldson to Lay, July 5, 1836, and to Robertson & Branda, October 7, 1836, Letter Book, BLIC.

39. Donaldson to James H. Causten, July 29, 1839, Letter Book, BLIC. See also Donaldson to John O. Lay, July 29, 1839, and to George Carle, January 4, 1843, Letter Book, BLIC.

40. James H. Causten to Donaldson, September 3, 1833, Correspondence 1, BLIC.

41. Richard Potts to Richard B. Dorsey, September 17, 1852, Correspondence 12, BLIC.

42. Richard Potts to Richard B. Dorsey, October 13, 1852, Correspondence 12, BLIC; and Policy Book, BLIC.

43. Noah Davis, *A Narrative of the Life of Rev. Noah Davis, A Colored Man* (Baltimore: J. F. Weishampel Jr., 1859), 37–42, 55–59.

44. James H. Causten to Donaldson, May 18, 1835, Correspondence 1, BLIC.

45. Donaldson to James H. Causten, May 19, 1835, Letter Book, BLIC.

46. Hugh C. Smith to Donaldson, April 30, 1836, Correspondence 2, BLIC.

47. United States Federal Population Census for Washington, DC, 1850.

48. George Lawry, Georgetown, to Donaldson, March 21, 1846, Correspondence 9, BLIC.

49. J. S. Wellford to Donaldson, December 7, 1855, Correspondence 12, BLIC.

50. R. Swann to Donaldson, October 6, 1859, Correspondence 14, BLIC.

51. Application 6379, NEMLIC.

52. James H. Causten to Donaldson, July 14, 1836, Correspondence 2, BLIC.

53. Charles Pairo to Richard B. Dorsey, August 24, 1852, Correspondence 12, BLIC.

54. Policy Book, BLIC.

55. Tadman, 140, 164–65, 179–80; Kolchin, 59–61, 129, 162; and Genovese, *Roll, Jordan, Roll,* 3–7, 89–91.

56. George Lawry to Donaldson, March 21, 1846, Correspondence 9, BLIC.

57. James H. Causten to Donaldson, September 3, 1833, Correspondence 1, BLIC.

58. R. Swann to Donaldson, October 6, 1859, Correspondence 14, BLIC.

59. James H. Causten to Donaldson, July 14, 1836, Correspondence 2, BLIC.

60. James H. Causten to Donaldson, May 18, 1835, Correspondence 1, BLIC.

61. James H. Causten to Donaldson, May 18, 1835, Correspondence 1, BLIC.

62. J. S. Wellford to Donaldson, December 7, 1855, Correspondence 12, BLIC.

63. Policy Book, BLIC; and United States Federal Population Census, 1850.

64. John Day to D. Robertson, September 4, 1835, Correspondence 1, John O. Lay to Donaldson, June 29, 1836, Correspondence 2, and B. W. Green to Lay, June 29, 1836, Letter Book, BLIC.

65. Donaldson to Robertson & Branda, December 17, 1836, Letter Book, BLIC. See also Donaldson to John O. Lay, July 29, 1839, Letter Book, BLIC.

66. Albin G. Saunders to John O. Lay, July 10, 1839, Correspondence 4, BLIC. See also James H. Causten to Donaldson, July 27, 1839, and W. F. Davis to Donaldson, January 15, 1839, Correspondence 4, and Donaldson to James H. Causten, July 29, 1839, Letter Book, BLIC.

67. Robertson & Branda to Donaldson, October 5, 1836, Correspondence 2, BLIC.

68. James H. Causten to Donaldson, March 12, 1838, Correspondence 3, BLIC.

69. Wilson Winfree to John O. Lay, July 27, 1839, Correspondence 4, BLIC.

70. See Richard B. Dorsey to Henry Stagg, April 14, 1849, Letter Book, BLIC.

71. Richard B. Dorsey to Corydon H. Sutton, December 9, 1851, Letter Book, BLIC.

72. Gwathmey Pine to Donaldson, June 22, 1844, Correspondence 8, BLIC.

73. Donaldson to Gwathmey Pine, July 3, 1844, Letter Book, BLIC.

74. Gwathmey Pine to Donaldson, July 31, 1845, Correspondence 9, BLIC.

75. Richard B. Dorsey to Gwathmey Pine, August 9, 1845, Letter Book, BLIC.

76. Franklin A. Slaughter to Donaldson, January 13, 1852, F. Johnston to Richard B. Dorsey, December 18, 1851, and Charles E. Beynroth to Dorsey, June 22, 1852, Correspondence 11, BLIC.

77. Franklin A. Slaughter to Donaldson, January 13, 1852, Correspondence 11, BLIC.

78. Richard B. Dorsey to Franklin A. Slaughter, January 16, 1852, Letter Book, and Charles E. Beynroth to Dorsey, August 10, 1852, Correspondence 11, BLIC.

79. *North Carolina Mutual;* Mutual Benefit Life and Fire advertisement, *De Bow's Commercial Review,* June 1852: 700; Greensboro Mutual Life Insurance Company policy, Joseph Adolph Linn Papers, UNC; and Savitt, 587.

80. Genovese, "The Medical and Insurance Costs," 146; and Starobin, 72.

81. Savitt, 594.

82. Richmond Fire Association circular, enclosed with Dr. Thomas Pollard to Henry F. Thompson, January 11, 1855, Correspondence 12, BLIC; *John W. Woodfin v. The Asheville Mutual Insurance Company,* 51 N.C. 558 (1859); California Department of Insurance Slavery Era Insurance Registry Report to the California Legislature (May 2002); and Savitt, 587.

83. C. J. Wills, Lynchburg Hose and Fire Company, to John H. McCue, Staunton, VA, December 9, 1853, Papers of the McCue Family, Albert and Shirley Small Special Collections Library, University of Virginia; and Richmond Fire Association Slave Insurance Policy, Albert and Shirley Small Special Collections Library, University of Virginia.

84. Franklin A. Slaughter to Donaldson, January 13, 1852, Correspondence 11, and October 12, 1853, Correspondence 12, BLIC.

85. D. Thompson to Sanford J. Smith, February 4, 1847, GA-14, NYL&T; William Bard to S. S. Cowdrey, May 29, 1838, GA-6, NYL&T; Charles E. Beynroth, to Richard B. Dorsey, June 22, 1852, Correspondence 12, BLIC; Gwathmey Pine to Donaldson, June 22, 1844, Correspondence 8, BLIC; National Loan Fund Life Assurance Company of London circular and National Safety Life Insurance and Trust Company circular, enclosed with Dr. Thomas Pollard to D. Thompson, January 11, 1855, Correspondence 12, BLIC; Mildred F. Stone, *Since 1845: A History of the Mutual Benefit Life Insurance Company* (New Brunswick, NJ: Rutgers University Press, 1957), 19; "Insurance on Negroes," *DeBow's Commercial Review,* February 1851: 241; *Life Insurance History, 1843–1910: Yearly Business of All Active United States Life Insurance Companies from Organization* (New York: Spectator Company, 1911), 81; J. Owen Stalson, *Marketing Life Insurance: Its History in America* (Cambridge, MA: Harvard University Press, 1942), 791; James Curtis Ballagh, ed., *The South in the Building of the Nation: A History of the Southern States Designed to Record the South's Part in the Making of the American Nation; to Portray the Character and Genius, to Chronicle the Achievements and Progress and to Illustrate the Life and Traditions of the Southern People,* vol. 5, *Economic History, 1607–1865* (Richmond,

VA: Southern Historical Publication Society, 1909), 643–44; Charter Oak Life Insurance policy, Sterling Neblett Papers, Rare Book, Manuscript, and Special Collections Library, Duke University.

86. California Registry Report, 2–3; and Illinois Department of Insurance, Slavery Era Insurance Policies Registry, http://www.insurance.illinois.gov/Consumer/SlaveryInformation/SlaveryReporting.asp, accessed November 2009.

87. Lawrence F. Abbott, *The Story of NYLIC: A History of the Origin and Development of the New York Life Insurance Company from 1845 to 1929* (New York, 1930), 36, 46; James M. Hudnut, *Semi-Centennial History of the New-York Life Insurance Company, 1845–1895* (New York, 1895), 22–23; California Department of Insurance Slavery Era Insurance Registry by Name of Slaveholder (May 2002); William Clendenin, "Brief Outline History of Life Insurance," in *The "Bible of Life Insurance" Being a Complete Photographic Reprint of the Original Studies and Official Reports of Elizur Wright* (Chicago: American Conservation, 1932), 62; *Life Insurance History*, 93; and Stalson, 791–92.

88. California Department of Insurance Slavery Era Insurance Registry by Name of Slaveholder (May 2002).

89. Martin, 1, 61–62.

90. Policy Book, BLIC.

91. Corydon H. Sutton to Donaldson, February 16, 1852, Correspondence 11, BLIC.

92. John Darracott to Donaldson, August 5, 1854, Correspondence 12, BLIC.

93. Policy Book, BLIC.

94. See Dr. Beverly R. Wellford to Donaldson, May 15, 1849, Correspondence 11, and Policy Book, BLIC.

95. *North Carolina Mutual*, 17; Virginia Life 1860 brochure: 43, University of Texas Libraries, Austin; brochures enclosed with Dr. Thomas Pollard to D. Thompson, January 11, 1855, Correspondence 12, BLIC; C. J. Wills to John H. McCue, December 9, 1853, Papers of the McCue Family, Albert and Shirley Small Special Collections Library, University of Virginia; Dr. Thomas Pollard to Baltimore Life Office, November 19, 1853, Correspondence 12, BLIC; and Richard B. Dorsey to Dr. Beverly R. Wellford, August 18, 1852, Letter Book, BLIC.

96. Brochures enclosed with Dr. Thomas Pollard to D. Thompson, January 11, 1855, Correspondence 12, BLIC; Charter Oak Life policy, Sterling Neblett Papers, Rare Book, Manuscript, and Special Collections Library, Duke University; and Greensboro Mutual Life and North Carolina Mutual Life policies, Joseph Adolph Linn Papers, UNC.

97. Dr. Josiah Clark Nott, "Statistics of Southern Slave Population, with especial reference to life insurance," *DeBow's Commercial Review*, November 1847: 275, 286–87; and Reginald Horsman, *Josiah Nott of Mobile: Southerner, Physician, and Racial Theorist* (Baton Rouge: Louisiana State University Press, 1987).

98. Manufacturing Schedule of the United States Federal Census, 1850 and 1860; Goldin, 26, 45–46; and Starobin, 14–17.

99. John Darracott to Richard B. Dorsey, March 26, 1853, Correspondence 12, BLIC.

100. Dr. Thomas Pollard to Baltimore Life Office, November 19, 1853, Correspondence 12, BLIC.

101. Corydon H. Sutton to Baltimore Life Office, December 14, 1852, Correspondence 12, BLIC.

102. Donaldson to Dr. Thomas Pollard, December 3 and 29, 1853, Letter Book, and Pollard to Donaldson, December 23, 1853, Correspondence 12, BLIC.

103. Dr. Thomas Pollard to Donaldson, December 23, 1853, and July 25, 1854, Correspondence 12, BLIC.

104. Only the names of the first five petitioners were listed. Loren Schweninger, ed., *Race, Slavery, and Free Blacks: Series I, Petitions to Southern Legislatures, 1777–1867* (Bethesda, MD: University Publications of America, 1999), 315.

105. J. S. Wellford to the Baltimore Life Office, March 29, 1856, Correspondence 13, BLIC.

106. Dr. Thomas Pollard to Donaldson, October 23, 1854, Correspondence 12, BLIC.

107. Policy Book, BLIC.

108. John Darracott to Donaldson, July 25, 1854, Correspondence 12, BLIC.

109. *Scudder v. Woodbridge*, 1 Ga. 195 (1846); Paul Finkelman, "Slaves as Fellow Servants: Ideology, Law, and Industrialization," *Journal of Legal History* 31 (October 1987): 279; and Martin, 73.

110. Starobin, 15–17, 28; James W. Ely Jr., *Railroads and American Law* (Lawrence: University Press of Kansas, 2002), 135–36; and Goldin, 21, 26.

111. Applications, BLIC. Employment information is available neither from 1858 to March 1859 nor after April 1860.

112. Henry F. Thompson to Dr. Thomas Pollard, January 9, 1855, Letter Book, BLIC.

113. Dr. Thomas Pollard to Henry F. Thompson, January 11, 1855, Correspondence 12, BLIC.

114. Tyler-McGraw and Kimball, 21. See also Sean Patrick Adams, *Old Dominion, Industrial Commonwealth: Coal, Politics, and Economy in Antebellum America* (Baltimore: Johns Hopkins University Press, 2004), 45.

115. Henry F. Thompson to Dr. Thomas Pollard, March 24, 1855, Letter Book, and Pollard to Thompson, March 2, 1855, Correspondence 12, BLIC. In many cases these policies were purchased by the hirer or hiring agent for the benefit of the owner, most likely as part of the terms of the hiring contract. For example, Thompkins & Co.—the hiring agent for the Black Heath Coal Pits in Chesterfield, VA—obtained policies on fourteen slaves in 1857. Thompkins was responsible for all premium payments, but any claim was to be paid directly to the owner. Applications, BLIC.

116. Dr. Thomas Pollard to Baltimore Life office, December 30, 1857, Correspondence 13, and M. M. Coulter to P. B. Price, January 11, 1860, Letter Book, BLIC.

117. James F. Jordon, North Carolina Mutual, to J. M. Horah, January 2, 1855, Orin Datus Davis Papers, UNC.

118. Brochure enclosed with Dr. Thomas Pollard to Henry F. Thompson, January 11, 1855, Correspondence 12, BLIC.

119. Tadman, 289–91.

120. Virginia Life 1860 brochure: 43, University of Texas Libraries, Austin.

121. A. B. Coulter to William Nourse, June 11, 1856, Letter Book, P. B. Price to Donaldson, January 3 and 11, 1860, Correspondence 14, and M. M. Coulter to Price, October 30, 1860, Letter Book, BLIC.

122. P. B. Price to Donaldson, January 3 and 11, 1860, Correspondence 14, BLIC.

123. Policy Book, BLIC.

124. Tadman, 289–91.

125. M. M. Coulter to P. B. Price, October 30, 1860, Letter Book, BLIC.

126. Virginia Life 1860 brochure: 8, University of Texas Libraries, Austin; and "The Virginia Life Insurance Company Advertisement," *Times Dispatch* (Richmond, VA), July 10, 1861.

127. John Darracott to Donaldson, August 5, 1854, Correspondence 12, BLIC. See also Dr. Thomas Pollard to Donaldson, December 5, 1853, Correspondence 12, BLIC.

128. Greensboro Mutual Life and North Carolina Mutual Life policies, UNC.

129. Donaldson to Dr. Thomas Pollard, December 8, 1853, Letter Book, BLIC.

130. M. M. Coulter to [illegible], January 12, 1860, Letter Book, BLIC.

131. Dr. Thomas Pollard to M. M. Coulter, October 20, 1860, Correspondence 14, BLIC.

132. Lucien Lewis to M. M. Coulter, November 12 and 17, 1860, Correspondence 14, BLIC.

133. Lucien Lewis to M. M. Coulter, December 26, 1860, Correspondence 14, BLIC.

134. Lucien Lewis to M. M. Coulter, November 17, 1860, Correspondence 14, BLIC.

135. M. M. Coulter to R. F. Lester, December 24, 1860, Letter Book, BLIC.

136. M. M. Coulter to Charles L. Mosby, December 24, 1860, Letter Book, BLIC.

137. Dr. Thomas Pollard to Henry F. Thompson, March 19, 1855, Correspondence 12, BLIC.

138. Dr. Thomas Pollard to Henry F. Thompson, January 11, 1855, Correspondence 12, BLIC.

139. M. M. Coulter to Lucien Lewis, November 19, 1860, Letter Book, BLIC.

140. M. M. Coulter to R. F. Lester, June 7, 1860, Letter Book, BLIC.

141. M. M. Coulter to R. F. Lester, December 24, 1860, Letter Book, BLIC.

142. M. M. Coulter to C. L. Mosby, December 24, 1860, Letter Book, BLIC.

143. Lucien Lewis to Secretary S. B. Coulter, November 17, 1860, Correspondence 14, BLIC.

144. M. M. Coulter to Lucien Lewis, December 24, 1860, Letter Book, BLIC.

145. Lucien Lewis to M. M. Coulter, December 26, 1860, and February 19, 1861, Correspondence 14, BLIC.

146. Lucien Lewis to M. M. Coulter, December 26, 1860, Correspondence 14, BLIC.

147. See J. Colston to John W. Magill, March 15, 1865, and Donaldson to C. B. Wellford, June 23, 1865, and to Dr. Thomas Pollard, June 28, 1865, Letter Book, BLIC.

148. William G. Harrison, to G. W. Phillips, Equitable Life Assurance Society, May 23, 1867, and to W. C. Alexander, Equitable Life Assurance Society, May 25, 1867, Letter Book, BLIC.

149. For a full overview of this debate, see Mark M. Smith, *Debating Slavery: Economy and Society in the Antebellum American South* (Cambridge: Cambridge University Press, 1998), chapter 6.

Chapter Eight · Acting *"in defiance of Providence"?*

1. See John Samuel Ezell, *Fortune's Merry Wheel: The Lottery in America* (Harvard University Press: 1960), chapters 10–11.

2. "The Relative Merits of Life Insurance and Savings Banks," *Hunt's Merchants' Magazine,* December 1851: 670–77.

3. "Mr. A. B. Johnson on Life Insurance," *New York Times,* December 26, 1851: 1.

4. "Life Insurance," *Hunt's Merchants' Magazine,* February 1852: 196–98.

5. "Life Insurance," *Hunt's Merchants' Magazine,* February 1852: 196–98.

6. "Mr. A. B. Johnson on Life Insurance," *New York Times,* December 26, 1851: 1.

7. Viviana A. Rotman Zelizer, *Morals and Markets: The Development of Life Insurance in the United States* (New York: Columbia University Press, 1979), 149–50.

8. Zelizer, 45–46, 164.

9. Charles Sellers, *The Market Revolution: Jacksonian America, 1815–1846* (Oxford: Oxford University Press, 1991), 30–31.

10. Stewart Davenport, *Friends of the Unrighteous Mammon: Northern Christians and Market Capitalism, 1815–1860* (Chicago: University of Chicago Press, 2008).

11. Mark A. Noll, introduction to *God and Mammon: Protestants, Money, and the Market, 1790–1860* (Oxford: Oxford University Press, 2002), 22.

12. "Life Insurance," *Boston Cultivator,* August 3, 1844: 244.

13. Alexander Mackie, *Facile Princeps: The Story of the Beginning of Life Insurance in America* (Lancaster, PA: Lancaster Press, 1956).

14. Corporation for the Relief of the Widows and Children of Clergymen of the Protestant Episcopal Church, *The Charters, with the Laws and the List of Members* (Philadelphia: Hall and Sellers, 1791).

15. Mackie, 120–24.

16. *The Charters,* 3–4.

17. Corporation for the Relief of the Widows and Children of Clergymen of the Protestant Episcopal Church, *Fundamental By-Laws and Tables of Rates for Reversionary Annuities, Annuities, and Endowment* (Philadelphia: Sherman, 1851), 5.

18. *Fundamental By-Laws,* 5.

19. *Fundamental By-Laws,* 14.

20. *Fundamental By-Laws,* 16.

21. John William Wallace, *Historical Sketch of the Corporation for the Relief of the Widows and Children of Clergymen* (Philadelphia: Sherman, 1870), 58.

22. William Bard to Alonso Potter, Schenectady, NY, September 20, 1833, GA-3, NYL&T.

23. Register of Life Insurance, EB-1, NYL&T.

24. Bard to Rev. John Brown, Newburgh, NY, March 23, 1844, GA-12, NYL&T.

25. Schedule of Insurance, FL-1, MHL.

26. Policy Books, BLIC.

27. Policy Books, NEMLIC.

28. Robert H. Abzug, *Cosmos Crumbling: American Reform and the Religious Imagination* (New York: Oxford University Press, 1994), 107.

29. The denominations represented include Episcopalians (both high and low church), Congregationalists (traditional Calvinists as well as the growing sects of Unitarians and Universalists), Presbyterians (of the Old School, New School, Reformed Dutch, and Reformed German persuasions), Baptists, Methodists, and even a Spiritualist.

30. Henry Perkins, *A Sermon Preached at the Funeral of George Holcombe, M.D.* (Trenton: George Sherman, 1828), 23–24.

31. 1 Timothy 5:8 (King James Version).

32. Thomas P. Hunt, *The Book of Wealth* (NY: Ezra Collier, 1836), 13.

33. Thomas Gray, *The Value of Life and Charitable Institutions. A Discourse Delivered before the Humane Society of the Commonwealth of Massachusetts* (Boston: Hosea Sprague, 1805), 10–11.

34. John Sylvester John Gardiner, *A Sermon Delivered before the Humane Society of the Commonwealth of Massachusetts* (Boston: Hosea Sprague, 1803), 12; Leonard Woods, *Duties of the Rich. A Sermon . . . On occasion of the death of Moses Brown, esq.* (Andover: Flagg and Gould, 1827), 10; Daniel Wise, *Bridal Greetings: A Marriage Gift, in which the mutual duties of husband and wife are familiarly illustrated and enforced* (New York: Carlton & Porter, 1850), 114; and Stephen Remington, *The Marriage Memento; A Treatise on the Nature of Matrimony, the mutual obligations of Husband and Wife* (New York: Edward H. Fletcher, 1852), 37.

35. Charles G. Finney, *Lectures to Professing Christians. Delivered in the City of New-York, in the years 1836 and 1837* (New York: John S. Taylor, 1836), 339.

36. James Foster, *The Married State; its obligations and duties. With hints on the Education of a Family* (Hartford: S. Andrus & Son, 1845), 47.

37. Proverbs 13:22 (King James Version).

38. Francis William Pitt Greenwood, *The Inheritance Which a Good Man Leaves to his Children. A Discourse Occasioned by the Death of James Freeman Curtis* (Boston: James Munroe, 1839), 5.

39. John Mather Austin, *A Voice to the Married; Being a Compendium of Social, Moral, and Religious Duties* (New York: J. Bolles, 1847), 66.

40. Eliphalet Nott, *A Discourse Delivered in the Presbyterian Church, in the City of Albany; Before the Ladies' Society, for the Relief of Distressed Women and Children* (Albany: Charles R. and George Webster, 1804), 34.

41. Archibald Alexander, *Practical Sermons; to be Read in Families and Social Meetings* (Philadelphia: Presbyterian Board of Publication, 1850), 433.

42. *The American Manual of Life Assurance. answering all questions necessary to a full understanding of the whole subject. By a clergyman* (Philadelphia: American Life Insurance and Trust Company, 1862), 70–74.

43. James William Thompson, *A sermon delivered by request of the Female Charitable Society in Salem* (Salem: Foote & Brown, 1832), 5.

44. John Williamson Nevin, *A Funeral Sermon with Reference to the Death of James Edgar Moore* (Mercersberg, PA, 1844), 12–13.

45. Alfred Lee, *Timely Preparation. A Sermon* (Wilmington: Henry Eckel, 1857), 4.

46. This examination was based on keyword searches for references to life insurance in two databases: America's Historical Newspapers and the American Periodical Series Online.

47. See Massachusetts Hospital Life advertisements, *Christian Register,* January 7, 1826: 3, and January 29, 1831: 19; Boston Equitable Life advertisement, *Zion's Herald and Wesleyan Journal,* July 6, 1842: 106; American Life and Trust advertisement, *New York Evangelist,* August 25, 1842: 135; Connecticut Mutual Life advertisements, *Christian Secretary,* December 18, 1846: 2, and *Christian Observer,* January 13, 1849: 7; and American Mutual Life advertisement, *Christian Register,* September 15, 1849: 147.

48. "To William Bard, Esq, President of the New York Life Insurance and Trust Company," *New York Evangelist,* August 21, 1830: 84.

49. "Benefits of Life Insurance," *New York Evangelist,* June 29, 1839: 103.

50. "Life Insurance," *Christian Register and Boston Observer,* September 3, 1836: 144. See also "Life Insurance," *Christian Register,* September 21, 1844: 151, reprinted from *New York Express;* and "Life Insurance," *Christian Reflector,* June 5, 1845: 92, reprinted from *New York Sun.*

51. *Trumpet and Universalist Magazine,* September 17, 1836: 51.

52. "Life Insurance," *Christian Secretary,* January 11, 1839: 3. See also the similar reference in "Life Insurance," *Christian Secretary,* January 31, 1840: 3.

53. "Fire and Life Insurance," *Christian Watchman,* April 8, 1842: 1.

54. "Mutual Life Insurance Company," *Christian Register,* April 11, 1835: 138.

55. Daniel Smith, "Life Insurance," *Christian Advocate and Journal,* October 18, 1849: 165.

56. "To the Editor of the Christian Observer on Communicating to the Dying a Knowledge of their Danger," *Christian Observer, Conducted by Members of the Established Church,* May 1831: 271–72.

57. "The Insurance Office," *Christian Secretary,* October 5, 1838: 2.

58. "Future Punishment," *Western Christian Advocate,* June 22, 1838: 33.

59. Reverend J. M. Dickey, "Sermon," *Baltimore Literary and Religious Magazine,* May 1835: 148.

60. Ohio Life 1835 brochure: 7, HCR.

61. Nautilus Insurance 1848 brochure: 10, HCR.

62. New York Life 1856 and 1858 brochures: 13, HCR.

63. Guardian Life advertisement, *Christian Advocate and Journal,* January 31, 1861: 40.

64. Equitable Life Assurance Society of New York advertisement, *New York Observer and Chronicle,* January 3, 1861: 7.

65. "Early Education," *Christian Advocate and Journal,* July 10, 1835: 181.

66. "Life Insurance," *Religious Intelligencer,* July 18, 1835: 103.

67. M. Spencer, "Life Insurance," *Zion's Herald and Wesleyan Journal,* April 8, 1846: 54; and Daniel Smith, "Life Insurance," *Christian Advocate and Journal,* October 18, 1849: 165.

68. "Life Insurance—Ministers," *Christian Secretary,* February 26, 1847: 2.

69. "Life Insurance—A Scruple," *Christian Secretary,* March 12, 1847: 2.

70. "Life Insurance of Ministers," *Christian Secretary,* April 23, 1847: 2.

71. "Life Insurance," *Christian Advocate and Journal,* February 9, 1848: 23.

72. "Life Insurance," *Christian Advocate and Journal,* April 19, 1848: 61.

73. "Life Insurance—Caution," *Christian Advocate and Journal,* November 22, 1849: 186.

74. "Life Insurance—Caution Continued," *Christian Advocate and Journal,* December 20, 1849: 203.

75. "Life Insurance—Caution," *Christian Advocate and Journal,* November 22, 1849: 186.

76. Jacob Ide, "Life Insurance," *Christian Register,* November 27, 1847: 1.

77. "Preachers' Widows and Orphans," *Universalist Watchman, Repository and Chronicle,* March 19, 1847: 284.

78. Philanthropos, "Life Insurance by, or for, Ministers," *Christian Inquirer,* May 27, 1848: 130.

79. "Methodism in the N.H. Conference," *Zion's Herald and Wesleyan Journal,* March 20, 1850: 1.

80. "Life Insurance," *Episcopal Reader,* November 25, 1848: 147.

81. "Life Insurance of Ministers," *Christian Watchman and Christian Reflector,* December 26, 1850: 206.

82. See also "The Way to Wealth," *Christian Register,* July 7, 1849: 1; Abner T. Ellis, "Life Insurance," *Christian Inquirer,* November 16, 1850: 3; "Life Insurance Companies," *Christian Watchman and Christian Reflector,* November 28, 1850: 191; and "Fund for Relief of Indigent Clergymen," *Princeton Review,* July 1856: 581.

83. Donaldson to C. L. Mosby, August 12, 1837, Letter Book, BLIC.

84. John O. Lay to Donaldson, September 11, 1837, Correspondence 3, BLIC.

85. See Donaldson to Somerville Pinkney, November 20, 1833, Letter Book, BLIC.

86. Dr. Beverly R. Wellford to Donaldson, November 15, 1836, written on Application 604, Policy Book, BLIC.

87. William Bard, *A Letter to David E. Evans, Esquire, of Batavia, on Life Insurance* (New York: William Van Norden, 1832), 4.

88. *Prospectus of the Union Insurance Company, Incorporated by the State of New-York, for Making Insurance on Lives, and Granting Annuities* (New York: J. Seymour, 1818), 3.

89. "Life Insurance," *Merchants' Magazine and Commercial Review,* March 1, 1840: 230.

90. Mutual Life of New York 1846 brochure: 30, HCR.

91. *Life Insurance: Its Principles, Operations and Benefits, as presented by the North Carolina Mutual Life Insurance Company* (Raleigh: Seaton Gales, 1849): 6.

92. *Life Insurance: Its Principles, Operations and Benefits, as presented by the Connecticut Mutual Life Insurance Company* (Hartford: Case, Tiffany & Burnham, 1846); and Connecticut Mutual Life 1847 brochure, HCR.

93. Connecticut Mutual Life 1851 brochure: 5, HCR.

94. Nautilus Insurance 1848 brochure and New York Life 1851 brochure, HCR.

95. New York Life 1856 and 1858 brochures: 12, HCR. See also New York Life 1861 brochure: 36–38, HCR.

96. New York Life 1861 brochure: 38, HCR.

97. *The American Manual of Life Assurance,* 70–74.

98. Donaldson, to C. L. Mosby, August 12, 1837, Letter Book, BLIC.

99. Mutual Life of New York 1846 brochure: 30, HCR.

100. *North Carolina Mutual,* 6.

101. Connecticut Mutual Life 1851 brochure: 5, HCR.

102. New York Life 1856 and 1858 brochures: 12, HCR.

103. Joseph Holt Ingraham, "The Romance of Broadway," in *The American Lounger; or Tales, Sketches, and Legends, Gathered in Sundry Journeyings* (Philadelphia: Lea and Blanchard, 1839), 29.

104. Charles Frederick Briggs, *The Adventures of Harry Franco,* vol. 1 (New York: F. Saunders, 1839), 35.

105. Nathaniel Parker Willis, *Dashes at Life with a Free Pencil* (New York: Burgess, Stringer, 1845); James Russell Lowell, "Letter From Boston, December 1846," in *The Writings of James Russell Lowell* (Cambridge, MA: Riverside, 1890); George Lippard, *The Killers: A Narrative of Real Life in Philadelphia . . . By a Member of the Philadelphia Bar* (Philadelphia: Hankinson and Bartholomew, 1850).

106. Herman Melville, *White-Jacket; or, The World in a Man-of-War* (1850), 410.

107. Herman Melville, *I and My Chimney* (New York: Dix & Edwards, 1856), 282.

108. Herman Melville, *Moby-Dick, or, The Whale* (New York: Hendricks House, 1851), 35–36.

109. F. A. Durivage, "Ruth Fairfax," *Ladies' Companion, a Monthly Magazine; Devoted to Literature and the Fine Arts,* March 1841: 213.

110. William Taylor Adams, *Little by Little, or, The Cruise of the Flyaway* (Chicago: Union School Furnishing, 1860), 38–40.

111. "Ella Winship," *New Mirror,* June 15, 1844: 164.

112. Mrs. A. M. F. Annan, "Marrying a Fool," *Graham's American Monthly Magazine of Literature, Art, and Fashion,* December 1845: 267.

113. See John Moore, *Mordaunt. Sketches of Life, Characters, and Manners, in Various Countries; Including the Memoirs of A French Lady of Quality* (1800); John Hamilton Reynolds, "The Fields of Tothill: A Fragment," *The Fancy* (1820); William Makepeace Thackeray, *The Newcomes. Memoirs of a Most Respectable Family* (1854), chapter 34; and Anthony Trollope, *Framley Parsonage* (1861), chapter 1.

114. "Insurance and Assurance," *Atheneum, or, Spirit of the English Magazines,* May 1, 1825: 103. Reprinted in *Providence Patriot,* September 3, 1825: 4; *Souvenir,* January 23, 1828: 233; *Pearl and Literary Gazette,* January 18, 1834: 95; and *Lady's Book,* April 1836: 175.

115. Charles Dickens, *The Life and Adventures of Martin Chuzzlewit,* vol. 2 (Leipzig: Bernh. Tauchnitz Jun., 1844), 16–35.

116. Charles Dickens, *Great Expectations* (1861; Boston: Estes and Lauriat, 1881), 209.

117. William Makepeace Thackeray, *Vanity Fair: A Novel without a Hero* (1848; Manchester: W. H. White, 1891), 293.

118. Thackeray, *Vanity Fair,* 291.

119. Charles Dickens, *Hunted Down and Other Reprinted Stories* (Philadelphia: T. B. Peterson, 1861), 12. See also Mrs. Emma C. Embury, "Our Library," *Ladies' Companion, a Monthly Magazine; Devoted to Literature and the Fine Arts,* December 1840: 71–76; and Wilkie Collins, *The Woman in White* (1860).

120. "An Extraordinary Story of Crime," *Insurance Monitor,* November 1872: 915.

121. "Frauds on Life Companies," *Insurance Monitor,* September 1869: 719.

122. See "Life Insurance—Or How to Make a Dead Man," *Brother Jonathan,* March 18, 1843: 328–329; "Our Foreign Gossip," *Harper's New Monthly Magazine,* April 1856: 704–7; "Notes of Charles Lamb to Thomas Allsop," *Harper's New Monthly Magazine,* December 1859: 92–93; and *Harper's New Monthly Magazine,* June 1867: 126.

123. "Our Foreign Bureau," *Harper's New Monthly Magazine,* November 1859: 849–50.

124. "Does a Man Shorten his Life by Insuring It?" *Hunt's Merchants' Magazine,* July 1856: 110–13.

125. "Henry Mayhew's Inquiries into Suspicious Deaths," *United States Insurance Gazette and Magazine of Useful Knowledge,* April–November 1856: 312–14.

126. "Life Insurances," *Atkinson's Saturday Evening Post,* January 24, 1835: 2.

127. Economical Mutual Life 1866 brochure: 47, HCR.

128. "Insurance Companies," *De Bow's Review,* April 1868: 448.

129. "Life Insurance—New Jersey Poisoning Case," *United States Gazette,* April–November 1859: 279.

130. "Angie Stewart, the Murdered Child," in J. B. Lewis and C. C. Bombaugh, *Remarkable Stratagems and Conspiracies: An Authentic Record of Surprising Attempts to Defraud Life Insurance Companies* (New York: G. W. Carleton, 1878), 282–300.

131. "The Brantley-Eskridge Romance," in Lewis and Bombaugh, 300–34.

132. "The Armstrong Murder Case," *Insurance Monitor,* March 1879: 121.

133. "Another Life Insurance Horror," *Insurance Monitor,* March 1879: 134–35.

134. "The Professor West Infamy," in Lewis and Bombaugh, 339–46; John N. Reynolds, *The Twin Hells: A Thrilling Narrative of Life in the Kansas and Missouri Penitentiaries* (Chicago: M. A. Donohue, 1890), 175–76; and "Hillmon Tells his Story: The Murderer Found in the Mountains of Utah," *New York Times,* January 2, 1894: 1.

135. Roland Marchand, *Creating the Corporate Soul: The Rise of Public Relations and Corporate Imagery in American Big Business* (Berkeley: University of California Press, 1998), 9.

136. Marchand, 37–38.

Chapter Nine · *Seeking Stability in an Increasingly Competitive Industry*

1. "The First American Life Underwriters' Convention," *United States Insurance Gazette and Magazine of Useful Knowledge,* July 1859: 113–37.

2. "Editorial Notes. The American Life Underwriters' Convention," *Insurance Gazette,* November 1858–April 1859: 177; and "Editorial Notes. American Life Underwriters' Convention, which is proposed to come off in May, 1859," *Insurance Gazette,* November 1858–April 1859: 375.

3. "Editorial Notes. The American Life Underwriters' Convention to be held in May, 1859," *Insurance Gazette,* November 1858–April 1859: 235.

4. "The First American Life Underwriters' Convention," *Insurance Gazette,* July 1859: 118.

5. American Temperance Life Insurance Company advertisement, *Portage County Democrat,* June 7, 1854: 4; George Larkin Clark, *A History of Connecticut: Its People and Institutions* (New York: Knickerbocker, 1914), 410; and "Boston Equitable Life Insurance Society," *Boston Medical and Surgical Journal,* August 3, 1842: 416.

6. John Gudmundsen, *The Great Provider: The Dramatic Story of Life Insurance in America* (South Norwalk, CT: Industrial Publications, 1959), 40–41.

7. R. Carlyle Buley, *The American Life Convention, 1906–1952: A Study in the History of Life Insurance* (New York: Appleton-Century-Crofts, 1953), xiii.

8. Buley, *The American Life Convention,* xiii.

9. Harvey G. Tuckett, *Practical Remarks on the Present State of Life Insurance in the United States. Showing the Evils Which Exist, and Rules for Improvement* (Philadelphia: published by the author, 1851), 59–62.

10. Tuckett, 47.

11. American Mutual Life advertisement, *American Agriculturalist,* February 1848: 71.

12. "A Comparative Table of the Rates of Twenty-Nine Life Insurance Companies," *Insurance Gazette,* May–October 1860. I have not found data on the rates for Kentucky Mutual Life in 1860.

13. By 1867, Kentucky Mutual had revised its rates to coincide with the rest of the industry, although American Mutual, Empire Mutual of Chicago, Economical Mutual Life of

Rhode Island, and New Jersey Mutual all quoted rates 10% to 16% less than the Carlisle Table. Rates for State Mutual of Worcester were not included in this 1867 list. "Comparative Table showing the Annual Rate of Premium," *Insurance Monitor,* June 1867: 346–48.

14. Steven Haberman and Trevor A. Sibbett, eds., *History of Actuarial Science,* vol. 1 (London: William Pickering, 1995), lxiv; and Shepard B. Clough, *A Century of American Life Insurance: A History of the Mutual Life Insurance Company of New York, 1843–1943* (New York: Columbia University Press, 1946), 58.

15. Clough, 69.

16. "A Comparative Table of the Rates of Twenty-Nine Life Insurance Companies," *Insurance Gazette,* May–October 1860.

17. "Valuation of Life Insurance Policies," *Hunt's Merchants' Magazine,* July 1860: 47; "Elements of Solvency in Life Insurance," *New York Times,* February 28, 1870: 5; John Hancock Life 1898 brochure, HCR; and James W. Glover, *United States Life Tables, 1890, 1901, 1910, and 1901–10* (Washington, DC: Government Printing Office, 1921), 20.

18. *Seventh Annual Report of the Massachusetts Commissioners of Insurance* (January 1862) in *The "Bible of Life Insurance" Being a Complete Photographic Reprint of the Original Studies and Official Reports of Elizur Wright* (Chicago: American Conservation, 1932), 164.

19. This is most likely because, following the British custom, life insurance companies only quoted premium rates for these three types of policies. See the 1820s brochure of the Crown Life Assurance Company, Early Insurance Circulars, HA-1, NYL&T.

20. "Proceedings of the Life Insurance Convention," *Insurance Gazette,* August 1860: 245.

21. Clough, 58.

22. The only difference in these rates was for policyholders aged 15, who were now charged $15.60 in lieu of the original rate of $15.30.

23. "A Comparative Table of the Rates of Twenty-Nine Life Insurance Companies," *Insurance Gazette,* May–October 1860.

24. "Comparative Table showing the Annual Rate of Premium," *Insurance Monitor,* June 1867: 346–48. Rates for State Mutual of Worcester were not included in this table.

25. "Life Insurance," *North American Review,* October 1863: 309.

26. "The Eleventh Annual Report of the New England Mutual Life Insurance Company of Boston," *Insurance Gazette,* May–October 1855: 48–49; "The Twelfth Annual Report of the New England Life Insurance Company of Boston," *Insurance Gazette,* May–October 1856: 37; "The Thirteenth Annual Report of the New England Mutual Life Insurance Company of Boston," *Insurance Gazette,* February 1857: 184–85; and "The New England Mutual Life Insurance Company," *Hunt's Merchants' Magazine,* February 1857: 225–26.

27. "The Thirteenth Annual Report of the New England Mutual Life Insurance Company of Boston," *Insurance Gazette,* November 1856–April 1857: 235.

28. "New York Life Insurance Company," *Insurance Gazette,* November 1855–April 1856: 287; and "State Mutual Life Insurance Company, of Worcester, Massachusetts. The Twelfth Annual Report," *Insurance Gazette,* November 1857–April 1858: 38.

29. Buley, *The American Life Convention,* 54.

30. "The First American Life Underwriters' Convention," *Insurance Gazette,* July 1859: 130.

31. *Statistics of the United States, 1860* (Washington, DC: Government Printing Office,

1866), xxiv–xxv; and "Vital Statistics. Importance of Registration," *Insurance Monitor,* May 1867: 605.

32. "The First American Life Underwriters' Convention," *Insurance Gazette,* July 1859: 134.

33. "Vital Statistics. Importance of Registration," *Insurance Monitor,* May 1867: 605.

34. *Statistics of the United States,* xxiv.

35. Michael R. Haines and Roger C. Avery, "The American Life Table of 1830–1860: An Evaluation," *Journal of Interdisciplinary History* 11 (1980): 81; and *Statistics of the United States,* xxiii–xxv.

36. "American Life Underwriters' Convention," *Hunt's Merchants' Magazine,* March 1859: 364–65; and "Editorial Notes. The American Life Underwriters' Convention," *Insurance Gazette,* November 1858–April 1859: 176–78.

37. "Editorial Notes. American Life Underwriters' Convention, which is proposed to come off in May, 1859," *Insurance Gazette,* November 1858–April 1859: 321–22.

38. "The First American Life Underwriters' Convention," *Insurance Gazette,* July 1859: 120.

39. "The First American Life Underwriters' Convention," *Insurance Gazette,* July 1859: 121; and Haberman and Sibbett, vol. 1, lxiii.

40. "Life Insurance—Wright's Tables," *Hunt's Merchants' Magazine,* December 1854: 735.

41. E. J. Moorhead, *Our Yesterdays: The History of the Actuarial Profession in North America, 1809–1979* (Schaumburg, IL: Society of Actuaries, 1989), 6.

42. "Proceedings of the Life Insurance Convention," *Insurance Gazette,* August 1860: 190–91.

43. "The First American Life Underwriters' Convention," *Insurance Gazette,* July 1859: 123.

44. "The First American Life Underwriters' Convention," *Insurance Gazette,* July 1859: 125.

45. "The First American Life Underwriters' Convention," *Insurance Gazette,* July 1859: 133. The *Insurance Monitor*'s report of the convention was entirely different from the *Insurance Gazette*'s. The former inexplicably opined that "the project . . . has met with no favor in the leading New York offices." Focusing on the absence of Mutual Benefit of New Jersey and New England Mutual (both of which publicly supported the first and sent representatives to the second convention), the journal asserted that their absence was the result of "a belief that the thing would not be much heeded in respectable quarters." The *Monitor* also seemed disappointed that most of the nine questions it claimed were originally put forth as the agenda for the convention were not addressed. These questions—including a vote on whether the stock or mutual plan was safest and most economical, the best manner for declaring dividends, whether English life companies should be allowed to do business in the United States, and whether pregnant women should be insured—were antagonistic to the interests of several of the companies invited and did not conform to any of the issues presented by Currie when calling for the convention or to the topics actually discussed. Because of these glaring discrepancies, I have chosen not to report the *Monitor*'s descriptions. They can be found in J. Owen Stalson, *Marketing Life Insurance: Its History in America* (Cambridge, MA: Harvard University Press, 1942), 777–79.

46. "Proceedings of the Life Insurance Convention," *Insurance Gazette,* August 1860: 190–91.

47. "Proceedings of the Life Insurance Convention," *Insurance Gazette,* August 1860: 192.

48. "Proceedings of the Life Insurance Convention," *Insurance Gazette*, August 1860: 193. Of the remaining five companies from the top twenty-five that had not responded, three were British firms with American offices, each of which charged rates significantly higher than their American counterparts. The tenth largest (Massachusetts Mutual) and the twenty-fifth largest (Mutual of Wisconsin, later renamed Northwestern Mutual) were the only two firms that inexplicably were unaccounted for on the list of participants (although Massachusetts Mutual had sent a representative to the 1859 convention and Northwestern was represented in 1860).

49. "Proceedings of the Life Insurance Convention," *Insurance Gazette*, August 1860: 193.

50. "Proceedings of the Life Insurance Convention," *Insurance Gazette*, August 1860: 185–212.

51. "Vital Statistics—The Combined Experience Mortality Table—When is it Forthcoming," *Insurance Gazette*, May–October 1861: 336–37.

52. "Life Insurance Combined Experience Table will be Forthcoming," *Insurance Gazette*, November 1861–April 1862: 105.

53. John Eadie, United States Life of New York, to Elizur Wright, April 22, 1864, WCP.

54. "First Annual Meeting of the Chamber of Life Insurance," *Insurance Monitor*, November 1867: 691.

55. Clough, 61; and Dan M. McGill, *Life Insurance* (Homewood, IL: Richard D. Irwin, 1967), 146–47. Several sources put this date at 1861 rather than 1868. However, the evidence does not seem to support this earlier date, as Mutual Life was still charging rates based on the Gill Table in 1867. See "Comparative Table showing the Annual Rate of Premium," *Insurance Monitor*, June 1867: 346.

56. Glover, 224.

57. See Stalson, 322.

58. Buley, *The American Life Convention*, 81.

59. Clough, 59.

60. "The First American Life Underwriters' Convention," *Insurance Gazette*, July 1859: 129.

61. "The First American Life Underwriters' Convention," *Insurance Gazette*, July 1859: 128–29. The committee went on to provide some of the most extreme examples of this legislation in action, including "a law . . . which expelled every Company that had complied with the law of a neighboring State." "The First American Life Underwriters' Convention," *Insurance Gazette*, July 1859: 130–31.

62. Lawrence B. Goodheart, *Abolitionist, Actuary, Atheist: Elizur Wright and the Reform Impulse* (Kent, OH: Kent State University Press, 1990), 146.

63. Goodheart, 146–47.

64. Kenneth J. Meier, *The Political Economy of Regulation: The Case of Insurance* (Albany: State University of New York Press, 1988), 46; Morton Keller, *The Life Insurance Enterprise, 1885–1910: A Study in the Limits of Corporate Power* (Cambridge, MA: Belknap, 1963), 199; and H. Roger Grant, *Insurance Reform: Consumer Action in the Progressive Era* (Ames: Iowa State University Press, 1988), 3–4. The creation of insurance departments parallels the establishment of similar commissions to oversee other industries such as railroads. See James W. Ely Jr., *Railroads and American Law* (Lawrence: University Press of Kansas, 2002), 84–85.

65. Goodheart, 141–43; Buley, *The American Life Convention*, 59; David Jenkins and

Takau Yoneyama, eds., *History of Insurance*, vol., *Life* (London: Pickering & Chatto, 2000), 2; and Elizur Wright, "Life Insurance," *North American Review*, August 1886: 145.

66. "Life Policies Not Subject to Forfeiture," *Hunt's Merchants' Magazine*, September 1861: 301.

67. Goodheart, 149.

68. "Proceedings of the Life Insurance Convention," *Insurance Gazette*, August 1860: 257.

69. "Life Policies Not Subject to Forfeiture," *Hunt's Merchants' Magazine*, September 1861: 301.

70. Buley *The American Life Convention*, 79.

71. "Proceedings of the Life Insurance Convention," *Insurance Gazette*, August 1860: 230.

72. "Proceedings of the Life Insurance Convention," *Insurance Gazette*, August 1860: 228.

73. "Proceedings of the Life Insurance Convention," *Insurance Gazette*, August 1860: 241.

74. "The First American Life Underwriters' Convention," *Insurance Gazette*, July 1859: 128–29.

75. "The First American Life Underwriters' Convention," *Insurance Gazette*, July 1859: 130–31.

76. "Proceedings of the Life Insurance Convention," *Insurance Gazette*, August 1860: 225.

77. "Proceedings of the Life Insurance Convention," *Insurance Gazette*, August 1860: 226.

78. "Proceedings of the Life Insurance Convention," *Insurance Gazette*, August 1860: 227–28.

79. "Proceedings of the Life Insurance Convention," *Insurance Gazette*, August 1860: 232–34.

80. "Proceedings of the Life Insurance Convention," *Insurance Gazette*, August 1860: 239.

81. "Proceedings of the Life Insurance Convention," *Insurance Gazette*, August 1860: 272.

82. Robert F. Dalzell Jr., *Enterprising Elite: The Boston Associates and the World They Made* (Cambridge, MA: Harvard University Press, 1987), 94–97; Bray Hammond, *Banks and Politics in America from the Revolution to the Civil War* (Princeton, NJ: Princeton University Press, 1957), 551–54; and Stephen Mihm, *A Nation of Counterfeiters: Capitalists, Con Men, and the Making of the United States* (Cambridge, MA: Harvard University Press, 2007), 134–37.

Chapter Ten • Insuring Soldiers, Insuring Civilians

1. F. M. Colston to C. B. Wellford, January 8, 1861, Letter Book, BLIC.

2. C. B. Wellford to F. M. Colston, January 22, 1861, Correspondence 14, BLIC.

3. F. M. Colston to C. B. Wellford, January 23, 1861, Letter Book, BLIC.

4. F. M. Colston to C. B. Wellford, January 8, 1861, Letter Book, BLIC.

5. Dr. Thomas Pollard to John J. Donaldson, February 20, 1861, Correspondence 14, BLIC.

6. C. B. Wellford to F. M. Colston, May 7, 1861, Correspondence 14, BLIC.

7. F. M. Colston to C. B. Wellford, May 13, 1861, Letter Book, BLIC. Reflecting Lieutenant Wellford's actual age of 27, Baltimore Life would reduce this rate even further to 4%— approximately 1% for the initial premium and 3% for the war and climate risks. C. B. Wellford to F. M. Colston, May 16, 1861, Correspondence 14, and F. M. Colston, to C. B. Wellford, May 20, 1861, Letter Book, BLIC.

8. F. M. Colston to C. B. Wellford, May 13, 1861, Letter Book, BLIC.

9. C. B. Wellford to F. M. Colston, May 29, 1861, Correspondence 14, BLIC.

10. F. M. Colston to C. B. Wellford, June 3, 1861, Letter Book, BLIC.

11. F. M. Colston to C. B. Wellford, June 3, 1861, Letter Book, BLIC.

12. Richard Franklin Bensel, *Yankee Leviathan: The Origins of Central State Authority in America, 1859–1877* (Cambridge: Cambridge University Press, 1990), 157; Mark A. Weitz, *The Confederacy on Trial: The Piracy and Sequestration Cases of 1861* (Lawrence: University Press of Kansas, 2005), 10–11; and Daniel W. Hamilton, *The Limits of Sovereignty: Property Confiscation in the Union and the Confederacy during the Civil War* (Chicago: University of Chicago Press, 2007), 6–7, 84, 87.

13. James M. Hudnut, *Semi-Centennial History of the New-York Life Insurance Company, 1845–1895* (New York: New York Life Insurance Company, 1895), 82.

14. Hudnut, 85.

15. "Northern Insurance Companies Expelled from the State of Mississippi," *United States Insurance Gazette and Magazine of Useful Knowledge,* May–October 1861: 115.

16. C. B. Wellford to F. M. Colston, secretary, October 25, 1861, Correspondence 14, BLIC.

17. F. M. Colston to C. B. Wellford, November 12, 1861, Letter Book, BLIC.

18. F. M. Colston to C. B. Wellford, May 13, 1861, Letter Book, BLIC.

19. F. M. Colston to J. W. Magill, June 4, 1861, Letter Book, BLIC.

20. F. M. Colston to C. B. Wellford, November 12, 1861, and to Dr. Thomas Pollard, March 11, 1862, Letter Book, BLIC.

21. Hamilton, 125.

22. Donaldson to C. B. Wellford, June 23, 1865, and to Dr. Thomas Pollard, June 28, 1865, Letter Book, BLIC.

23. In December 1862, the company felt it necessary to inform its agents that "slaves emancipated during the existence of their policy, renders it void." Secretary pro tem to J. W. Magill, December 9, 1862, Letter Book, BLIC.

24. See George W. Turner, and attached note from C. L. Mosby, to Donaldson, October 14, 1865, Correspondence 14, BLIC.

25. George W. Turner to Donaldson, October 14, 1865, Correspondence 14, BLIC.

26. Donaldson to C. L. Mosby, November 1, 1865, Letter Book, BLIC.

27. Henry F. Thompson to Sheppard Homans, November 9, 1866, Letter Book, BLIC. See also Homans to Thompson, November 6 and 22, 1866, Correspondence 14, BLIC.

28. Henry F. Thompson to Sheppard Homans, February 14, 1867, Letter Book, BLIC.

29. William G. Harrison to G. W. Phillips, Equitable Life Assurance Society, May 23, 1867, and to William C. Alexander, Equitable Life, May 25, 1867, Letter Book, BLIC.

30. J. Owen Stalson, *Marketing Life Insurance: Its History in America* (Cambridge, MA: Harvard University Press, 1942), 750–51.

31. The Mexican-American War of 1846–48 shed only limited light on this problem. Approximately 78,700 men participated in that war, which lasted less than two years, compared with the 3.9 million men who would participate during the four years of the Civil War.

32. Stalson, 329.

33. Connecticut Mutual Life 1846 and 1851 brochures: 19, HCR. See also Mutual Life of New York 1847 brochure: 22–23, Albion Life 1845 brochure: 5, and Mutual Life of Baltimore 1849 brochure: 16, HCR.

34. "Life Insurance in the United States," *Hunt's Merchants' Magazine*, March 1843: 231. See also "American Life Insurance Companies Opposed to Granting 'Days of Grace,'" *Insurance Gazette*, May–October 1858: 99; and *Life Insurance: Its Principles, Operations and Benefits, as presented by the North Carolina Mutual Life Insurance Company* (Raleigh: Seaton Gales, 1849), 16.

35. Located one mile from Fort Sumter on the southern tip of Sullivan's Island in Charleston Harbor, Fort Moultrie was a pre-revolutionary fortification served by the First United States Artillery garrison. The garrison was relocated to the still incomplete Fort Sumter in late December 1860.

36. "Patriotism and Liberality of our Life Insurance Corporations—The Fort Moultrie Policyholder," *Insurance Gazette*, November 1860–April 1861: 329.

37. "Exciting Scenes in the City," *New York Herald*, April 19, 1861.

38. "How to Aid Volunteers," *New York Times*, April 24, 1861: 5.

39. "War Risks of Life Insurance—Letter from Elizur Wright," *Hunt's Merchants' Magazine*, July 1861: 103–4.

40. "War Risks of Life Insurance—Letter from Elizur Wright," *Hunt's Merchants' Magazine*, July 1861: 103–4.

41. "Third Annual Report of Honorable William Barnes," *Insurance Gazette*, May–October 1862: 82.

42. "Life Insurance War Risks," *Insurance Gazette*, May–October 1862: 330.

43. Abram T. Collier, *A Capital Ship, New England Life: A History of America's First Chartered Mutual Life Insurance Company, 1835–1985* (Boston: New England Mutual Life Insurance Company, 1985), 47; William Cahn, *A Matter of Life and Death: The Connecticut Mutual Story* (New York: Random House, 1970), 58–59; Wendell Buck, *From Quill Pens to Computers: An Account of the First One Hundred and Twenty-five Years of The Manhattan Life Insurance Company of New York, N.Y.* (New York: Manhattan Life Insurance Company, 1975), 20–21; Hudnut, 75; and R. Carlyle Buley, *The American Life Convention, 1906–1952: A Study in the History of Life Insurance* (New York: Appleton-Century-Crofts, 1953), 72–73.

44. "Mutual Life Insurance Company of the State of Wisconsin," *Insurance Gazette*, May–October 1861: 279; Cahn, 58–59; Buck, 20–21; R. Carlyle Buley, *The Equitable Life Assurance Society of the United States, 1859–1964* (New York: Appleton-Century-Crofts, 1967), 76–77; and Buley, *The American Life Convention*, 72–73.

45. "The Third Annual American Life Underwriters' Convention," *Insurance Gazette*, August 1862: 179.

46. "The Third Annual American Life Underwriters' Convention," *Insurance Gazette*, August 1862: 178.

47. New York Life 1863 brochure: 24, and New York Life 1866 brochure: 64–65, HCR.

48. Buley, *The Equitable Life*, 77.

49. "Life Insurance War Risks," *Insurance Gazette*, May–October 1862: 288–89.

50. "Life Insurance War Risks," *Insurance Gazette*, May–October 1862: 288–89.

51. "Life Insurance War Risks," *Insurance Gazette,* May–October 1862: 288–89.

52. "Mutual Life Insurance Company of the State of Wisconsin," *Insurance Gazette,* May–October 1861: 279.

53. "Life Insurance War Risks," *Insurance Gazette,* May–October 1862: 330.

54. Quoted in Hudnut, 102.

55. "Reflections—New York Life Insurance Co.," *Insurance Gazette,* November 1861–April 1862: 146.

56. Marquis James, *The Metropolitan Life: A Study in Business Growth* (New York: Viking, 1947), 19–20; Stalson, 329; and Hudnut, 119, 389.

57. "Life Insurance War Risks," *Insurance Gazette,* May–October 1862: 330.

58. Hudnut, 101–2; and Lawrence F. Abbott, *The Story of NYLIC: A History of the Origin and Development of the New York Life Insurance Company from 1845 to 1929* (New York, 1930), 64.

59. James, 19–20; Stalson, 329; and Hudnut 119, 389.

60. Collier, 47; and "Commission on War Risks," *Insurance Monitor,* November 1861: 258.

61. Policy Applications, NEMLIC. Unfortunately, most of the other extant policy applications, policy books, and policy registers of the company exclude the war years, so it is impossible to compile more complete data on its war risks.

62. "New England Mutual Life Insurance Company," *Insurance Gazette,* November 1861–April 1862: 260.

63. "Insurance Advertiser," *Insurance Gazette,* May–October 1864.

64. "North America Life Insurance Company, N.Y.—Unparalleled Success," *Insurance Gazette,* May–October 1863: 296–97.

65. See Iver Bernstein, *The New York City Draft Riots: Their Significance for American Society and Politics in the Age of the Civil War* (New York: Oxford University Press, 1990), 7–8.

66. James, 23.

67. Bensel, 138.

68. "National Union Life and Limb Insurance Company of New York—Commenced Operations with a Capital of $500,000," *Insurance Gazette,* May–October 1864: 242–43. See also "National Union Life and Limb," *New York Times,* August 1, 1864: 6.

69. James, 22; and Buley, *The American Life Convention,* 74–75.

70. James, 24; and Buley, *The American Life Convention,* 74–75.

71. James, 26.

72. Hudnut, 119.

73. Mildred F. Stone, *Since 1845: A History of the Mutual Benefit Life Insurance Company* (New Brunswick, NJ: Rutgers University Press, 1957), 67.

74. "United States Life Insurance Company, New York—Its Rapid Extension of Business and Increase of Assets During the Past Six Months," *Insurance Gazette,* May–October 1863: 293; Buley, *The American Life Convention,* 74; and James, 20. It is unclear how these war risks were distributed between existing policyholders and new risks.

75. Shepard B. Clough, *A Century of American Life Insurance: A History of the Mutual Life Insurance Company of New York, 1843–1943* (New York: Columbia University Press, 1946), 88.

76. Cahn, 59–60.

77. *Historical Statistics of the United States, Colonial Times to 1970* (Washington, DC:

Government Printing Office, 1975), 1057. All amounts in 1860 dollars, adjusted according to the consumer price index in Paul A. David and Peter Solar, "A Bicentenary Contribution to the History of the Cost of Living in America," *Research in Economic History* 2 (1977): 16.

78. Stalson, 786.

79. Lester W. Zartman, "History of Life Insurance in the United States," in Lester W. Zartman, ed., *Personal Insurance: Life and Accident* (New Haven, CT: Yale University Press, 1914), 86.

80. "Mutual Life Insurance Company of New York—Its Conduct Toward Policyholders in Seceding Southern States," *Insurance Gazette*, November 1860–April 1861: 329.

81. Hudnut, 70.

82. Stalson, 329; Hudnut, 117; and Collier, 47.

83. Quoted from a letter submitted as evidence in *Manhattan Life Insurance Company v. Warwick*, 61 Va. 614 (1871).

84. Quoted from a letter submitted as evidence *Manhattan Life v. Warwick* (1871).

85. "Mutual Benefit Life Insurance Company of Newark, N. J.—Circular to Southern Agents in Relation to their Operations," *Insurance Gazette*, May–October 1861: 337.

86. "Mutual Benefit Life Insurance Company of Newark, N. J.—Circular to Southern Agents in Relation to their Operations," *Insurance Gazette*, May–October 1861: 337.

87. Buck, 26.

88. Stone, 69.

89. The companies involved in these lawsuits included Charter Oak Life, Connecticut Mutual Life, Manhattan Life, Mutual Benefit, Mutual Life of New York, New York Life, and Penn Mutual Life.

90. See the language of Manhattan Life's policy, as quoted in *Manhattan Life v. Warwick* (1871).

91. *W. C. Statham v. New York Life Insurance Company*, 45 Miss. 581 (1871).

92. *Manhattan v. Warwick* (1871); *Statham v. New York* (1871); *The New York Life Insurance Company v. Hendren*, 65 Va. 536 (1874); *John W. Smith v. The Charter Oak Life Insurance Company*, 64 Mo. 330 (1876); *Connecticut Mutual Life Insurance Company v. Duerson's Executor*, 69 Va. 630 (1877); *Tait v. New York Life Insurance Company*, 23 F. Cas. 620 (1873); and *Davis v. New York Life Insurance Company*, 7 F. Cas. 150 (1879).

93. *Statham v. New York Life* (1871); *Henrietta Hillyard v. The Mutual Benefit Life Insurance Company*, 35 N.J.L. 415 (1872); and *Maria Worthington v. The Charter Oak Life Insurance Company*, 41 Conn. 372 (1874).

94. *Statham v. New York Life* (1871). This was similar to the policy adopted by the Confederacy based on its Sequestration Act. Continued residence within the Union, regardless of where a person claimed to be legally domiciled, was sufficient evidence of enemy status for the Confederacy to confiscate any southern property belonging to that person. As one Confederate judge asserted, if a person "desired to establish or to retain his domicile or citizenship here, and to prevent the status of alien enemy being charged against him, it was his duty, as soon as he reasonably could do so, to come into the Confederate states and bear his share of the burdens, and take his chances of the perils of this war." Hamilton, 105.

95. *William D. Robinson v. The International Life Assurance Society of London*, 42 N.Y. 54 (1870); and *Stephania Lucy Sands v. The New York Life Insurance Company*, 50 N.Y. 626 (1872).

96. *New York Life Insurance Company v. Clopton,* 70 Ky. 179 (1870); *Manhattan Life v. Warwick* (1871); *Statham v. New York Life* (1871); *Mutual Benefit Life Insurance Company v. Atwood's Administratrix,* 65 Va. 497 (1874); *Smith v. Charter Oak Life* (1876); *Tait v. New York Life* (1873); and *Davis v. New York Life* (1879).

97. *New York Life v. Clopton* (1870).

98. *Mary H. Dillard v. The Manhattan Life Insurance Company,* 44 Ga. 119 (1871); and *Hillyard v. Mutual Benefit Life* (1872).

99. *Henrietta Yates Cohen v. The New York Mutual Life Insurance Company,* 50 N.Y. 610 (1872); *Manhattan Life Insurance Company v. Eliza P. LePert,* 52 Tex. 504 (1880); and *Abell v. Penn Mutual Life Insurance Company* 18 W. Va. 400 (1881).

100. *Mutual Benefit Life Insurance Company v. Hillyard,* 37 N.J.L. 444 (1874).

101. *Cohen v. New York Mutual Life* (1872).

102. For a comprehensive discussion of the law of incomplete contracts, see Roy Kreitner, *Calculating Promises: The Emergence of Modern American Contract Doctrine* (Stanford, CA: Stanford University Press, 2007), part 3.

103. *New York Life v. Clopton* (1870).

104. *Cohen v. New York Mutual Life* (1872).

105. *Cohen v. New York Mutual Life* (1872).

106. *Hillyard v. Mutual Benefit Life* (1872).

107. *Statham v. New York Life* (1871).

108. *Manhattan Life v. Warwick* (1871).

109. Kreitner, 218.

110. *Worthington v. Charter Oak Life* (1874).

111. *New York Life Insurance Company v. Statham, New York Life Insurance Company v. Seyms, Manhattan Life Insurance Company v. Buck,* 93 U.S. 24 (1876).

112. *New York Life v. Statham, New York Life v. Seyms, Manhattan Life v. Buck* (1876).

113. *New York Life v. Statham, New York Life v. Seyms, Manhattan Life v. Buck* (1876).

114. *New York Life Insurance Company v. Davis,* 95 U.S. 425 (1877).

115. Kreitner, part 3.

Chapter Eleven · *The Perils of Success during the Postbellum Years*

1. "Life Insurance," *North American Review,* October 1863: 301–13.

2. "Life Insurance," *North American Review,* October 1863: 307–21.

3. "Life Insurance," *North American Review,* October 1863: 315–19.

4. Guardian Life advertisement, *Christian Advocate and Journal,* January 31, 1861: 40.

5. Harry N. Scheiber, "Federalism and the American Economic Order, 1789–1910," *Law and Society Review* 10 (1975): 116.

6. Philip L. Merkel, "Going National: The Life Insurance Industry's Campaign for Federal Regulation after the Civil War" *Business History Review* 65 (1991): 540–41.

7. Merkel, 542.

8. "The Life Insurance Convention," *New York Times,* November 23, 1866: 8. See also "Life Insurance Convention," *New York Times,* November 22, 1866: 2.

9. "Life Insurance Convention," *New York Times,* November 22, 1866: 2. Only 17% of

the companies and six of the top fifteen would be represented in November 1867. "First Annual Meeting of the Chamber of Life Insurance," *Insurance Monitor,* November 1867: 688.

10. "First Annual Meeting of the Chamber of Life Insurance," *Insurance Monitor,* November 1867: 694.

11. "Life Insurance Statistics," *DeBow's Commercial Review,* August 8, 1868: 687–88.

12. "Fortieth Congress," *New York Times,* January 30, 1868: 8; and Merkel, 542–43.

13. Merkel, 544–45.

14. "The Chamber of Life Insurance," *New York Times,* November 24, 1866: 2.

15. *Paul v. Virginia,* 75 U.S. 168 (1869); Kenneth J. Meier, *The Political Economy of Regulation: The Case of Insurance* (Albany: State University of New York Press, 1988), 53; and Merkel, 546.

16. *Paul v. Virginia* (1869); and Edmund W. Kitch, "Regulation and the American Common Market," in A. Dan. Tarlock, ed., *Regulation, Federalism, and Interstate Commerce* (Cambridge, MA: Oelgeschlager, Gunn & Hain, 1981), 26–27.

17. *Paul v. Virginia* (1869).

18. *Paul v. Virginia* (1869).

19. *Liverpool Insurance Company v. Massachusetts,* 77 U.S. 566 (1871); *Ducat v. Chicago,* 48 Ill. 172 (1868); *Ducat v. Chicago,* 77 U.S. 410 (1871); *Philadelphia Fire Association v. New York,* 119 U.S. 110 (1886); *Hooper v. California,* 155 U.S. 648 (1895); *Cravens v. New York Life Insurance Company,* 148 Mo. 583 (1899); *New York Life Insurance Company v. Cravens,* 178 U.S. 389 (1900); *Nutting v. Massachusetts,* 183 U.S. 553 (1902); *New York Life Insurance Company v. Deer Lodge County,* 43 Mont. 243 (1911); and *New York Life Insurance Company v. Deer Lodge County,* 231 U.S. 495 (1913).

20. *United States v. South-Eastern Underwriters Association,* 51 F. Supp. 712 (1943); *United States v. South-Eastern Underwriters Association,* 322 U.S. 533 (1944); *United States v. South-Eastern Underwriters Association,* 323 U.S. 811 (1944); Spencer L. Kimball and Ronald N. Boyce, "The Adequacy of State Insurance Rate Regulation: The McCarran-Ferguson Act in Historical Perspective," *Michigan Law Review* 56 (1958), 553; and Meier, 67.

21. John Gudmundsen, *The Great Provider: The Dramatic Story of Life Insurance in America* (South Norwalk, CT: Industrial Publications, 1959), 49.

22. H. Roger Grant, *Insurance Reform: Consumer Action in the Progressive Era* (Ames: Iowa State University Press, 1988), 166.

23. Tom Baker, "On the Genealogy of Moral Hazard," *Texas Law Review* (December 1996): 8–9.

24. "American Mutual Life Insurance and Trust Company," *Insurance Gazette,* November 1859–April 1860.

25. "Statement of the United States Life Insurance Co.," *Insurance Gazette,* April–November 1861 and April–November 1864.

26. "British Commercial and British Nation Life Assurance Association," *Insurance Gazette,* April–November 1864.

27. "The Charter Oak Life Insurance Company," *Insurance Monitor,* January 1867: 24, and February 1869: 101.

28. "The Manhattan Life Insurance Company," *Insurance Monitor,* January 1867: 51; "Empire Mutual Life Insurance Co.," *Galaxy,* January 1870; "Atlantic Mutual Life Insurance

Company," *Insurance Monitor,* January 1872: 90; and "Hope Mutual Life Insurance Company," *Insurance Monitor,* January 1872: 102. See also "Great Western Life Insurance Co.," *Insurance Monitor,* February 1867: 104; "Metropolitan Life Insurance Company," *Insurance Monitor,* February 1869: 132; and "Commonwealth Life Insurance Company," *Insurance Monitor,* September 1869: 706.

29. "Phoenix Mutual Life Insurance Company," *Insurance Monitor,* February 1869: 156.

30. Empire Mutual Life Insurance Company advertisement, *Galaxy,* January 1870: 148.

31. "The Two Sides of the Indisputability Question," *Insurance Monitor,* August 1879: 396–97.

32. "Unjust Toleration. A Warning to Life Insurance Companies," *Insurance Monitor,* June 1867: 341.

33. "Joseph Cochrane vs. The Knickerbocker Life Insurance Company," *Insurance Monitor,* November 1861: 254.

34. "Unjust Toleration. A Warning to Life Insurance Companies," *Insurance Monitor,* June 1867: 341.

35. "The Litigiousness of Life Companies," *Insurance Monitor,* October 1879: 485.

36. "Chamber of Life Insurance," *The Insurance Monitor,* December 1867: 767.

37. "First Annual Meeting of the Chamber of Life Insurance," *Insurance Monitor,* November 1867: 694. This committee appears to have been modeled on the British system whereby all disputed claims in fire and life insurance were submitted to arbitration before being brought before a court of law. "The Law of Fire and Life Insurance," *Insurance Gazette,* November 1860–April 1861: 7.

38. "Chamber of Life Insurance," *Insurance Monitor,* December 1867: 767.

39. "The Commission System in Life Insurance," *Insurance Monitor,* June 1869: 451.

40. J. B. Lewis and C. C. Bombaugh, *Remarkable Stratagems and Conspiracies: An Authentic Record of Surprising Attempts to Defraud Life Insurance Companies* (New York: G. W. Carleton, 1878).

41. "Attempt to Swindle a Life Insurance Company," *Insurance Monitor,* January 1867: 36.

42. "A Philadelphia Life Ins. Fraud. A Singular Story," *Insurance Monitor,* October 1867: 620.

43. *Historical Statistics of the United States, Colonial Times to 1970* (Washington, DC: Government Printing Office, 1975), 1057. All amounts in 1860 dollars, adjusted according to the consumer price index in Paul A. David and Peter Solar, "A Bicentenary Contribution to the History of the Cost of Living in America," *Research in Economic History* 2 (1977): 16.

44. Lawrence F. Abbott, *The Story of NYLIC: A History of the Origin and Development of the New York Life Insurance Company from 1845 to 1929* (New York, 1930), 102.

45. Louis I. Dublin, *A Family of Thirty Million: The Story of the Metropolitan Life Insurance Company* (New York: Metropolitan Life Insurance Company, 1943), 36.

46. R. Carlyle Buley, *The American Life Convention, 1906–1952: A Study in the History of Life Insurance* (New York: Appleton-Century-Crofts, 1953), 129; and B. H. Meyer, "Fraternal Beneficiary Societies in the United States," *American Journal of Sociology* 6 (1901): 650.

47. Buley, *The American Life Convention,* 107.

48. *Report of the Commission on Old Age Pensions, Annuities and Insurance* (Boston: Wright

& Potter, 1910), 178–79; and William H. A. Carr, *From Three Cents a Week . . . The Story of The Prudential Insurance Company of America* (Englewood Cliffs, NY: Prentice-Hall, 1975), 14.

49. Walter McElreath, *History of the Industrial Life and Health Insurance Company* (Atlanta: Industrial Life and Health Insurance Company, 1935), 32; Anita Rapone, *The Guardian Life Insurance Company, 1860–1920: A History of a German-American Enterprise* (New York: New York University Press, 1987), 80; and Buley, *The American Life Convention,* III.

50. *McClure's Magazine,* October 1896.

51. *McClure's Magazine,* May 1896.

52. *McClure's Magazine,* June 1896.

53. Dublin, 57–58; and Buley, *The American Life Convention,* III. According to Viviana Zelizer, at least seventy attempts were made to ban insurance on the lives of children. Viviana A. Rotman Zelizer, *Morals and Markets: The Development of Life Insurance in the United States* (New York: Columbia University Press, 1979), 63n.

54. Earl Chapin May and Will Oursler, *The Prudential: A Story of Human Security* (New York: Doubleday, 1950), 84.

Conclusion · *"Have you provided for your Family an Insurance on your Life?"*

1. "Life Insurance—A Dream," *Harper's New Monthly Magazine,* January 1856: 284–85. Courtesy of Cornell University Library, Making of America Digital Collection.

2. National Life of Vermont 1868 brochure: 8, HCR.

3. Home Life advertisement, *Christian Advocate and Journal,* September 19, 1861: 303.

4. "Life Assurance," *Atlantic Monthly,* September 1866: 314.

Upon entering graduate school, I intended to focus my research on nineteenth-century financial institutions. I was particularly interested in the interaction of commercial and savings banks with both their immediate clientele and with American society at large. As I began exploring this area of inquiry, my advisor (Mark Thomas at the University of Virginia) mentioned my interests to banking historian Eugene White at Rutgers University. It was White who initially suggested that I instead consider studying life insurance, an important financial intermediary whose history had heretofore been overlooked by most academics.

Intrigued by the idea of applying my original set of research questions to a similar yet largely unexplored industry, I immediately obtained the few major academic works on the history of life insurance: J. Owen Stalson's 1942 tome *Marketing Life Insurance: Its History in America* (Cambridge, MA: Harvard University Press) and Viviana A. Rotman Zelizer's 1979 sociological analysis *Morals and Markets: The Development of Life Insurance in the United States* (New York: Columbia University Press). Both of these studies begin with the premise that life insurance was an unpopular, unsuccessful industry prior to its sudden ascendancy in the 1840s. While Stalson argues that the innovative marketing techniques of newly established mutual life insurance companies accounted for this shift, Zelizer attributes this reversal to a cultural revolution in the public's attitude toward underwriting lives—largely fueled by religious beliefs that initially proscribed but then (around 1843) abruptly started to promote the industry. When I read these studies in conjunction with the numerous corporate histories of specific life insurance companies, most of which were written during the 1940s and 1950s to commemorate the centennial anniversaries of extant institutions, I too was convinced of this general time line, and it seemed any useful study of nineteenth-century life insurance would necessarily focus on the second half of the century.

More recent scholarship has explored the unique regulatory history of the insurance industry as a whole, especially its contribution to Gilded Age scandals and Progressive Era reforms. Most notable among these works are *The Life Insurance Enterprise, 1885–1910: A Study in the Limits of Corporate Power* by Morton Keller (Cambridge, MA: Belknap, 1963), *Insurance Reform: Consumer Action in the Progressive Era* by H. Roger Grant (Ames: Iowa State

University Press, 1988), and "Going National: The Life Insurance Industry's Campaign for Federal Regulation after the Civil War" by Philip L. Merkel (*Business History Review* 1991). In his 1952 article "Capital Accumulation in Life Insurance between the Civil War and the Investigation of 1905," Douglass North offers the first financial analysis of the importance of postbellum life insurance (in William Miller, ed., *Men in Business: Essays on the Historical Role of the Entrepreneur*, New York: Harper & Row), while B. Michael Pritchett's 1977 dissertation (republished in 1985 as *Financing Growth: A Financial History of American Life Insurance through 1900*, Philadelphia: S. S. Huebner Foundation for Insurance Education) utilizes early computer technology to quantify the impact of the industry on specific areas of the economy. Finally, Roger L. Ransom and Richard Sutch's 1987 article in the *Journal of Economic History*, "Tontine Insurance and the Armstrong Investigation: A Case of Stifled Innovation, 1868–1905," details one instance in which Progressive Era reforms directly hindered the financial advancement of the industry. These works further convinced me that the most important developments in life insurance occurred during the postbellum period.

With this historiography under my belt, I had a working research plan. I would examine the regulatory and financial histories of life insurance within a larger social and cultural framework in order to create a comprehensive postbellum account of life insurance through the 1920s. On one hand, I would employ the traditional tools of the business historian to identify the managerial, marketing, and financial developments of the major firms and their interaction with the various political, economic, and social events of the day. On the other, I would analyze the people who were actually buying and selling life insurance to understand why this industry became so successful. With these goals in mind, I excitedly marched into Baker Library at Harvard Business School and began poring over its collections—including the Hyde Collection, containing Equitable Life Assurance Society of New York records, and the Historic Corporate Reports Collection, with its numerous brochures from various companies—and the library's copies of the *United States Insurance Gazette and Magazine of Useful Knowledge* and the *Insurance Monitor and Wall Street Review.*

While at Baker Library, I also could not resist the seductive allure of the oldest life insurance records at the archive: those of Massachusetts Hospital Life Insurance Company and New York Life Insurance and Trust Company. As I read through the letter books of these two firms, I realized that they little resembled the life insurers portrayed by Stalson and Zelizer. Massachusetts Hospital Life seemed vibrantly engaged with the religious community during the 1820s and 1830s, while the rapidly growing and profitable New York Life and Trust had an aggressive marketing plan in the 1830s. Likewise, some of earliest extant insurance brochures seemed to belie the accepted historiography. Armed with these sources, I decided to jettison my initial project (along with my foundational assumptions about the state of life insurance prior to 1843) and engage in a thorough reexamination of the antebellum origins of life insurance in the United States.

Primary Sources

By far the most important sources for this study were the records of the antebellum life insurers themselves. While I was never able to locate any documents of the first for-profit company, Pennsylvania Company for Insurances on Lives and Granting Annuities, archival sources for the remaining three major early companies provided a treasure trove of information. The records of Massachusetts Hospital Life (Baker Library Historical Collections, Harvard Business School) include copies of all outgoing letters written by the company starting from its incorporation in 1823; the first three hundred policies issued; a detailed listing of the name, place of residence, occupation, and age of all policyholders through 1832; and the research notes taken in conversation with older insurance firms prior to the company's incorporation. While incoming letters to Massachusetts Hospital Life have also survived, their fragile condition meant that I was only allowed to view specific letters and could not browse through the whole collection. Baker Library Historical Collections also houses the records of New York Life and Trust, the nation's largest life insurer during the 1830s. In addition to a substantial number of outgoing letter books and a detailed list of policyholders from its incorporation in 1830 through its suspension of insurance sales in the 1860s, this collection includes the insurance circulars of earlier British and American companies used as models by the firm as well as the records of its individual agencies.

The records of Baltimore Life Insurance Company—the second-largest insurer in the 1830s—are found at the H. Furlong Baldwin Library at the Maryland Historical Society. The collection is unique in its comprehensiveness, including all incoming and outgoing letters, all accepted policy applications, and a detailed list of policyholders from its inception in 1830 through its demise in 1867. Unlike the New York Life and Trust and Massachusetts Hospital Life collections, which show only the standpoint of the firm, the records of Baltimore Life highlight the beliefs, attitudes, fears, and expectations of the insured public through the incoming letters and applications included in the collection. This is also the largest known extant source on slave insurance policies.

After the completion of my dissertation, but prior to its revision for this book, Baker Library Historical Collections obtained the records of New England Mutual Life Insurance Company—the fifth-largest company during the late 1840s and 1850s—which the staff graciously allowed me to examine before they had even completed its formal cataloging. The value of this archive is twofold. On one hand, as New England Mutual began selling policies after Stalson's "revolution of 1843," it offers a critical point of comparison with the practices of the earlier firms. On the other, its extensive collection of policy applications—including the commentary of agents, medical examiners, and members of the board of directors—provides an indispensable window into the process of evaluating applicants as well as an extension of the demographic knowledge of policyholders further into the 1850s.

The numerous company brochures found in the Historical Corporate Reports Collection at Baker Library appear throughout this study. These were supplemented with the published works of several companies, including literature of the Corporation for the Relief of the

Widows and Children of Clergymen of the Protestant Episcopal Church (*The Charters, with the Laws and the List of Members* [1791] and *Fundamental By-Laws and Tables of Rates for Reversionary Annuities, Annuities, and Endowments* [1851]); Pennsylvania Company (*An Address to the Citizens of Pennsylvania, Upon the Subject of a Life Insurance Company* [1813]; *An Address from the President and Directors of the Pennsylvania Company for Insurances on Lives and Granting Annuities to the Inhabitants of the United States, upon the Subject of the Beneficial Objects of that Institution* [1814]; and *Proposals of the Pennsylvania Company for Insurances on Lives and Granting Annuities* [1837]); Union Insurance Company (*Prospectus of the Union Insurance Company* [1818]); New York Life and Trust (*Rates and Proposals of the New-York Life Insurance and Trust Company* [1830] and William Bard's *A Letter to David E. Evans, Esquire, of Batavia, on Life Insurance* [1832]); Massachusetts Hospital Life (*Proposals of the Massachusetts Hospital Life Insurance Company, to Make Insurance on Lives, to Grant Annuities on Lives and in Trust, and Endowments for Children* [1835]); Mutual Life Insurance Company of New York (*Are Accumulative Life Policies Superior to Savings Banks in Providing for Families?* [1854] and *Life Insurance Illustrated* [1868]); Connecticut Mutual Life Insurance Company (*Life Insurance: Its Principles, Operations and Benefits* [1846]); and North Carolina Mutual Life Insurance Company (*Life Insurance: Its Principles, Operations and Benefits* [1849]).

The published works of several insurance theorists also contributed to this study. The Baker Library Historical Collections contain the correspondence of Elizur Wright, a major life insurance promoter and reformer at midcentury. Several of his reports as Massachusetts insurance commissioner are also available in *The "Bible of Life Insurance"; Being a Complete Photographic Reprint of the Original Studies and Official Reports of Elizur Wright* (1932). Harvey G. Tuckett's *Practical Remarks on the Present State of Life Insurance in the United States. Showing the Evils Which Exist, and Rules for Improvement* (1851) and Moses L. Knapp's *Lectures on the Science of Life Insurance* (1853) both provided great insight on the attitudes and concerns of the public toward life insurance. Statistical data were gleaned from several other works, including *A Comparative Atlas and Graphical History of American Life Insurance* (1880), *Life Insurance History, 1843–1910: Yearly Business of All Active United States Life Insurance Companies from Organization* (1911), and "Fifty Years of American Life Insurance Progress: Tables" (*Publications of the American Statistical Association*, 1911). Finally, Steven Haberman and Trevor A. Sibbett have reprinted the works of several prominent actuaries in *History of Actuarial Science* (London: William Pickering, 1995).

The chapter on slave insurance benefited greatly from the Joseph Adolph Linn Papers and the Orin Datus Davis Papers in the University of North Carolina at Chapel Hill's Southern Historical Collection, the Sterling Neblett Papers at Duke University's William R. Perkins Library, and the Papers of the McCue Family at the University of Virginia's Albert and Shirley Small Special Collections Library. Although the information available through the California Department of Insurance Slavery Era Insurance Registry Report to the California Legislature (May 2002) and the Illinois Department of Insurance, Slavery Era Insurance Policies Registry (http://www.insurance.illinois.gov/Consumer/SlaveryInformation/Slavery

Reporting.asp, accessed November 2009) is far from complete, these sources provide some baseline data on the involvement of northern firms in the business of slave insurance.

For advertisements, articles, editorials, and fictional accounts of life insurance, I relied heavily on several databases, including America's Historical Newspapers, the American Periodical Series Online, the Making of America digital collection at Cornell University and the University of Michigan, the University of Virginia Library Electronic Text Center, Project Gutenberg, and Google Books. These were supplemented with old-fashioned research in several newspapers and periodicals, including the *New York Times, Hunt's Merchants' Magazine and Commercial Review,* the *Insurance Monitor and Wall Street Review,* the *United States Insurance Almanac,* and the *United States Insurance Gazette and Magazine of Useful Knowledge.* Most of the sermons and marriage manuals consulted for this study are from the collection at the Library Company of Philadelphia, while the numerous court cases were accessed through the LexisNexis database. Biographical information on William Bard was obtained through the Bard College Archives.

Secondary Sources

In addition to the handful of general works on life insurance and the numerous corporate histories, the context for this book includes studies of the development of the middle class, the culture of capitalism in the early republic, the history of fatherhood, women in the nineteenth century, advancements in scientific and statistical knowledge, urban slavery and the slave trade, and the regulatory state. Timothy Alborn's *Regulated Lives: Life Insurance and British Society, 1800–1914* (Toronto: University of Toronto Press, 2009) nicely parallels this work by addressing many similar social, cultural, economic, and regulatory issues from the British perspective. Unfortunately, Alborn's well-argued book was not released in time for me to incorporate these British comparisons.

A central argument of this book is that life insurance marketing tapped into both the fears and the aspirations of the emerging urban middle class. Particularly useful in defining the characteristics of this elusive group are Stuart M. Blumin's *The Emergence of the Middle Class: Social Experience in the American City, 1760–1900* (New York: Cambridge University Press, 1989), Mary P. Ryan's *Cradle of the Middle Class: The Family in Oneida County, New York, 1790–1865* (Cambridge: Cambridge University Press, 1981), Paul E. Johnson's *A Shopkeeper's Millennium: Society and Revivals in Rochester, New York, 1815–1837* (New York: Farrar, Straus & Giroux, 1978), and Cindy Sondik Aron's *Ladies and Gentlemen of the Civil Service* (New York: Oxford University Press, 1987). Although Edwin J. Perkins's *Wall Street to Main Street: Charles Merrill and Middle-Class Investors* (Cambridge: Cambridge University Press, 1999) is a twentieth-century analysis, it had a significant influence on my thinking about the relationship between the middle class and the financial services industry.

Recent scholarship on the shifting role of fathers within the family has highlighted the responsibility of middle-class fathers in ensuring that their offspring continue to rise up the socioeconomic ladder. E. Anthony Rotundo's *American Manhood: Transformations in Masculinity from the Revolution to the Modern Era* (New York: Basic Books, 1993), Stephen M. Frank's *Life with Father: Parenthood and Masculinity in the Nineteenth-Century American North* (Baltimore: Johns Hopkins University Press, 1998), and Shawn Johansen's *Family Men: Middle-Class Fatherhood in Early Industrializing America* (New York: Routledge, 2001) are especially useful in detailing this trend.

Even as life insurers were targeting middle-class fathers, they recognized that the women in the household would be the true beneficiaries of their policies. Among the works consulted for understanding the precarious legal and economic position of women in the early republic are Norma Basch's *In the Eyes of the Law: Women, Marriage, and Property in Nineteenth-Century New York* (Ithaca, NY: Cornell University Press, 1982), Jeanne Boydston's *Home and Work: Housework, Wages, and the Ideology of Labor in the Early Republic* (New York: Oxford University Press, 1990), Nancy Cott's *The Bonds of Womanhood: "Woman's Sphere" in New England, 1780–1835* (New Haven, CT: Yale University Press, 1977), Marylynn Salmon's *Women and the Law of Property in Early America* (Chapel Hill: University of North Carolina Press, 1986), and Elizabeth Bowles Warbasse's *The Changing Legal Rights of Married Women, 1800–1861* (New York: Garland, 1987). The potential plight of the urban middle-class widow is contrasted with the rural ideal as set forth by Joan M. Jensen in *Loosening the Bonds: Mid-Atlantic Farm Women, 1750–1850* (New Haven, CT: Yale University Press, 1986) and Nancy Grey Osterud in *Bonds of Community: The Lives of Farm Women in Nineteenth-Century New York* (Ithaca, NY: Cornell University Press, 1991).

To establish a viable business model, the early companies needed to create mortality tables that accurately predicted the risks they faced in underwriting lives. While several works address the actuarial profession specifically, including Lawrence B. Goodheart's biography *Abolitionist, Actuary, Atheist: Elizur Wright and the Reform Impulse* (Kent, OH: Kent State University Press, 1990) and E. J. Moorhead's *Our Yesterdays: the History of the Actuarial Profession in North America, 1809–1979* (Schaumburg, IL: Society of Actuaries, 1989), these developments arose during a time of increasing infatuation with numbers, as detailed by Patricia Cline Cohen in *A Calculating People: The Spread of Numeracy in Early America* (Chicago: University of Chicago Press, 1982) and Theodore M. Porter in *The Rise of Statistical Thinking, 1820–1900* (Princeton, NJ: Princeton University Press, 1986).

Insurers also sought to supplement general mortality data with a greater understanding of the individual risks arising from disease or personal habits. Particularly helpful in demonstrating antebellum knowledge of morbidity are W. F. Bynum's *Science and the Practice of Medicine in the Nineteenth Century* (Cambridge: Cambridge University Press, 1994), Georgina D. Feldberg's *Disease and Class: Tuberculosis and the Shaping of Modern North American Society* (New Brunswick, NJ: Rutgers University Press, 1995), and Hervé Bazin's *The Eradication of Smallpox: Edward Jenner and the First and Only Eradication of a Human Infectious Disease* (San Diego: Academic Press, 2000). The oft-cited literature on shifting attitudes toward the consumption of alcohol includes W. J. Rorabaugh's *The Alcoholic Republic: An Amer-*

ican Tradition (Oxford: Oxford University Press, 1981), Jack S. Blocker Jr.'s *American Temperance Movements: Cycles of Reform* (Boston: Twayne, 1989), Ronald G. Walters's *American Reformers, 1815–1860* (New York: Hill and Wang, 1997), and Thomas R. Pegram's *Battling Demon Rum: The Struggle for a Dry America, 1800–1933* (Chicago: Ivan R. Dee, 1998).

The extensive research on the culture of capitalism necessarily had a profound influence on this book. A prominent recent trend in the historiography—which dovetails perfectly with the marketing tactics of life insurers—is studies of the losers in the capitalist game. Most notable among these are Edward J. Balleisen's *Navigating Failure: Bankruptcy and Commercial Society in Antebellum America* (Chapel Hill: University of North Carolina Press, 2001), Bruce Mann's *Republic of Debtors: Bankruptcy in the Age of American Independence* (Cambridge, MA: Harvard University Press, 2002), and Scott A. Sandage's *Born Losers: A History of Failure in America* (Cambridge, MA: Harvard University Press, 2005). A second relevant theme in this literature is the relationship between religion and capitalism. While Charles Sellers indirectly broached this topic in *The Market Revolution: Jacksonian America, 1815–1846* (Oxford: Oxford University Press, 1991), it is the central premise of both Mark A. Noll's edited volume *God and Mammon: Protestants, Money, and the Market, 1790–1860* (Oxford: Oxford University Press, 2002) and Stewart Davenport's *Friends of the Unrighteous Mammon: Northern Christians and Market Capitalism, 1815–1860* (Chicago: University of Chicago Press, 2008).

There are also a substantial number of works analyzing the motives and activities of corporate capitalists. Specifically applicable for an understanding of life insurance entrepreneurs are Robert F. Dalzell Jr.'s *Enterprising Elite: The Boston Associates and the World They Made* (Cambridge, MA: Harvard University Press, 1987), Conrad Edick Wright and Katheryn P. Viens's edited volume *Entrepreneurs: The Boston Business Community, 1700–1850* (Boston: Massachusetts Historical Society, 1997), and Naomi R. Lamoreaux's *Insider Lending: Banks, Personal Connections, and Economic Development in Industrial New England* (Cambridge: Cambridge University Press, 1996). Finally, like other entrepreneurs of the early nineteenth century, life insurers were concerned with projecting and maintaining a respectable reputation. This infatuation with image is also apparent in Roland Marchand's unparalleled study *Creating the Corporate Soul: The Rise of Public Relations and Corporate Imagery in American Big Business* (Berkeley: University of California Press, 1998) as well as Rowena Olegario's *A Culture of Credit: Embedding Trust and Transparency in American Business* (Cambridge, MA: Harvard University Press, 2006) and Stephen Mihm's *A Nation of Counterfeiters: Capitalists, Con Men, and the Making of the United States* (Cambridge, MA: Harvard University Press, 2007).

Life insurers were also attempting to navigate within an evolving regulatory environment. Most directly influencing my conceptualization of the relationship between business enterprises and the state are William J. Novak's *The People's Welfare: Law and Regulation in Nineteenth-Century America* (Chapel Hill: University of North Carolina Press, 1996) and Charles W. McCurdy's 1975 study in the *Journal of American History,* "Justice Field and the

Jurisprudence of Government-Business Relations: Some Parameters of Laissez-Faire Constitutionalism, 1863–1897." The comparative experience of other corporations is apparent in James W. Ely Jr.'s *Railroads and American Law* (Lawrence: University Press of Kansas, 2002), Herbert Hovenkamp's *Enterprise and American Law, 1836–1937* (Cambridge, MA: Harvard University Press, 1991), and Ronald E. Seavoy's *The Origins of the American Business Corporation, 1784–1855: Broadening the Concept of Public Service during Industrialization* (Westport, CT: Greenwood, 1982).

This regulatory environment became even more complicated with the onset of the Civil War. The impact of sequestration and nonintercourse acts on corporations is most notable in two recent books, Mark A. Weitz's *The Confederacy on Trial: The Piracy and Sequestration Cases of 1861* (Lawrence: University Press of Kansas, 2005) and Daniel W. Hamilton's *The Limits of Sovereignty: Property Confiscation in the Union and the Confederacy during the Civil War* (Chicago: University of Chicago Press, 2007). Finally, Roy Kreitner's captivating book *Calculating Promises: The Emergence of Modern American Contract Doctrine* (Stanford, CA: Stanford University Press, 2007) compelled me to rethink the nature of the insurance contract and the relationship between the company and the policyholder.

The involvement of some life insurance companies with the institution of slavery forced me to delve into an almost mind-numbing historical literature. Beyond the two lone articles on insuring slaves—Todd L. Savitt's "Slave Life Insurance in Virginia and North Carolina" (*Journal of Southern History*, 1977) and Eugene D. Genovese's "The Medical and Insurance Costs of Slaveholding in the Cotton Belt" (*Journal of Negro History*, 1960)—I relied on Mark M. Smith's fine historiographical essay *Debating Slavery: Economy and Society in the Antebellum American South* (Cambridge: Cambridge University Press, 1998) to help me grasp the major sources. My first area of inquiry was industrial slavery, which led me to Ronald L. Lewis's *Coal, Iron, and Slaves: Industrial Slavery in Maryland and Virginia, 1715–1865* (Westport, CT: Greenwood, 1979), Robert S. Starobin's *Industrial Slavery in the Old South* (London: Oxford University Press, 1970), and Paul Finkelman's article "Slaves as Fellow Servants: Ideology, Law, and Industrialization" (*Journal of Legal History*, 1987). I next examined the literature on urban slavery, especially Claudia Dale Goldin's *Urban Slavery in the American South, 1820–1860: A Quantitative History* (Chicago: University of Chicago Press, 1976), Jonathan D. Martin's *Divided Mastery: Slave Hiring in the American South* (Cambridge, MA: Harvard University Press, 2004), and Jonathan Daniel Wells's wonderful study *The Origins of the Southern Middle Class, 1800–1861* (Chapel Hill: University of North Carolina Press, 2004). The particulars of the slave trade itself were best described in Michael Tadman's *Speculators and Slaves: Masters, Traders, and Slaves in the Old South* (Madison: University of Wisconsin Press, 1989).

Finally, I revisited the origins of the classic debates over the economics of slavery by consulting Ulrich Bonnell Phillips's *American Negro Slavery: A Survey of the Supply, Employment and Control of Negro Labor as Determined by the Plantation Regime* (New York: D. Appleton, 1918), Kenneth M. Stampp's *The Peculiar Institution: Slavery in the Ante-Bellum South* (New

York: Alfred A. Knopf, 1961), Eugene D. Genovese's *Roll, Jordon, Roll: The World the Slaves Made* (New York: Random House, 1972), Gavin Wright's *The Political Economy of the Cotton South: Households, Markets, and Wealth in the Nineteenth Century* (New York: W. W. Norton, 1978), and Robert William Fogel's *Without Consent or Contract: The Rise and Fall of American Slavery* (New York: W. W. Norton, 1989).

Abbott, Lawrence, 196
Abell v. Penn Mutual Life Insurance Company (1881), 279
Actuaries Table. *See* Combined Experience Table (England)
Adams, William Taylor, 229
adverse selection, 43, 48–49, 53, 57, 75, 286
Aetna Life Insurance Company (Hartford), 196, 250, 258, 308
age. *See under* premium
agents: and commissions, 59–60, 68, 286, 291, 326n59; definition of, 112–15; role of, 48–50, 60–67, 74, 76–78, 224, 263–65, 278–79, 291; selection of, 47–49, 58–60, 67, 76; and underwriting of slaves, 189, 194–95, 197, 199–200. *See also* principal-agent problem
Albion Life Insurance Company (London), 39, 91, 155, 173
Allen, Stephen (NYL&T president), 98–99, 101–2
American Experience Table, 252–53
American Life and Trust Insurance Company (Maryland), 37, 162–63
American Life and Trust Insurance Company (Philadelphia), 21, 226
American Life Underwriters' Convention: Committee on Legislation, 258–59, 362n61; Committee on Vital Statistics, 249–52; and federal insurance tax, 116; in *Insurance Monitor*, 361n45; and lapsed policies, 246; and mortality tables, 241–43, 248–54, 260, 271, 288; participation of companies in, 251, 288, 362n48; and uniform state regulation, 241–43, 249, 254–60, 285–87; and war risks, 266, 269–71, 283

American Mutual Life Insurance Company (New Haven), 85, 87–88, 91, 244, 251, 258, 269
American Temperance Life Insurance Company (Hartford), 56–57, 242
American Temperance Society, 71
application. *See under* policy; *names of individual companies*
Armfield, John, 191
artisans, 2, 28–30, 129, 177–79, 182
Asheville Mutual Insurance Company (North Carolina), 195
Association for the Relief of Respectable or Aged Females, 130
Astley, Thomas (Pennsylvania Company), 20
asymmetric information, 51
Atkinson, George, 27
Atkinson, William, 35

Babbage, Charles, 24
Balleisen, Edward J., 127, 137, 339n52
Baltimore Life Insurance Company: agency system of, 50, 53, 58–59, 61–64, 68–69, 194–95, 197, 199–202; application form of, 51, 53, 55, 70; charter provisions of, 103–6; closure of, 205, 265; contract terms of, 156; geographic expansion of, 50, 112–15; incorporation of, 4; loans through, 106, 157–61, 165; marketing campaigns of, 21–22, 132, 168; and marriage, 40; and middle-class applicants, 133–34; mortality tables of, 18, 20–21, 243; payment of cash surrenders by, 162–64; policy length of, 246, 311; policy sales of, 14, 21, 146–47, 160–61, 176–77, 180, 194, 199–201, 219, 317n32; policy size of,

CPSIA information can be obtained
at www.ICGtesting.com
Printed in the USA
LVHW031742281122
734201LV00022B/355